THE WAY OF MUSIC

Second Edition

THE WAY OF MUSIC

Second Edition

WILLIAM E. BRANDT

DEPARTMENT OF MUSIC
WASHINGTON STATE UNIVERSITY

ALLYN AND BACON, INC.
BOSTON

PREFACE

WHAT IS THE PURPOSE of a study of music literature? To learn amusing anecdotes about composers? To hear a variety of music? To learn to recognize the orchestral instruments by the sounds they produce? Or is it to learn how the music functions, how it is put together, how the composer was affected by his times and how he expresses his time as well as himself in the music? I feel that the last question most nearly states the requirements necessary to allow the serious listener to penetrate the music, become involved in it and to examine it "from the inside." For that reason, this book spends considerable time upon the constructive elements of the art—melody, harmony, rhythm, form and style—so that the person with curiosity and interest in the great music of Europe and America may better understand the universality and importance of these works.

The listener is probably aware that there are many different ways of responding to compositions. We may daydream when certain pieces are played, or become excited. We may "see" in our mind scenes or landscapes, or we may feel our blood tingling in response to the force or the grandeur or the rhythm of the music. Or again, we may follow the drama unfolding in sound in much the same way as we attend a play in the theater, with intellectual and emotional satisfaction over the dynamic progression of events, penetration into the "message" of the work, and appreciation of the structural balance. All of these ways are legitimate, but some yield more profound enjoyment than others. In general, the more one knows about the processes of a work, the more intensely he understands the final accomplishment, whether it be a skyscraper, a round of golf, a piano recital or a symphony. And, best of all, the addition of new ways of understanding does not invali-

v

date the old ones: emotional and intellectual appreciation go hand in hand, each enhancing the other.

In order to attain these ends, this book has been organized in a careful way. After the first chapter, devoted to the establishment of some important basic concepts and terminology, each of the succeeding chapters treats in chronological order the periods of music history from the Medieval to the present, exploring the important components of the style of each as exemplified in the works of that period's great composers. This exploration is contained in the same five sections of each chapter, the first of which provides an historical and biographical background, the second a discussion of the musical style, the third an exposition of formal and generative principles, the fourth a series of analyses of representative works, together with musical examples, and the fifth a comparison of the abstract style of the music with the visual arts of the time, wherever these run parallel. There is no attempt made to integrate the arts, but rather to assist comprehension of the music by showing similarities in line, rhythm, color and emotional content with paintings, sculpture and architecture. Also included at the end of each chapter is a list of important terms which have been explained and used in the chapter and suggestions for additional listening. The whole study is cumulative in the use of terms as well as in the degree of listening and analytical skill required. For that reason, thorough familiarity with vocabulary and formal diagrams is of the utmost importance.

In order to learn to swim, one must get into the water. In order to increase one's perceptions of music, one must immerse himself in it via phonograph, radio, television and—most important of all—concerts. Recorded music, while a great benefit, can never rival the vividness of a live concert where the interrelation of performer and audience charges the atmosphere with an electric stimulation. One leaves the concert hall with the feeling that he has experienced something ennobling and spiritually rewarding. In our complex civilization with its emphasis upon material values, the arts, and especially music by virtue of its abstract quality, symbolize a whole world of the spirit, organized, harmonious and humane. Let us not ignore them.

I am indebted to my colleagues Peter DeLone and Robert Miller for many useful suggestions concerning this book, and to Kemble Stout, chairman of the Music Department at Washington State University, for the opportunity to test the book in class before publication. And not least, I feel that the many classes in music literature deserve my gratitude for being the unwitting "guinea pigs" during the book's development period.

William E. Brandt

PREFACE TO THE SECOND EDITION

THE APPROVAL WITH WHICH the first edition of *The Way of Music* was generally received has encouraged the publication of this second edition. The reader familiar with the former version will find essentially the same approach in the present book, with the addition to certain chapters of important material dealing with opera, keyboard and chamber music. The chapter dealing with the twentieth century has been thoroughly revised, brought up to date and, it is hoped, generally improved. Chapter II of the first edition, dealing with musical instruments, has been deleted on the grounds that most university students are familiar with the appearance and sound of the usual instruments through participation in bands and orchestras in high schools and through recordings, radio and television. Ample material in the form of charts and recordings is available to any instructor who wishes to include a unit dealing with the instruments, and his colleagues who are performers may dramatically supplement these aids. However, a discussion of the instruments and ensembles stylistically appropriate to each of the historical periods has been included in every chapter except the one dealing with theory, and it is to be hoped that recordings used to exemplify the musical style will also employ the authentic instruments, for it must be realized that the timbres and capabilities of these instruments deeply influenced the music written for them.

While there is somewhat more material in each chapter, the analyses have been reduced in most cases, sometimes to outline form. They are intended to reinforce the classroom work by providing a guide for the student's outside listening. The technical terminology has not been expanded more than is necessary to explain some of the new material. To those who object to using these terms and concepts, I can only say that the students at the state university in which this book evolved seem wholly capable of understanding them. This is as one would expect from students who deal with calculus, nuclear chemistry and physics, and the "new criticism" of literature.

In any course which offers a survey of a field, one is always faced with the problem of covering the material in enough depth to be significant. Music literature is no exception, and many of us wish for the equivalent of an academic year for such a course. Usually only half that amount of time is available, and we are forced to compromise. Three suggestions which I have tried may be of use to those faced with this dilemma, although I make no particular claim to originality for them. The first is to begin the survey, after dealing with the theory of music, with Chapter IV, the Baroque Period, since the greatest amount of music heard in concert by the general public was composed from 1600 to the present. The five chapters may thus be divided as experience deems best over the semester or the usual two quarters. A second method is that of careful selection among the items offered, using those which seem most important and appropriate. In conjunction with both of these methods, the use of specially prepared tapes dealing with some important phase of a style may significantly increase the student's exposure to the material, and may legitimately be required as a phase of his class preparation. An ideal solution would be one which would permit sufficient class discussion of the music in terms of style, practice and aesthetic, yet allow time for group "laboratory" listening guided by the instructor. So often the student is called upon for a response only in tests, and this is not enough. Reports on concerts, recitals and biographies, while onerous for the instructor to read in addition to other paper work, have the advantage of requiring the student to verbalize about music; this should be encouraged, for not only is the self-teaching aspect valuable, but also the airing of information, insight, opinion, vocabulary and enthusiasm is part of the fun of being knowledgeable about music.

In conclusion, I wish to thank those persons who have endured the rigors of this revision, particularly my wife; and those colleagues whose suggestions have reshaped the presentation in some respects. I am especially grateful to Mr. Nelson M. Jansky and the editors of Allyn and Bacon who have been unceasingly patient and cooperative in bringing out both editions of this book. And finally, I dare to hope that this edition is an improvement over the preceding one, and will prove at least as serviceable and useful in the classroom as that one did.

William E. Brandt

CONTENTS

THE WAY OF MUSIC

Second Edition

I THEORY FOR
THE LISTENER

SOUND, PITCH, AND SCALES

PROBABLY THE FIRST element of music of which we are conscious is sound: music consists of sounds arranged in order—not just any
sounds, but tones of definite highness or lowness. These tones are said
to have high or low pitch. Sound results from rapid vibration of an elas-
tic substance; anyone who has snapped a bowstring or a rubber band
knows this. The string vibrates back and forth: this we see. What we
do not see are the ranks of air molecules jostled together then pulled
apart by the motion of the string. The air waves formed in this way
travel from the vibrating string to our ear drum and by alternately
pushing and pulling it at the same rate of speed as the bowstring
cause it to vibrate at the same pitch. This vibratory motion is then
transmitted via the apparatus in the ear to the auditory nerve and
thence to the brain where it is experienced as sound.

The tones which supply the sound material of music are selected
from a systematized sequence of definite pitches ranging from low to
high which is another way of saying that they vary from slow vibrations to very rapid ones. Instruments that produce the slow vibrations
which we hear as low pitches are generally large, like the tuba or
double-bass, whereas those producing high-pitched sounds with rapid
vibratory rates are small, like the piccolo. A glance at the different

1

Harmonic series: ratio of whole length to number of vibrating parts (harmonic series)

Schemetic diagram shows only the partial vibration.

Tone produced by the vibration shown.

a. 1/1

A, 110 vibrations per second

Vibration over whole length, producing the fundamental tone of the string.

b. 1/2

a, 220 vibrations per second

Vibration in halves, each section moving twice as fast as the rate of the fundamental, thus producing the pitch one octave above it.

c. 1/3

e1, 330 vibrations per second

Vibration in thirds, at a rate three times that of the fundamental, producing a pitch an octave plus a fifth above the fundamental.

d. 1/4

a1, 440 vibrations per second

Vibration in fourths, at a rate four times that of the fundamental, producing a pitch two octaves above the fundamental.

EXAMPLE I-1: *Whole and partial vibrations of a string.*

The string vibrates in all of these ways, and more, as given by the ratios of the harmonic series (1/1, 1/2, 1/3, 1/4, 1/5, 1/6, 1/7, . . . 1/n), all simultaneously, thus producing a sound which is a mixture with the fundamental predominating.

lengths of string used in a grand piano will make this association of size and pitch quite clear. Each pitch has a definite number of vibrations per second, however, regardless of the instrument which produces it. Thus, an a' played on the violin, the flute, the piano or the trumpet consists of vibrations at the rate of 440 per second. Why, then, do each of these instruments sound different when they play the same tone? The explanation of this is a bit more complicated but still dependent upon the vibratory nature of sound-producing instruments.

If we stretch a wire or string between two fixed points and pluck it gently we produce the lowest tone of which that length of string at that tension is capable. This is called the *fundamental tone*, and represents the largest component of the sound when the tone is played by an instrument. If we were to substitute an air column, such as exists in the bore of a wind instrument, and set it in vibration with a reed, the same situation would obtain, and it would sound the fundamental tone. In producing it, the string or air column vibrates *as a whole* over its entire length, as is indicated in Example I-1a. In reality, however, the string set in motion by the violinist's bow, for example, vibrates in a combination of ways simultaneously—in halves, thirds, quarters and so on. Each of these *partial vibrations* produces its own higher pitch——higher because the vibrating length of string or air is shorter than the original string or air column. The relationship of their pitches to that of the fundamental is that of the vibrating lengths to the whole string or air column. If the string vibrates in halves each section moves at twice the rate of the fundamental vibration and produces a tone which is called the *octave* of the basic one. If the string vibrates in four parts the rate is four times that of the fundamental and the tone is two octaves higher (Example I-1b and d). Other tones, more than we have shown in the diagram, produce a whole series of pitches which become closer and closer together as the vibratory rate increases (theoretically infinite in length) and which are called the *harmonic* series, or the *overtone* series. None of these harmonics is as loud as the fundamental——and they vary in loudness among themselves——but all are present, blended into the total sound of the instrument when it is played. Each instrument has its own definite pattern of overtones with fairly constant ratios of loudness among the members of the series; it is this which gives each kind of instrument its individual *quality* and enables us to recognize it by its sound. In some cases, such as the trombone (and the brass instruments generally) the overtones provide the variety of pitches which the instrument can play.

A tone and its octave blend smoothly together when sounded simultaneously. Indeed, the upper tone seems to be a duplication of

the lower one on a higher level; as we have seen, this has a mathematical basis. The various musical systems of the Orient and Occident
developed through the division of the octave into smaller units with
tones closer together and more suited to melody. The musical culture
of Western Europe used a division of the octave into twelve equidistant pitches called *semitones*, or *half-steps*. This system becomes clear
when we examine the piano keyboard (Example I-2). The tones are
named for the letters of the alphabet from A through G. Starting on
any tone, C for example, and counting all of the keys within the span
of an octave, both white and black, we find a total of twelve. These
half-steps are the smallest pitch divisions used in our music except

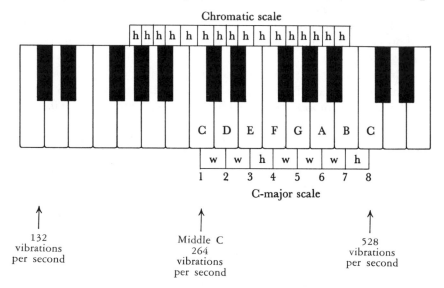

EXAMPLE I-2: *The piano keyboard.*

w indicates a whole step between adjacent tones

h indicates a half step between adjacent tones

Pattern of whole and half steps in the major scale:

Tone:	C	D	E	F	G	A	B	C
Number:	1	2	3	4	5	6	7	8
Interval:		w	w	h	w	w	w	h

Note that the major scale consists of the pattern w-w-h twice,
with a whole step between.

for certain Balkan folksongs, jazz and twentieth century electronic music.

The half-steps are named in two ways. A tone one half-step *above* a white key receives the name of that key plus the word *sharp*, or the symbol ♯ (C-sharp, or C♯). A tone one half-step *below* a white key receives the name of that key plus the word *flat*, or the symbol ♭ (B-flat, B♭). A half-step occurs between two white keys in two places ——between E and F, and B and C. Thus, the white key E is also F♭, and the white key F is also E♯. Each of the black keys also has two names: for example, the one just higher than C is C♯ or D♭. The custom is to use the sharp designation when a passage is ascending in pitch (C-C♯-D-D♯), and the flat for descending pitch (E-E♭-D-D♭-C). The tones of the half-step arrangement can be clearly located in this way.

When a series of pitches is arranged according to some prearranged pattern of whole steps (two half steps, *e.g.*, C to C♯ + C♯ to D = C to D, a whole step) and half steps, a structure called a *scale* is formed (from *scala*, a ladder). The one constructed of the twelve half steps (C, C♯, D, D♯, E, F, F♯, G, G♯, A, A♯, B) is called the *chromatic* ("colored" scale).

Notice that when the chromatic scale is played it has no tendency to stop on any particular note, but may continue on and on, the choice of the final pitch being at the option of the player. When the white keys from C up an octave to the next C are played, we have an arrangement called the *major scale* (Example I-2). Notice how this scale contains half and whole steps in a definite pattern; if this pattern is reproduced using any other pitch as the starting point, regardless of

Major scale on E

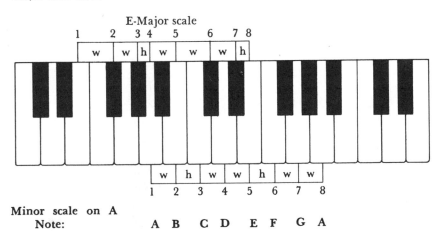

Minor scale on A

Note:	A	B	C	D	E	F	G	A
Distance:		w	h	w	w	h	w	w

EXAMPLE I-3: *The major and minor scales.*

whether that note is a black or white key on the piano, we still have as the result a major scale. (Example I-3). Another important quality of the major scale is its tendency to want to use that starting note as its final tone. This tone, then, is the ruler of the other tones. There are two other notes, the fifth and sixth scale tones, upon which we may come to rest, but they do not sound final. Always the basic note of the scale draws the others to it. This *stable* pitch is said to be the *keynote* or *tonic note* of the scale. The temporary resting places may be said to be *conditionally stable* while others, particularly the second, fourth and seventh notes of the major scale, are *unstable* and wish to move to either the *conditionally stable* pitches or the *stable keynote* of the scale.

If we begin a scale on the sixth note of the C-major scale and continue it upwards one octave the result is an arrangement of half and whole steps different from that of the major; it is called the *minor scale* (Example I-3). This scale, like the major, has a keynote; while this tone represents the main point of stability in the scale, its attraction is far weaker than that of its major counterpart. The total sound of the minor scale is quite different from that of the major as a result of the different arrangement in the sequence of whole and half steps. Because the distance between the seventh tone and the tonic is a whole step, the tendency of this seventh tone, or "leading tone" to rise to the tonic is not strong. To improve this situation the seventh tone in minor is often raised one half step *(sharped)* thus making it only a half step from the tonic, analogous to the relationship of these two notes in the major scale.

The notes of these scales, when arranged in a chosen order by a composer, furnish the pitches for a melody. Another basic element of music must be considered and applied, however, before this series of pitches can come to life as a melody.

METER AND RHYTHM

As we have applied a measuring scale to pitches, so now we use the yardstick on that important but elusive dimension of music——time. First of all, we realize that the flow of time may be broken up into small divisions, either noted on a watch dial, or experienced as sound in the regular dripping of a leaky faucet, the ticking of a clock, or the tapping of our foot. The time distances between successive sounds must be equal to be useful, and may be closely or more widely spaced resulting in either a rapid stream of pulsations or a slower series. This speed of pulsation is called *tempo* in music, and requires a qualifying adjective to render it meaningful; thus, we speak of a fast, moderate or slow tempo. The Italian words printed at the beginning of compositions are the traditional way to indicate to the performer the approximate tempo of the music (a list of the most common of these appears at the end of this chapter).

The human mind tends to try to impose order on regularly recurring events in order to reduce them to a system; the endless, even flow of pulsations described above is no exception. Perhaps you have noticed, when listening to that leaking faucet, you tend to feel more emphasis on every other drip? Soon you find yourself counting 1-2, 1-2, 1-2. If you have an experimental nature, you might try counting 1-2-3, 1-2-3, 1-2-3-, always with the emphasis on number 1. You find that this works also, although perhaps not as comfortably as the duple counting. What you have done here is to apply the phenomenon called *meter* to this stream of pulsations, reducing it into units of two or three pulsations, with a stress on the first one in each group.

The conductor of an orchestra makes clear to the players the metric design of the composition they are playing by using certain stylized gestures to indicate the metric beats. The curves which the tip of his baton traces in the air are shown in the figures of Example I-4.

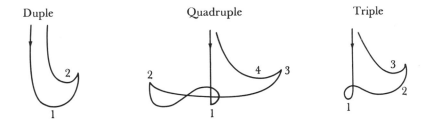

EXAMPLE I-4: *Conducting patterns of three common meters.*

It will be noticed that the first beat of each metric pattern is vertical and downward (the "downbeat"), and that this motion and direction give emphasis to the beat. Just the opposite feeling occurs on the last beat of any of the metric patterns, when the motion is upward (the "upbeat"), and seems to heighten our anticipation for the downbeat. The four beat pattern (quadruple meter) has a secondary stress on the third beat which is represented by a long horizontal motion. It is interesting and helpful to be able to execute these simple motions in time with the music in order to determine the meter; merely move the right hand in the directions shown, making sure that the beats are all equidistant in time. In this way the feeling of up and downbeats becomes physically more meaningful than a page of explanation could make them.

The larger unit formed by the number of beats from the count of *one* to the next count of *one* is called a *measure,* and represents an entire conducting pattern as shown above. In music notation, it is represented by the distance between vertical "bar-lines" across the horizontal staff lines.

What we have just defined is meter. What, then is *rhythm?* One encyclopedia defines it as "the element of music concerned with the relative duration of tones and with the stress or accent placed on certain tones." Thus meter itself is also rhythmic, for the stress placed on the first beat of the measure and the equal duration of each of the counts thereafter would qualify it under the definition. It is an especial kind of rhythm, then, which we shall call *metric rhythm.* This term also applies, in a larger sense, to the patterns formed by dividing each beat in half or in thirds, and placing a tone or a light pulsation on each of these subsidiary points. If we conduct one of the basic patterns, duple for example, and count aloud, inserting the syllable *te* (tay) halfway between the numbers (1-te-2-te-1-te-2-te), we have produced duple *simple* time. The term *simple* means that the basic beat has been divided in half: this may be applied to triple, quadruple, or any other meter in the same way that we did with duple meter. When the basic beat is divided in three, the division is said to be *compound,* and the syllables *la-lee* may be used to show where the divisions begin: 1-la-lee-2-la-lee is duple compound meter, for example. Further subdivision of both the simple and compound varieties is common and may be illustrated by following each of the syllables given above by *ta* (tah): 1-ta-te-ta-2-ta-te-ta; or 1-ta-la-ta-lee-ta-2-ta-la-ta-lee-ta. Further subdivision is also possible, but for our purposes this is complicated enough! These, then, are all varieties of metric rhythm, dependent upon the accented first beat of the measure and the subdivision into evenly spaced pulses.

The continuation of an even stream of tones in metric rhythm may become monotonous after awhile, and more irregular patterns derived from lengthening the durations of some of the beats, divisions and subdivisions often are more interesting. One which is very common is indicated by a note followed by a dot, after which a note one-half the value of the first one appears (♪. ♪ , or more commonly, ♩. ♪):

this *dotted rhythmic* pattern may be read using our rhythmic syllables; the pulses in parentheses are not spoken, but the proper time is allowed for them.

1 - (ta - te) - ta - 2 - (ta - te) - ta

This jerky rhythmic pattern lends solemnity or pompousness to slow music, while at a faster tempo it creates great rhythmic excitement. A similar effect in compound meter, although smoother and less vigorous, may be created by prolonging the numbered beat through the first syllable:

1 - (la) - lee 2 - (la) - lee

This rhythmic *cliché* may be heard in the "Barcarolle," or "Boat Song" from the opera *The Tales of Hoffman* by Offenbach, but it occurs frequently in other music. Other irregular patterns, some of which are listed below, occur in music to give more rhythmic variety and sometimes an especial propulsive force to melody and harmony.

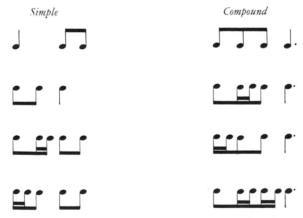

In all of the rhythmic examples discussed so far the accents and beats of the measure follow regularly with no dislocations. Once such rhythmic patterns are started, they tend to go on repeating and soon become monotonous. Such an unchanging regularity we call *stable* rhythm. If, however, an accent is placed upon a beat or some division of a beat which does not normally have a stress, an unbalanced, *unstable* situation is obtained. This can be demonstrated easily by counting and conducting a series of measures in triple meter in which the first beat of the measure is strongly accented. After four or five such measures shift the accent to the second or third beat for two measures, then return it to the first beat. The unstable in contrast to the stable rhythm thus becomes dramatically clear. Such a displaced accent is often called a *syncopation*, a much abused word during the jazz era of the 1920's. If the accent is placed upon one of the divisions or subdivisions of any of the beats the effect, while still unstable, becomes more subtle and less obviously dramatic. One may try this effect by conducting and counting using the *te* or *ta* in either simple or compound meter. A similar effect of instability may be achieved by substituting a silence for one of the beats of a measure, especially the first one, or by prolonging a beat over such an accented beat. (*e.g.*, 1-te-(2)-te; or 1-te-2-te-(1)-te-(2)-te; The beats in parentheses are not to be counted aloud, but space allowed for them through the conducting pattern.)

We have noted the tension in the major scale due to the attraction of the other tones by the tonic tone. When this tone finally is arrived at after moving through the other tones, the tension relaxes and a *cadence* thus is formed. An analogous situation often appears in the rhythmic aspect of music, usually in conjunction with tones of melody or harmony or both. A rhythmic cadence may be created by the progression from highly unstable patterns to stable ones often with a simplification of the patterns to the most basic beats of the measure. The approach to such a cadence and its resolution might be illustrated by the following:

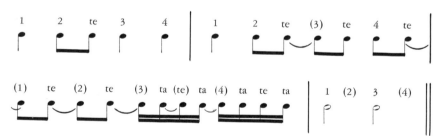

We frequently shall be aware of the general formula for a cadence:

high tension   →   lower tension

and the artistic ways in which it may be used by great composers.

When a relatively short rhythmic pattern is repeated a number of times in a piece of music it seems to assume a certain importance.

The same is true of a pattern of tones if treated with similar emphasis. These patterns are called *motives* and may be either rhythmic or melodic, or both at the same time. The descending three notes of "Three Blind Mice" constitute an important melodic motive which, at "See how they run—" collects a definite rhythmic motive. The opening measures of the first movement of the *Fifth Symphony* by Beethoven constitute perhaps the most well-known rhythmic motive in all music— the "V for Victory" symbol of the Second World War. The tones first associated with the rhythm, however, give way to other ones and are not repeated as a pattern very many times during the movement. Hence, the rhythmic motive is of greater significance here than the melodic. Because of the very numerous repetitions of this motive which occur in the first movement of this symphony the rhythmic motive may be said here to have important structural qualities. We shall explore these ideas more thoroughly when we come to the music of the Baroque, Classic and Romantic periods.

We now have the means to create melodies by applying the regulating and propelling force of meter and rhythm to a series of tones. Two dimensions of music thus are accounted for: the vertical movement of pitches as the tones of a melody vary upward and downward, and the horizontal movement through time (that factor is made perceptible by meter and eventful by rhythm). Let us now examine the phenomenon of melody a little more closely in order to find out what factors contribute to the feeling of satisfaction and perception of beauty which comes to us upon hearing an artistically formed melody.

MELODY

The melody of a piece of music is its most important element. Not only is the melody the most immediately attractive feature to the listener, but in a very real sense the harmony, rhythm and form of the entire composition depend upon it. These other factors support, clarify, modify and intensify the melodic element, and while it may exist without them, they cannot go on for long without it.

To provide variety and interest, generally speaking a melody must traverse a number of tones, whether it revolves in a narrow orbit around a central tone or strides vigorously up and down the scale in leaps. The span of tones which a melody covers is called its *range*. The range of "America," for example, is comparatively narrow, while that of "The Star Spangled Banner" is wide. In traversing the notes within its range, a melodic line may move smoothly in steps, or what is known as *conjunct* motion; again "America" is a good example. Or, like "The Star Spangled Banner," it may have a large number of skips, *disjunct* motion, which gives vitality and excitement to the composition. During the course of its travels, a melody usually reaches a high point, a *climax,* then subsides. Sometimes there are several climaxes if the feeling expressed is very intense, but most melodies because of their relative brevity do not have room for more than one. The climactic point usually is approached and departed from by waves of smaller climaxes—foothills, as it were—to the peak which have the function of intensifying or relaxing the energy needed for the high point.

One cannot define all of the qualities of a good melody but only describe what they consist of in an objective manner. As soon as a definition is decided upon it is found to apply to only one class or style of melody and excludes beautiful examples which were written at other times when different fashions prevailed. Part of our examination of the styles of the various historical periods of music will be to characterize the melodic fashion of those times.

If, as we have said, the melodies of these various styles are so different, what generalizations can we make about them which will clarify our concepts? The first is the fact that all melody is organized into sections, called *phrases*, which measure it off into understandable units. This kind of division probably first resulted from the limitations of the human breath capacity in singing; certainly the convenient pause at the end of a phrase allows time for a breath to be taken in order to go on with the following phrase. Instead of interrupting a continuous line of melody to gasp for breath, the artistic creators of melody in all ages have turned the melodic line at these points so that it comes to rest momentarily upon a tone of some stability before continuing. Such a cadence satisfies the musical requirement for a logical rest point as well as the physical one for breath. Some phrases require a sense of finality, especially if they conclude the melody, and must come to rest upon a tone which arouses no expectation of continuation. The tonic tone of the major and minor scales provides just such a feeling, and the melodic cadence which concludes upon it may be termed a *final* cadence. During the course of a melody, such a final cadence may be used for interior pauses without implying complete finality (the first phrase of "America," for example) mainly because we sense that the form of the melody requires continuation. If the melody comes to rest momentarily upon any other tone of the scale, the cadence is *nonfinal,* and implies continuation (the phrase of

"Way Down upon the Swanee River" which ends "far, far away," for example). Some of these tones, particularly the fifth (dominant) and sixth degrees of the scale, provide a somewhat more stable rest point than the others, and we might term a cadence upon them *conditionally stable.* In our discussion of harmony we shall treat the subject of cadences again, finding that the harmony verifies the quality of the cadence in a more complete way than is possible for the melody alone.

Most melodies, then, consist of a number of phrases each ending with some kind of cadence. For some reason, probably psychological, the melody of Western European music is predominantly organized in phrases of four measures, regardless of the meter. Two of these combine to form an eight measure *period,* and two of such periods create a section of music which is frequently complete and independent in itself. By such additive procedures a larger composition may be constructed. The four measure phrase may consist of a more or less continuous melodic strand, or divided into two shorter ideas, the second of which may be a repetition of the first. This often is the case when the melodic idea itself consists of melodic or rhythmic motives, as in the French folk song "Frère Jacques," or "America." Such repetition welds the phrases together, imparting *unity* to the whole structure. In the same way that a sentence must have a subject, to which all of the other words refer, so a central musical idea——a motive—— acts as a musical subject which, due to the nature of musical communication, is repeated rather than referred to more indirectly. Such repetition, however, may become wearisome if prolonged; contrasting motives and patterns are needed to provide variety. An example of this on a very low level is the round "Three Blind Mice." The first section consists of the descending three note motive presented twice and is followed by a similar repetition of it in slightly varied form at a higher pitch level (through "see how they run"). The central contrasting phrase appears three times, after which the opening motive concludes the piece. Not only the repetition of the melodic-rhythmic motive in the first section, but also its return to literally close the song, illustrates the role of repetition and contrast to secure musical unity and form. The concept of variation is also at work, providing variety and unity at the same time. All works of art use the techniques of repetition, contrast and variation in their structures, but none more so than music, which is, to quote an eminent aesthetician, *"sounding form,"* for it consists objectively of nothing else.

The following diagram, which refers to Example I-5, may be used to show in quite a clear way the construction by phrases and the use of repetition, contrast and variation in a musical composition.

EXAMPLE I-5: Dvořák: slow movement, *Symphony No. 9* ("From the New World").

Location	Musical structure
measures 1 through 6	Introduction: unstable harmony, reaching a final cadence in measure 4. Tonic chord prolonged in measures 5-6, allowing intensity of measure 4 to dissipate.
measures 7-8, 9-10	Slow 2-measure phrase so constructed as to give impression that it requires four duple measures to complete. Note the frequent use of the dotted-note figure and the rhythmic motive which contains it. Nonfinal cadence in measure 8, final cadence in measure 10.
measures 11-12, 13-14	Unstable varied repetition of motives of measure 7-8. Contrast through variation and instability of melody and harmony.
measures 15-18	Varied repetition of measures 7-10, leading to final cadence weakened by being one octave higher than before.
measures 19-21	Repeated cadences confirming that of measure 18. Note the expansion of time values in measure 20.
measures 22-26	Varied repetition of introduction, now on different tones, two octaves higher and with different instruments.
measures 27-30	Variation and expansion of principal material.
measures 31-35	Repetition of melodic pattern of measure 28 and 30, creating a certain amount of tension which is relaxed by the slow motion of measure 35 and the resolution into measure 36.
measures 36-39	Repetition of measures 15-18.
measures 40-41	Repetition of measures 19-20.
measures 42-45	Repetition of the principal musical idea, serving both to give the feeling of finality to the section of music as well as to provide a connection to the next section, measures 46 *et seq.*

The part of the composition following measure 45 consists first of a rather large contrasting section in a new key which exploits themes which sound new but are related to those of the section we have exam-

ined. This is followed by a varied repetition of the section which we
have just examined, with the omission of the introductory material
until the end of the movement.

TEXTURE

Music may be compared to the weaving of threads together in
needlework or tapestry. The simplest example might consist of a single-
colored thread outlining a design on a neutral background. This cor-
responds to melody alone, and is called *monophonic texture*. But in
music as well as tapestry this seldom happens. More often we have
a series of threads of different colors combined in pictorial or abstract
designs. Such is sometimes the case in music. Separate yet compatible
melodic lines are woven upon the background of time, regulated by
the metric warp and woof of the organization. Such music is said to
be *polyphonic* in texture. Examples may easily be found. Almost
everyone has sung a round such as "Row, Row, Row Your Boat," "Frère
Jacques," or "Three Blind Mice." Musically, this procedure is called a

EXAMPLE I-6a: Canon: *Frère Jacques.*

canon, which means a law. The law of such rounds is that everyone
shall sing the same melody, but not simultaneously; rather, the
entrance of each group occurs after a certain number of measures of

the preceding group have been sung, giving a staggered series of beginnings (Example I-6a). This very old musical device is often used by composers to lend intensity, development, or interest to a composi-

EXAMPLE 1-6b: Fugal imitation: Handel's *Messiah*, Part II, "Behold the Lamb of God."

tion. Sometimes, only the first phrase is presented by an instrument or voices; when it has been played or sung, that particular instrument continues freely using melodic phrases which combine with the other parts. Because they all begin alike, these parts are said to enter in imitation (Example I-6b). These parts may also be said to exist in a *contrapuntal* relationship to each other. Counterpoint is the process which creates *polyphony.*

Suppose, however, the composer wishes to use a simpler procedure than polyphony so that his melody may stand out more clearly. He may resort to what is called *homophonic* texture, or, more simply, melody with accompaniment. Let us see how this is accomplished.

If we examine the tones which sound simultaneously in either of the polyphonic examples (I-6a,b), we find that they are a certain pitch distance apart. Musically, this distance is called an *interval,* and we have already dealt with intervals in the whole and half steps of the scale. In that discussion, however, they were treated one after another ——melodically——while here our concern is with their simultaneous combination——harmonically. Such a combination is a byproduct of the process of polyphony, as it were; for, here the primary attention is focussed on the melodic lines, horizontal, as they extend through time, rather than vertical which is a cross section of the texture at any one moment. Of course, the harmonic byproduct in most styles of polyphony is strongly controlled even though the emphasis is elsewhere. When the tones are grouped into *chords,* however, by the selection of certain intervals with desired qualities, and these are used to support a melody, *homophonic* texture is the result. Here, the movement from chord to chord and the relation of these to the melody is the important

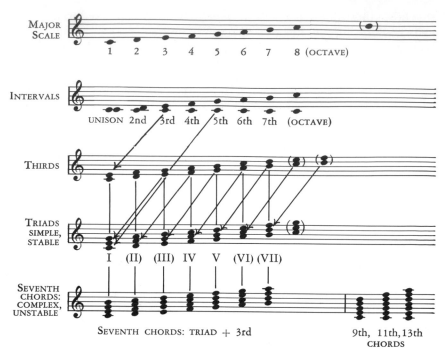

EXAMPLE I-7: *Derivation of intervals and chords from the scale.*

thing. A constant process of selection and refinement went on during the Medieval Period with the resultant establishment of certain tone combinations (chords) which we recognize as general structures with rather well-defined properties. Without recapitulating the history of harmony, let us examine the more important of these structures and try to define their qualities.

Example I-7 is a chart showing the traditional combinations and their derivation from the materials provided by the major scale. With a few exceptions, what is generally true of the major scale also applies to the minor. When one plays the intervals shown in the second line of the example, one is sure to be struck by the varying qualities of the harmonic combinations. The 3rd and 6th, for example, sound smooth and pleasant to the ear, while the 2nd and 7th have considerable tension, and the tones do not blend together but can be heard separately vibrating. The 4th partakes somewhat of this quality, but with more blend, and forms an intermediate value between them and the smooth but rather hollow-sounding 5th. The 5th and the octave were called the *perfect consonances* by theorists in the Middle Ages because of the smoothness of blending of the tones. Somewhat less smooth, although more pleasant to our ears, are the *imperfect consonances* of the 3rd and 6th. The *dissonances* are the 2nd and 7th, and one which is not shown in our chart, called the *tritone*, consisting of three whole steps, which may be exemplified by the interval F-B, either up or down. These dissonances, when encountered in music, are unstable and show a tendency to move to one of the consonances, usually by downward stepwise motion of one tone to the pitch below, which in most cases is a consonance with the retained lower tone (the 7th C-B moving to the 6th C-A, for example). This kind of *resolution* of dissonance causes a corresponding lessening of tension as well as a point of harmonic interest in the music. One composer compared dissonance to salt and pepper, and said that like well-seasoned food, music should contain a certain amount of dissonance. Each of the intervals shown on the chart may be created on any tone of the chromatic scale, thus multiplying the number of them by twelve.

It soon will be seen, if one experiments with the greater resources of the chromatic scale, that there are two sizes of the imperfect consonances and of the dissonances. C-D is a 2nd, but so is C-D♭ and a much sharper dissonance as well. C-E is a 3rd, but so is C-E♭ and both are recognizably related in quality. This is also true of the 6ths and the 7ths, with the smaller of the latter being less sharp than the larger. Other intervals are possible, but are too complex for our present discussion. The smaller interval in each case is called minor (*e.g.*, C-B♭ is a minor 7th), while the larger is major (C-A, a major 6th). Essentially, the size of the 3rd between the tonic and the third tone of a scale determines whether it shall be called a major or a minor scale.

If we erect a series of 3rds upon the tones of a scale, then add another 3rd above the previous upper tone (C-E + G) the result is a *triad,* a three-tone harmonic unit which has come to be the traditional basic chord in the music of western Europe since about 1600. These are shown in the fourth line of the example. If we should play them, a difference in quality would be perceptible from triad to triad. Those based upon the first, fourth and fifth scale degrees would differ from those on the second, third and sixth. This difference essentially is due to the size of the bottom interval of the chord: if the third is a major third, made up of four half-steps, the triad is said to have a major quality. If, however, only three half steps constitute the third, it is minor in quality, and so is the triad based upon it. The triad upon the 7th degree is of still different quality because it contains the restless tritone as its outer interval, and is named *diminished,* since that tritone lacks a half-step of being a perfect fifth, which is the "outside" interval of all the other triads. The triads of any major or minor scale consist basically of these varieties, and to generalize them they are named by the scale degrees upon which they are based and are indicated in writing by the use of Roman numerals. The most important, of course, is the I, or *tonic triad,* which enlarges the influence of the tonic tone and acts in a way exactly similar, drawing all other tones and chords towards itself as a kind of magnetic or gravitational center——a point of rest for all of the unstable tendencies inherent in chords and tones other than tonic in the major-minor scale system.

Second in importance are those triads built upon the fourth and fifth degrees of the scale, the IV and V, called the *subdominant* and the *dominant* triads. They lead most strongly to the tonic in such sequences as V-I, IV-I, or IV-V-I. Harmonic movement of this kind gives the sensation of movement in one of the mysterious dimensions of music, and successions of chords which create this feeling are known as harmonic *progressions.* Many melodies may be satisfactorily accompanied by using only the IV-V-I chords, either in major or minor. For example, "Way Down Upon the Swanee River" uses the following progression in the first phrase, ending with a nonfinal cadence: I-IV-I-V.

Upon examining the harmony found in a musical composition, we should find that not all of the chords seem to be built of neat little stacks of thirds, but contain fourths and sixths as well in addition to more complicated harmonies that we shall discuss shortly. These seemingly new formations are the results of rearranging the vertical order of the tones, and are named *inversions* of the original triad. The *root* position of the C triad (so-called because the foundation tone is on the bottom of the harmony) is spelled C-E-G, always from the bass tone upward. The *first inversion* is spelled E-G-C, and the *second* inversion, G-C-E. Each of these rearrangements is recognizable to the ear as a C chord, but each has a flavor of its own, and neither of the inversions is as stable as the root position—the second inversion least of all. Such variation within the chord makes possible fine shades of sonority and tension in harmonic progressions, a potent means for subtle expression in the hands of a good composer.

Through the past periods of music, composers have devised many ways of elaborating harmonies to create various rhythmic and sonorous effects. Example I-8 suggests some of the many ways in which the rhythmic treatment of the I-V-I progression might be used for the opening two measures of Mozart's familiar piano sonata. The first four sections employ the chords in "chunks," spaced throughout the measure in such a way as to emphasize the squareness of the meter. The fifth one is Mozart's own version, spreading the harmony throughout the measure by breaking up the triads into their component tones which are then played one at a time. This *diffusion* of a harmony through all or part of measure can be accomplished in many ways, and the next section illustrates how it was frequently done in the nineteenth century. The last example indicates how such rhythmic treatments of harmony might be arranged for orchestra.

EXAMPLE I-8: *Harmonic accompaniments.*

COMPLEX HARMONY

We have noted that most of the triads derived from the major scale are individually stable, since they contain no dissonance, but in a series together with other chords from the same scale tend to progress toward the tonic and thus may be characterized as *tonally unstable* in nature. Certain musical styles which employ no chords more complex than triads sound bright and clear to present-day listeners, accustomed as we are to a larger degree of tension in the music of the nineteenth and twentieth centuries. Some of this earlier music has little interest for us for exactly the reason that it is too predictable in its harmonic content. This is not because dissonance was entirely absent, for there has never been a style of which this was true, but rather because the dissonance was not emphasized and was absorbed in the prevailing consonance. The increase in harmonic complexity during the past centuries reflects the growing acceptance of dissonance by the human ear and mind.

This complexity, as an outgrowth of the logical use of dissonance, revealed itself first in the seventh chord whose basis was the V triad of the major/minor scale. If a triad is extended upward another interval of a 3rd, a chord results in which the highest tone is a 7th above the foundation tone, or *root*. If the upper 3rd is major, a chord of some tension is created; there is less tension if the third is smaller. Were one to count intervals in the latter chord, he would note the presence of a tritone in those seventh chords based upon a major triad thus adding to the already strong tendency of the 7th to resolve. Historically, it would seem that the first seventh chord to be used to any extent was that formed from the V triad, and hence known as the *dominant seventh chord* (V^7). The tendency of this chord (in context of course, for only then does a chord have significance) was even more strongly toward resolution on the tonic chord. Later, more such complex chords were added to the vocabulary of music until, at the end of the nineteenth century, much music employed no other kind of harmony. The basic qualities of these chords also became varied through chromatically changing one or more tones up or down by half-steps until they were no longer recognizably part of a major/minor key system. As we shall see, this development precipitated a revolution which is not completely over yet. Other thirds were piled atop the seventh chords to create ever more dissonant complexes of ninth, eleventh and thirteenth chords. New ways were found to resolve these, although eventually this device was dispensed with, and the chord became regarded as an entity which was free to move in any direction——not only that of lessening tension, but also to other harmonies of the same or greater dissonance. We shall explore these perilous regions more fully when our survey reaches the twentieth century.

Harmonic Cadences

The harmonic support for a melody must enhance the rise and fall of the melodic line, and, most important of all, must verify the kind of cadence at the end of each phrase of the melody. We have, then, not only *melodic* cadences, but also *harmonic* cadences. These may also be divided into two classes: *final* and *non-final*. The final cadence represents arrival at complete stability, with no need to move further. (Sing the first phrase of "America": this concludes with a final cadence.) The non-final cadence implies that there is more to come, and represents an arrival at a plane of conditional stability (first phrase of the "Star-Spangled Banner"). In either case, the general formula for a cadence is: unstable chord → to → more stable chord. Everything we have discovered about the importance and function of the melodic cadence is emphasized when the harmony is added.

The most important final cadences may be represented by the chord progressions of V-I and IV-I. The former is the cadence at the end of the phrase of "America" ("—of thee I sing"). The second is the familiar "Amen" cadence used after hymns. An especially strong final cadence may be created by combining these two into IV-V-I, or V-I-IV-I. Of course, if the V^7 chord is substituted for the plain dominant in any of these cadential progressions, the finality of the cadence is increased.

The non-final cadences are comparatively numerous, but two deserve specific mention. One is the arrival at conditional stability on the V chord, and is called a *half-cadence*. It is the kind used at the end of the first phrase of "The Star-Spangled Banner," and of Dvořák's "Largo" (Example I-5). The second is the *deceptive cadence*, and consists of the substitution of a chord other than tonic for the final chord of a strong cadential progression (for example: IV-V^7-VI). It has a certain shocking and surprising effect, and usually signals that the selection is about to end——but not just yet! The most common chord which replaces that I in this situation is VI, although a number of others may be used when varying inflections of deception are desired.

Harmonic cadences, while important as artistic punctuation for melodic phrases, have another important function: they define the key at the moment of cadence by their feeling of finality or the opposite. This key-defining function is not so strongly felt nor so important in music written before about 1630, since the scales used during the Middle Ages and Renaissance were *modal scales* (see p. 46) whose tonic, or *final* tones did not exert the strong pull on other scale tones characteristic of the major/minor scale tonics in general use after that date. But in the music of the Baroque, Classic and Romantic periods (1600 to 1900), the *tonality* (or scale in use at any particular moment) became the basis for the structure of the music, thus making the key-defining function of cadences highly important. The strongest of these cadences is the IV-V-I progression, for it presents all of the tones of the scale in a series of harmonies, allowing in this way no ambiguity of key feeling.

One of the ways to indicate in tonal music the change from one structural area, A, to a different one, B, is by changing from scale A to scale B. To accomplish this, the necessary sharps or flats are added or subtracted from scale A to result in scale B. Referring to Example I-3, we may see that to change from the a-minor scale indicated below the keyboard to the E-major scale above, we should have to introduce F♯,G♯,C♯ and D♯, replacing those unaltered tones in the a-minor scale. This process is known as *modulation,* and usually occurs in an intermediate section of music, between A and B, in which the necessary changes are smoothly introduced. It also may be accomplished abruptly, with a strong sense of movement to the new key, or sometimes shock. We shall call attention to modulation in our survey when it becomes important in the music and devote more explanation to it at that time.

SONORITY

Music, as heard by the attentive listener, has another attribute which is called *sonority.* This term describes the quality of sound at a given moment in a piece of music, or as a generalization of the character of sound representative of a particular style or period. It is a product of a number of contributory factors which includes the texture, the complexity (or simplicity) of the harmony, the spacing and repetition of tones in a chord, the combined sound of the instruments or voices engaged in a composition, or the individual quality of the instruments themselves. It is, in part, a product of subjective judgment, but it seems to be a matter of general agreement that the sonority of a

Baroque orchestral composition is quite characteristic and recognizably different from that of a symphony by Beethoven, Brahms or
Stravinsky; and, all are of a totally different sound quality from the
choral music of the Renaissance, not only because the latter is formed
exclusively of voices, but also because of the polyphonic texture and
the simple harmony which is produced as its byproduct. Thus, the
sonority of a composition often will lead to an educated guess as to its
stylistic period, opening the door on information about composers,
forms and other specific features leading to more complete understanding of the work.

MUSICAL FORM

Form in music is pervasive. It is the expression of time and tone,
and is created by the operations of rhythm throughout the whole realm
of sound combinations. At the lowest level, it is the rhythmic vibration
which begets sound itself, but on higher levels it is responsible for the
meter, the repetitions of musical ideas, sections and eventually the
entire movements of compound forms such as the mass, the symphony
and the opera. A composer, it is plain to see, must have a clear knowledge of the workings of these aspects of rhythm in order to write even
a simple composition. Let us examine the most important general
qualities of musical form as it has been used over the centuries in the
music of western Europe, the seat of our musical tradition since about
600 A.D. What we find may then be used by the listener to understand
the larger as well as the smaller characteristics of the music which he
hears. It is clear that there is no real comprehension of music without
insight into the pervasive qualities of its rhythmic formal structure.

Form is, first of all, the expression of a particular style in music,
which in turn is the expression of its age in history. Music at any time
conforms to the requirements of society whether these spring from the
church, the court or the concert hall. Just as do the other arts, music
expresses its time. A change in style indicates that the former period is
passing, and a new style is being evolved out of innovations and usable
remnants of the old practices, resulting in a synthesis based upon historical precedents but satisfying the new requirements.

Secondly, musical form is also a function of its material, particularly the scale and metric organizations which it uses. The history of
western European music may be divided into three eras on the basis of
the type of scale which each employed. The period of the modal scales

embraces the first thousand years or so, from about 600 to 1600. These will be discussed in the relevant chapters of our survey, but suffice it to say here that they have no strong organizing element comparable to the magnetic pull of the tonic tone and triad of the major/minor scale system. For this very reason, their forms must be different from those of the next era——that of these tonal scales (major/minor). The years between 1600 and 1900 saw music organized upon the principles of *tonality* and the creation of new forms which were its expression. From 1900 to the present, the tonal principle has been challenged by the introduction of tones of the chromatic scale into the major/minor system, weakening the attraction by the tonic tone, and therefore tending to destroy the forms based upon this principle. It became necessary to create new musical techniques to produce forms which were the embodiment of the chromatic scale. The advent of electronic music with its freedom from any restrictions of scale and meter has caused a serious crisis which has not at this writing been successfully dealt with. The beginnings and conclusions of these periods are transitional and show increasing use of the new style factors and corresponding weakening of the old ones.

The third factor influencing form is the performing *medium* for which the music was written. Here there is a strong relation to the periods described in the previous paragraph, for the modal period was predominantly a time of vocal and choral music, the tonal one of instrumental music, and the chromatic twentieth century a time of mixed media which included traditional instruments as well as the new electronic ones. In the same way that a sculptor chooses different materials to suit the requirements of his creations, so the composer creates different forms each adapted to the peculiarities of the medium for which it is intended. To be sure, this is often a flexible rule, and many a work is "apt for voyces or viols," for a great deal of traditional music is an imitation of the singing voice. But instrumental music consistently has exploited its capabilities of facile movement by any size of step or skip over a wider range of tones than possible to the voice and thus has drawn away from the highly expressive but limited range and movement of the human voice. Indeed, one of the criteria in judging music, new music especially, is that of how well it is written to exploit the medium, be it voice, piano, string quartet, symphony orchestra or electronic sound synthesizer. While each may borrow techniques from the other, they must be made to sound genuine in the new medium.

The requirements of vocal music are quite different from those of instrumental music largely because the extramusical element of words is present. In many cases the sense of the text supersedes the necessity for purely musical logic, and the form of the text dictates that of the music. This was true repeatedly of some of the vocal music of the Middle Ages and Renaissance and has been characterized by the German term *durchkomponiert,* or "through-composed." Most composers, however, think in musical terms predominantly and therefore try to make their music independently strong and unified, whether it carries a text or not. During the modal period they accomplished this by the repetition of motivic patterns, phrases or sections thereof, or whole sections consisting of several phrases. Using short patterns or sections of phrases, a composer could create a tight musical relationship among the parts of what otherwise would be classified as a through-composed piece of music. The repetition of larger sections, of course, gives rise to forms characterized by letter sequences as A-B-A-C-A-D. Since each new thought in the text of this music required a different musical idea, such a structure was necessary to give musical coherence to the whole.

The necessity of developing musical forms which did not depend upon words resulted in many of the structures characteristic of the tonal age of music. These forms also required more sharply defined rhythmic and melodic ideas for their material than did the style of the previous century. Instead of flowing, melodic phrases, the new *theme* (or *subject,* depending upon its use) was characteristically short, with a well defined melodic and/or rhythmic character, and a sense of incompletion requiring some sort of process of expansion and growth to fulfill its possibilities.

To be sure, the so-called lyric or song forms of previous times were retained. These essentially simple structures usually employ extended melody as their material, and depend upon more or less simple repetition and contrast for their structures. Therefore, if we characterize two different and complete melodies by A and B, the simplest form will be A-B, which, however, is not generally satisfying as a closed form which concludes with the repetition of A: A-B-A. In the tonal period, to heighten the contrast and to emphasize the newness and freshness of melody B, the central section was placed in a tonality different from that of A which was the same at the end as at the beginning. This three-part, or *ternary* form may be extended by the addition of other contrasting material, but usually is closed by a repetition of the A section (for an example of this, see the final movement of the *Concerto for Violin in E-major* by Bach.). In some cases, the sections other than A employ themes for their material rather than fully developed melodies and use them in ways which we are about to discuss.

The other more complex and cohesive instrumental forms are cast in sections devoted to the processes of *presentation, extension* and *summation*. They use a mixture of themes and melodic phrases, the one throwing the other into relief by effective contrast of smoothness of melodic character or sharply defined ryhthm. In general, sections devoted to different themes or processes are in different keys, sometimes with modulations providing smooth and logical transitions between them.

The presentation of thematic material, literally the *subjects* of the musical discourse, usually is done as simply as possible so that the listener may hear them undisturbed by complexities of harmony, rhythm or instrumentation, and thus memorize them so as to be able to recognize them when they recur. The recognition of form in music depends upon this memory, and to reinforce the first impressions, a composer often repeats his presentation, sometimes in a slightly varied way so as to sustain interest. The greater the complexity of the subsequent music, the greater is the necessity of clear presentation.

The extension process occupies the central and often the most interesting portion of the composition, just as in a sermon or lecture it is what the speaker says about his subject, rather than the subject itself, which is of the greater interest. Musical extension employs repetition, usually in new and unexpected yet logical ways, and often with more or less rapid changes of key to suggest motion through tonal space. Variation and contrast play a large role in this kind of extension, and impart a sense of growth and realization to the material, which may have seemed rather fragmentary and ordinary when it was first heard. It is in the extension of the material that the imaginative and creative ability, as well as the craftsmanship of the composer is most evident. It is here that his right to the title "composer" is won.

The summation usually provides a clear restatement of the material out of which the movement has been constructed and should have a sense of gathering in all of the threads of the preceding music, showing their relationships and concluding in a manner which resolves the tensions of the central sections. In some cases, a more or less exact repetition of the presentation section is all that is needed. In others, a more elaborate and varied reprise must be written to give that sense of balance and symmetry, resolution and conclusion so necessary to the summation of a large and complex discourse.

A number of compositions may be used to illustrate these general processes of music. The masses of Palestrina and other Renaissance composers of sacred music show the formal dependence upon words, for the most part, although other unifying devices may be present;

these usually are not apparent to the listener, however. The fugues of Bach, as well as the opening movements of the first and second *Brandenburg Concertos* provide examples of polyphonic presentation, extension and summation; the first movements of the *Symphony No. 40* of Mozart, *Symphony No. 5* of Beethoven, and the *Symphony in C* of Stravinsky are more homophonic. The song forms find ample illustration in the short piano pieces of Chopin and Schubert, and in some of the latter's songs (see the pages devoted to this composer).

Most of what has been said about form was derived from traditional practice employing voice and instrument, and does not apply generally to the new electronic music. This art is in its infancy and has not yet evolved structures which can be regarded as formal procedures other than the ones inherited from twelve-tone serial music. Let us postpone discussion of these until their proper place in our survey, when our listening experience and accumulated information will help us to deal more justly with them.

AESTHETICS

Practically everyone nowadays is a music critic. He may not realize it and may disclaim all knowledge of the art, but he is even more ready to hand down opinions on everything from rock-and-roll to electronic music. He may never have heard of the philosophical examination of beauty and meaning in the arts which is called *aesthetics*. Nevertheless, he is entitled to his opinion. If required to defend that opinion, however, our critic would be wise to learn what conclusions and theories have been advanced in aesthetics, especially in the last hundred years. These have ranged from speculations on the nature of beauty in music, the nature of the art and how and why it affects us as it does, and the problem of judging the value and significance of a composition.

In the matter of beauty itself, it seems to be the result of the mind's intuition of orderliness in musical composition, the feeling that, to quote Thomas Aquinas, "the senses delight in things duly proportioned as in something akin to them." Eduard Hanslick (1825-1904), in his highly influential book *On the Beautiful in Music*, reiterates a similar idea but extends it to include comments on the nature of music. He coined the aesthetic definition of music as "sounding form" (*tönend bewegte Form*), and affirmed that music was incapable of expressing anything else other than this——its intrinsic nature. "By this we mean that the beautiful is not contingent upon nor in need of any subject introduced from without, but that it consists wholly of sounds artistically combined. . . . A musical idea reproduced in its entirety is not only an object of intrinsic beauty but also an end in itself and not a means for representing feelings and thoughts." He would not readily admit as music, then, imitations of cuckoos and other birds, steam locomotives, or thunderstorms unless they made good sense as abstract music to begin with. His book appeared during the second half of the nineteenth century at a time when, through the Wagnerian opera and the Lisztian tone poem, composers sought to create "pictures" and other nonmusical effects through harmony, rhythm, melody and tone color. This descriptive art Hanslick opposed with his appeal to abstract music, represented then by the music of the composer Brahms. With the reaction against nineteenth century ideals and standards which came during the second decade of the twentieth century, many composers and critics agreed with Hanslick's view.

But, if music expresses nothing but itself, how can we account for the fact that it affects us emotionally? Modern psychological research has attempted to explain this, and philosophers, using these results together with their insights and reasoning have extended their hypotheses in many directions. Suzanne Langer, in her book, *Philosophy in a New Key,* calls music a symbolic language, since it does not convey scientific information upon which action can be based and hence is a language of *unconsummated symbols.* In *Music as Metaphor,* Donald N. Ferguson relates the fluctuations of tension and relaxation in music to those caused in the human organism by the impact of sensory experience. Human response to music is thus a sympathetic reflection of the stresses of the music, but the physical tensions are inhibited before active responses are initiated, and so turn into sensations of feeling. Presumably, the composer writes tensions and relaxations into his music through his past experience; his audience finds points of contact with him through his expression, although their experiences may not be exactly those which he has reflected in his music, but ones which call forth similar tensions. Thus, each person has a relatively unique response based upon his experience; certainly there are enough common experiences to provide also a similarly common response to some music. The slow, dark music which reminds most people of sadness in terms of a "funeral march" is one of these, and may be recognized as a kind of *cliché* whose response is quite firmly established. Dissonance is always effective in one way or another, since it calls forth considerable tension, often reminiscent of unpleasant experiences, and may explain the general dislike of music whose dissonance saturation is rather high. Conversely, much choral music from the sixteenth century possesses little tension, and, unless controlled by a skilled director, leaves an impression of bland monotony. The degree of emotion received by the listener may be due in a large part to these factors as well as to the presence of *clichés* to which he has been habituated, knowingly or not. A composer whose nature is to persuade his audience to "feel" with him, and therefore creates his music out of *clichés*——perhaps radically altered in outward appearance according to his musical personality, but still *clichés* at the core——such a composer essentially is a romantic writer, appealing to the heart. Another, whose interest is in the controlled expression of feeling, stated in a strongly formal manner, may use *clichés* also, but these are more abstract in nature, and seldom have the connotations common to the romantic ones. This is the classic attitude, an appeal to the intellect, to "the delight in things duly proportioned." Because even the most romantic music must have structure, else it ceases being music, and because no music written by human beings can be wholly abstract and without significance to others, romanticism and classicism are the two faces of the same coin, and become a matter of degree. The pendulum of musical style swings now toward one, then back toward the other as the eras of history pass by; it is the constant struggle that the Greeks recognized between Apollo, the epitome of intellect and radiant abstraction, and Dionysius, the intoxicating spirit of the senses and emotions. It is the play between head and heart, and, as in human action, the music is usually based upon a combination of the two.

However interesting, these speculations do not always prove of value in our attempts to evaluate what we hear. What may we use to judge music, aside from the physical criteria of the lump in the throat, the knotted stomach muscles and the shiver up and down the back?

Fortunately, there are a number of quite objective characteristics of music which the attentive listener may pick out, and which, combined with a certain imaginative insight increased by experience, will enable him to do justice to most traditional music. Contemporary music poses a rather different problem which we shall deal with when we come to it. A large number of the musical characteristics which may be used as criteria depend upon the style of the music. In our use of this term, we shall limit it to mean the preference by composers and listeners during a historical cultural period for certain types of melody, harmony, rhythm, texture and sonority.

Music does not exist in a vacuum, but is shaped by the common experiences, needs and tastes of the composer and his audience living in a clearly defined intellectual and physical environment. In past centuries, up to about the middle of the nineteenth century, almost all music was commissioned and paid for by persons whose preferences guided the composer in his work. If the music did not please the patron, who often times was a sort of cultural standard-bearer of his time, the music was not performed, the composer was not paid, and the manuscript was more than likely used to start a fire! Thus, in the music which survived such harsh treatment, we deal with two interconnected styles——that of the composer and of his time, the differences and likenesses of which become ever clearer and more characteristic upon repeated listening to the compositions.

Each of the elements of music plays a part in shaping the style: melody, by its smoothness or angularity, for example; harmony in its degree of complexity; rhythm in its degree of stability; texture in the predominance of the linear-horizontal or the columnar-vertical structure; sonority in the use of particular instruments or in the total effect, and form in revealing the musical logic (or lack of it, or dependence upon it) of the composer and the style. Unfortunately, the names of the historical style periods of music are not always as accurately descriptive as they might be since most of them were taken from the sister arts of literature and architecture. Thus, the so-called "Classic Period" (1750-1825) has nothing to do in music with the songs and symphonia of ancient Greece and Rome in the way that the architecture of the period revives the structural ideals of the ancient classical buildings. So, we must treat such terms merely as names for certain spans of time during which a particular synthesis of musical elements arose, flourished, and then gave way to a different one. Our journey through this book will be undertaken with the idea of establishing the general manner of treatment of the elements of musical compositions which are particular and peculiar to each stylistic period in the history of music. It will, perforce, be somewhat technical but not more so than is necessary. Definitions will be advanced, and hopefully, upon listening to particular works, illustrated in the music. Certainly, generalizations must be made and must be recognized as being true in the whole picture even if contradicted by a few specific instances. After some listening one should be able to fix his attention upon specific characteristics of a work which define its style and turn his judgement toward defining in his mind how well (craftsmanship) and how imaginatively (artistry) the composer has employed them. In these days of widespread recording of music which is not all made up of imperishable masterpieces, this kind of critical judgement may be exercised easily to the greater appreciation of the really great works of our musical heritage.

Like language, music deals with ideas: patterns of tones, of rhythms or of harmonies. The basic form for a good essay or lecture revolves around the statement, development and summary of the leading ideas. That of a musical composition, as we have seen, may do exactly the same thing. If the ideas are small, not necessarily trivial, then the work will be brief and the scope of expression limited to the size of the work. If the composition is to be large, the ideas will be more numerous and provocative, inviting extension and development. There must be unity gained by repetition in various ways, and variety by contrast and comparison of musical materials. Most superior composers try to use a minimum of material and to create a maximum of variety, interest and extension from it. The form is engendered by the natural unfolding of the material, as an inevitable result of the kinds of material used in the work. Indeed, in great art works of any kind, there seems to be an inevitability about the structure, reminding one of the shape of a tree on a mountain ledge, growing against the tensions of wind and gravity, but assuming its natural generic form and characteristics.

To say some things, simple words simply put together suffice. To say more difficult things as simply as possible, more complicated words and meanings must often be related in a less straightforward manner. There are degrees of simplicity, depending upon what is to be said. So it is in music: complex statements require complex structures. Great composers, however, always see to it that the work is as simple as it can be. If it is complex, then the musical concept and statement must be complex. But one must remember, form is of the essence in music and therefore with sufficient listening and creative attention, even the most labyrinthine musical thoughts may be understood. Such perception of the organization of parts, their derivations, interrelations and contrasts depends upon the faculty of memory. The cardinal rule to abide by in listening to music, especially if it is the first exposure to a composition, is: remember the first musical idea which you hear when the music begins. Very often in music, as in literature, the important characters appear immediately. Their recurrences, extensions and developments may then be recognized. Additional musical ideas will begin to reveal themselves in relation to the established one and rank themselves in importance by the repetitions and developments to which they are subjected. The sequence of musical events becomes clearer, and the formal logic begins to emerge until finally one perceives the whole structure and can look both ahead and behind as he is immersed in the work, comparing, noting, and appreciating ever finer distinctions which the composer has created. If a composition will bear this kind of scrutiny, it is safe to say that it is a durable work——one of value. And, if the listener can find new things of interest each time he hears it, his reward for the painstaking effort will be so much the greater. This book will be devoted to just such scrutiny, up to a point, for the listener needs no guide after a certain level is reached. The necessarily somewhat wordy analyses are no substitute for listening to the music. They merely serve as guides to style, forms and techniques which, it is hoped, will facilitate the listener's recognition of what is happening in the music. No guide book can chart all of the interesting locations in a region! This is for the traveller to discover for himself. Using this book to locate the landmarks, the musical traveller may then set out on his own.

RELATIONSHIPS BETWEEN MUSIC AND THE OTHER ARTS

While it is dangerous to make comparisons on a one-to-one basis between the various arts of a period, certain aspects of one of them may assist in the comprehension of another. In the case of music, parallels drawn from the other arts are open to disagreement if for no other reason than the fact that they are spatial and relatively enduring in nature while music is evanescent and exists only in time or recollection. Nevertheless, the insights obtained by this comparison seem valuable enough to attempt such a venture.

In the largest aspect, certain resemblances of formal treatment might be pointed out. In each, music and painting as well as architecture and sculpture, sections are apt to be repeated, either literally or with variations, separated by some differing material. The original section may comprise, in painting, a color area of a certain intensity which may be repeated elsewhere with a different intensity, or even with a different color if the intensities are comparable. Or it may be made up of a certain pattern of lines, the general character of which may recur elsewhere, thus resembling the melodic and thematic elements of a piece of music. In the case of sculpture, the correspondences are more difficult to point out since this involves the comparison between a one-dimensional art—music, which exists only in time—with a three, or actually four-dimensional art. Certain parallels will be noticed, however, depending upon how obviously the sculptor has used his formal elements. In architecture, the balancing and symmetrical parts of buildings, the proportions, heights, ornaments and other features often make comparison quite obvious and easy, but one must always take into account that exactness of correspondence is neither to be looked for nor expected.

Because of the spatial nature of painting, artists have long employed a formal device which became a conscious factor in musical composition only near the end of the seventeenth century. This is the use of structural elements to "lead the eye" to the most important object or area of the painting—the "subject" really, of the whole effort. A correspondence may be seen in literature also, consisting of the sections in a play or novel—argument, complication, denouément. Opera, since it is dependent upon dramatic literature often is built upon such a principle. In music, compound forms, such as the cantata, the symphony, the sonata and the string quartet, offer valid comparisons. The cantatas of Bach, as well as other works by this master, show definite, well worked-out conceptions of centralization of important moments or movements in the structure, as do the later quartets of Beethoven and Béla Bartók, and many other works between. Even the asymmetric placement of the "subject" on the canvas is paralleled by the off center location of the climactic spot in a movement of music or in a series of movements. Certain characteristics of music, literature and the drama may warrant calling them the "time arts." The most important of these characteristics is that of emotional progression, in which the observer is carried along toward the climactic moment upon a tide of time. The progression of the Beethoven Fifth Symphony, or the Prelude to *Tristan und Isolde* are excellent examples of this. In the other arts, the painter and sculptor are obliged to accomplish this by a series of separate pieces showing developments of an action or drama, although this is rather crude compared with the time-arts, and precisely so because of the natural limitations of the medium. But examples of this do exist, particularly in art of the Middle Ages, where the painter often places multiple views of his subject under different circumstances within one frame (see Chapter II, Plate II).

When we descend from the larger realm of form to more elemental components of the arts, we find again that certain congruences occur. Melodic line, for example, is quite comparable to line, or often outline, in painting and sculpture, sometimes in architecture. All may contain either "lyric" lines which are smoothly curved, or more or less angular lines which stride about with a feeling of boldness or tension. Or, in painting and architecture, the lines may be diffused by minute irregularities, the use of shading or the application of profuse ornamentation. Similarly in music, the skeletal structure of the line may be obscured and the line itself diffused by ornamentation—turns, trills, grace notes of various kinds—or by rapid stepwise movement around the skeletal structure, sometimes scalewise, sometimes with the use of a recurrent melodic or rhythmic pattern.

Harmony in music has often been compared to the phenomenon of perspective in painting as a means of adding depth. It must be added that the degree of intensity is in both art forms another potent factor in this illusion of depth. Any beginning painter knows how hard it is to make objects recede in his painting, for not only must the laws of diminishing perspective be used, but also those of diminishing intensity. A similar situation occurs to a conductor when he "balances" an orchestra by cautioning the oboe not to play too loudly—that is, to stay in the background—while another less sonorous instrument plays a "foreground" solo. Very often in an analogous way, harmony is used to provide the background to a foreground solo, especially in homophonic texture. The tones of the background blend in such a way as to provide a "canvas" upon which the nearer and brighter solo color may trace its line. If the background contains too many dissonances, and is too unstable or active, it will call attention to itself and not fulfill its primary function. These non-blending dissonances are like bright flashes of too intense color in a painting, intended to be background, but not receding because of their intensity.

Rhythm, too, has a complex but somewhat comparable role in both painting and music. Unfortunately, the use of the word in the graphic arts is not entirely the same as it is in music. Painters tend to use it in terms of repetition or "eye motion" of some element in the painting, whereas in music, it more often designates an onward-moving factor which, together with the subtle qualities of tension variation inherent in harmonic progressions, seems to cause the music to travel down the time dimension in an almost physical way. But in the larger aspect, rhythm has a similar function in both arts: it creates or relaxes tension by means of the degree of activity it possesses. A musical composition may be agitated due to the great profusion of rhythmic motives and their continuous motion, just as the lines and color factors of a painting may give a swirling or chaotic effect by allowing no quiet area to appear upon which the eye may rest. Rhythmic activity of line is one of the more important aspects of comparison between these art forms.

The factor of repetition is an interesting and somewhat ambiguous element in both arts. When used discreetly, it tends to create form. When overused, it tends to deaden the senses by sheer cumulative power resulting in, at worst, monotony, or at best, an effect of massive grandeur. In some medieval structures, for example, the endless repetition of undifferentiated statues or other figures, such as rows of small, Roman-arched windows, lends a certain immobility, sometimes impressiveness, to the structure, just as the long drawn-out repetitions of only a few chords over a held bass note make Notre Dame organum of the Perotin variety static, massive, and eventually by cumulative effect, almost overpowering.

In art, the word "tone," when used to describe the general effect of a painting, may find a counterpart in the term "sonority" in music. We may say that the tone of a painting is bright, just as the opening of the Bach *Magnificat* is bright. And, by extension, works in both media may be monochromatic—using shades of the same color, or tone color—or polychromatic, sharply defined or blended, brilliant or dull. But we must realize that these are only generalizations, and therefore dangerous and inaccurate when extended too far. Proceed cautiously and, as always in this area, at your own risk.

To this observer, the various media employed in music and painting have a certain correspondence. The transparent quality of a chamber ensemble, consisting of from two to a dozen players, is comparable to paintings done in watercolor, or other transparent media, which, we must not forget, like chamber music may have strong contrasts and emotional quality. In the same way, the larger musical groups tend toward thickness and opacity—here also a function of how the instruments are used—so do oils, gouache, and other basically opaque forms of paint add thickness to the picture. Drama, too, is more inherent in these heavier materials, it would seem.

A final consideration of the formal structure suggests itself— whether the music or picture is closed and classical in nature, or open and romantic. Many pictures are completely closed in that they presuppose nothing relevant outside of what is shown. The eye is led inward and around, never to the edges and thence outside the frame. Musical form in the Classic period has this same quality of completeness, whereas in the Renaissance the motet-style forms are each inconclusive and, by the avoidance of repetition, are open in nature; any composer, working in the style, could add other sections on to those already in existence without doing damage to the work. Of course, these are text-based forms, and this single fact makes a great difference.

In the final section of each of the chapters devoted to the great historical epochs of music, we shall suggest comparisons between certain art works of that period and the music which we have examined. It is hoped that these interrelations will have the effect of offering visual interpretations not only of the cultural ideals of a period, but also of more specific parallel techniques of composition. The fleeting and abstract flow of music often profits by such comparison, and it is in this spirit that these sections are included.

FREQUENTLY USED ITALIAN TEMPO
AND EXPRESSION INDICATIONS

Tempo

Presto. Very fast
Vivace. Lively
Allegro. Fast, often followed by a qualifying term of which the following
are the most common:
  Allegro vivace. Somewhat slower than *vivace* alone, still very fast.
  Allegro molto. Very fast, but not as rapid as presto.
  Allegro assai. Very quick
Animato. Animated, less rapid than allegro
Allegretto. Literally, a "little *allegro*", *-etto* being a diminutive suffix.
Moderato. At medium speed.
Andantino. Again a diminutive suffix, *-ino* thus meaning "a little *andante.*"
Andante. Literally, "going," less fast than *moderato.*
Adagio, Lento, Largo and *Grave* signify increasingly slow tempos, often
qualified by *molto* (very), *assai* (extremely), or the comparative and
superlative suffixes, *-issimo* (*largissimo,* "most slowly") and *-ississimo*
(*largississimo,* "most slowliest").

Expression

Very often one of the tempo indications given above is modified by another
term in order to convey to the performer the manner in which the piece
is to be played. Such words are:

Affettuoso. With warmth, affectionately.
Agitato. Agitated, excited.
Appassionata. Impassioned.
Con brio. With spirit.
Cantabile. In a singing manner.
Capriccioso. In a humorous or capricious manner.
Dolce. Sweet and soft.
Dolente, Doloroso. Sadly, dolefully.
Frenetico. Frenzied.
Giocoso. Playful.
Grazioso. Graceful.
Lamentando. Mournfully, lamenting.
Leggiero. Light and graceful.
Lusinghando. Flattering, coaxing, intimate.
Maestoso. Grandly, with Majesty.
Marziale. Martially, march-like.
Ma non troppo. Not too much so (*e.g., Allegro ma non troppo:* fast, but not
extremely so).

Mesto. Mournful.
Con moto. With motion.
Non tanto, non troppo. Not too much (*e.g., Allegro non troppo*)
All' Ongarese. In Hungarian style.
Pesante. Heavily.
Quasi. As if, or almost: *e.g. Allegro quasi presto—allegro,* almost *presto.*
Risoluto. Resolutely, with decision.
Scherzando. Playfully.
Scorrevole. Freely flowing.
Sempre. Always, *e.g. sempre pesante*—always heavily.
Semplice. Simply.
Soave. Suavely, gently.
Sostenuto. Sustaining the tone or slackening the tempo, *e.g. allegro sostenuto* somewhat slower than *allegro.*
Spiritoso. Spirited, lively.
Teneramente. Tenderly.

Certain other terms relate to the dynamic level or to tempo changes. The most commonly used are these:
Dynamic level increasing from very soft to the loudest possible.

Pianississimo	*pianissimo*	*piano*	*mezzo-piano*		
(abbr.) ppp	pp	p	mp		
	mezzo-forte	*forte*	*fortissimo*	*fortississimo*	
	mf	f	ff	fff	

"*Piano*" (p) is the Italian term for soft: the endings make superlative and double-superlative degrees: similarly with "*forte*" (f), the Italian term for loud (literally, strong). The word "*mezzo*" signifies "medium."

The terms "*crescendo*" and "*diminuendo*" are frequently used, and denote a growing and a diminishing in dynamic level, respectively.
The most common terms relating to the change of tempo are these:

Accelerando. To accelerate, or speed up, often preceded or followed by "*poco a poco,*" meaning wherever used, "little by little."
Meno mosso. Less motion, more slowly.
Piu mosso. More motion, faster.
Ritardando, rallentando. Gradually slackening the speed. Abbreviated *rit.* and *rall.*

Most terms used in the above situations are derived from the Italian due to the fact that in the early Baroque era, when these terms first gradually came into use, most composers were trained in Italy. Hence Italian became the language most common among musical performers and was readily understood by them. Since Beethoven, German has appeared as a nationalistic substitute for Italian, and the same is true of French since Debussy, possibly somewhat before him. Some American and English composers use English terms as well as the Italian ones. Certainly there are no substitutes for the dynamic abbreviations as commonly used.

LIST OF IMPORTANT TERMS IN CHAPTER I

pitch
vibration
fundamental tone
partial vibrations
octave
harmonic series, overtone series
quality (of sound)
half step, semitone
whole step, whole-tone
musical alphabet
sharp, ♯
flat, ♭
scale
chromatic scale
major scale
minor scale
keynote, tonic tone
stable, unstable scale tones
tempo
meter
conducting patterns
measure, bar-lines
rhythm
simple time: 1-ta-te-ta
compound time: 1-la-lee
dotted rhythm
stable, unstable rhythm
syncopation
cadence: melodic, rhythmic,
    harmonic
motive
range (melodic)
conjunct, disjunct motion
final, nonfinal cadences,
phrase, period, section
texture: monophonic, polyphonic,
    homophonic

round, canon
counterpoint, polyphony
imitation
interval
chord
perfect consonances, imperfect
    consonances, dissonances
resolution (of dissonance)
triad
tritone
Tonic triad, I; Dominant triad, V;
    Subdominant triad, IV.
harmonic progression
root position, 1st and 2nd
    inversions of triads
harmonic diffusion
complex harmony
tonally unstable
7th chords
Harmonic cadences: final, nonfinal,
    half-cadence, deceptive
    cadence
tonality
modulation
sonority
musical form, structure
performing medium
durchkomponiert
    (through-composed)
theme, subject
song form
ternary, three-part, A-B-A
presentation, extension, summation
repetition, development
aesthetics
classicism, romanticism

BOOKS AND MUSIC

Ferguson, Donald N., *Music as Metaphor.* University of Minnesota Press, Minneapolis, 1960.

Hanslick, Eduard, *On the Beautiful in Music,* Liberal Arts Press, Bobbs, New York, 1957.

Langer, Suzanne, *Philosophy in a New Key.* New American Library, Mentor Books, New York, 1961.

Dvořák, Antonin: *Symphony No. 9, in E-minor, Op. 95* ("From the New World").

Beethoven, Ludwig van: *Symphony No. 5, in C-minor, Op. 67.*

Handel, George Frederick: *Messiah.*

Bach, Johann Sebastian: *Concerto for Violin and Orchestra, in E-major.*

Bach, Johann Sebastian: *Brandenburg Concertos Nos. 1 and 2.*

Mozart, Wolfgang A.: *Symphony No. 40, in G-minor.*

Stravinsky, Igor: *Symphony in C-major.*

II THE MEDIEVAL
PERIOD, 600-1450

PART I: THE ROMANESQUE ERA, 600-1100

Historical Perspective

THE HISTORY OF Western music begins with the medieval period—the Middle Ages, between antiquity and what we are pleased to call modern civilization, usually regarded as beginning with the Renaissance (c. 1450). For all practical purposes, we may regard the centuries from 600 to 1450 as the medieval period, although it is obvious that no specific date is really accurate when large cultural changes involving decades or even centuries are being considered. Furthermore, this long epoch may be conveniently subdivided into two periods of contrasting culture: the Romanesque, (600-1100) and the Gothic (1100-1450). The first embraces the period of slow recovery from the barbarian invasions and the resultant disruption of both the *Pax Romana* and the laws by which it was maintained. This culture, almost completely dominated by the ascetic Christian church, is marked by a religious mysticism exemplified by the low, horizontal lines and dark interiors of the Romanesque churches (Plate I), and by the subdued and meditative plainchant, as impersonal and other-

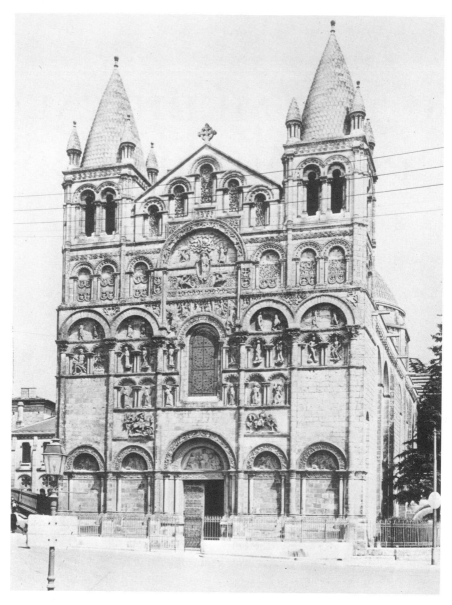

PLATE I. *Romanesque Church of St. Peter at Angoulême, France. (Courtesy of French Government Tourist Office.)*

worldly as the sculptures and paintings which adorn the churches. To the men of these times, the earthly life was an interlude to be endured until death opened the doors to eternal bliss in heaven. The church was the sole power which held this world together, for civil power could not rule without the sacred sanction.

In the artistic realm, all forms of representational and musical art were marshalled by the church to teach its laws to the illiterate populace. To accomplish this, stylization, resulting in the submergence of the individuality of the artist, prevailed in order that the images and pictures by the uniformity of their symbols, would always be intelligible to the unlettered beholder. For example, St. Paul was always depicted as a bald man with a long beard. When such a figure appears in a painting, stained glass window, or as a statue, we can be sure who it is, just as could the man of the Romanesque era. Thus, by bowing to these rules, individuality was lost in the interest of intelligibility, and the artist of the period is largely anonymous. It would almost seem that man had no individual will of his own at this time, for he dared not invent or discover something without the sanction of some kind of authority, usually religious. The authorities for the musical science of the time were Boethius and Cassiodorus, through whose books the knowledge of the Greeks was passed on to the monastic musicians of these early days. It was a philosophical and scientific examination of the phenomenon of sound rather than an "art" in the modern sense of the term, one of the "quadrivium" of arithmetic, geometry, music and astronomy deemed necessary for any student before he studied the ultimate subject, theology. Let us take a moment to review in general the achievements of the ancient Greeks in music.

Only a few decipherable examples of music have come down to us from antiquity, and these are mostly Greek. In contrast to them, the writings about music by the philosophers and scientists of this great civilization are numerous and illuminating. Pythagoras discovered the laws governing the vibration of stretched strings some 600 years before Christ, and his followers raised upon his work a mystic and speculative philosophy which often clouded the scientifically valuable part of the investigation. By means of these laws, however, as transmitted by Boethius, the medieval investigator could construct a "gamut" or scale of whole and half steps like that which we use today. In Greek times, the scales thus constructed were called "modes," and the medieval musician took over this term as well as the more specific names for each of the four modes he used. These were originally the names of the various Greek tribes, but now indicate what are usually called the "medieval modes," or the "church modes." Let us examine them.

Suppose we have series of tones arranged in whole and half steps exactly like the white keys of the piano (Example I-2). The half steps will occur between E and F, B and C. We may begin upon any tone of this series, F, for example, and by including the seven tones from this note up to its octave (F-G-A-B-C-D-E-) create a modal scale, in this case, the Lydian mode. Those modes beginning on C and A are our familiar major and minor modes. The others sound less familiar, since the arrangement of whole and half steps differs from major or minor, although they bear a certain resemblance in quality to these. The scale on B was never included in the medieval modes because of its instability, but the other four provided the material for the melodic, and later, harmonic constructions of music from the early Middle Ages up to the end of the Renaissance. The following tabulation shows the name of the scale, its fundamental note which was called the "final," from its cadential function at the close of a composition, and the dominant tone, next in importance to the final. (See Example II-1.)

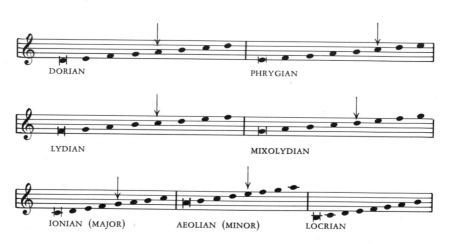

EXAMPLE II-1: *The modal scales.*

NAME	DOMINANT	FINAL
Dorian	A	D
Phrygian	C	E
Lydian	C	F
Mixolydian	D	G

PLATE II. *St. Francis of Assisi by Berlinghieri from the Church of San Francesco, Pescia, Italy. Note the Byzantine impersonality of the figure in which all irregularities are omitted, thus creating a symbol rather than a portrait. (Photo Alinari, Florence.)*

The Musical Style of the Romanesque Period

The music of the early Middle Ages is predominantly monophonic, and is exemplified on the sacred side by *plainchant*, sometimes called *plainsong* or *Gregorian chant*, and on the secular side by the lusty or courtly songs of the minstrels, *trouvères* and *troubadours*. Both kinds employ modal scale material and have strong points of resemblance in their melodic construction, and both are monophonic, although it seems likely that some sort of simple accompaniment was used with the secular music. Let us first examine plainchant.

This music is devotional and rather impersonal in nature, devised to carry the all-important words of church ritual and therefore generally subservient to them. But it is highly artistic in the way it subtly heightens the meaning of the words——an artistry similar to that of folk song. Melodically, it is exceedingly vocal in character, with no wide leaps, and usually moves within a rather restricted range of tones, seldom greater than an octave in span.

In the square notation which has come down to us (Example II-3), the notes, called *neumes*, are written on a four-line staff with a clef-sign to indicate the line upon which the tone C, or in some cases, F, is placed. The square, or Gregorian notation, provides possibilities for vocal interpretation of plainchant which are not easily indicated in modern notation, and thus is retained in chant books. The various complicated shapes of these notes would require considerable space and time to explain, so that we shall not pursue them further. If one is interested, the introduction to the *Liber Usualis**, a useful collection of many chants, provides information about them and the performance of plainchant.

Let us examine some examples of these various settings of sacred words and see what else we can learn from them. Example II-2 is the famous Easter sequence *Victimae paschali laudes*, written by Wipo (d.ca 1048), chaplain to King Henry III. It is in the Dorian mode, and the formal arrangement is clear from the way in which the example is written; less obvious, however, is the use of unifying motives which give organization to the melody by their reappearance. These are indicated by brackets and letters. This composition should not only be listened to, but also sung if one is to get the feeling of the subtle flow of groups of two or three syllables in each small metric unit. This *prose rhythm*, while it lacks the evenly spaced pulse of poetic rhythm, still propels the melody very satisfyingly.

---

* Published by Desclée et Cie., Tournai, Belgium, 1950.

EXAMPLE II-2: *Victimae paschali laudes.* Easter Sequence by Wipo (*Liber Usualis* 780).

A.

1. Ví - cti mae pas - chál - i láu - des * ím - mo - lent Chri - sti - á - ni.

B.

2. A - gnus re - dé - mit ó - ves: Chrís - tus ín - no - cens Pá - tri
3. Mors et ví - ta du - él - lo con - flix - é - re mi - rán - do:

re - con - ci - li - á - vit pec - ca - tó - res.
dux ví - tae mór - tu - us, rég - nat ví - vus.

C.

4. Dic nó - bis Ma - rí - a____, quid vi - dís - ti in ví - a?
5. An - gé - li - cos tés - tes, su - dá - ri - um, et vé - stes.

Se - púl - crum Chrís - ti vi - vén - tis,
Sur - réx - it Chrís - tus spes mé - a:

et gló - ri - am ví - di re - sur - gén - tis:
prae - cé - det sú - os in Ga - li - laé - am.

D.

6. Scí - mus Chrís - tus sur - rex - ís - se a mór - tu - is ve - re:

tu   nó - bis,   víc - tor Rex,   mi - se - ré - re.

A   -   men.   Al - le - lú - ia.

Motives which recur in this chant, providing unity through repetition and
variation:

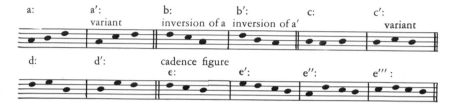

Note the repetition of phrases: B_1-D_1 and the variation of phrases: A_2-B_2-
C_3-D_2. The two patterns marked f are rearrangements of the tones of a, b and,
consisting of the important interval of a 4th, with an auxiliary tone.

The text may be translated as follows, with letter showing the poetic
form:

A. Let Christians dedicate their praises to the Easter victim.
B. The Lamb has ransomed the sheep: The innocent Christ has reconciled
   the sinners with the Father.
B. Death and life have contended in wondrous battle: after death the living
   Leader reigns.
C. Tell us, Mary, what you saw upon the way?
   The sepulchre of the living Christ, and the glory of His rising.
C. The angelic witnesses, and the veil and garments.
   Christ, my hope, is risen, and goes ahead of us into Galilee.
D. We know in truth that Christ has arisen from the dead: to us, victorious
   king, be merciful. Amen. Alleluia.

Example II-3 is the Introit which opens the Easter Mass. The first
section (lines 1 through 5) is called an *antiphon,* and introduces the
psalm (marked Ps.) which is, for the most part chanted with one note
per syllable in two phrases provided with beginning figures and
cadences. When the Psalm is finished, the *Gloria Patri* ("Glory be to
the Father . . .") is chanted to the same tones as the Psalm, after which
the antiphon is repeated. Thus, an A-B-A structure is created. Originally, more verses of the Psalm were used, but these disappeared in

the early Gothic ritual leaving only the antiphon and one psalm verse. Notice the decorative setting of the antiphon words in what is known as *melismatic* style with many tones to each syllable. This kind of music was used for the high feasts of the church, while plainer settings were sung on more ordinary occasions.

EXAMPLE II-3: *Introit to the Easter Mass.* Antiphon and Psalm.

Translation:
Antiphon: I am risen and am now with thee, alleluia; thou hast placed thy hand on me, alleluia; thy knowledge is made wonderful, alleluia, alleluia. *Psalm:* O Lord, thou has searched me out and known me; thou knowest my downsitting and my uprising.

The most significant compound form in which plainchant is used is that of the Mass, or celebration of the Last Supper, sometimes called Holy Communion. This ritual may be divided into two main

parts, the Ordinary and the Proper. The texts of the Ordinary, set to
various chants, form part of every celebration of the Mass, while those
of the Proper change according to the seasons of the church calendar.
For example, a Christmas and an Easter Mass will have the same
Ordinary, but different Propers. Because of this invariability of the
Ordinary, composers from the fourteenth century to the present time
have set these texts to more or less elaborate music. There are five
main sections to the Ordinary named by the first few words of the
Latin text:

1. *Kyrie eleison* ("Lord have mercy")
2. *Gloria in excelsis Deo* ("Glory to God in the highest")
3. *Credo in unum deum* ("I believe in one God," the Nicene creed)
4. *Sanctus* (Holy, holy, holy); *Benedictus* ("Blessed is he who cometh in the
   name of the Lord")
5. *Agnus Dei* ("Lamb of God, that taketh away the sins of the world")

A striking example of the subtle feeling for unity and formal
coherence in plainchant is to be found in the Kyrie shown in Example
II-4. This chant is in the Dorian mode, and consists of threefold repetitions of *Kyrie eleison, Christe eleison* and finally *Kyrie eleison* again,
outlining a simple A-B-A structure. In this chant, the design is made
richer and more interesting by the varied repetition of certain melodic
figures tabulated below the music.

An important expressive element in the design is the sense of
organic growth toward the climax of the whole composition which
occurs in lines 7 through 10. The climax is reached in two waves, the
smaller in line 7 and the greater in lines 9-10. The word setting here
becomes more melismatic, and a longer portion of the chant revolves
around the dominant tone, A, before descending to the final.

EXAMPLE II-4: *Kyrie (cum jubilo),* 12th century.

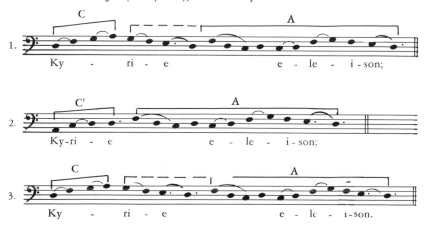

Repetitions:
Of motives or groups of motives:
        A repeated in lines 2, 3, 5, 8, 9
        B   ”   ”   ”   4, 6, 7, 9, 10
        C, C'   ”   ”   ”   1, 2, 3, 7, 9, 10
        D   ”   ”   ”   5, 8, 11

E   ”   ”   ”   7, 9, 10
Of entire lines or major portions of them:
   Line 1 repeated in line 3
   Line 4   ”   ”   ”   6; in part in lines 7, 9, 10
   Line 5   ”   ”   ”   8, 11
   Line 7   ”   ”   ”   9, 10

Secular compositions often are related to dance songs, and show verse-refrain divisions. As usually transcribed from the all too obscure notation of the period, they are modal, predominantly in triple or some variety of compound time, have clear, rather short phrases, are vocal in character and employ syllabic text settings. The words are typical of popular songs through the centuries, devoted to praise of a beloved, lamentation at the loss, estrangement or failure to win the smile of a sweetheart, drinking songs, martial airs (this is the time of the Crusades), and religious texts, often directed toward the Virgin Mary as the epitome of earthly and heavenly adoration. These pieces continue in much the same style well into the Gothic period, and exist side by side with the advancing polyphonic art of the church music as well as with somewhat more sophisticated court music.

The troubadours, wiped out by the Albigensian Crusade of 1209, practiced their art in southern France, the trouvères were located in northern France, and the Minnesänger were the Teutonic counterparts of the French composers (Examples II-5, 6, 7). Minstrels, jongleurs and goliards were traveling performers, not composers, for the most part.

EXAMPLE II-5: Richard Coeur-de-Lion (1157-1199), *Ballade: Ja nuns hons pris* (Trouvère style).

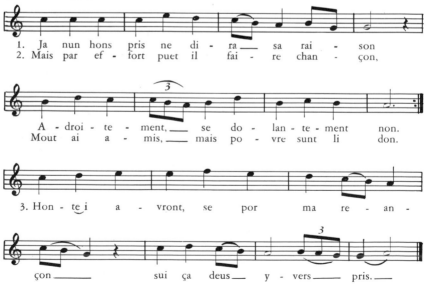

1. Ja   nun hons pris   ne   di - ra___ sa   rai - son
2. Mais par ef - fort puet il   fai - re chan - çon,

A - droi - te - ment,___ se do - lan - te - ment non.
Mout ai   a - mis,___ mais po - vre sunt li   don.

3. Hon - te i   a - vront, se por   ma   re - an -

çon ___   sui ça deus ___ y - vers ___ pris. ___

1. To be sure, no prisoner can relate his tale but sadly.
2. But with effort, he can make a song.
   Many friends have I, but poor are their gifts.
3. They will be shamed if, for my ransom,
   I am imprisoned here two winters.

Attributed to Richard the Lionhearted during his imprisonment by Leopold of Austria following Richard's return from the Third Crusade. Eventually his subjects ransomed him for a huge sum.

EXAMPLE II-6: Moniot d'Arras: *Ce fut en Mai* (Troubadour style 13th century.)*

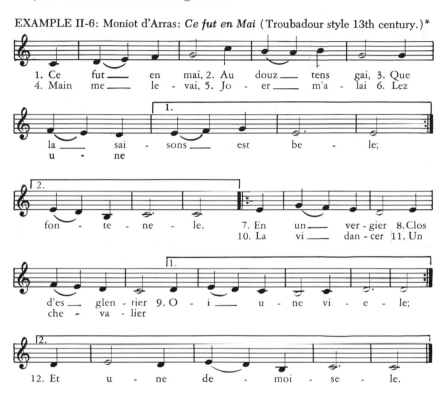

1. It was in May (2) Sweet time and gay (3) when all is fresh and gleaming; (4) I rose to play (5) and took my way (6) to where a fount was streaming. (7) Where blossoms white (8) hedged fruit trees bright (9) I heard a vielle entrancing; (10) Before my sight (11) a gallant knight (12) and noble maid were dancing.

* Trans. Gustave Reese, in *Music in the Middle Ages,* Norton, 1940.

EXAMPLE II-7: Neidhart von Reuenthal (d. 1245): *Mayenzeit one neidt* (Minnesinger song).

1. May - en - zeit   o - ne neidt freu-den geit   wi - der streit 2. Sein
2. Uff dem plan   o - ne wan   sicht man stan   wol - ge - than _____

    wi - der ku - men   kan uns al - len   hel - ffen.
4. Lich - te präu - ne   plüm - lein bey den   gel - ffen.

5. Durch das gras sind sie schon uf ge - drun - gen,

6. Und der walt   ma - nig - valt   un - ge - tzalt

ist der schalt. 7. Das er ward mit dem nie bas ge - sun - gen.

1. Maytime spiteless, joytime spotless
2. Coming back to ease us all
3. On the plain far and wide
4. Flowers countless, white or gold,
5. Already in the grass.
6. In the wood, from every nook
7. Song resounds.

The reader is urged to sing the foregoing examples, despite any misgivings about performance technique! Many recordings are available of both the sacred and secular music of this period, a few of which are listed at the end of this chapter (page 75).

LIST OF IMPORTANT TERMS

Romanesque	Prose rhythm
Modal Scales	Antiphon
Dominant	Mass, Proper and Ordinary
Final	Troubadour, Trouvère
Plainchant, plainsong,	Minnesinger
Gregorian chant	Neume, square notation

PART II: THE GOTHIC PERIOD, 1100-1450

By the time of the Gothic period, Europe had largely recovered from the anarchy which followed the decline of the strong rule of Rome. She was now ready to resume more actively the cultural and social development which culminated in the brilliance of the Renaissance.

Of the many political, chivalric, literary and artistic achievements of this time, we may mention a few. These were the years of the Crusades, those fruitless but rewarding attempts to wrest the Holy Land from the Moslems—fruitless because no real gains were made, and much blood and money were wasted, but rewarding because the ventures into the Near East brought the travelling warriors into contact with two highly developed cultures, the Byzantine and Islamic civilizations, which had not suffered the fate of Rome at the hands of barbarians. In addition to bringing back the exotic trade goods, such as spices, silks and skillfully worked metal, they also returned with outlandish foreign customs such as regular bathing and the use of the fork in eating instead of the hands, as well as such aids to philosophy and science as the decimal system, arabic numbers and many translations of the Greek philosophers which were non-existent even in the best European libraries of the time. It will be noted that the search for the goods of these countries initiated many of the explorations of the fifteenth and sixteenth centuries, and that the books of the pagan Greeks, Aristotle particularly, led to the development of scholastic philosophy and thence to the founding of the universities.

The great cathedrals were built in these centuries (Plate IV). Few were the decades that passed without the cornerstone of some major church being set in place—Durham Cathedral in 1093, in 1133 the rebuilding of the Abbey of St. Denis; 1154, York Minster; 1163, Notre

Dame de Paris; 1175, Canterbury Cathedral; 1185, Bamberg Cathedral; 1195, Bourges Cathedral; 1201, Cathedral of Rouen; 1211, Rheims Cathedral; 1220, Amiens and Salisbury Cathedrals, and so on for yet another century.

There were also the years of great kings—William the Conqueror, Frederick Barbarossa, Richard the Lion-Hearted, Saladin, St. Louis of France, John of England; of notable philosophers—Abelard, St. Thomas Aquinas, Roger Bacon, Duns Scotus; of men of letters—Hartman von Aue, Gottfried of Strasbourg who wrote one of the Tristan stories later used by Wagner, Joinville the historian, Dante; of missionaries and travelers—Giovanni Carpini in Mongolia, and Marco Polo in Asia; of important human documents—the Domesday Book, the Magna Carta; of the great universities of Paris, Montpellier, Cambridge, Naples and Salamanca; and of meaningful stories and legends for future times—the *Chanson de Roland,* the *Nibelungenlied,* the *Roman de la Rose, Aucassin et Nicolette* and *El Cid.* These are but a few of the noteworthy items in the rich catalog of the "Age of Faith."

Early Gothic Style: 1100-1300

Because of the multiplicity of styles in this long period, we shall content ourselves with a chronological narrative, mentioning along the way the outstanding features of each style and indicating the line of development throughout the period.

With the rise of polyphonic composition in the eleventh and twelfth centuries, the center of musical investigation moved northward to France. Little by little, music began to free itself from the bonds of ecclesiastical authority and to enter the secular world. At first, the music itself was dependent upon the "authority" of plainchant, for the early polyphony consists of a section of chant with which is combined a composed part. The two progress in parallel motion at the interval of a fifth or fourth apart (Example II-8), and because of the con-

EXAMPLE II-8: Musica enchiriadis (ca. 850), *Parallel organum.*

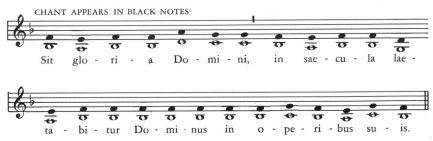

tinuous use of the same interval, this music has an unmoving quality resembling the static harmony studied earlier. Soon, however, the composed voice freed itself from this rather unimaginative combination and began to move in contrary and oblique motion in relation to the fixed plainchant or *cantus firmus* part (Example II-9). These were all varieties of what was called *organum*, a term which has nothing to do with the instrument, organ.

EXAMPLE II-9: *11th century organum.* Perfect consonances only.

Melodically, the newly composed part was often very much like plainchant in its use of steps and skips, although in some cases the line became rather angular with comparatively large skips in order to satisfy the rules concerning the basic consonances which appeared at important points in the texture. These foundation intervals were the so-called "perfect consonances" of the fourth, fifth and octave. The thirds, sixths, seconds and sevenths were not yet admitted to the hierarchy of important intervals, and sufficed as means to progress from one consonance to another. Often such a progression, when it occurs in two or three voices simultaneously, results in a clash of considerable proportions which relieves the "openness" of the harmonic structure. In addition, the dissonances between the parts above the *cantus firmus* were not regulated in relation to each other, but only in regard to the *cantus.*

Both the plainchant and secular music of the Romanesque was first written in a notation which indicated pitch but not meter or rhythm —that is, proportional durations among the notes. This simple notation began as a means of remembering long chant melodies, and consisted of ascending, descending or other types of curved lines which indicated the motion of the music. Later, the square symbols, less graphic in nature were developed and a four line staff was used so that pitch indication became precise. The record of the various other early experiments in the development of notation is a fascinating study in ingenuity, but too long for our present account.

The rise of polyphonic music in which the rhythms in the parts were different from each other necessitated a system of measured time values in order to keep the parts together. Using two different durations, one worth two beats and another worth one beat, a system was worked out called the *rhythmic modes.* The rhythms derived from these combinations were all triple in nature, best transcribed in our duple compound meter. The rhythmic modes held sway over sacred and, presumably, secular music from the eleventh to the middle of the thirteenth century. Modal rhythm was particularly used at the church of Notre Dame (not the present one) in Paris, where two choirmaster-composers, Leonin (latter twelfth century) and Perotin (ca. 1183-1238) set parts of many chants in what was known as "discant style." In the case of Leonin, the sections employing modal rhythm are prefaced and followed by sections of a species of polyphony which developed at St. Martial Monastery, near Limoges (Example II-10). The plainchant *cantus firmus* progresses in very long, sustained notes in this style, while the upper part weaves arabesques in more rapid notes, often vocalizations on a vowel syllable of a text. The modal rhythms of the chant part—the "tenor," from Latin *tenere* (to hold)—in Leonin

EXAMPLE II-10: St. Martial and Compostela (c. 1175), *organum.*

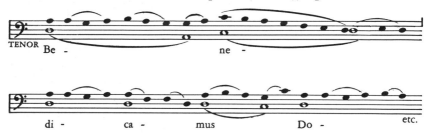

organum move rather slowly, but in the style of his successor, Perotin, they are cast into short, rather rapid rhythmic patterns, yielding a dance-like quality to the music (Example II-11).

While the harmonic structure of this music theoretically is based upon the perfect consonances, the use of other intervals, particularly thirds and sixths, tends to create major and minor triads in considerable quantity, especially in the rather few examples by Perotin in four parts. The harmony is not functional as yet, and cadences, if such they can be called, are merely arrivals at more "open" consonances than those occurring during the course of the music; there is no hint of intended V-I or IV-I, although these sound complexes do occur as a result of the polyphonic combinations of voices. A discography of this music appears at the end of the chapter.

EXAMPLE II-11: Perotin (ca. 1200), *organum: Hec dies.*

Historical Anthology, Harvard University Press, 1949

Middle Gothic Style: 1300-1400

As might be expected, music began to cast off its restraining bonds —the modal rhythmic system and the use of plainchant as a compositional basis—and began to develop forms and techniques exploiting the new freedom. The triply-divided rhythmic modes were replaced by a new system which admitted duple subdivision of note duration—the *Ars nova,* or new art of music, as compared with the *Ars Antiqua* of the Notre Dame school. At first, it abounded in bewildering rhythmic complexities still difficult for musicologists to unravel and agree upon, but after this exuberant experimentation mensural notation settled down to substantially the system in use today.

In secular music, which far outweighed in importance the sacred music of the time, the use of a pre-existing melody or *cantus firmus* was largely abandoned, and all parts became original with the composer. In the small amount of church music written, however, this conservative and traditional method still was employed, but with a certain difference. We have mentioned above the fact that Perotin used short repeated patterns in modal rhythms for the part carrying the plainchant *cantus*. Now, in the procedure called *isorhythm*, not

EXAMPLE II-12: Guillaume de Machaut: *Notre Dame Mass* (Kyrie).

only a series of tones—a plainchant section—is chosen, but also a rhythmic phrase some measures in length is set up as a standard pattern to be repeated throughout the composition. The rhythmic phrase is usually not extensive enough to arrive at its completion when the *cantus* does. When this point is reached, the rhythmic phrase repeats, using up the remaining notes of the *cantus* which then, in turn, begins its repetition, now in a different rhythmic guise from its former appearance. The process is repeated until the composer chooses to terminate it, or until the composition, as determined by the text, is finished (Example II-12). The whole process is undetectable by the listener, and may be regarded as in the same class as the many mystifications and scholastic hidden meanings which delighted the medieval mind.

Most of the forms of this time are word-based. That is, they depend upon a text for their length, not upon purely musical procedures. To be sure, the composer could expand the musical setting of the text by writing more than one note to each syllable, sometimes expanding a vowel sound into a lengthy melismatic passage. But the text was still the determining factor. This remained so for some time in musical Europe, but across the Channel, the English, along with some other unusual practices, produced the first written canon, "Sumer is icumen in, lhude sing cuccu" (Plate III). This is no simple piece, such as "Three Blind Mice," or "Frère Jacques," but a four part canon accompanied by a two part canon! The date of this surprising work is a source of some argument, but dates from 1240 to 1310 have been advanced. It would seem, from the complexity of this music, that the English had probably been practicing this technique for some time previous. It has been transcribed in both duple and triple meter, but in either one retains its folk-song quality and dance-like charm.

The French music of the fourteenth century is largely courtly and elegant in nature, and finds its most famous exponent in Guillaume de Machaut (ca. 1300-1377), who, however, is also responsible for writing the first setting of the Ordinary of the Mass completely composed by one person. The music of the Mass is isorhythmic in some movements, and is unified in style as well as by a short melodic fragment which recurs frequently in all parts of every movement of the work (Example II-12). The polyphony of this composition, like that of the secular ballades and chansons, is very transparent, almost ascetic sounding to modern ears. Despite the fact that he was a churchman, Machaut's secular poetry and music reflect a worldly attitude acquainted with the graces of the dying age of chivalry.

The sweet expressiveness of the Italian music of this time, especially as exemplified in the works of the blind Florentine organist

PLATE III. "Sumer Is Icumen In" (ca. 1310). *Facsimile of first page, from British Museum (Harley 978).*

Francesco Landini (1325-1397), is in sharp contrast to the spiky Gothic elegance of the French music. It is simpler, warmer and more direct, an emotional rather than intellectual approach to the setting of poerty. For example, Landini used little or no isorhythm, while Machaut, in addition to employing this device, enjoyed working out somewhat mathematical puzzles in some of his compositions. Such is the rondeau, "Ma fin est mon commencement" ("My end is my beginning"), a complicated triple canon in which two of the parts are the exact reverse of each other. The key to the solution of the canon lies in the text——a kind of double unification as well as mystification.

Both the French and Italian styles used similar sonorities, especially at cadence points. The cadence formulas found in Landini's beautiful ballata "Gram piant agli' ochi" are typical, and were called Landini cadences. This was not yet an example of functional harmony, but soon evolved into a rudimentary V-I progression, usually with the third of the final chord omitted.

It probably has become apparent by now to the thoughtful reader that the rise of polyphony and mensural notation in the early and middle Gothic period in a sense parallel the architectural developments of that time, especially the Gothic cathedral. In contrast to the dark and earth-hugging aspect of the Romanesque churches (Plate I), largely due to the round Roman arch and the emphasis on weight and horizontal lines, the Gothic structure is a vertical, upward-thrusting manifestation of the growing realization of the beauty of the earth and man, and the exaltation of the spirit in its yearning for the infinite (Plate IV). The balanced complexity of these webs of stone, in which the removal of one pier of an arch would cause the entire building to collapse, is paralleled by the webs of polyphonic sound so composed that each tone bears its share of the structure and is similarly indispensable. The conduct of the melodic lines, no longer smooth and rounded in contour, but containing upward and downward leaps, resembles the points of the Gothic arches and towers; and the polyphony, too, with open spaces between the constituent voices (transparency), brings to mind the sense of "openness" of the Gothic cathedral, where windows form the greater part of the walls. Even the growing emphasis upon secular music is reflected by these "poems in stone," for such churches exhibited not only the religious feeling of the people, but also their pride, their realization of worldly knowledge and skill necessary to raise such structures, and a competitive spirit in trying to create a more beautiful work than other cities. Civilization had emerged from the dark mysticism of the Romanesque

PLATE IV. *A Gothic church: the Cathedral at Amiens, France. (Courtesy of the French Government Tourist Office.)*

into the more worldly light of the Gothic, well on the way to the Renaissance.

That this period saw the first signs of the Renaissance is evidenced by the decay of scholastic philosophy and the rise of humanism, by the weakening power of the Church in many of the affairs of men (especially of the power of Rome over the heads of states resulting from the fragmentation of the Holy Roman Empire), and by the development of literature in the common tongue and painting in an uncommon manner. These are the times of Petrarch and Boccaccio, Giotto and Orcagna, the Black Death, Chaucer, the Hundred Years War, the growing interest in classical antiquity and the rise of the ruling families of Italy which were to play such an important part upon the glittering stage of the Renaissance.

The Late Gothic Period: 1400-1450

The third step toward the typical style of the Renaissance is largely a harmonic one—the recognition of the intervals of the third and sixth as usable consonances, not merely as passing or "non-harmonic" sounds. The English had long shown a liking for this interval, but it seems not to have been shared by their colleagues on the continent until the English composer John Dunstable (c. 1385-1435) accompanied the Duke of Bedford, Regent of France who fought against Jeanne d'Arc, to that country in 1422. It would appear that Dunstable and other visiting English composers did much to change the French, or to be more exact, the Burgundian style during these years, for not long after, at the court of the Duke of Burgundy, there appeared one of the foremost composers of the time, Guillaume Dufay (c. 1400-1472).

The graceful and courtly secular works of this master composer depend less upon canonic and imitative devices than do the works of the preceding period, or those which follow. The lines are smooth and vocal, expressive with a warm, rather romantic sentiment which often reflects the meaning of the text. The sound ideal of the Burgundian group of composers, of which Dufay was a part, seems to have been a transparent, rather high-pitched sonority, ideal for the presentation of beautifully written polyphonic lines. Much of the church music, particularly that of the early part of the period, is composed in the same manner as the secular *chansons*, but a more reserved sacred style begins to develop in the late works of Dufay and others, a manner which is the forerunner of the polyphonic sacred style of the Renaissance. While Dufay wrote both sacred and secular music, his most famous contemporary, Gilles Binchois (1400-1460) largely confined himself to the secular and sensuous *chanson*. These miniatures are in keeping with the manuscript illuminations of the time, depicting with almost photographic clarity, if not fidelity, scenes of lovers, courtly dances and peasant frolics.

The lovely rondeau "Adieu m'amour" is representative of one facet of Dufay's work. In it, the technique of using full triads consecutively has been mastered, and, while polyphonic devices make their appearance, there is no insistence upon them for their own sakes. In this composition, however, notice how the expressive element is enhanced by the technique of imitation, usually regarded as an "intellectual" device.

If further proof were needed of the expressive power of musical devices in the hands of a clever composer, the gay chanson "Files à marier," of Dufay's compatriot, Binchois, should set all doubts at rest. Here the imitations are presented with such a deft hand and such a lighthearted spirit that they cannot fail to be delightful in their effect.

The next generation of composers carried on the development of a church style, each in his own individual fashion, to be sure, but tending toward a unified style which we shall call "Netherlands style" in the next chapter. Among these composers, Ockeghem (c. 1425-1495) and Obrecht (1430-1505), wrote much music that is all too seldom heard today. They were given to exploiting the possibilities of complex canonic and imitative writing, a trait which did not endear them to many historians, particularly those of the nineteenth century, who characterized these works as dry, complicated exercises in ingenuity rather than music. The modern listener, more accustomed to today's complex procedures is apt to find them beautiful, moving compositions, despite—or perhaps because of—the complexities of mirror canons, retrograde imitations and the like.

All of the musical tendencies of the preceding fifty years culminate in the art of Josquin des Près (1450-1521), a composer who, said Martin Luther, was "master of the notes," instead of being mastered by them. In his music we find the consistent use of various kinds of imitative techniques, ranging from strict canons to the free imitation which often opens a section of music. This is combined with beautiful polyphonic writing, a sense of full and rich sonority and a most lively imagination. His text settings, whether they are full of secular wit or expressive of solemn sacred ritual, are always appropriate, often using descriptive musical devices to portray the sense of the words (*e.g.*, "*eternam*" in long, "unending" tones, or the chirp of "*El Grillo*," the cricket, in short ones).

Most of the advance in style achieved by these three composers depends upon the treatment of dissonance. Whereas, in earlier compositions, all parts agreed with the bass but not necessarily with each other, now all dissonant intervals are controlled, deriving from motion of the parts or from the use of stylized figures which resolve the dissonance to a consonance on the next metric pulsation. The general quality is one of consonance, for with this treatment the dissonance tends to be absorbed, and functions largely as a sonority which supports the rhythmic pulse. We shall try to define the style more clearly in its several aspects in the next section, where such a discussion is more appropriate.

The delightfully wry chanson, "*Faulte d'argent*" ("Lack of money is painful beyond measure"), exhibits one side of Josquin's production. Especially notable is the rhythmic life of the piece, in part the result of the entrances of the voices as well as their individual rhythms. The structural basis for the work is a concealed canon between two of the inner voices which begins in the sixth measure, and around which the other voices play in imitative counterpoint. The form is A-B-A'. The whole affair is carried off with the wit and dash so characteristic of Josquin in his lighter moments.

At this time, the use of plainchant sections for the *cantus firmus* of sacred compositions was broadened to include quotations from secular music. These *chanson* melodies were treated in much the same way as the chant had been, providing a structural basis for the music. The work using them included the title of the song in its name; one of the most popular tunes for *cantus firmus* treatment from Dufay's time well into the seventeenth century was a grim little song entitled "L'Homme armé" ("The Armed Man"), and masses using it were entitled "Missa l'homme armé." Those employing plainsong *cantus firmus* were similarly named, and Josquin's beautiful "Missa pange lingua" shows what this genius could accomplish with the technique.

Josquin's work marks an end and a beginning: with it, the Middle Ages were over and the Renaissance begun. It is, in a sense, the culmination of the developments of earlier styles, and represents the final control of both consonance and dissonance in the harmony and the subtle balance between linear polyphony and vertical harmony that were to characterize much of the music of the Renaissance, and, in a somewhat different way, music of all succeeding styles.

COMPARISON OF MEDIEVAL MUSIC
WITH THE OTHER ARTS

When we examine the European architecture, sculpture and painting of the centuries between 600 and 1450, we are confronted with
such a dazzling wealth of material that choices of individual works for
commentary are difficult. It becomes obvious from an examination of
this art that masterpieces may occur at any time, and that art from
1450 to the present becomes not necessarily any better, but only
different.

A few generalizations may be made about these centuries, however. We have noted the preponderance of church music; a similar
situation exists in all of the other arts, for the Church employed them
to present important religious teachings clearly and symbolically to the
generally illiterate populace. Thus we have the hundreds of depictions
in paint, stone or glass of the Annunciation, the Crucifixion, the Resurrection and the Ascension, as well as scenes from the lives of the
Apostles and saints which adorn the altars, walls, windows and door-
ways of churches throughout these two periods. At first, the figures are
impersonal—the portrait does not exist—but later, there is a change
from the stiff ceremonial figures to characterizations consistent with
the historical personality of the saint or sinner represented. Perspective, almost entirely absent in the Romanesque, develops as we move
toward the Renaissance, until, with Leonardo de Vinci, Michelangelo
and others, it forms a highly important part of the painter's technique.
Much of the art of both periods is dominated by architecture, and we
find the subjects enclosed in arches or alcoves which are essentially
part of the picture, not the frame. Little by little these give way to
encircling bands of angels or cherubs whose structural function is
similar. Both the arches and the angels do much to enhance the symmetry of these pictures, a quality which had the mystical significance
in the Middle Ages of demonstrating the order of the universe and the
harmony of all things therein.

Romanesque art is a development of the Byzantine mosaic, a
medium in which small pieces of highly colored glass or pottery were
set in cement to form designs and pictures. The mosaic representations
of religious figures were highly stylized and impersonal, symbolic in
the strongest sense of the word. When painters of the Romanesque
illustrated Biblical stories, they copied these symbols, making them
hardly less austere and impersonal. The outlines of the figures were

clear, the faces were shown either in profile—a favorite pose—or full face, and perspective was nonexistent (Plate II). In these respects, this art resembles the coexistent plainchant, for it is music in profile, with no harmonic perspective, impersonal, meditative and otherworldly. The earthbound church architecture of the time, dark because of the small windows which did, not weaken the strength of the massive walls required to uphold the heavy horizontal roof, was full of dim corners where man could be alone with his meditations and his God. The dark color of male voices singing in the narrow and limited range of tones allowed to plainchant, itself meditative and prayerful, is the natural sound-parallel to the architectural style (Plate I).

PLATE V. "Maria im Rosenhag" ("*Mary in the Rosegarden*") by Leonard Lochner (d. 1450). *Note the late Gothic profusion of decoration similar to that used in illuminating manuscripts. In the original the predominating colors are rose, blue and gold. (Archive-German Information Center.)*

In the Gothic era, the spirit of man began to expand in both earthly and heavenly directions (Plate IV). The sloping cathedral roof, shaped like an inverted V, was upheld by flying buttresses and supported upon a series of pointed Gothic arches pierced with large windows, so that the entire structure had a lightness and airiness both inside and out. No longer resting heavily upon the earth like the Romanesque church, it seemed ready to ascend to heaven like the prayers of the worshippers inside. We find a parallel in the music of the times, ranging from the massiveness of Perotin's quadruple *organa* to the transparency of Machaut's isorhythmically supported polyphony.

The Perotin polyphony, consisting of the rhythmic progression of quite individual voice lines above an equally rhythmic plainchant *cantus firmus*, strongly resembles the concentric bands of the tympanum above the doorway to a church (cf. Plate IV) or the long rows of statues such as those found in Chartres. In each, the individuality of the figure, whether it is rhythmic or statuesque, is lost in the endless sequence of similar figures. And the lines of the later *Ars Nova* style quite clearly call to mind the pointed and decorated Gothic arch not only in shape, but also in firmness of structure; like the apparently too slender piers of the arches which support the building, so does each note of the fragile polyphony exert its strength to uphold the structure built on the firm but inaudible isorhythm.

By the end of the Gothic age, architecture, art and music have become exceedingly elegant and decorated. Indeed, the period is called "flamboyant" in most histories of architecture. Here we have the suave music of Dufay and the winding traceries of Ockeghem and Obrecht. The sweetness of the third has entered music, and a similar sweetness, albeit somewhat artificial at times, permeates some of the painting, along with a trend toward a certain degree of naturalness. Like the art, music gained a warmth and humanity which was missing in the Romanesque and early Gothic periods. In the painting by Lochner (Plate V), we see a charming Madonna, ensconced in a Gothic rose garden surrounded by small musical angels, holding the infant Jesus who is no longer represented as a miniature man, as He was in earlier times, but now as a real baby. The colors are clear and transparent, the lines are sharp, the composition is closed and the counterpoint of straight, parallel, horizontal and vertical lines versus the enclosing curves and the curved lines of the figure are all closely comparable to the music of the Burgundians, with Dufay as the chief example.

Thus both painting and music during these centuries added new dimensions of perspective and harmony, color and sonority, individuality and humanistic expressiveness. Representation of the artist's and composer's world became an increasingly major factor.

LIST OF TERMS

Gothic	perfect consonances
melismatic chant	Adam de la Halle
mensural notation	Leonin
rhythmic modes	Perotin
organum	Guillaume Machaut
polyphony	Francesco Landini
Ars Nova	John Dunstable
canon	Guillaume Dufay
imitation	Gilles Binchois
cantus firmus, cantus firmus Mass	Josquin des Près
isorhythm	

BIBLIOGRAPHY

There is a great number of technical books concerned with medieval music, most of which are too erudite for the layman. Of more interest and of considerably greater value are those essays which portray various facets of the culture of these far-off and essentially foreign times. The following is a short list of books, mostly paperbound, which have been found to be helpful and interesting. It by no means pretends to be complete, but may be used as a point of departure.

Briffault, R., *The Troubadours*, Indiana University Press, Bloomington, 1965.

Coulton, G. C., *Medieval Village, Manor and Monastery*, Harper & Row, TB1022, N.Y., 1960.

Dawson, Christopher, *The Making of Europe*, Meridian Books, M 35, N.Y., 1956.

Frost, Wm., ed. *The Age of Chaucer*, Prentice-Hall, N.Y., 1950.

Huizinga, J., *The Waning of the Middle Ages*, Doubleday & Co., Garden City, N.Y., 1956.

Joinville, Villehardouin de, *Memoirs of the Crusades*, E. P. Dutton, N.Y., 1958.

Kubler, George, *The Shape of Time*, Yale University Press, New Haven, Conn., 1962.

Liber Usualis, Desclée & Co. Tournai, Belgium, 1950.

Mâle, Emile, *The Gothic Image,* TB 44, Harper & Row, N.Y., 1958.

Morey, C. R., *Christian Art,* Norton, N.Y., 1958.

Medieval Age, Flores ed., Dell, N.Y., 1963.

Medieval English Verse. Penguin Books, Baltimore, Md., 1964.

Mott, G. F. and Dee, H. M., *College Outline Series: Middle Ages,* Barnes & Noble, N.Y., 1954.

Neill, T. P., ed. *The Building of the Human City,* Doubleday, Garden City, N.Y., 1960.

Panofsky, E., *Gothic Architecture and Scholasticism,* World (Meridian Books), Cleveland, Ohio, 1957.

Pevsner, Nikolaus, *An Outline of European Architecture,* Penguin Books, Baltimore, Md., 1963.

Pirenne, Henri, *Medieval Cities,* Doubleday, Garden City, N.Y., 1956.

Power, Eileen, *Medieval People,* Doubleday, Garden City, N.Y. 1954.

Seay, Albert, *Music in the Medieval World,* Prentice-Hall, Englewood Cliffs, New Jersey, 1965.

Strunk, Oliver, ed. *Source Readings in Music History: Antiquity and the Middle Ages,* Norton, N.Y., 1965.

Temko, Allan, *Notre Dame of Paris: The Biography of a Cathedral,* Viking, N.Y., 1959.

Waddell, Helen, trans., *Mediaeval Latin Lyrics,* Penguin Books, Harmondsworth, Middlesex, England, 1962.

Waddell, Helen, *The Wandering Scholars,* Doubleday, Garden City, N.Y., 1961.

Of interest also are the books dealing with illuminated manuscripts, of which *The Belles Heures of Jean, Duke of Berry, Prince of France,* published by the Metropolitan Museum of Art, New York, 1958, is an example. New Yorkers may view this beautiful manuscript at the Cloisters. Other museums often have examples of this art unique to the Middle Ages, and sometimes pages from old codices may be purchased at antiquarians, although the deplorable habit of cutting up such treasures should certainly be discouraged.

In addition to the above books, a number of anthologies of Medieval and Renaissance music have been published in paperback form, some with recordings. *An English Songbook* (Anchor A360), edited by Noah Greenberg is an interesting anthology of English vocal music from about 1170 to 1600. Unfortunately——or perhaps not so unfortunately, since it is intended for use by singing amateurs——it is not accompanied by recordings. Two other anthologies, both published by Norton, *Masterpieces of Music before 1750*, by Parrish and Ohl, and Ohl's *Treasury of Early Music* are available with recordings of their contents, Haydn Society 9038 and Haydn Society S-1900/3 respectively. The Victor *History of Music in Sound* is an anthology of recordings, each volume of which is accompanied by a scholarly booklet. The two volumes pertaining to the material in this chapter are *Early Medieval Music*, Victor LM 6015, and *Ars Nova and the Renaissance*, Victor LM 6057. The following list presents, for the most part, miscellaneous recordings covering the period.

A PARTIAL DISCOGRAPHY OF THE MEDIEVAL PERIOD

Plainchant
   (See anthologies listed above)
   1. *Plainchant Easter Mass:* DDG ARC 3001
   2. *Requiem Mass:* DGG ARC 3031
   3. *Easter Liturgy:* DDG ARC 3088/3090
   4. Miscellaneous chants by the Mount Angel Choir: MA-LP- 1, 2.
      Chants of the Church: WLSM 7, 8. *Chants:* Vic LSC 2786
Secular Monophonic Music
   (See anthologies listed above)
   1. *Minnesong and Prosody:* Telefunken S 9487
   2. *Music of the Middle Ages:* Lyr. 85
   3. *French Troubadour Songs:* West. 9610
   4. *German Songs:* West. 9621
   5. *Troubadour Songs:* West. 18683
   6. *Music of the Middle Ages:* Vol. I, EA 12 and Vol. III, EA 23.
   7. *Minnesinger and Meistersinger:* DGG ARC 73222
   8. *Music of the Minstrels:* 17 Dances, and 10 Rondeaux of Adam de la Hale DGG ARC 3002
   9. *English Medieval Songs:* EA 29
   10. *The Play of Daniel* (a miracle play with music): Dec 79402
   11. *The Play of Herod:* Dec DXS-7187
Polyphonic Music of the Middle Ages
   Early:
   1. *Notre Dame Polyphony, and Songs and Motets of the 13th Century:* DDG ARC 3051
   2. *Music of the 12th and 13th Centuries:* EMS 201
   3. *Notre Dame Organa:* EA 21
   4. *Works of Perotin and Machaut:* Bach 5045
   5. *French Ars Antiqua:* EA 35

Middle:
1. *Spanish Medieval Music:* Dec 79416
2. *Carols and Motets of Medieval Europe:* Bach 70680
3. *Medieval France:* Bach 70656
4. *English Polyphony:* EA 24, EA 31.
5. *Florentine Music* (*Ars nova* and Renaissance): DL 79428 (S)
6. *Eight Madrigals and Caccie by Landini:* DGG ARC 3003
7. *Machaut: Mass and Ten Secular Works:* DGG ARC 3032
8. *Works of Perotin and Machaut:* Bach 5045

Late:
1. *Music from the Court of Burgundy:* Nonesuch 71058
2. *Music of the Burgundian Court* (Dufay, Binchois *et al.*):
   Bach 634
3. *Six Motets by John Dunstable:* DGG ARC 3052
4. Dufay: *Five Sacred Songs:* DGG ARC 3003
5. Dufay: *Sacred and Secular Music:* EMS 206
6. Dufay: *Missa Se la face ay pale:* Bach 70653
7. Dufay: *Missa L'Homme armé:* Lyr. 7150
8. Dufay: *Motets:* Vox 500990
9. Ockeghem: *Chansons* (see item 3, this list): DGG ARC 3052
10. Ockeghem: *Missa Mi-mi, Chanson and Missa Fors seulement:*
    Lyr. 108
11. Ockeghem: *Instrumental and Vocal Motets:* Mus-Guild S 134
12. Obrecht: *Missa Fortuna desperata* (see item 6, this list): Bach
    70653
13. Josquin des Près: *Secular Works:* EMS 213
14. Josquin des Près: *Missa Pange lingua:* DGG ARC 73159, and
    Dec 79410
15. Josquin des Près: *Motets and Instrumental Pieces:* Dec 79410
16. Josquin des Près: *Missa Hercules dux Ferrariae:* Mus-Lib. 7075
17. Josquin des Près: *Motets:* Tel (S) 9480

III THE RENAISSANCE PERIOD, 1450-1600

HISTORICAL PERSPECTIVE

THE RENAISSANCE WAS a time of expansion in the physical, historical, intellectual and spiritual horizons of man and his world. Certainly this process had been going on to some degree throughout the Medieval Period, creating in the twelfth century a renaissance movement. But the crest of the wave seems to have occurred between the dates 1450 and 1600, when the activity surpassed any that had come before. The feudal system had finally broken down under the pressures of international commerce, the rise of the middle class and the city, and the weakening of the bond between the church and the ruling class. Finally, medieval ways of thought had been gradually abandoned, philosophy moved from scholasticism to humanism, and reliance upon ancient authority gave way to scientific experiment and empirical observation.

The expansion of the physical horizon began with the voyages of discovery and exploration around Africa and to the Far East, but reached their most significant point with the discovery and exploitation of the New World by Columbus and others after 1492. The fact that there were new and uncharted areas of the earth engaged men's imaginations and inclination toward adventure; the lure of new sights

and the untold wealth of the West Indies affected literature, politics
and mapmaking alike. The power of Spain rose to its greatest height
until the defeat of the Spanish Armada in 1588, when England became
mistress of the seas. The beginnings of the Portuguese, English, French
and Spanish colonial empires——horizons beyond the seas!——date
from this time.

Other physical horizons expanded too, in a skyward direction.
After some 1400 years of belief that the sun and planets revolved
around the earth according to the system of Ptolemy, Copernicus
(1473-1543), Galileo (1564-1642) and Kepler (1571-1630) proved
mathematically according to astronomical measurements with instruments which they invented that the sun was the central body of the
solar system. Indeed, Galileo is credited with being the father of the
experimental scientific method which has revealed so many secrets of
Nature to man. His work with gravitation laid the mathematical foundation upon which Newton's later work was partly based. No longer
was it necessary to accept blindly an ecclesiastical or ancient authority
to explain natural phenomena.

Nevertheless, the ancient writers possessed great fascination for
the scholars of the Renaissance, for the authors of Greece and Rome
revealed a new concept of man and his place in the universe. The
harmonious proportions of their sculptures and buildings, as well as
their philosophies suggested ways to create anew the "golden age" of
antiquity. And the basis of this creation was man, the "measure of all
things," not the suppliant of medieval times with his eye bent on
heavenly salvation, but a physical being endowed with life and imagination, ready to enjoy the world which seemed created expressly for
him. This humanistic philosophy, aiming for the highest ideals in the
recreation of the golden age was expressed in the writings of Erasmus
of Rotterdam, Sir Thomas More and Francis Bacon. Others instructed
their readers in manners and the bearing of a gentleman, foremost of
which were Castiglione's *The Courtier,* and Giovanni della Casa in
The Perfect Gentleman. No less a part of this was Macchiavelli's book
of instruction, *The Prince,* a realistic political catechism for the ideal
Renaissance ruler.

These books and numerous others were widely disseminated by
perhaps one of the most important inventions in man's history: the
printing press with movable type. This machine, developed by
Gutenberg about 1436, made possible the rapid, inexpensive printing
of books, and authors took up the challenge immediately. It is reported
that the printers took each page of Thomas More's books as quickly as
he could write it! Not only philosophical works, but also religious

tracts of the Reformation, scientific reports, and entertaining or instructive works by such authors as Cervantes, Boccaccio, Rabelais, Ronsard and Shakespeare were produced by this invention. The importance of Gutenberg's press can hardly be overestimated.

But scientific and philosophical expansions of the horizon sorely tried the conservative and medieval church, for embarrassing questions began to be asked, questions which scholastic theology had no means of answering and which thus weakened the credibility of the church. In addition to this, the rift between church and state, already wide in the fourteenth century Babylonian Captivity of the church, continued to increase until the papacy became a pawn in the political intrigues of the great powers despite the efforts of such warlike popes as Julius II to give it real power. During the fifteenth century, weak and venal popes had allowed bureaucracy, inefficiency and corruption to develop within the structure of the church. By the beginning of the sixteenth century it had reached alarming proportions, and, in 1517, a monk by the name of Martin Luther called upon the church to reform its ways. But rather than a reformation, the church became divided into Catholics and Protestants with much strife, bitterness and persecution on both sides. The two Protestant sects, Lutheran and Calvinist, altered or completely changed the rituals of their churches to conform with their ideas of a personal, "pietistic" worship. Reform of the Catholic Church finally did take place, however, as a result of the Council of Trent (1545-63), and a movement called the Counter-Reformation was launched to win back the Protestant congregations to the mother church. The Anglican Reform under Henry VIII was not of the same kind as the Protestant Reformation, however, but was essentially political, a step on the way toward the despotism desired by that monarch and his minister Cromwell. Not entirely good, the Protestant Reformation was inevitable, considering the parallel developments in humanism and the woeful state of the church.

In this new "golden age," the arts flourished in providing lavish surroundings for the princes and prelates, the city-states and their governors. Painting, sculpture and architecture were most important, for buildings and their adornments were necessary and should be imposing. Music was a lesser, if essential art, still an adornment to the court of a prince or aristocrat, and, of course, an integral part of the church ritual. To this end, not only did the church patronize the composer and performer, but also wealthy men of the nobility and aristocracy sought famous musicians to add to their household or court.

It was generally agreed that every lady and gentleman should be able to play passably upon an instrument and to carry a part in a madrigal or *chanson*. To this end, self-instruction books were numerous, telling how to play the lute or harpsichord, or, like Thomas Morley's *A Plaine and Easie Introduction to Practicall Musicke*, even to compose! The ability to make music extremely well was not expected; indeed, it was rather discouraged as being undesirably professional, although Lorenzo de'Medici, Henry VIII and Elizabeth I reportedly both composed and played with enviable skill.

Italy was one of the major sources of music during the Renaissance, but she achieved this distinction through the efforts of musicians imported from the Netherlands by her nobility. The scarcity of music by genuine Italian composers until the middle of the sixteenth century is quite amazing. The Netherlanders brought their polyphonic style with them and grafted it upon the tree of Italian culture so firmly that it remained a part of Italy's tradition for several centuries, particularly in church music. In the same way, they influenced Italian secular music with their *chansons,* which also helped to shape Italian instrumental music. And when we consider that the English received the models of their renaissance style from the Italians, we begin to see the far-reaching influence of the men from the Low Countries. Germany was slow in entering the cultural trends of the times, but she too profited by having these men in important musical posts in the courts, cathedrals and towns.

For the purposes of our study, we shall divide the music of the Renaissance into three important categories: sacred music, secular music and instrumental music. The sacred music consisted, as heretofore, of the Masses, motets and psalm settings, plus the chorales of the new Protestant churches which were destined to be of greater importance in the seventeenth and early eighteenth centuries. The secular music of Italy and England produced as its most typical form the madrigal, matched in many ways by the *chanson* in France. Originally, vocal music provided literature for instruments, and was transferred to them with no change. Toward the end of the Renaissance, however, these vocal works became only models for compositions written to fit more closely the style, tone or idiom of certain instruments, and thus began an important branch of the art which in later centuries tended to overshadow in significance music for the voice. Lurking behind each of these divisions, more visible in some than others, is the unifying technique of the Netherlands polyphonic style. It becomes slghtly modified in the works of composers with strong personalities, such a Josquin, Victoria and Lassus, and is heard in probably its most refined form in the works of Palestrina.

PLATE VI: *"A Concert" by Costa. The center figure plays a lute, while in the fore-ground are a fiddle and bow, a straight cornet and a book of music. (Reproduced by courtesy of the Trustees, The National Gallery of Art, London.)*

THE MUSICAL STYLE OF THE RENAISSANCE

Melody

Melody as such is probably of less importance in this style than in many others for the simple reason that it becomes submerged in the polyphonic flow. Often dramatic melodic ideas are not desired, especially in the sacred music. Many times the composers seem to have been more interested in the total texture than in any individual part. For these reasons, the melodic ideas usually are not memorable. They are eminently singable, however, with rather close restrictions upon the size and direction of skips, the requirement that the line shall turn back when it has made one of these skips, and similar tendencies which unite to produce a refined vocal line. This line often reaches its highest point near its beginning and descends gently in a succession of short arcs to its final note.

Harmony

The harmonic combinations in this style are all triads—major, minor, rarely the more unstable diminished or the chromatically derived augmented triad—and they are obtained from the various modal scales, often including the Ionian mode, or major, and the Aeolian mode, or minor (Example II-1). The triads are used in their most stable positions, with either the root or the third of the chord in the bass, hence the music is predominantly consonant and stable. The harmony is not functional; that is, we feel little sense of movement toward a cadential goal in this music, not only because the triads built upon the modal finals do not exert the strong pull characteristic of our major and minor tonal scales, but also because the chord succession seems absolutely free, unmotivated, and, to modern ears, wandering. The only point at which the harmony tends to take on functional motion is at final cadence points where the V, IV, and I chords are often made major, if they are otherwise minor, in order to create a strong cadence. The interior cadences are usually left in their purely modal state, and weakened by the overlapping of sections, thus creating a continuous flow of music. Often these interior cadences seem entirely incidental and unimportant to the total composition.

Dissonance is very strictly controlled in the Netherlands style, and is one of the least obvious features of the music, although it is present to a considerable degree, at least when the written music is examined. In performance, it seems to be absorbed into the general consonance, and creates little instability. It is derived from the motion of the voice parts through the formula *consonance-dissonance-consonance,* and may appear only as a result of certain standard usages which, in part, help to create the style (Example III-1).

Rhythm

The rhythm of this music is individual with each voice line. The note durations follow the syllabic accentuation according to a general rule which specifies a long note for each accented syllable, thus creating accents of duration rather than dynamic stress. In polyphonic texture, these "agogic" accents create a subtle and interestingly random interplay among the voices.

Otherwise, the music moves to a steady unaccented pulse in simple duple or triple meter, the former preferred in polyphonic sections, the other in homophonic portions. The rhythm is preponderantly stable, like the harmony, and pervades the gentle flow of metric pulsations which move at about the speed of the human heartbeat. There are no indications in the music that this tempo is ever intended to accelerate or retard.

Texture

Polyphony is the preferred texture for church music, relieved by rather short sections of homophony, usually in triple meter. Most polyphonic compositions begin imitatively and frequently employ this device rather consistently throughout. Often two parts are written in canon with polyphonic accompaniment by the others. Writing in four parts (soprano, alto, tenor, bass) had become quite standard, but for purposes of greater sonority, five and six parts often were employed, usually resulting from the addition of one or two new parts for the soprano (thus, soprano I and II), alto or tenor, rarely the bass. For interesting three-dimensional effects, polychoral writing sometimes was used; that is, compositions were planned for two or more spatially separated choruses which answered each other, or from time to time combined their forces. We shall find this technique to be a traditional

EXAMPLE III-1: Palestrina, excerpt from "Agnus Dei" of Parody Mass *Veni sponsa Christi.*

LEGEND

a. First motet section ends at beginning of measure 5 of this example; new section actually begins on third count of measure 4 by tenor announcement of the subject, which is then imitated in all parts (see bracketed notes).

b. C-D-C refers to suspension figure in which note is first consonant, then dissonant due to the movement of the other voices, then moves downward a step ("resolves") to create a consonant triad.

c. * indicates full triad constructions.

one at the Cathedral of St. Mark in Venice, a technique which foreshadowed and led to the style of the Baroque in the seventeenth century.

Sonority

The Renaissance sound ideal is one of light-colored, transparent music of medium dynamic level, with few dramatic contrasts. The tone colors were secured by the ranges of the voices employed and by the spacing and quality of the harmony. Both sonority and harmony tended toward expressive extremes as the period drew to a close, but were balanced, mild and classical for the greater part of the era.

FORMAL AND GENERATIVE PRINCIPLES

All of the forms of renaissance music are what might be termed "text-based" in that the lengths of musical sections are dependent upon the phrases, clauses or sentences of the text. These texts, in sacred music, consisted of the words of the Mass (especially the Ordinary), psalms and other biblical selections used in the rituals. Settings of this kind, exclusive of the Mass texts, were called *motets* or, in England, *anthems*. In secular music, any poem, however light or serious its subject matter, was material for the composer of madrigals. However, this poetry became very stylized during the first century of the Renaissance in order to make it more suitable to the elegant manners and music of the mid-century culture.

The *motet-style* of composition, as it is called, generally consists of overlapping imitative sections, each with its own melodic subject which bears the beginning words of a new phrase of the text (Example III-1). Usually these melodic subjects are not repeated later in the work, but suffice to provide beginnings for only their section. In addition, there is generally no thematic development of these subjects in the sense that motives are reworked and varied, although in some of the compositions of Josquin both repetition and a small amount of thematic development occur. The smaller sections of a composition are welded together by the introduction of the subject of the next section in one voice while the others are closing the previous one with a modal, and therefore usually somewhat indecisive, cadence. This procedure may be used throughout an entire composition, with the only strong cadence appearing at the end.

In order to unify this "run-on" series of sections in some degree, many devices were developed. One of these was the use of canonic writing in each of the several movements of a Mass—a large structure which needed more than the consistency of melodic and harmonic style to hold it together musically. Such a technique recalls Machauts's use of isorhythm for the same purpose. And another device of that composer was also adopted, that of using a melodic or rhythmic fragment repeatedly in fairly prominent parts of each of the movements. The old *cantus firmus* technique was a frequent means of unification, although now the composers did not always use plainchant for the *cantus,* but often adopted popular songs for this purpose. Perhaps the most complicated, most "modern" technique aimed at unification of the movements of the mass was one in which the entire musical structure—melody, harmonic successions and rhythms—of a pre-existent motet or secular composition was varied and extended to form each of the movements of the Ordinary. Such a *parody mass,* as it is called, is also named after the source of the material used in it. (Example III-1). Both the *cantus firmus* masses and the parody masses are examples of *cyclic structure,* so called because of the return of the basic material in each of the movements. We shall hear this term again when we study the symphonies of the Romantic period.

The methods and techniques of performance had a considerable effect upon the construction of the music also. The composers wrote for an ideal chorus of unaccompanied voices—the so-called *a cappella* style. Thus, the combined voice parts had to make complete and euphonious musical sense without relying upon a "fill-in" accompaniment. In practice, however, it seems quite certain that instruments were often employed to render the parts more secure in pitch or to reinforce the sound. In addition, it also seems quite certain that the singers took what we feel to be unwarranted liberties with the music, adding flourishes and freehand ornaments to the long-drawn, serene lines of the polyphony. This aroused ecclesiastical wrath, but seems to have left the composers unmoved! We must understand that written music in this period, and for the following two centuries was regarded by performers as the skeleton upon which they were licensed to hang any amount of decoration their fancies and tastes suggested. However, we now perform the music exactly as written—even more strictly, without accompanying instruments, than did the people of the Renaissance.

SACRED MUSIC

We have already examined the work of Josquin des Prés in the preceding chapter, but to remind ourselves again of his important position in the Renaissance, it would be well to listen to his motet *"Ave Maria"* (MM Vol. I, band 19), which is written in a manner similar to the movement of the Mass *"Pange lingua,"* but which incorporates a homophonic section about two-thirds of the way through.

"Tristis est anima mea," by Orlando Lassus (MM Vol. II, band 1).
This motet, representative of sacred music of the High Renaissance, exhibits many of the stylistic features of the preceding one. However, it is written for five voices rather than four, and has a sonority of greater richness. There is no insistence upon clearly defined imitations, and, except for a few places in the scond half, the imitations employ only two notes: the sound is rather chordal for this reason. Lassus uses text-painting to some degree in this motet, although this technique is more frequent in secular than sacred music. An outstanding example is the musical pun on the word *"fugum,"* which, in the text means "to flee." The musical meaning implies imitation—eventually crystallizing in the form known as *fugue*—and Lassus treats it so repeatedly, using a descending scale figure of five notes imitated every other beat for a total of eleven imitations! Evidently he does not want us to miss it! The whole piece is written in the Ionian (major) mode.

"Agnus Dei" (1) from the Mass *Veni sponsa Christi* by Palestrina.
(MM Vol. II, band 2; Example III-1 in part).
The mass from which this movement is drawn is a parody mass based upon Palestrina's own motet, *"Veni sponsa Christi,"* which in turn is written on the plainchant melody of this antiphon. Palestrina usually begins a movement, as here, with two voices in canon for a longer period of time than did either Josquin or

Lassus. The imitation is then taken up by the other voices, here bass and tenor, while the other parts sing free (non-imitative) counterpoint above them. The overlapping-section technique is plainly in evidence here. Now and then a voice drops out of the texture, but not with the regularity with which Josquin does it: in this work we expect the re-entry of the missing voice, whereas in the music of Josquin, it is obvious that there is to be a short section for only two (or three) voices.

"Ego sum panis vivus," by William Byrd (MM Vol. II, band 3).

This music, by perhaps the greatest English composer of church music during the Renaissance, exhibits his personality within the narrow range in which this is possible in the style. Particularly noticeable after the smoothly flowing rhythms of Lassus and Palestrina is the more broken quality of Byrd's treatment, enlivening the texture with cross rhythms and elongating the phrases until the even duple pulsation is lost or changed into sextuple. Notice the text-painting on the words *"descendit"* (came down), *"vivus"* (living—in faster note values) and *"coelo"* (heaven—on a high note). The concluding "Alleluia" uses repeated note-patterns beginning on scale-wise ascending or descending steps (sequence), a device which is rather rare at this time.

The three examples discussed above should illustrate the style; they only hint at the multitude of works of the Catholic church composers of this period. Other works by these composers should be explored, and many are available on recordings. The *Missa Brevis* and the *Missa Papae Marcelli* of Palestrina, the *Lamentations of Jeremiah* by Lassus, the masses and motets of De Monte, Byrd, Tallis, Gibbons, and the emotional fervor of the works of the Spaniards Victoria and Morales —all these are available in their full richness of devotional expression.

The Protestant churches which arose during the Reformation turned away from the elaborateness of the Catholic service music in one degree or another, and often sought for church music which would be closer to the people. The most important kind of this music to survive to modern times is the Lutheran chorale which was derived from many sources. Luther is said to have remarked that "the devil should not have all the best tunes," and thus popular and folk songs were rearranged and given Reformation texts, as were some plainchants familiar to the congregation. Luther himself, it is said, composed some of the tunes, most noteworthy of which is *"Ein feste Burg"* ("A Mighty Fortress") with which we shall have to do later. These chorale melo-

dies were used as the basis of many instrumental preludes and postludes to be played in church services, and were also harmonized homophonically for congregational singing by many Protestant composers up
to J. S. Bach. We sing them today in church: at Christmas, "Lo How
a Rose E'er Blooming," "From Heaven High," "How Brightly Shines
the Morning Star," and at Easter, the Passion chorale "O Sacred Head,"
"Christ Lay in Death's Dark Prison," "Christ Is Arisen" and many
others. The real development of these chorales, however, belongs to
the succeeding era, the Baroque.

The Calvinists felt quite differently about music and replaced the
elaborate Catholic liturgy with one in which music played a fairly
small part. The hymns sung by the congregation were in the simplest
homophonic style and were based on a hymn-tune placed in the tenor
part like a *cantus firmus*. We still sing some of these in church, most
notable the Doxology "Praise God from Whom all blessings flow."
Oddly enough, elaborate, motet-like arrangements were made for family devotional use. But it may be safely said that in general, the Calvinists distrusted what seemed to them to be pagan and Romish power
of ritual music, thus retarding the progress of this branch of the art for
many years in Switzerland, Scotland and some of the American colonies.

SECULAR MUSIC

When we think of popular music in this period, the term *madrigal*
comes first to mind, as well it should, for it was assiduously cultivated,
first in Italy, the land of its birth and later in England. The contem-
poraneous French *chanson*, similar in many respects to the madrigal,
is the other important secular form of the time (Plate VI).

The Italian madrigal began as the *frottola*, a short, homophonic
choral work for four voices, with dance-like rhythms and a simple
text, often pastoral in nature. Example III-2 shows the typical appearance of this kind of composition. Note the chordal style, the absence of
imitation or other polyphonic devices, the dance rhythm and the pastoral text. This piece, although called a madrigal, is very close to the
original frottola. Costanzo Festa, (C. 1490-1545) the composer, was
one of the few native Italians to compete with the Netherland musical
invasion which brought such men as Philippe Verdelot (1480-1540),
Jacob Arcadelt (C. 1514-C. 1557) and Adrian Willaert (1490-1562) to

the sunny peninsula. The works of these men usually are somewhat more polyphonic than our first example and establish the style of the madrigal for the remainder of the period.

EXAMPLE III-2: Costanzo Festa, *Quando ritrova.**

Quan - do ri - tro - va la mi - a pas - to - rel - la

Al   pra - to con   le pe - cor' in pas - tu - ra,

etc.

Io mi   gli a - cos - t'e pres-to la sa - lu - ta

When I discover my little shepherdess
In the meadow with the sheep at pasture,
I go to her and quickly greet her.

* Historical Anthology, Harvard University Press, 1949

The main features of early madrigal style are these: (1) the use of modal scales, although a tendency toward major is evident; (2) the parts are easily sung; (3) the usually amorous text is carefully set so that the accents of the words become musical accents of height, duration or metrical accents; (4) there is somewhat more emphasis upon metrical or "bar-line" rhythm, and dance-like rhythmic patterns often appear, especially in homophonic sections; (5) the text is treated in the manner of a motet, one line per section, sometimes with slightly varied repetition in order to expand the section; (6) there is frequent use of overlapping parts at cadence points in order to weaken the finality of the cadence and promote the flowing movement of the music; (7) there is a free alternation between polyphonic and homophonic texture, depending upon the expression of the words or the desire of the composer to emphasize the text; and finally, (8) the music interprets the symbolism or description of each line or phrase by means of text-painting. Example III-3, by Jacob Arcadelt, illustrates a number of these points. Here the piece begins with an imitation of the rising skip of the tenor part, followed by a scale line which descends in the bass and tenor, but pulls away from them to the soprano and alto, illustrating by this contrary motion the concept of "going heavenward." There is a cadence on the first beat of measure 4, but the next phrase begins immediately in the bass, followed by a change to homophonic texture in measures 5 and 6. Again the overlapping and imitation begin the new phrase "with your bright light," concluding with a cadence on the first beat of measure 12. Since this is the final phrase of the line, followed by a period and requiring an important structural cadence, Arcadelt repeats the phrase *Co'l vostro chiaro* . . . ("With your bright light and my songs"), and reaches the end of the first section at measure 16. The intervals used in the parts are "natural" skips of thirds, fourths and fifths, plus much stepwise motion. The vocal lines are graceful and flowing, and the modal harmony exhibits several pleasant spots, even though the piece is centered about the F-major scale.

The middle period, so-called "classical madrigal," shows little change from the foregoing, except possibly more polish and expressive writing, and somewhat more emphasis upon text-painting. Generally, there is a more liberal use of sharped and flatted notes to widen the harmonic range (*i.e.*, a chord naturally minor in the mode may now be made major, and vice-versa), as well as to increase the finality of structural cadences. The composers of this period are still predominantly Netherlanders—Cipriano de Rore (1516-1565), Philippe de Monte (1521-1603) and the peripatetic Orlando Lassus (1532-1594).

EXAMPLE III-3: Jacob Arcadelt, *Voi ve n'andat' al cielo.**

* Historical Anthology, Harvard Univ. Press, 1949

† Translation not intended for singing.

Balanced between the classicism of the middle period and the expressionism of the third, is Luca Marenzio (1533-1599), called the "sweetest swan of Italy" by one of his contemporaries. His wedding madrigal, "*Scendo dal paradiso*" (Descend from paradise) forms the excerpt of Example III-4. Here are the same general devices as before, but noteworthy is the way Marenzio increases upward the range used by the upper voices. Observe the falling scale line which depicts the descent of Venus from paradise (measures 1-4) and the E♭ in measure 12 on the word *guida* (literally *guide*), a tone which strongly "guides" the chord toward the resolution on the next chord. This is the first such chromaticism to appear in this madrigal, a fact which lends it special significance in conjunction with the text, for these composers write for the eyes of their singers as well as for their voices! Later, the Graces are given properly graceful lines (measure 15), and the laughter is dealt with quite realistically (measures 21-23). Note the change to homophony for the portrayal of serenity near the end of the printed excerpt (measures 25-28). In this madrigal, there is much more text-painting than in the previous one, and the text is richer in illustrative words: just such texts were sought for madrigals by the composers of this period. They deal with approximately the same subjects as popular music does today, except that there are frequent allusions to mythological gods and goddesses, places and happenings, and the style of the poetry is apt to sound rather artificial and stilted to us. Nevertheless, the emotional Italian temperament treated many of these verses, especially if they dealt with some aspect—any aspect—of love, with the utmost intensity of expression current in the musical vocabulary.

Indeed, the final period of the madrigal is one of romantic expressionism, for the composers turned away from the representation of the most obvious nouns and verbs of their texts, and lavished their imaginative and technical resources upon the delineation of emotional states. Now, while "ascending," "laughter" and even "serenity" have obvious musical interpretations, how shall such terms as "death," "life" and "unhappiness" be translated into tones? Not by musical patterns or figures, but by that unique dimension of music which moves the emotions quickly—harmony. But this is only a part, although important, of the whole picture, for effective harmony must be combined with exactly the right melodic, rhythmic and textural components to achieve the desired effect. The two outstanding madrigal composers of the late Renaissance, Carlo Gesualdo (1560-1613) and Claudio Monteverdi (1567-1643), possessed the genius to do this. These romantic compositions which hint at the imminent end of an era, are really miniature music-dramas whose intensity is all the greater for being

EXAMPLE III-4: Luca Marenzio, *Scendi dal paradiso.*

(Original note-values halved)

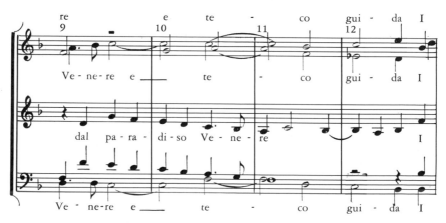

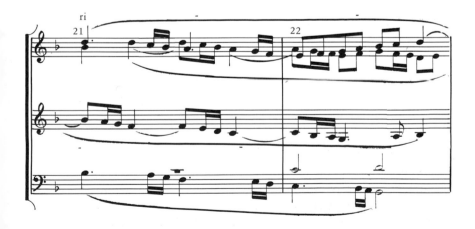

Translation:
Descend from Paradise, O Venus, and bring with you your little
Cupids. May the Graces and laughter be gayer than is their wont,
and beneath a tranquil sky may the Tiber bear to the Tyrrhenian
Sea his horn adorned with pearls instead of water.

compressed into a few measures. Melodic and harmonic chromaticism,
strangely twisted chord progressions, difficult vocal writing, obsession
with the interpretation of a single key word and morbid texts: these
are all components of the mannerist madrigal of the passing Renais-

sance. One of the most famous is *"Moro lasso"* ("Let me die") by
Gesualdo (Example III-5), which has hardly been surpassed as a
tonal portrait of despair since its publication in 1611. Gesualdo goes
beyond mere text-painting here, for what he is seeking to depict are
the psychological states suggested by important words of the text. The
means are largely harmonic, and consist of progressions of unrelated
chords such as that which opens the piece. Here the composer goes
beyond not only the modal system of his time, but also beyond the
tonal system of the next three hundred years to achieve a startlingly
modern effect. Listen to the melodic and harmonic chromaticism which
appears on the words *morta* and *moro* (death, die). More conventional text-painting is reserved for *vita* (life), consisting of rapidly
moving notes. Note the striking despair of the unprepared chromaticism on *Ahi* (alas) each time it occurs, and the clash of the soprano
part of the word *darmi* in the phrase *"e non vuol darmi vita."* After
this point, the whole verse is repeated with minor changes in text but
with considerable alteration and expansion in the musical treatment,
which is still, however, roughly parallel with the music of the previous
verse. The concluding two lines, beginning *O dolorosa sorte* ("O
unhappy fate") provide an ending which abounds in dissonance (the
soprano *Ahi* on the high F), unexpected resolutions, and chromatic
voice-leading. To modern ears, the final chord sounds almost a little
too tame, coming as it does after such emotional intensity, but upon
recollection, one finds that most of the chords in the piece are just such
major triads!

Not all of the madrigals of this composer are so intense in feeling,
for he wrote many of the more conventional kind, but those by which
we remember him best are the advanced ones like *"Io pur respiro"*
("I still breathe in such deep sorrow"), *"Io tacero"* ("I shall keep
silent"), or *"Mercei grido piangendo"* ("Mercy! tearfully I plead").
The personal, "inside," expressionistic view of life and suffering is
obvious from these first lines, and the music matches it.

The madrigals of Monteverdi, the great transition composer, reveal
a similar mastery of depicting emotional and dramatic situations. But
the attitude of Monteverdi is healthier, more given to outward dramatic
gestures rather than the almost psychopathic expressionism of
Gesualdo. He uses less conspicuous chromaticism, and then only where
it will be most effective. His chord progressions seem less arbitrary,
and, while he often sets poetry similar to that which Gesualdo used,
his music is less morbid. Often, in Monteverdi's later works, dramatic
effects are achieved by the rapid declamation of the text upon repeated
notes of the same pitch, called by him the *stile concitato*, or excited

EXAMPLE III-5: Carlo Gesualdo, *Moro lasso.*

style. This device passes into the baroque lexicon of affects with hardly a change. A good example of Monteverdi's madrigal style may be heard in one from Book Four (1603) entitled "*A un giro sol*" (To but one turning of the beautiful shining eyes), which consist of two stanzas. The first is conventional in its harmonic and melodic qualities, and is mostly devoted to text-painting with such words as "laugh," the "sea" and "winds." But the second section begins on a foreign note, and the first sentence, "I alone have eyes weeping and sorrowful," is set to a drooping, exhausted line: while it is being finished, the tenor declaims rapidly in "*stile concitato*," "Yes! When you were born so cruel and guilty, my death was born!" This outburst is imitated in the other voices, and the piece ends with a feeling of helpless rage, excited and defiant.

The English madrigal has many representatives, but by common consent, the masters of this form are John Wilbye (1574-1638), and Thomas Weelkes (1575-1623), with Thomas Morely (1557-1602) coming close behind with a handful of madrigals and a goodly number of dance songs with fa-la refrains called "balletts" after the Italian *balletti*. The English were introduced to the madrigal in 1588 by a printed edition of the classical Italian works in this form called *Musica Transalpina* and adopted the genre wholeheartedly. During the Elizabethan period, there were literally hundreds of these compositions produced and printed. Much of the poetry was created expressly for the music, and often by the composer himself. The musical settings follow the middle-period Italian examples with which the Elizabethans were familiar in that they interpret the text phrase by phrase. There is a certain difference from the Italian style in sonority, however, even in compositions which are rather parallel otherwise. The English seem to favor a lighter, less emotional setting and harmonic style, although feeling is often present, especially in melancholy examples. Much of the poetry is highly artificial, with references to the stock figures of Grecian mythology, especially nymphs and shepherds with names like Phyllis, Cloris, Flora, Daphnis and Amaryllis. The underlying ideas, too, are often what Shakespeare called "pretty conceits," and as such are treated with a light hand by the composers. Many of the printed editions indicated that the music was "apt for voyces or viols," and was undoubtedly often performed wholly or partially by instruments. Not transcriptions, which they sometimes resembled, but written expressly for solo voice and lute were compositions by John Dowland (1563-1626) and Thomas Campion (1567-1620). Dowland's genius is most evident in his melancholy songs which touch a depth of emotion rarely encountered in English or even Italian music of this period.

The English madrigal is easily understood on these terms, and one need only observe the text-painting, the light touch in the setting of the text, the tripping counterpoint and its fascinating cross-rhythms and the general elegance of the whole proceeding to derive considerable enjoyment from this music.

The French *chanson* is roughly the equivalent of the English and Italian madrigals, although simpler and always entrusted to four voices. The most striking difference lies in the frequently strophic treatment of the text in the *chanson*, where several verses (strophes) may be sung to the same music, a repetition which seldom happens in a true madrigal. These songs frequently begin with a characteristic rhythm (long-short-short) which found its way into the instrumental transcriptions so important at the time, and thereby became a trademark of the later, purely instrumental *canzona*. One of these *chansons*, the Christmas piece "Allons gay bergeres" (Hasten, shepherds) by Guillaume Costeley (1531-1606) is performed rather frequently. Other composers of this music are Clement Janequin (1485-1560), Claudin de Sermisy (d. 1562), Claude le Jeune (1528-1600) and Jacques Mauduit 1557-1627).

INSTRUMENTAL MUSIC

While the Renaissance is often regarded as the period in which the composition of *a cappella* choral music flourished, we must not lose sight of the fact that both the sacred and secular vocal music often were accompanied by instruments in order to render the ensemble more powerful or more secure in pitch. At times, especially in the soloistic music of the madrigal, when a performer was missing, it often was necessary and quite permissible to play that part on a suitable instrument. In fact, during the late Renaissance, pieces entitled madrigals were written for a solo voice with instrumental accompaniment. In addition, we must remember also that this was an age of social dancing, requiring much music. There were three sources for instrumental music at the beginning of the Renaissance: vocal pieces performed instrumentally just as written, transcriptions of vocal music for instruments in which certain procedures more native to the voice were changed so as to be more effective when played, and unharmonized dance tunes or basses upon which a group of players could improvise or have a "jam session." As the sixteenth century passed, more music for instruments was written and printed, although improvisation was still important. Music constructed upon vocal models such as the *chanson* or the motet, drew away from servile imitations of these forms and was eventually conceived in the composer's mind especially for instruments and their peculiarities.

Many of the wind instruments were the ancestors of those we have today, such as the flute, oboe, bassoon, trumpet and trombone. The latter brass instruments were made of narrow bore tubing, and the trumpet had no valves to enable it to play chromatically. The tones of these were lighter, less sonorous than those of today, and they were used frequently to double voice parts without overpowering them. The woodwinds, of course, had only primitive key systems, but this difficulty seems to have been conquered acceptably by the players. Two kinds of flute were to be found: the transverse, or "German" flute of wood, looking much as it does now, and the vertical or "fipple" flute, now called the *recorder*. This instrument, built in several sizes to give a variety of pitch ranges, was very popular. It consists of a whistle mouthpiece attached to a wooden tube bored with finger holes, much like the whistle flutes which children play today. The tone is soft, "hooty" rather than shrill, and mixes well with the generally low dynamic level of the other Renaissance instruments.

The popular double-reed instruments, ancestors of our oboes, English horns and bassoons, were the *krummhorns* (Ger. "bent horn" sometimes spelled *cromorne*), the shawms and the dulcians. The krummhorn family consisted of narrow, L-shaped instruments whose double reed was enclosed in a tube through which the breath traveled on its way to the bore of the instrument. The player's lips had no contact with nor control over the action of the reed. The pitch was controlled by stopping the finger holes bored into the tube of the instrument. Their sound was soft, resembling a muffled oboe tone. The shawms and dulcians, forerunners of the oboe and bassoon, had an unenclosed reed and were straight rather than bent, although the dulcian appeared much like the modern bassoon. They were somewhat louder and coarser in tone than our modern double-reeds, and were employed when loud music was desired. Together with trombones, they appear frequently in pictures of the period, furnishing music for dancing.

The cornetts, also part of the "loud consort" and usually matched with the trumpets or trombones, have very little resemblance to the modern cornet. They were straight or slightly curved wooden or ivory tubes, comparable to the recorders in size, but played with a cup-shaped mouthpiece, that is, like the trumpets, with the vibration of the player's lips producing the sound to which the air column of the instrument vibrated. The pitch was controlled by finger holes similar to those of the recorder. The tone was rather brilliant and high-pitched, and often doubled the upper voices of vocal music.

The stringed instruments were quite different, for they belonged to the viol and lute families, rather than to the modern violin and guitars. The viols had the shape of the modern double-bass viol: round shoulders and flat backs. In addition, there were frets on the fingerboard like the ukelele or guitar, thus making the pitch secure for the player. They were played with a bow, and produced a pleasant nasal sound, much less loud and brilliant than our modern strings. It was customary to build these instruments in families, sometimes storing such a group in a cupboard especially made for this purpose. This was known as a "chest of viols," a term found frequently in the literature of the day. The plucked stringed instruments belonged to the lute family, and were characterized by a pear-shaped body with a long fingerboard bent back at right angles at the peg end (Plate IX). These were plucked by the fingers, later with a pick for special effects, and sound much like the modern "classic guitar."

The keyboard instruments were the organ, clavichord and harpsichord. Often they were made in small sizes whose correspondingly quiet sound was suitable for solo chamber music, such as the "Bible Regal," a small reed organ built in the shape of a large book, and the virginal, a small harpsichord popular in Elizabethan England. The larger organs were located in churches as they are today, and followed the same principles of sound production, but without the romantic richness we associate with the modern instrument. In addition, most renaissance organs had no pedal keyboard, except for those in Germany and the Netherlands, and therefore the music is simpler, being limited to two hands on the manual keyboards.

Of the stringed keyboard instruments, there were two main types, constructed in various sizes to suit the need and pocketbook of the player. The first, the clavichord, produced a weak, but sweet tone by striking a metal string with a brass blade or "tangent." This tangent not only produced the sound, but, by its position on the string, determined the pitch of the sound. The harpsichord, on the other hand, utilized a device which plucked the string when the key was depressed, and produced a comparatively louder and more brilliant sound. While the clavichord could produce a small variation in loudness dependent upon the force with which the tangent struck the string, the harpsichord was more limited, and depended upon a series of stops which added sets of strings in order to vary the intensity of sound.

Much accurate information has come down to us concerning these instruments in books which sought to include pictures and descriptions of all the known kinds, as well as some highly imaginative devices for making music. Such works are Sebastian Virdung's *Musica getutscht und ausgezogen* (*Music taught and explained*), and Michael Praetorius' *Syntagma Musicum* (*Treatise on Music*), 1618.

The Canzona

Many of the instrumental compositions show little divergence in type of writing and style from the vocal models, the *chanson* and motet. In the transference from voice to instrument, however, the names become somewhat different: the gayer *chanson* became *canzona,* the Italian equivalent, and was characterized by a light sectional style, with a textural balance between polyphony and homophony. Such works frequently began with a rhythmic motto of a long note followed by two short ones, and thus have a certain dance quality. As the period advanced, the differences between the vocal models and their instrumental equivalents became greater, largely through the adoption of a more idiomatic style for the instruments, which featured trills, rapid scales and revolving clusters of notes, all difficult for the voice, but suited to the bowed string or the keyboard.

"Pour ung plaisir," chanson by Thomas Crequillon, with keyboard transcription by Andrea Gabrieli. (MM Vol. I, bd. 20, 21)

Here we have a typical French *chanson,* with imitative polyphony, the typical rhythmic beginning, the repetition of some sections (the first one repeats after a nonfinal cadence at measure 14 and closes with a final cadence at measure 27), and new melodic material at the beginning of each new section. It is obvious to even the unskilled eye and ear that A. Gabrieli, while retaining the essential harmony and line of the original, has made quite a new piece out of the vocal model by using figures which are idiomatic to the keyboard, and which, on a harpsichord, would sustain or make more brilliant the tones of the original. See the Harvard Anthology of Music, Vol. I,* for a similar transcription of Josquin's *Faulte d' Argent* by Cavazzoni.

* Harvard University Press, Cambridge, Mass., 1949.

The Ricercar and Fantasie

The more serious motet adopted the names of ricercar or fantasie, although there is often no clear distinction made in this period between the two, nor, for that matter, is there often one to be found between the ricercar and the canzona. Both were composed of sections in imitative counterpoint with new thematic material for each section. However, it would seem that the development of the ricercar led toward the use of fewer themes, eventually only one, and that all of the contrapuntal devices of augmentation and diminution of note values, inversion and retrograde, stretto and canon were applied to this subject, thus forming a species of what was later known as *fugue*. In distinction, the canzona's sections tended to become separated as individual movements and fewer in number, to retain their polythematic construction, and to remain relatively simple in texture. This developed eventually into the seventeenth century *sonata da camera* and *sonata da chiesa*.

The Elizabethan composers were especially attracted by the fantasie, or in the English of that day, *fancy*, and we find large numbers of them in the Fitzwilliam Virginal Book by Byrd, Bull, Farnaby and others, as well as in other sources written for viols by Byrd, Ferrabosco and Gibbons. Some of the latter are called *In Nomines* and include a long-note plainchant *cantus firmus* in addition to the expected imitative counterpoint. The Spanish composers Milan and Ortiz also wrote fantasies, and those of Henry Purcell, written in his youth, are modeled after the earlier Elizabethan style.

The Variation

The English and Spanish keyboard music developed the technique of variation, especially that of the *cantus firmus* variety in which the melody is accompanied and supported by repetitive rhythmic figures which are easily played upon the keyboard. The English favored a small harpsichord called the *virginal* which was placed on the top of a table, rather than being a free-standing large instrument. Its tone was correspondingly weak, and, to remedy this, composers developed a style which made use of rapid scale figures, trills and other ornamentation designed to present a great many tones in a short time.

Another frequent form of variation, not only for the keyboard instruments but also for consorts of viols, was based upon a repetitive pattern in the lowest part. When short, this was called a *ground*, and in England such variations were termed "divisions on a ground." If the bass pattern were fairly long, four to eight measures, it resembled an older dance called the *passacaglia,* and was so called, although the English composers often stubbornly retained the name "ground." Both the ground and the passacaglia, since they are only bass lines, allow considerable melodic and harmonic freedom above them, usually in polyphonic texture. If, however, a chord pattern of four to eight measures in length is employed, with or without the same bass line on each repetition, the variations are called a *chaconne,* again an ancient dance, related, as we see, to the passacaglia. We shall come upon the chaconne and passacaglia again in the next chapter, where they become somewhat more important than in the Renaissance. Again, the *Fitzwilliam Virginal Book* (Dover Press, N.Y., 1963) is an excellent source for the variation.

Dance Music

Dances in the Renaissance tended to come in pairs, a slow one followed by a lively one as, for example, the common *Pavane-Galliard* combination. Many times, a number of dances were based upon the same theme, but treated in each according to the metric and rhythmic character of that dance. This was the *variation suite.* Others, however, were entirely different from each other. The following dances are encountered most frequently during this period, and also during the early seventeenth century.

Pavane, also *"pavana," "pavian,"* and *"pavin."* A slow dance in duple time from Spain. Often followed by a *Galliard* which used the same theme. (See *My Ladye Nevell's Booke,* Nos. 20, 21).

Galliard, Fr. *Gaillarde;* It. *Gagliarda.* A lively French dance in triple meter.

Allemande, Eng. *Alman.* A moderately slow German dance in duple meter.

Courante, It. *Corrente,* Eng. *Coranto.* A lively dance in triple time.

Gigue, from Eng. *Jig.* A rapid dance in duple compound meter, often with upbeats to the strong beats of the measure.

Miscellaneous Compositions

While many works with fanciful titles from this period would seem to fall into this classification, they often will be found to be dances in disguise. The others, such as the toccata, prelude, popular song, descriptive piece or religious composition (e.g., Bull's *Miserere*), which really belong to the miscellaneous category, are to be found illustrated especially well in the English virginal books and the recordings of them, particularly the *Fitzwilliam Virginal Book* (Dover Press, N.Y., 1963, *Parthenia* (Broude Bros., N.Y, 1951) and *My Ladye Nevell's Booke* (H. Andrews, ed., London, 1926). The lute music is also a fertile source for all types of Renaissance music.

Choral-Instrumental Music

We have seen so far the progress of separate classifications of music and the styles which grew from them; now let us look at the fusion of vocal and instrumental music in the work of the Venetian composers, particularly those appointed to the influential position of choirmaster at that city's great Cathedral of St. Mark (Plate VII). From the early years of the Netherlander Willaert, until the end of the Renaissance and beginning of the Baroque, the musical performances of this church had emphasized the pomp and splendor characteristic of the strong, proud and cosmopolitan city. Noteworthy in the succession of choirmasters after Willaert were the two Gabrielis, Andrea and Giovanni, uncle and nephew. Andrea had studied with Willaert, and Giovanni was Andrea's pupil. During the years of writing music to be performed in the great cathedral, the composers had drawn farther away from the classic Netherland style of the Romans as exemplified by Palestrina, and had created a brilliant, massive, largely homophonic style which employed not only voices, often divided into two or more choirs, but also brass and woodwind instruments and organ. These instrumental and choral ensembles were disposed in various locations of the great church, creating three-dimensional musical effects which became renowned for their spatial and sonorous interplay. The opulence and color of these compositions is characteristic of what has been called the "Venetian style," comparable in effect to the style of such painters as Titian and Veronese.

Together with Monteverdi, Giovanni Gabrieli shares the credit for assigning certain instruments to each of the musical parts of a composition. Formerly, the instrumental forces used in concerted music were not prescribed, but the orchestra was a somewhat fortuitous gathering. As the score of *In Ecclesiis* shows, Gabrieli definitely wrote parts for the three cornetti (wooden or ivory horns with fingerholes, blown with a cupshaped mouthpiece), the violino

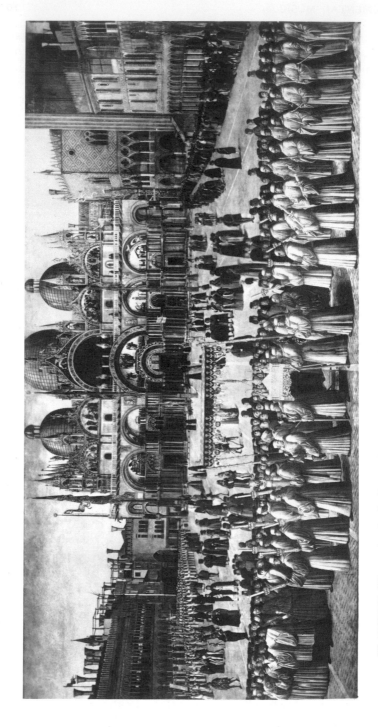

PLATE VII. "Procession in the Piazza San Marco, Venice" by Gentile Bellini (1430-1516). (Photo Alinari, Florence.)

(usually now played on the viola), and the two trombones; in addition, of course, to those for the two choirs, one of soloists, and one of the normal grouping. He was also one of the first composers to indicate in his scores the degree of intensity he desired. His *Sonata pian'e forte* (c. 1600) carry these indications, although there is evidence that the idea was not original with him.

Let us examine more closely the work of Giovanni Gabrieli and Claudio Monteverdi in order to demonstrate clearly that they are transition figures, bridging in their development the stylistic change from Renaissance to Baroque. And, more than merely fulfilling this function, we shall find that they are vital composers whose music is alive and exciting to us today.

In Gabrieli's magnificent motet, *In ecclesiis*, we find a number of traits which, while native to the music written to be performed at San Marco, are definite models for certain elements of Baroque style. In most performances, there is an improvisatory organ prelude——frequently found in the seventeenth century style——although it is not indicated in the score. This serves the purpose of fixing our attention and arousing our expectations of a large work. When the soprano soloist begins, we have an immediate feeling of the expansion of musical dimensions which impresses the listener in a spatial way due to the sound coming from different locations. This feeling is later reinforced when, from a still different point in space, a chorus intones repeated *Alleluias* in impressive major chords. The later entrance of the instrumental choir expands the spatial effect even more, in addition to presenting golden designs like the ornamental volutes and cascades of Baroque church architecture. Not only do we hear these sounds from different locations, implying musical and physical space, but they also are contrasted——solo voice against chorus, chorus versus instruments, line against mass, mass versus mass and color against color. Such compositions emphasizing these contrasts even at the close of the sixteenth century were named *concertos*. This technique becomes elevated to a stylistic principle in the following century.

The motet is further organized as a series of increasingly massive and colorful sections alternating with the choral *Alleluia*, which by its return, unifies and gives musical form to the succession of parts. Recurring sections of this kind, called *ritornellos*, become important means of formal organization in the Baroque period. The compositions of Gabrieli, then, already achieve several important traits of the coming style: a spatial element, contrast in sonority and mass, ornamentation and organization by recurrent sections.

Let us now turn to the works of Monteverdi written during the same period. Our last mention of this composer was in the section of this chapter dealing with the madrigal of the late Renaissance. In compositions of this type, Monteverdi and others had sought to define emotional states sharply through melodic and harmonic formulas, a practice which became prevalent in the next century and gave rise to the esthetic principles rather grandiosely named the "doctrine of the affections." In addition, madrigals with instrumental accompaniment were written, usually including a bass instrument which played the harmonic foundation of the chords, a lute or harpsichord to fill in the harmonies and often a pair of violins which added decorative upper parts or played ritornelli. In many of these works, Monteverdi shows his dramatic instinct through the use of strong contrasts or rapid declamation of the words on repeated notes. But his dramatic conceptions remained bound to the chordal-polyphonic music of the late sixteenth century until he was commissioned to write a musical stage work in 1607. This work was entitled *L'Orfeo: Favola in musica* (Orpheus: A Fable in Music), and became the first masterpiece of the new operatic style. But first, let us see how opera came to be.

A group of humanists in Florence during the last decades of the century, mostly literary men interested in the culture of the ancient Greeks and Romans, formed a club which they called the *Camerata*. They met at the house of one Count Bardi, and discussed classic literature, read new poems and essays by the members and performed music by Jacopo Peri (1561-1633), Giulio Caccini (c. 1546-1618) and Vincenzo Galilei (c. 1520-1591), the father of the astronomer. They speculated about the great power which the Greeks had ascribed to music, and wondered why the music of their own time seemed so feeble in comparison. The practice of polyphony was at fault, they concluded, for by its overlapping of text and music it rendered each unclear and diluted the effect. They therefore set out to create a kind of music which would reproduce in tones the passions of men and evoke in the listener a vibration sympathetic and strongly persuasive. Such a style must needs use the simple means of the ancients: a single voice part declaiming the text clearly, the melody of which would be fitted to the words to express as exactly as possible their emotional connotations, the whole supported with sparse but appropriate harmonies. They felt that the music existed only for the sake of the words, as was true of Greek music, and tried to limit the melody so as not to obscure the all-important text. The result was called *monody,* and represents the triumph of melody over polyphony——at least for a short time! The supporting bass and harmony was the forerunner of the Baroque *basso continuo,* of which we shall learn more in the next chapter, and the transformation of emotion into musical figures was again the precursor of the doctrine of the affections, which we already have met. Peri, Caccini and others wrote operas embodying these esthetic theories, but no really vital work appeared until Monteverdi's *Orfeo* in 1607.

This opera consists of five acts, and the music includes Monteverdi's extremely expressive monody, madrigal choruses, instrumental introductions and ritornelli, and formal solo song. The use of ritornelli to give formal coherence to entire acts is a forecast of the Baroque style. So also is the contrast of freedom and strictness; in the Second Act, the formal plan is interrupted by freely emotional monody at the announcement of Euridice's death, and forms a stunning dramatic stroke. Again, in Act Three, Orfeo's pleading with Charon makes use of impulsive interruption for a dramatic moment. In both instances the voice line rushes forward, staggers in syncopations, creates expressive dissonance——sometimes unresolved——with the accompaniment, and, in a word portrays the passionate state of the character. Thus, it derives its *Stile nuovo,* Monteverdi's most important contribution, from the expressive elements worked out through the madrigal, and looks forward to the less free but still expressive recitative of Baroque opera.

In listening to this opera, one is constantly struck by the appropriateness of the orchestration. Following the custom of the time, the composer accompanies happy scenes or those illustrating the power of Orfeo's music with viols, lutes, keyboard instruments and high woodwinds. The heavier and darker brasses and the cool, impersonal tones of the organ are reserved for tragic emotion and the realm of Pluto. Monteverdi stated what instruments were to be used, and in doing so followed a tradition which later become standardized.

With the Venetian style and the new monodic composition so masterfully illustrated by Monteverdi we have touched the beginnings of the style of the seventeenth century. With these purely musical devices one characteristic needs to be united: the form-building power of tonality through the use of the functional harmony afforded by the major and minor scales. With this addition, composers for some two hundred years will work, writing some of the greatest masterpieces of European music. In the succeeding two chapters we shall examine the life history of the tonal system.

PLATE VIII: *"Madonna del Granduca" by Raphael. Note the purity of line, the balance of the composition and the general classical serenity of this painting. Compare with Plate IX. (Photo Alinari, Florence.)*

COMPARISON OF RENAISSANCE MUSIC WITH THE OTHER ARTS

Almost all Renaissance art sings a paean of praise to the earth and its creatures; adoration to God and the panoply of heaven is inevitably cast in artistic parables formed out of human experience. Only in the exalted music of the Roman style and in the ecstatic medieval longing for God portrayed in the Byzantine paintings of El Greco does one sense that humanity and the earth have become subordinate. For now the artists have cast off the asceticism of the Middle Ages and the unhuman stylizations which it produced, and begun to look around them at the colors and shapes of the physical world.

The warmth and sensuous beauty of all the arts increases in the Renaissance. Matching the rounded contours and curved lines of Da Vinci, Bellini and Botticelli are the arcs of the polyphony, whether they be the short ones found in the madrigal or the longer, more flowing lines typical of the Netherlands polyphony. In secular music, especially, there is a tendency toward greater activity of the parts, comparable in painting to the inclusion of many figures and details in the depiction of such scenes as the Last Judgement. There is an increasing secularization of religious subjects in painting, and we need only recall the structure of the parody mass for a musical counterpart. At the same time there is the classicism of Holbein, and the clear and clean draughtsmanship of the Dutch and Flemish painters. Here one might discern a parallel to the simplicity of the homophonic French chanson and the Italian frottola, especially since the texts of these compositions, like the subjects of the pictures, dealt with experiences of the middle and lower classes, not necessarily the nobility.

It must be admitted, however, that there was a good deal more of romantic feeling in the painting of the period than in most of the music which has come down to us—at least until the High Renaissance, where we encounter Gesualdo, Monteverdi and Gabrieli. But, side by side with these daring spirits is found the sober classicism—almost mysticism—of the Roman school of sacred music, dominated by Palestrina, and including Victoria and Morales. Perhaps the translation of their classicism onto canvas may be found in the works of an earlier painter, Raphael (Plate VIII), or closer to them in time, Bronzino or Botticelli. Their mysticism has a parallel in the works of El Greco, a spirituality embodied in upward straining lines, unearthly colors and distortion of figures (Plate IX). The last element—distortion—if found in less spiritual surroundings, might well be chosen to represent the harmonic and melodic strangeness found in Gesualdo. In pioneering spirit and sheer audacity, we might easily find comparisons between Michelangelo and Monteverdi, with the realization, however, that Monteverdi did not have at his disposal a medium as massive as did the great sculptor.

In point of color and mass, perhaps the Venetians stand out most significantly. Gabrieli, in his ceremonial music for organ, brass and double choir, handles these colorful media in broad and magnificent strokes. His fellow Venetians, Titian, Tintoretto and Veronese reflect similar attitudes in their love of color, solid composition and the dynamic balance of line and mass to be found in many of their works. Few changes in these are needed to enter the world of Rubens and

Caravaggio, the Baroque. In fact, with these Venetians, we have already crossed the threshhold.

PLATE IX: "St. Jerome" by *El Greco*. *Note the elongation of the extended arm and leg, the mystery of the dark background and the sense of strain as the saint turns his face upward to the light of heaven to receive divine guidance in his translation of the Bible into Latin. Mark the contrast with the repose of Lochner's Mary and Raphael's Madonna. (National Gallery of Art, Washington, D.C., Chester Dale Collection, gift.)*

LIST OF TERMS AND NAMES

Renaissance
Netherlands polyphony
Venetian style
Baroque

Imitation
Cantus firmus
Text painting
Stile concitato

Motet

Parody Mass

Chorale

Frottola

Madrigal

Accompanied madrigal

Chanson

Canzona

Ballett, *balletti*

Ricercar

Fantasy, fancy

Variations on a ground

Concerto

Opera

a cappella

Idiomatic instrumental writing

Transcription

Chromaticism

Monody

Ritornello

Musica Transalpina, 1588

Orlandus Lassus (or Orlando
de Lasso)

Palestrina

William Byrd

Costanzo Festa

Jacob Arcadelt

Luca Marenzio

Carlo Gesualdo

Thomas Morley

Giovanni Gabrieli

Weelkes

Wilbye

Monteverdi

Victoria

BIBLIOGRAPHY

As mentioned before, anthologies of Renaissance music, especially when accompanied by recordings are of use: the two historical series mentioned in the bibliography to Chapter III are good. The two paperback anthologies edited by the late Noah Greenberg (*An English Songbook,* Anchor 360; *An Elizabethan Songbook,* Anchor 56) are highly approachable, the second more so than the first because of the simpler nature of solo song and lute (arranged for keyboard) accompaniment. *The Penguin Book of English Madrigals,* (Q33) may also prove interesting and useful. The following list includes general references to the period as well as the all-too-few biographies in English of important composers.

Burckhardt, Jacob, *The Civilization of the Renaissance in Italy,* Harper Torchbooks 40 and 41.

Cellini, Benvenuto, *Autobiography,* Bantam FB404. Many other translations are available.

Fellowes, E. H., *The English Madrigal Composers,* Oxford, N.Y., 1948.

Fellowes, E. H., *William Byrd,* London, 1948.

Finney, G. L., *Music: A Book of Knowledge in Renaissance England,* No. 6 of *Studies in the Renaissance,* 1959.

Fitzwilliam Virginal Book, ed. Maitland and Squire, in two volumes, Dover, N.Y., 1963.

Gray, Cecil and Heseltine, Philip, *Carlo Gesualdo, Prince of Venosa, Musician and Murderer,* London, 1926.

Kerman, Joseph, *Opera as Drama,* Vintage Book K88.

Mattingly, Garrett, *The Armada,* Sentry Books 17.

Mattingly, Garrett, *Catharine of Aragon,* Vintage Books V92.

Morley, Thomas, *A Plaine and Easie Introduction to Practicall Musicke* (1597) ed. R. Alex Harman, N.Y., 1952.

Panofsky, Erwin, *Studies in Iconology: Humanistic Themes in the Art of the Renaissance,* Harper Torchbook 1077.

Plumb, J. H., *The Italian Renaissance: A Concise Survey of its History and Culture,* Harper Torchbook 1161.

Redlich, H. F., *Claudio Monteverdi: Life and Works,* Oxford, N.Y., 1952.

Roeder, Ralph, *Catherine de'Medici and the Lost Revolution,* Vintage Books 263.

Roeder, Ralph, *The Man of the Renaissance,* Meridian Book MG 17. A study of Savonarola, Castiglione, Machiavelli and Aretino.

Ross, J. B. and McLaughlin, M. M., eds. *The Renaissance Reader,* Viking P. 61.

Santillana, Giorgio de, *The Crime of Galileo,* Phoenix Books P40.

Strunk, Oliver, *Source Readings in Music History: The Renaissance,* Norton, paperback.

Schevill, Ferdinand, *The Medici,* Harper Torchbook 1010.

Schrade, Leo, *Monteverdi, Creator of Modern Music,* Norton, N.Y. 1950.

DISCOGRAPHY

This list is by no means complete, but contains suggestions. The first grouping consists of recordings in which the music of several composers is collected on one record.

Lute Music from the Royal Courts of Europe Cr. 22160066

English Lute Music Vic. LDS 2560

Elizabethan and Jacobean Ayres, Madrigals and Dances Dec. 79406

A Lover and His Lass Dec. 79421

The Triumphs of Oriana Mus-Lib. 7000/2

Music for Recorder from Shakespeare's England Mer 90397

Virginal Music from "Parthenia" and "My Ladye Nevells Booke" DGG ARC 73 201

Music from the Fitzwilliam Virginal Book Vox SVBX 572

The Renaissance Band Dec. DL 79424

Spanish Renaissance Music Dec. 79409

Songs of the Spanish Renaissance Ang. (S) 35888

9 Chansons from the Notebook of Marguerite of Austria DGG ARC 3071

The second list is by composers. If two composers are recorded on one disc, and both are important Renaissance musicians, the name of each will appear: if one of the composers belongs to a different period, or is less famous, his name will be given second in one item.

William Byrd (English)
Ave verum corpus; Magnificat; Nunc dimittus, Mass in Five Parts: Lon 25725
Fantasies for Strings: Tel (S) 9481
Madrigals, Motets, Anthems: Lyr 7156
Mass for Four Voices: ARC 73 201

Dowland (English)
Ayres for the Lute: Bach 70673
Dances for the Lute: West 18429
Two Songs, with Campian, Ten Songs: DGG ARC 3004

Gabrieli, G. (Italian, Venetian School)
Sacrae Symphoniae: Bach 5037
Gabrieli and His Contemporaries: Canzonas and Sonatas: DGG ARC 73 154

Gesualdo (Italian)
Six Madrigals: DGG ARC 3073

Gibbons, Orlando (English)
Anthems, Madrigals and Fantasies: DGG ARC 3053

Isaac, Heinrich (Netherlands)
Music for the Court of Lorenzo the Magnificent: Dec 79413

Jannequin (French)
Seven Chansons: DGG ARC 3034

Lassus, Orlandus (Netherlands by birth, international in style)
Seven Penitential Psalms: DGG ARC 73 134/35
Missa VIII toni, "Puisque j'ai perdu": Eight Latin Motets: DGG ARC
3077
Neue teutsche lieder, Chansons, Madrigals, Villanelles: DGG ARC
3076

Marenzio, Luca (Italian)
Six Madrigals: DGG ARC 3073

Milan, Don Luis, and Ortiz, Diego (Spanish)
Música de vihuela de mano; Música de Violones: DGG ARC 3078

Monteverdi, Claudio (Italian)
L'Orfeo: DGG ARC 3035/36
Lamento d'Arianna; Sonata à 8 sopra "Sancta Maria"; with Carissimi,
Jephthe: DGG ARC 3005
Seven Madrigals; with Banchieri, Madrigal comedy La Pazzia Senile:
DGG ARC 73 136
Il Ballo delle Ingrate: Bach 567

Morales, Cristóbal de (Spanish) and Cabezón, Antonio de
Magnificat, Motets: None. 71016

Morley, Thomas (English)
Harpsichord Lessons: DGG ARC 73209
Madrigals: Van 157SD
Four Little Short Songs: DGG ARC 3004

Palestrina (Italian)
Missa Papae Marcelli; Eight Motets: DGG ARC 73 182

Rhaw, Georg (German)
Eleven Secular Songs in Two Parts; with Praetorius, Eight Sacred
Songs in Three Parts: DGG ARC 3072

Victoria, Tomas Luis (Spanish)
Messa da requiem: Ang. 35668

Wilbye, John (English)
Madrigals: Bach 678
Madrigals: Van 157SD

IV THE BAROQUE
PERIOD, 1600-1750

HISTORICAL PERSPECTIVE

TO ACHIEVE EVEN a moderately detailed *résumé* of the one hundred and fifty years of this period without major omissions and slights is a well-nigh impossible task, so full is it of important events and men, the repercussions of which have been of lasting importance in all of the following centuries. Perhaps we can make a summation of the ideals and motivations of the time, however, by choosing a word representative of them, a blanket term such as *humanism*, when applied to the Renaissance. For the Baroque, this word is *power*.

Power is the key word in understanding the Baroque, whether it is applied to the realm of politics, religion, philosophy or the arts. Thomas Hobbes (1588-1679), the English materialist philosopher, wrote in his political treatise *The Leviathan*,* "So that in the first place, I put for a generall inclination of all mankind, a perpetuall and restlesse desire of Power, after Power, that ceaseth only in Death." . . . "for Riches, Knowledge and Honour are but severall sorts of Power."

Politically, this quest for power and honor gave rise to the wars of the period, and the emergence of the absolute monarchy and the modern state. The English Civil War, with the rise of Cromwell and the

* Everyman's Library, 691A, Dutton, N.Y., 1950.

Commonwealth, the execution of Charles I, the religious strife between Anglican and Catholic, the Restoration and subsequent establishment of the House of Hanover in the person of George I are all manifestations of the power struggle. The Seven Years War, the Thirty Years War, so devastating to German culture, and the War of the Spanish Succession may all be counted in this roster. In France, we find the state turning to the absolute monarchy of the "Sun King," Louis XIV, attaining during his reign a degree of power which succeeding rulers found difficult to maintain. The decline ended in the revolution of 1789, an event which, like the American Revolution, effectively changed many facets of the older culture. The power of knowledge, both scientific and philosophic, was eagerly sought after by many men whose achievements have been of lasting importance to the following centuries. In science, we need only repeat the names of Galileo (1564-1642), Francis Bacon (1561-1626), Johannes Kepler (1571-1630), and add to them René Descartes (1596-1650), Leibnitz (1646-1716) and Isaac Newton (1642-1727). There are important names in philosophy, both social and political, during this time: Thomas Hobbes (1588-1697), John Locke (1632-1704), Bishop Berkeley (1685-1753), David Hume (1711-1776), Jean-Jacques Rousseau (1712-1778), Adam Smith (1723-1790), Immanual Kant (1724-1804) and Voltaire (1694-1778).

The power to move the emotions of men lay in the dominion of the arts, and was extensively cultivated. In literature, how the memorable names crowd in! Beginning the age were the most illustrious writers of the tardy English Renaissance, already verging on the Baroque in some of their works: Shakespeare (1564-1616), John Donne (1573-1631), and Ben Jonson (1573-1637). In Spain, literature was graced by Cervantes (1547-1616) and Lope de Vega (1562-1635). Then arrive the greatest of the truly Baroque writers, in England, Milton (1608-1674), in France, Corneille (1606-1684) and in Spain, Calderón (1600-1681). Later, in England, we have the polished verse of Dryden (1631-1700) and Pope (1688-1744), the chatty and informative diaries of Samuel Pepys (1633-1703), and the biting social satire of Defoe (1660-1731) and Swift (1667-1745). France continued the great age of the theater inaugurated by Corneille with Molière (1622-1673) and Racine (1639-1699), and produced among others, two quite different men of letters, La Fontaine (1621-1695), famous for his *Fables,* and Voltaire (1694-1778), whose fame needs no description.

The arts were supported during this time by the aristocracy or the state. The patronage system, which began in the Renaissance with Lorenzo de'Medici had by now become widespread, and petty princes as well as great ones employed painters, sculptors, architects and musicians to lend splendor to their courts and give outward show of their power. Louis XIV, who said *"L'etat, c'est moi,"* gathered together what was perhaps the most outstanding group of artists ever to reflect the glory of a king. From their productions, French taste and culture became regarded as the ultimate in splendor and refinement, and were slavishly imitated in the courts of other, lesser rulers. Interior and exterior decoration, music, dress and even the speech of innumerable little courts in Germany, Austria and Scandinavia reflected French style. Frederick the Great of Prussia summed up the princely opinion of the times when he remarked that French was the only language suitable for cultured people, that German was fit only for peasants and coachmen.

Only church music and opera remained relatively free from the control of aristocratic patronage, although to be sure, many a nobleman had a private chapel or theater and a "name" composer to produce music for it. Opera was, in a large measure, supported by the well-to-do middle class, and opera houses soon appeared in all of the larger cities after the opening of the first one in Venice in 1637. Except in France, Italian opera had a monopoly on these theaters, and the works presented were either written by Italian composers imported for the purpose, or by native composers who had learned their art in Italy. Even English opera, developed from the *masque* (a play with music), and which reached a memorable high point in the works of Purcell, succumbed to the popularity of the Italian product. In France, opera was not particularly popular until Lully (1632-1687) proved that the French language could be set satisfactorily to music in a style that reflected the pomp and ceremony of *"le roi soleil."* It became official then and gained in snob appeal among the members of the aristocracy and the rich commoners.

The paintings of the official French court artists, Boucher (1703-1770), Fragonard (1732-1806) and Watteau (1684-1721), are delicate summations on canvas of the exquisite and hedonistic life of the aristocracy, and are representative of only a transitional and local phase of the Baroque. The most typical painters to embody the Baroque spirit are Rubens (1577-1640), Poussin (1594-1665) and Rembrandt (1606-1669) who filled their canvases with the energy, movement, contrast and power so typical of this time. Architecture, which produced some of the most enduring monuments to the glory and power of state and ruler (including the church), established the last of the true grand styles until the twentieth century. The geniuses responsible for this were Bernini (1598-1680), who was also a sculptor of no mean quality, Borromini (1599-1667), both from Italy; Inigo Jones (1573-c.1652) and Christopher Wren (1632-1723) in England, and Mansart (1646-1708) in France. These were the years of the completion of the great cathedrals of St. Peter in Rome and St. Paul in London, the finishing of the Louvre and Versailles in France, to single out only a few of the important structures, public and private, that mark this period.

So—power and the exhibition of power is the key. Let us now see how this concept shapes the music and forms the style for composers as widely separated in time and attitude as Purcell and Bach.

THE BAROQUE SPIRIT

Frederich B. Artz, in his excellent book, *From the Renaissance to Romanticism,* writes a summation of the artistic tendencies of this period which will give us more aesthetic insight into not only the music but all the arts. He says:

The artistic styles of the Baroque——in comparison with those of the High Renaissance——show the same admiration for classical Roman grandeur, the same love of harmony and symmetry, and the same self confidence. But the Baroque is at the same time more exuberant, dynamic, and ornamented. The High Renaissance style is one of being; that of the Baroque is one of becoming. Moreover, the scale of the Baroque, in all the arts, is much larger, and the rhythmic phrase inside a whole unit is bigger than in the arts of the High Renaissance.

And later:

The audacities of the Baroque are boundless; in art, letters, and music masses are piled one on the other; in literature, descriptive adjectives and declamatory nouns are heaped on; and the most exaggerated contrasts are attained. . . . But its sweeping extravagances, its vitality, its heaven-scaling grandeur, and its complexity were usually controlled and unified. . . . The style is, at once, robust, positive, forceful, demonstrative, exuberant, and superlative. It is addressed even more to the imagination and the emotion than to reason, but to an imagination and emotion that recognize the order that reason can work.[1]

---

[1] Frederick B. Artz, *From the Renaissance to Romanticism,* University of Chicago Press, Chicago, 1962, pages 161-163. Used by permission.

PLATE X: "St. Theresa in Ecstasy," *by Bernini. This dramatic sculpture is the altarpiece of the Coronaro Chapel in the Church of Santa Maria della Vittoria, Rome. Here the baroque sense of drama and motion is expressed in stone and metal. The emotional element is heightened by the activity implied by the folds of the dress, the clouds and the tense, expectant poses. (Photo Alinari, Florence.)*

Let us now see how the reason worked in the realm of musical compositions, the ordering of lines and masses, colors and qualities, to move the emotions of the listener. And let us examine the means used by the great Baroque composers such as Frescobaldi, Corelli, Scarlatti, Purcell, Lully, Handel and Bach, always keeping in mind that their techniques, however complex, were directed toward the imagination and the emotion.

FORMAL AND GENERATIVE PRINCIPLES

In the last chapter we noted the emergence of the polychoral style of the Venetian composers and the development of the opera at the close of the sixteenth century. Many of the characteristics of this music were to become hallmarks of the Baroque style which ensued. Those derived from the opera were the *basso continuo,* the use of monody, the organization of a body of melodic figures which depicted emotional states into an aesthetic system called the *Doctrine of the Affections,* the ritornello as a form-giving device, the use of ornamentation by soloists, the song or variation over a repeated bass, and the use of heroic, larger-than-life subject material. From the Venetians, the style derived the element of contrast of mass and color, the sense of space through placement of the performers, the contrast of massive chordal movements with clear imitative polyphonic ones, and again, the ritornello. Let us discuss these factors in relation to their use during the one-hundred and fifty years in which the Baroque style held sway.

Tonality

By about 1680 the modal scales had generally ceased to be used, and the major-minor tonal scale system had evolved (See Chapter I). In the major scale there exists a strong tendency for all of the tones and the triads built upon them to move toward the tonic tone and triad, much like the force of gravitation. Like that force, which gives organization and form to the solar system, for example, tonality provided an organizing element which was lacking in the modes. This attraction by the tonic made all other tones and chords more or less unstable, thus providing the general formula which had been realized mostly at cadence points in earlier music:

Instability, creating tension ──────────→ stability, relaxation.

Expanding this principle to apply to a whole composition,

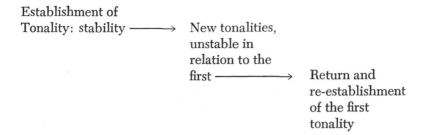

Establishment of
Tonality: stability ⟶ New tonalities,
unstable in
relation to the
first ⟶ Return and
re-establishment
of the first
tonality

This general principle became the guiding rule through all forms used in the 17th, 18th and 19th centuries; the forms themselves differ only in the ways in which the principle was applied.

The means of establishing a tonality are principally harmonic, and depend to a large degree upon the use of the chords IV, V, I of the key. These chords together contain all of the tones of the scale, and, in a sense, define that scale harmonically; when they are used, there can be no doubt of the tonality. The other chords also function to define the key, however, although less strongly; and, just as the solar system is defined by the sun and all of the bodies which rotate around it, so a key is defined by the tonic center and its satellite chords. The Baroque Period was devoted musically toward clarifying the function of the tonal system in musical forms and therefore demanded that every composition state the key clearly at its beginning through the use of tonally functioning harmony. This provided a stable area from which to depart. Similarly, the return and re-etablishment of the key had to be equally obvious. The sense of form for the listener, then, depends upon his memory of the opening tonality. This memory is assisted by recognition of the principle themes which characterize the tonality, as well as the attendent sonority, texture, rhythm, etc.

The structures found in a Baroque music may be classified as (1) "free" forms, (2) repetition forms, and (3) continuation forms. The first results from the improvisation by one person, usually at the keyboard although possible for any performer. The written music entitled prelude, toccata or fantasie is intended to sound as though it were being made up on the spur of the moment. They are, however, clearly organized in some loose way within the practice of the tonal system, and only appear to be free because of the capricious use of thematic material, sudden changes of tempo or manner, and the use of idiomatic figuration for the particular instrument. The improvisatory forms are almost always linked to some more strictly defined form or procedure for contrast and formal balance. Thus, typically, the prelude is followed by a *fugue,* and, in opera, the recitative by the formal song called the *aria.*

The repetition forms depend upon the recognizable return of key and thematic material. This may be simply the recurrence in a set of variations of the theme, and may be symbolized by A A' A'' . . . etc. Or, there may be intervening material of more or less importance between the recurrences of the principal key and theme. If it is of lesser importance, short and containing no clearly defined themes of its own, it is called *transitional* or *episodic* material. If, however, it is of some length, compared to the principal section, and is characterized by its own themes, it is signified by the name *section,* and is assigned an alphabetical letter different from that of the main section, which is usually A. Thus, a three-part form would be A-B-A; larger extensions, called song-forms or rondos, might be A-B-A-C-A, etc.

The simplest, yet most frequently encountered of the repetition forms in the Baroque is the *binary form.* Because of its importance, and because it cannot be clearly indicated by an alphabetical symbol, let us examine it more closely. As the name suggests, it consists of two sections, I and II, each of which concludes with a cadence. Usually each section is immediately repeated (*i.e.,* I-I-II-II). The first section presents some clearly recognizable thematic material in the tonic key, and concludes with either a final or nonfinal cadence, as shown in the following diagram:

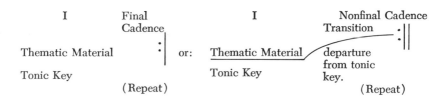

The second section usually begins where the first stopped, either in the tonic key, or away from it, as suggested by the nonfinal cadence. The principle tonality is then re-established and the section closes with a final cadence.

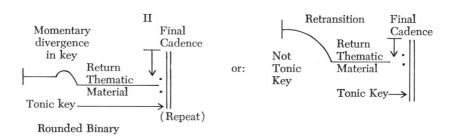

In some cases, the return of the tonality in section II is accompanied by a similar presentation of the theme that occurred in section I: the structure is then called *rounded binary form*. Example IV-1 is an example of this, in which the first section ends with a final cadence in the tonic key, and Section II begins in the same key, moves away momentarily (measures 5-8, Section II), then returns to the main key and theme in

EXAMPLE IV-1: *Menuett* by Handel.

measure 9. The Bach *Sarabande* (Example IV-2) illustrates another procedure. The whole form is organized by a strong dotted rhythmic motive, and, in a sense, this is the only "theme." By the use of complex harmony, Bach postpones the return of the main key until the last two measures of Section II, creating a long arch of unstable harmony from the first key area of Section I (measure 1-4) to the concluding measures. This is obviously a more elaborate view of the form and is frequently encountered in the music of Bach.

EXAMPLE IV-2: *Sarabande* by Bach.

The binary form often is used as a component of larger forms as well as independently, and is a most important basic structure of the Baroque and Classic Periods. It should be thoroughly understood, both intellectually and through analytical listening.

The continuation forms, while essentially adhering to the tonal principles outlined above, result from the application of a procedure. There are three procedures common to the Baroque style: the *cantus firmus principle*, the *fugal principle*, and the *concerto principle*. We have met all of them before in modal music, but in the Baroque they are totally organized and employ clearly defined themes and recognizable repetitions of those themes. *The cantus firmus principle* depends upon the elaboration of a superstructure above a given melody, itself possessing a clearly defined form. It is, in a sense, a variation procedure, and produces in this period the chorale-prelude and the repetitive variations of the ground, passacaglia and chaconne.

The fugal principle operates only in polyphonic texture and depends upon the process of imitation and contrapuntal manipulation and combination of the thematic material while following the general tonal plan of structure in some way. Thus, the fugue itself is the *result of a procedure* and is necessarily *variable in its use of the material and its manipulation of tonal principles*. Do not expect to find two fugues which are alike, for this very reason.

The concerto principle depends to a large extent upon homophonic texture, since it tends to oppose masses of sound of different qualities in the Venetian style. Forms resulting from the application of this principle are often called *ritornello* forms because of the use of this device to emphasize the arrival of a new key, or to signal the return of the principal tonality. Polyphony is not excluded, however, from compositions employing the concerto principle, often being used between the ritornelli by a small number of soloists in combination.

The Doctrine of the Affections

The portrayal of emotion in the opera and other vocal music was of the utmost importance to the Baroque composer, just as similar representation of texts had been to the Renaissance composer of madrigals. But to the 17th century composer, the modern concept of dynamic, changing emotion was foreign, at least when applied to the stage, and the feelings——*affections*, as they were known——remained static in any situation. When the character "burned with rage," there was no room for any other feeling, nor was it possible for any change to take place until he had delivered his rage in a more or less lengthy speech. These affections were really a set of stereotyped emotional states, such as rage, jealously, anger, love, timidity, pathos and so on, which made the classification of passages in a play or opera quite easy. The task of the composer was to find musical figures which corresponded to the affection of the passage. Gradually there grew up a lexicon of such figures or affective motives, which were the common property of all composers. Since the meaning of the musical figure is explained by the words, many such figures were capable of being used in different situations; trembling with rage is not so different musically, in this respect, from trembling with love! One would certainly be louder and faster than the other, but the figure used might be the same.

Since the representation of the emotion was static, the same figure would be repeated throughout the section of the composition devoted to that affection, only changing when the affection changed. And for the same reason, the tempo could not deviate from that established at the beginning of the section. Both of these characteristics aided in unifying the music, and in creating strong formal sections. The emphatic beat often established by the repetition of the motives may also create an athletic and propulsive effect called *motoric rhythm.*

Although the doctrine of the affections originated in vocal music, it soon passed into purely instrumental music and became one of the guiding principles in the creation of musical themes and the spinning out of whole movements. Without the words to make the emotion explicit, the listener must use his imagination to correlate other elements of a work——such as the tempo, harmonic complexity and instrumentation——in order to approximate the affection which the composer intended to convey in his music.

NATIONAL STYLES

In listening to a large number of Baroque works by different composers, it will be noticed that some are more homophonic than others, simpler to comprehend in melody and harmony. These characteristics are often the hallmarks of the national style of the music. Italian music, with its basis in the vocal style, is represented by less elaborate melodies, simpler chords and less variety in harmony, a tendency toward homophony and the general disinclination to continue counterpoint for very long. These traits are, on the whole, shared by the French music, together with a more formal, less subjective quality. The German style, on the other hand, is more involved: the melody tends to be instrumental in nature, even when intended to be sung, the harmony makes use of more chords and explores their relationships more thoroughly (compare Handel's Italian style in the aria "I know that my Redeemer liveth," from *Messiah,* with Bach's German style in the aria "Come within my heart," *Cantata No. 80*), and once begun, polyphony of a rather elaborate kind persists throughout a composition. Interestingly enough, both the Italian and German styles may be profoundly moving in their effect upon the listener.

THE MUSICAL STYLE OF THE BAROQUE PERIOD

Melody

The melody of a musical composition may be compared to line in a drawing or painting, on in architecture. In these sister arts of the Baroque period the line is usually decorative, often ornamented heavily, and frequently quite active, suggesting motion. These qualities are easily seen in the pictures in this chapter. Motion and ornamentation appear in the folds of St. Theresa's robes, the jagged outline of the crowd in Rembrandt's painting, and in the play of light and shadow upon the facade of San Carlo alla Fontana. In the music, much of this activity is due to repetition of the small melodic and rhythmic affective motives and by ornamentation of an otherwise only moderately active melodic line with trills, turns and other such figures (Example IV-4). Very often the motives integrally ornament and partially obscure such plain melodic skeletons as the tones of triads (Example IV-3) in much the same way as architectural ornamentation of the period hides the straight lines and right angles of the intersections of columns with roof beams. Such ornamentation, in both cases, also provides continuity between the structural members, which, in the case of music, are the functional chords. The passion for ornament was so great during the seventeenth and eighteenth centuries that the study of improvised embellishment of the melodic line became an important part of the training of singers, violinists, flutists, oboists and keyboard executants. Many of the long-breathed melodies of such works as Handel's Messiah, for example, would be unrecognizable to us today if we heard them sung in this manner. In many cases, however, as noted above, the ornamentation is "built in," requiring nothing from the performer other than that he play the notes (Example IV-3). In the music of the substyle called Rococo which prevailed in France from about 1715 to 1720, we find that the ornaments are not always integral to the melody, but are applied to rather simple melodic skeletons resulting in a quality less vigorous, miniature, intimate and fussy.

In order to create a sense of logic and direction in these ornate melodies, the composers developed certain techniques. One, which we have already mentioned, was the use of functional harmonies as the

EXAMPLE IV-3: *Ornamentation.*

Asterisks indicate broken chord skeleton of melody. X's indicate possible cadence points which become nonfinal. Roman numerals indicate chords.

EXAMPLE IV-4: *Ornamentation.*

EXAMPLE IV-5: *Common sequence patterns.*

basis for the melody. A second device was that called *sequence* in which melodic patterns were repeated upon successively higher or lower scale degrees with appropriate harmonizations (Example IV-4). Some of the sequence patterns are quite brief while others may extend to two measures. The danger inherent in the sequence is that of monotony if the pattern is repeated too many times; usually three repetitions is the limit, although Bach constructed an entire section of twenty-seven measures in the *F Sharp Minor Toccata* for harpsichord out of a one-measure sequence pattern!

We may distinguish two national styles in melody, as we have in harmony. These are the Italian and German and represent generally simplicity and complexity in melodic formations. The Italian ideal was that of the singing voice, the so-called *bel canto* (beautiful singing), with relatively smooth lines containing easily sung skips, occasional graceful and fanciful ornamentation usually at cadence points (in the written music, probably more embellished in practice), and phrases of moderate length, designed to be sung in one breath. The German composer tended to write instrumental melodies, often with skips between tones which are not easily and accurately sung, "built in" ornamentation which is often affective in character, and exceedingly long melodic spans which drive through their intermediate cadences and were conceived for the "nonbreathing" instruments such as the violin, not for the singer.

Melodic character, often idiomatic to certain instruments, particularly the violin and the voice, was often transferred to other instruments. Thus, we find vocal, harpsichord and organ works employing the melodic idioms of the violin, while in others the violin sings like a superhuman soprano with an enormous reserve of breath. The former case we shall encounter in an aria in Bach's *Cantata No. 80*, to be studied later, while the vocal style transferred to the instruments may be found in the second movement of the *Italian Concerto* and in the "Aria" of the *Third Suite for Orchestra,* both by Bach.

Harmony

Three important developments related to harmony made possible the characteristic quality of this element of Baroque music. The first, the adoption of the tonal system, we have already discussed. The second was the concept of the triad or chord as a unit, not as a grouping of intervals which the Renaissance and Medieval composer had regarded it. The chord was an entity now, the notes of which could be rearranged——*inverted* is the technical term——without changing its identity. This harmonic concept had been realized by earlier theoreticians, but it remained for the great French composer Jean-Philippe Rameau (1683-1764) to systematize it in his *Traité de l'Harmonie* of 1722. Thus, instead of treating the simultaneous intervals as byproducts of the polyphony, the vertical harmonic groups became independent individuals, free to move from beat to beat according to the dictates of tonality. Homophonic texture therefore was created when they were used to support a melody. Rameau even went so far as to say that the melody was created by the harmony and was only the upper surface of it.

The lower surface of the music consisted of the lowest notes of the chords, and was so written that it formed a melodic partner to the upper melody in two part counterpoint. It had, therefore, two functions: to provide a melodious lowest part, and to provide the basis of the harmonic foundation. Between these two surfaces the rest of the harmony was filled in by a keyboard instrument. The bass melody usually was played by a stringed instrument, or the bassoon, or in some cases the pedal of the organ. The *combination* of such a bass melody instrument and the keyboard harmonic instrument was known as the *basso continuo,* and is an integral part of all Baroque music. The concept of two outer surfaces and a harmonic middle is even carried into keyboard music.

In writing the music, the composer notated carefully the one or more upper polyphonic melodies and the bass melody. Under the notes of the latter he wrote numbers indicating the harmonic formula of the chord for the guidance of the keyboard player who in performance "realized" these in sound (Example IV-6). Such continuo playing was quite different from merely "plunking out" the chords, for around these

EXAMPLE IV-6: Figured Bass (from Bach: *Flute Sonata No. 1*).

The small notes indicate the tones dictated by the figures under
the bass line. When no figure appears, the bass tone is the root
of the triad. A ♯ indicates that the third above the bass note is to
be raised a half-step. The line through the 6 directs a similar procedure. 7's and 2's indicate seventh chord dissonances. x indicates
a cadence through which the music moves.

the skilled player wove a quasi-polyphonic web of improvised figuration which added detail and sonority to the ensemble. The basso
continuo concept is still vital in the jazz combo of today, although
now the combination of piano, guitar, string bass and drums is usually
known as the rhythm section. As in jazz improvisation, the Baroque
melody was able to create previously unheard-of dissonant figures
over the strong chordal underpinning as long as these dissonances
eventually resolved. This was an extension of the Renaissance technique of the suspension, but it also applied to other dissonant patterns
which became an integral part of Baroque melodic style. The poly-

phony created by this combination is known as *continuo polyphony,* and is a basic texture of Baroque music.

As with earlier "pure" polyphony, continuo polyphony inclines toward flow and continuity of motion. This tends to weaken the interior cadences of a composition since the flow passes through them without stopping to give them any quality of punctuation, or any real emphasis (Examples IV-3, 6). Only the most important structural cadences——that is, cadences which mark the end of a section or an important modulation——only these halt the flow of music. The function of the cadence in defining tonality is important, for it indicates in this way the structure of the composition. The I, IV and V cadence chords, it will be remembered, contain all of the tones of their scale, and a sequence of these chords functionally outlines the scale in harmony. In compositions based upon the concerto principle, the ritornelli often appear at such cadence points.

The third important development in the seventeenth century was the advance toward the use of equal temperament in the tuning of keyboard instruments and, subsequently, all instruments with more-or-less fixed pitch such as the flute and oboe. Equal temperament implies that all of the half-steps in the chromatic scale are the same size. This seems a foregone conclusion to us, but it was not always so. Other systems of tuning had been in use during earlier times and were reasonably satisfactory as long as the music used few sharps or flats. But with the adoption of the tonal system it was theoretically possible to move freely from key to key. With the older tuning systems, however, the more sharps or flats added to produce the new keys, the more out of tune the chords became. Musicians in the Baroque period solved this by "tempering" the old tunings into an approximation of what we know as equal temperament. When this was done, modulation from one tonality to another could be accomplished with ease and the new keys were in tune. The process of adjustment in tuning is referred to in the title of one of J. S. Bach's most important works, *The Well-Tempered Clavier:* in other words, a keyboard instrument whose tuning has been carefully adjusted.

The firm tonal basis created by the functional harmony of this music made possible the art of improvisation as an important characteristic of Baroque style. Just as the trumpeter in a jazz group of today, when he knows the chord progression of a song, may create melodic patterns from these chords without reference to the tune, so the Baroque musician (usually a harpsichordist or organist) could create out of the common chord progressions of his day the preludes, toccatas and fantasies which, when written down, still carry the flavor of music made up on the spur of the moment. The improvisation of wholly melodic instruments, such as the voice, flute, oboe and stringed instruments, of necessity was confined to melodic improvisation and embellishment of given melodies. But this was a fine art in the seventeenth century, and singers especially vied with one another in the art of improvised ornamentation which showed off the brilliance of their voices or almost instrumental dexterity. Nothing was ever repeated without the addition of more ornamentation, and cadence points were pried apart for the insertion of scales, decorative figures, trills and other showy flights of fancy before the final chord. The name of this cadence ornamentation, *cadenza*, now includes any extended passage of virtuosity inserted anywhere in a composition, but it originally came from the improvisation at the cadence point. Originally deriving from the opera of the Baroque period, these techniques quickly were adopted by instrumentalists. Later they were systematized, and shorthand symbols adopted so as to show them in written music. Much dispute has taken place over their interpretation, despite explanations in books of the time by Couperin, J. S. Bach, J. J. Quantz and Bach's oldest son, Karl Philip Emmanuel. Certainly the correct interpretation of this music depends upon scholarly research, but in an equal degree the development of an aesthetic understanding, a sense of taste, is important. We can only recapture a portion of the past, and it must always be seen through twentieth century eyes, heard through ears which have come to accept Wagner, Schoenberg, Webern, Stockhausen. What the performer of Baroque music must do is to synthesize a version which satisfies modern taste without doing violence to the nature of the music. And this is a formidable task.

Certain tension devices of this style emphasize its "becoming" quality. Constant motion, repetition of a motive and increased ornamentation do this effectively. In melody, ascending sequences seem directed toward a climax, and increasingly unstable harmony tends to build tension. Bach employs the last device most skilfully in the first movement of *Brandenburg Concerto No. 2*. Handel often is fond of bringing a movement to a climactic close by an emphatic deceptive cadence upon a complex harmony followed by a rhetorical pause after which a complete final cadence ensues. In polyphonic texture, the shortening of the time interval between successive imitations of a theme, causing it to overlap itself, is a device frequently employed in fugues. It is known as *stretto*. The use of a sustained bass tone may create tension directed toward a strong cadence if the tone is the dominant or subdominant of a key. Paradoxically, this device also may be used to create tonal security and affirmation if the sustained tone is the tonic of the key.

Texture

Continuo polyphony is the prevalent texture of Baroque music, although some national styles (particularly the Italian) emphasize the homophonic element, especially in choral and vocal works in which polyphony with its overlapping parts tends to obscure the words. Strongly rhythmic music, such as the dances in suites, also tends toward homophony so that the rhythm will not be diluted by the interaction of individually rhythmic parts. The German style, for the most part, inclines toward polyphony, even in choral and dance music. This is particularly true of the music of Bach. In the case of choral-vocal compositions, the text often becomes merely a vehicle for the music and supplies the vowel sounds upon which the singers vocalize the long, decorative baroque garlands of affective melody.

THE BAROQUE ORCHESTRA

In this period, we find the nucleus of the modern orchestra taking shape. This is the string quintet consisting of first and second violins, violas, cellos and double-bass viols. The violin family had little by little replaced the older viols, beloved by the Renaissance composers, until only the double-bass remained. The more brilliant tone of the new instruments made them more suitable for the opera and chamber concert, and the techniques for playing them developed rapidly in the hands of such mid and late Baroque violinists as Corelli, Geminiani and Vivaldi. These stringed instruments, then, together with the harpsichord, formed the core of the orchestra. This was occasionally altered, to be sure, by leaving out a section, such as the second violins, or replacing a section with violas to secure a darker and richer sonority.

To the strings were added, as required, the woodwind, brass and percussion. The recorder and the flute were both popular instruments and appear frequently in the ensemble and concerto literature, as does the oboe and its tenor cousin, the oboe d'amore, and its bass relative, the bassoon. The clarinet does not seem to have been accepted into the polite society of orchestral music of this time and was obliged to wait until the latter years of the eighteenth century. The favorite brass instruments were the hunting horns and the trumpets, the latter instruments representative of nobility and often associated with the equally royal kettledrums. These brass instruments, as well as the trombones, were smaller in bore than our modern instruments, and produced a softer tone. The horns and trumpets were without the modern valves that make it possible to play the chromatic scale and were therefore limited largely to bugle-call melodic formations, at least in their middle and lower registers. In the upper range the tones producible without valves were close enough together to allow scale patterns to be played if the performer were expert enough. The trumpets and drums lent a truly festive and brilliant sound to the Baroque ensemble. The trombones seem to have seldom been used as solo or orchestral instruments except in operatic and church music, a situation which prevailed until the late eighteenth century.

The baroque orchestra, for various reasons, seems never to have been very large, comprising what we today would call a chamber orchestra of about twenty players. Similarly, choruses were of comparable size, not the huge aggregations now assembled to perform the *Messiah* or the *B-Minor Mass!*

An outcome of the concerto principle of contrast of a large body of instruments——the *tutti,* or entire group——with a small one—— the soloists, or *concertino*——and their relative masses of sound and differences in sonority, was the phenomenon of *terrace dynamics.* Presumably, the Baroque orchestra observed no gradations in dynamics, playing probably at a level of *forte.* The addition or subtraction of other instruments to the group would cause the immediate step-like change in the dynamic level. This terrace effect also resulted from the manipulation of stops in the baroque organ or harpsichord. It seems doubtful that solo singing and playing by other solo wind and stringed instruments were limited in this way, however.

THE MUSICAL LITERATURE
OF THE BAROQUE PERIOD

The parent forms of the music of the Baroque period are the opera and concerto. If we recognize that the dance music of the period was included in the scope of opera as ballet, particularly in French opera, the cohesiveness of the music of this period becomes even more striking. For our examination of the musical literature of the period, however, it is necessary to make some reasonable division into categories which can be handled more easily. We shall first study the most important form of the period, opera, followed by some of its close relatives.

The second large division, instrumental music, will include compositions written for orchestra, chamber ensemble and keyboard instruments.

The Vocal Forms: Opera and Cantata

The chart (Example IV-7) may help to establish the relationship
between opera and some of its derivative forms. All of these have

EXAMPLE IV-7: *Vocal Compositions.*

OPERA
A drama in music;
acting, staging;
depends heavily
on recitative and
aria.

ORATORIO	CANTATA
A sacred "opera" or meditation; no acting or staging; recitative and aria, chorus; story sometimes narrated.	A small dramatic moment related by a character in it; usually not more than two soloists involved; recitative and aria.

PASSION
A sacred oratorio
relating the story
of Christ's betrayal
and crucifixion.
Forms and methods
same as oratorio;
may use chorale.

CHURCH CANTATA
More elaborate cantata,
often orchestra, soloists, chorus; recitative,
aria, sometimes use of melody
and text of hymn tune (chorale)—a
"sermon" in song.

suitable instrumental accompaniment, sometimes more or less elaborate introductions, internal instrumental movements, and sometimes
concluding ones also. There may be orchestra, solo instruments or
only basso continuo.

We already have examined the beginnings of opera in the late
Renaissance and early Baroque periods. Let us now trace the history
and influence of this important form. The operas of Monteverdi and
others established a tradition early in the seventeenth century of treating elevated subjects——the adventures of kings and queens, gods and
goddesses. This variety of musical drama was known as *opera seria*
and was practiced by most of the composers of the time. The short,
sometimes improvised comedy interludes which appeared between

the long acts of the opera seria were little by little furnished with music, often parodistic of the larger work, and eventually (around the turn of the eighteenth century) became a species of opera themselves called *opera buffa*. As we shall see, opera buffa with its witty plots, easily understood by the people of the middle class, gradually replaced the opera seria during the eighteenth century. Very often the mythological or historical plots of the opera seria seem to have been regarded by composers merely as convenient excuses upon which to hang their music with little regard for dramatic characterization——an attitude ably abetted by the singers who in turn felt that the music was merely a sketch for them to fill out with the improvisatory embellishments suitable to their voices. So, the opera seria at its lowest point was essentially a concert with scenery, costume and stage effects; the public attended mostly to hear its favorite singers, not to be moved by the drama.

The ingredients of the opera had also changed, for instead of the melodious and flexible monody, clear divisions were made between the active and reflective elements of the drama, creating on the one hand a species of declamation in which the words were important, the *recitative*, and on the other hand the song, or *aria*, in which the music had control. In both, a certain degree of text-painting was used, and the aria was, of course, ruled strongly by the doctrine of the affections. The typical opera, then, consisted of action carried on in recitative, and lyrical moments, rather comparable to the Shakespearian soliloquy, set in musical forms, usually with rather few words which were repeated to allow the music time to take shape and expand. Duets, trios and choral ensembles were also sometimes treated in the manner of arias.

The opera essentially was an Italian product, and the Italian style was dominant all over Europe except for France, as we have explained. Certain procedures adopted by the first composer of French opera, Lully (1632-1687), became popular in England and Germany, however. These were the *French overture* and the *aria over a strophic bass*. They, plus recitative and the typical Italian aria structures, will be encountered in our study of the music, so let us pause here to examine them.

French Overture

This is a large binary structure the first section of which is slow in tempo, largely homophonic, employs a pompous, angular "dotted" rhythm, and ends on a half-cadence (V). The second section is rapid, fugal, and sometimes uses concerto-like alternations of solo instruments, ending either with an abbreviated return of the slow first section, or an emphatic and impressive cadence arrived at by slowing down the tempo considerably. The overtures to both *Dido and Aeneas* and *Alcina,* which we shall study, are of this variety.

Aria over a Strophic Bass (Example IV-8)

This is a type of variation called the *passacaglia* when it appears in instrumental music. The theme is a bass pattern of usually four to eight measures in length which is repeated with only slight changes throughout the aria. The voice part is combined with it in such a way as to comply with the chords it suggests, creating consonances or dissonances which resolve in the usual way. The chordal fill-in is supplied by the continuo, and may vary from repetition to repetition, since the

EXAMPLE IV-8: Aria over Strophic Bass, Purcell: *Dido and Aeneas.*

bass tone may be interpreted as the root, third, fifth or even the seventh tone of a chord. If the chord series remains the same throughout, the variation type is given the name of *chaconne*, this being, as it were, a kind of harmonized passacaglia. If the bass is shorter than four measures, it is called a *ground bass*.

The Binary Form Aria

We have already investigated this form on page 126 as used in keyboard music. Its application to vocal music is exactly parallel, modulations, cadences and all, except that the melodic line is supplied with words to be sung. In the interests of variety, the composer may write out the sectional repetitions, using slightly different turns of melody or of figured bass, thus avoiding the exact repetition dictated by the musical repeat sign. When performed, improvised ornaments and cadenzas were added to the repeated section by the singer.

The Ternary, or Da Capo Aria

This form may be symbolized by the formula A-B-A, signifying that the tonality and melodic material of B is different from that of the two A sections, which are alike. In many cases both the A and B sections are organized internally in binary forms, in which event a more accurate name for this ternary would be *compound* ternary form. In arias, the A section usually is preceded and followed by a thematic ritornello, thus providing an introduction and a coda, the latter separating it clearly from the following B section. The B section usually is without these ritornelli, although there may be one or two within it depending on its length. The B section usually closes with a firm final cadence, after which the introductory ritornello of A is heard. At the end of the B section, the Italian words appear: *Da capo al fine*, or *Dal segno*. The first signifies that the performers are to play section A once more until they arrive at the word *fine*, the end. The second provides for a shortening of A by directing them to play from a sign ($\S$) in that section to the end of it. In some cases only the introductory ritornello is repeated. The diagram in Example IV-9 should make these procedures clear. Not only are the A and B sections distinguished from each other in key, but they also differ in the "affection" upon which they are based and usually in the fullness or sonority of the accompaniment.

EXAMPLE IV-9: The *da capo* (ternary) Aria.

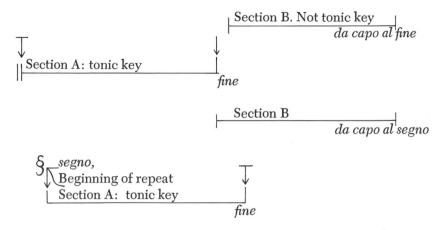

Both the A and B sections may include ornamentation and cadenzas, but the most brilliant display is usually saved for the *da capo* repeat of A.

Recitative

Derived from the older monody, this is the operatic equivalent of speech through which the action of an opera is accomplished, or the commentary or message of a cantata is conveyed. It may be accompanied by only the basso continuo (Example IV-10) in which case it is called *secco* recitative ("dry" in the sense of not being particularly expressive), or increasingly melodious in line and using text painting with richer orchestral accompaniment, in which case it is called *recitativo accompagnato*. In both, the inflections and tempos of speech are imitated musically, sometimes for increased expression of the affect of the passage. It is based entirely upon the text, and the musical elements are subordinated entirely to the words; it is also intended to sound improvisatory, thus resembling speech more closely.

A type of declamation half-way between the improvisatory recitative and the formally organized song in which the musical element is predominant is the *arioso*. At the point where repetition of words begins——signifying usually that the music is becoming more important as an organizing force instead of the logic of the words——a more melodious quality may be observed, together with the rhythmic pulse, which in recitative is usually absent or weak (Example IV-10, at b).

In the French and English style, however, the metric pulse may be present even in recitative (rather seldom true of the Italian style). Bach freely uses both practices, but tends toward the Italian.

EXAMPLE IV-10: Recitative and Arioso.

EXAMPLE IV-10: Recitative and Arioso (Continued).

Note that the firm beat of the arioso part supports the confidence expressed in the text, especially at the final cadence on "secure."

Dido and Aeneas by Henry Purcell (1659-1695)

Opera in England had its origin in the masques, plays with music, but had adopted many French traits through the studies of English composers on the continent. Thus, we find a French overture and a number of arias set over a strophic (passacaglia) bass in this moving work by the last outstanding English composer before the twentieth century. After Purcell's death Italian opera became the rage, reaching its height of achievement in the works of Handel which, paradoxically, fell before the popular ballad opera *The Beggar's Opera* and others.

Dido and Aeneas, taken from Vergil's *Aeneid,* relates the tragic story of the love of Dido, queen of ancient Carthage, for Aeneas, the prince of Troy, lately destroyed by the Greeks. Aeneas is on his way to found a city in Italy at the behest of the gods, and, when he forgets this celestial order, is spurred to leave Carthage by certain witches who hate Dido and seek thus to cause her downfall. In this they are successful.

Sufficient for our purposes is an examination of the third act, although it is hoped that the reader will listen to the entire opera, for it contains much beautiful and interesting music. The following *résumé* analyzes this act, the climax of the opera which sees the triumph of the malevolent witches, the quarrel between Dido and Aeneas, and Dido's resolve to die.

1. Orchestral prelude, rapid tempo, partly imitative in texture, based on the coming sailor's song.
2. Sailor's song, solo and chorus: "Come away, fellow sailors." A humorous and bright beginning to an act that ends in darkness.
3. Sailor's dance. Binary form.
4. Sorceress and witches: recitative and stagily fiendish laughing duet in arioso style. Leads to binary aria by Sorceress: Section I, "Our next motion must be to storm her lover on the ocean," repeated. Section II: "From the ruin of others" forms the transition, and the tonic key is regained at the repetition of "Elissa bleeds tonight and Carthage flames tomorrow!" Note the text-painting.
5. Chorus: "Destruction's our delight," polyphonic laughter; deliberately fantastic dance by witches and sailors. This closes the first scene.
6. Recitative: Dido, Belinda, Aeneas. Dido reveals her grief in a magnificently pathetic recitative: note the affective downward steps and skips. Belinda hails Aeneas with a fanfare figure, followed by affective motives of sorrow in the recitative. Aeneas, a cardboard figure in the opera, expresses a stylized grief in a rather chromatic recitative, followed by Dido's acid comment that his tears are those of the "deceitful crocodile," with exquisitely mocking text-painting on "weeps." The following quarrel rises to a climax in an arioso duet.
7. Chorus: "Great minds against themselves conspire." This consists of two sections: the first, a setting of the above sentence, is in major and is homophonic; the second is in minor and is polyphonic, stating "And shun the cure they most desire." The two halves are equal in size and importance, but have differences which imply motion and continuity ——an example of the same kind of dynamic symmetry often encountered in art and architecture of the period. Dramatically, this chorus moves from the excitement of the dispute to the tragic calm of the closing action; musically, a modulation from the major to the minor key of the close. The quietness and air of inevitability increase the human quality of the queen and her tragedy.

8. Recitative and aria over a strophic bass: "Thy hand, Belinda" and "When I am laid in earth" (Example IV-8). The recitative is built on a descending chromatic scale, always an effective expressive technique. The five measure bass pattern is also chromatic; the phrases of the melody overlap the beginnings and endings of the pattern, creating a continuity of flow and a sense of melodic freedom. The melodic line struggles to rise, but is turned downward at the close of each phrase, imparting a sense of grief and doom. The harmonization, which is rather consistent, is very rich, with many dissonances and unexpected chords. The coda, by the orchestra, leads to the closing chorus.

9. Chorus: "With drooping wings, ye Cupids, come, and scatter roses on her tomb." One writer compares this chorus to a Baroque funeral monument, solemn yet ornate, decorated with cherubs whose wings are limned by the graceful downward curves of the polyphonic lines. This is exactly the right way to close this opera, far more dramatically potent than to set Dido's immolation as a dazzling orchestral finale in the nineteenth century manner!

Alcina by Handel

Our second opera is quite different from *Dido and Aeneas* in that it is a fully developed opera seria in the Italian style of the late Baroque. First performed in 1735, it was one of the operas with which Handel hoped to recoup his losses of the preceding season caused in part by *The Beggar's Opera* and by the withdrawal of the patronage of the Prince of Wales. In order to court popular support, Handel abandoned the high heroic tragedy in favor of somewhat lighter plots, a characteristic of *Alcina*. Not that this is an opera buffa by any means! The plot revolves about Alcina, an enchantress like Circe in her power to change men to animals and rocks. She somehow has ensnared the affections of Ruggiero, the former betrothed of the maiden Bradamante who has come to Alcina's island in search of him. The story essentially is concerned with the defeat of Alcina and the reunion of the lovers, but complications in the form of subplots, disguises and mistaken identities not only prevent a straightforward presentation, but also afford many opportunities for arias of various kinds, ensemble numbers and magical transformation scenes. Other characters are: Oronte, Alcina's military commander, in love with Morgana, her assistant; Oberto, who has come in search of his father whom Alcina has turned into a lion; and Melisso, Bradamante's tutor and advisor. Some of these parts were sung during the Baroque period by *castrati*, boys who were emasculated before puberty, and thus grew up retaining the range and quality of boys' voices, but otherwise with the resonance and power of an adult. They often were extremely famous,

PLATE XI: *George Frederick Handel. Painting by Thomas Hudson. (The Metropolitan Museum of Art, gift of Francis Neilson, 1946.)*

and commanded fabulous salaries. Today these parts either are rearranged for tenor voices or taken by women. The following is a descriptive condensation of the opening scene of the first act.

1. French Overture, with short cadential slow section at the close.
2. The scene is a deserted hollow enclosed by hills, at the foot of which there is a small cave. Bradamante, (in disguise as a young warrior) and Melisso, are accosted by Morgana, who tells them that they are in the realm of the enchantress Alcina. The secco recitative is accompanied only by the harpsichord. Morgana takes a liking to the young man (Bradamante) and sings an aria to him.
3. Aria: "Wreathed in smiles, speaking or silent, your comely face has a certain something which appeals too greatly, dear one, to my heart." As is usual in arias, the orchestra plays an introduction composed of the thematic affective motives. It appears again in a short ritornello and the coda, both fashioned from the thematic material. The aria, having only one affection, is cast in binary form. The words are repeated in Section II, which is more elaborately ornamented than Section I, and the singer embellishes the closing cadence of her part with a brilliant cadenza. A diagram of this aria would appear thus:

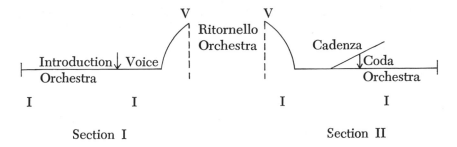

4. Thunder and lightning demolish the hills and reveal the palace of Alcina. Courtiers, Ruggiero and Oberto are present. Chorus: "This is the heaven of delight, this is the center of enjoyment." Orchestral introduction, ritornello and coda. Homophonic chorus in brilliant and vigorous rhythms.

5. Recitative: Bradamante recognizes Ruggiero as her faithless lover, but before she reveals her identity, the diplomatic Melisso greets Alcina, introducing the disguised Bradamante as *Ricciardo*. She welcomes them, and instructs Ruggiero to show them the palace, the countryside, and curiously enough, the spot where she and Ruggiero discovered their mutual love. This is, of course, a pretext for the following aria by Alcina!

6. Aria. This is a grand da capo aria, as befits the first appearance of the *prima donna* of the opera. The text for the A section, begins: *"Di', cor mio, quanto amai"* (Tell, dearest heart, how much I have loved you), and is set to a broad, vigorous but not rapid melody in major tonality. The formal design of this section is exactly like the binary aria above. The B section is in minor and employs a florid vocal line toward the end of the verse as an affective device. The text of B is: *"Dove fisso ne' miei rai . . ."* (Where, gazing sighing in my eyes, . . . you told me with a look; I suffer and burn just as you do). At the conclusion of the B section, the A section is repeated in its entirety, but with more elaborate embellishments in the voice part.

7. While Alcina withdraws, the chorus sings a homophonic song of praise. *Ricciardo* (Bradamante) reproves Ruggiero for abandoning Bradamante, and for living this slothful existence. Ruggiero, annoyed by them, sings the following aria.

8. Aria: *"Di te mi rido, semplice stolto. Sieguo Cupido, amo un bel volto, ne so mancar di fe"* (You make me laugh, stupid simpleton. I am Cupid's follower; I love a beauteous face, and am incapable of playing false). This aria, employing a laughing motive in both voice and orchestra, is in binary form as indicated above.

9. The minor character, Oberto, now comes forward to inquire of the newcomers if they have heard of Astolfo, his father (who also happens to be Bradamante's cousin). Alcina saved them from shipwreck, says Oberto, and loaded his father with honors, but now he has vanished. Bradamante confides to Melisso in an aside that Astolfo has probably been changed into a wild beast. Oberto then sings the following pathetic aria.

10. Aria: Section A: *"Chi m'insegna il caro padre?"* (Who will show me where my dear father is?) Section B: *"M'abbandona la speranza;"* (Hope abandons me). *Da capo.* Section B has some beautiful florid writing for the voice, restrained enough not to spoil the melancholy mood of the aria.

11. Oberto withdraws, weeping, as Oronte, Alcina's commander-in-chief, angrily challenges *Ricciardo* (Bradamante) to a duel for stealing the love of Morgana away from him. The lady in question hurriedly enters to defend *Ricciardo,* and tries to placate the two antagonists in her first full-dress aria as *seconda donna* of the opera.

12. Aria *da capo.* Section A: *"E gelosia, forza e d'amore, ch'il sen t'affanna"* (It is jealousy, the power of love, that vexes your breast). The full orchestra accompanies the A section, using as thematic material affective motives and rhythms suitable to the emotion of jealousy. These are first presented in abrupt, short phrases, then spun out in long stretches in the voice part. Section B: *"Per un bel volto, che ne vien tolto, tu mesto gemi"* (For a lovely face which has been snatched from you, you sadly sigh. We are full of anger, we are all in love and know not pity). This part, set in the dominant key, is accompanied by the continuo only, and has a pathetic quality, especially near the close of the second sentence quoted in translation above. The *da capo* reprise is somewhat more highly ornamented than in its first presentation.

Thus ends the first scene of the opera. The remainder is well worth hearing, for, like Handel's patrons, we enjoy the brilliant arias while not bothering a great deal about the plot, which gets more involved as it progresses.

A comparison of the music of this work with the beloved *Messiah* reveals that, except for more choral numbers, and the use of polyphony in them, the alternation of recitative and aria and the use of the *da capo* aria are the same in both. Bach's monumental musical settings of the story of the betrayal and crucifixion of Christ also are based upon the opera style, and progress in scenes interspersed with choruses employing hymn melodies familiar to his congregation in order to make the dramatic effect and the religious message more immediate.

The Cantata

This form was a development of monody, and, in the works of early and middle Baroque composers such as Peri (1561-1663), Carissimi (1605-1674) and Cesti (1623-1669) it developed from a series of arias over a strophic bass to a succession of recitatives, ariosos and arias separated by instrumental ritornelli. It is essentially this latter type of structure which was brought to its highest point by Alessandro

Scarlatti (1660-1725), the Neapolitan opera composer whose works served in a large measure as models for Handel. Scarlatti, who did much to establish the *da capo* aria form, composed more than six hundred of these chamber cantatas for one or two voices and varying instrumental ensembles. Typically, his cantatas consist of a pair of recitatives and arias, sometimes with arioso sections and instrumental ritornelli. They resemble a short section of an opera in this way, but in the cantata the story, rather than being acted, is told by a narrator who may be one of its characters.

The cantata we shall examine is entitled *Su Le Sponde del Tebro* (On the Banks of the Tiber), by Alessandro Scarlatti, and is scored for solo soprano, trumpet, strings and continuo. It opens with a moderately rapid orchestral movement called "Sinfonia," employing the high trumpet somewhat in the manner of a concerto. The text of the cantata in translation follows:

1. Recitative
   "On the banks of the Tiber, where the goddesses of Latium wove their hair into cords for bows, the faithful Amintas, scorned by Cloris, with infinite grief cried to heaven, cried to earth, 'I am betrayed.'" This is a melodious recitative, less anguished and dramatic than the words might lead us to think. The continuo provides a rhythmic and melodic coda.
2. A short and brilliant Sinfonia follows, as if to set off the central thought of the cantata, Amintas' betrayal.
3. Aria
   "Content yourselves, O faithful thoughts, with remaining guardians of my heart, which is stormed by sorrows, gigantic warriors whose leader is pain." The affective note of this brilliant *da capo* aria is that of war, and the fanfare figures in the solo, as well as the martial sound of the trumpet, support this attitude.
4. Recitative
   "Sad, weary and sighing with the grief that oppressed him, he thus addressed his eyes:"
   Arioso
   "Unhappy eyes of mine, since we remain alone, make way for tears, and let my heart trace its sorrow on your lids."
   After the melodious and expressive recitative, the arioso which follows presents the most emotional movement of the cantata. The trumpet is omitted, and the strings are treated polyphonically, with chromatic dissonances and unexpected harmonic changes. The mood of intense grief, beautified through the power of music, is sustained throughout, with the vocal part leading among the interweaving strings.
5. Aria
   "Say at least, cruel stars, when did my life offend you, that now you fill it with sorrow. Become a martyr to love, through the tears of faith, it is forced to hope alone."

A plaintive *da capo* aria whose unity of mood is preserved by the gradual modulation to very closely related keys in the B section. The A section is binary with a short ritornello at the midpoint.

6. Ritornello

A short, moderately polyphonic movement by the string orchestra, in the same key as the preceding aria. This movement, together with the earlier Sinfonia, serves to frame the central and musically climactic section of the cantata, dividing it, as it were, into Introduction, Catastrophe and Resolution.

7. Recitative

"To the air, to the sky, to the winds, spoke the gentle shepherd. But perceiving at last that no tears, no prayers could soften a heart of stone, resolutely and constantly the desolate lover spoke to his heart:"

8. Aria

"Cease then to weep, poor afflicted heart, since, despised by fate, nothing is left thee but to bewail the cruelty of an unfaithful one."

The lover's address to the air, the sky and the winds is represented by the ascending vocal line, while at the word "resolutely," the music takes on rhythmic pulse and motion, representing the change of mood of Amintas. This change is also reflected in the following *da capo* aria in which martial and optimistic figures in the trumpet and voice provide a brilliant conclusion to the work. It is apparent from this work, and from other Italian chamber cantatas, that like the opera, they were intended as showpieces for virtuoso singers.

The Church Cantata

In the Protestant North, the cantata was adopted not only as a secular form, but also as religious music, sometimes presenting a Biblical situation, but more often as a musical exhortation embodying Christian doctrine and serving to amplify the verbal sermon. To bring the main musical portion of the long Lutheran service closer to the congregation, the composer often used familiar hymn-tunes and their words in the cantatas. These hymns were called *chorales,* and the practice of basing organ preludes and choral works upon them had a long tradition in the German Baroque, extending from Praetorius (1572-1621) through Schein (1586-1630) to Bach's predecessor in Leipzig, Kuhnau (1660-1722). The organization and structure of the church cantatas vary, some being entirely based upon the chorale (Bach's *Cantata No. 4, Christ lag in Todesbanden,* for example), some using the chorale and its text interspersed with other verses more suitable for recitative and aria (Bach's *Cantatas No. 140, Wachet auf,* and *No. 80, Ein feste Burg*), and finally cantatas not based in any way upon chorales, either for solo voice or vocal ensemble (Bach, *Cantata 152, Tritt auf die Glaubensbahn,* for soprano, bass and small orchestra; Bach, *Cantata No. 63,*

PLATE XII: *Johann Sebastian Bach. Painting by Elias Gottlob Haussmann (1746). (Museum Geschichte der Stadt Leipzig.)*

Christen, ätzet diesen Tag, for soprano, alto, tenor and bass soloists, chorus, strings with trumpet, timpani oboe and bassoon—an elaborate work without chorale.)

The musical treatment of the chorale melody varied, almost always as a result of the interpretation of the text according to the doctrine of the affections. In Bach's works, great care is taken to select a single word as point of reference in the text and to build affective accompaniment or ornamentation of the chorale around it. These words, such as *sin, death, atonement, redemption* and *resurrection* are treated with such depth in Bach's religious music that we cannot doubt their reality to him, especially the concepts of atonement and redemption through Christ's sacrifice. Let us see how Bach treats them in his *Cantata No. 80,* based on "the Marseillaise of the Reformation," as Heine called it, Luther's own chorale, *Ein feste Burg ist unser Gott* (A Mighty Fortress is Our God). Bach composed this work for the bicentennial celebration of the Augsburg Confession, and therefore used a festival orchestra including trumpets and timpani, vocal soloists and chorus. Movements

EXAMPLE IV-11: Chorale from Bach's Cantata No. 80, *Ein feste Burg ist unser Gott.*

Text attributed to Luther
Translated by Henry Drinker

1, 2, 5 and 8 are based upon the chorale melody and text, while the others are commentaries set in recitative, arioso and aria. The chorale melody and a translation of the texts used (with the number of the movement in which they appear) is shown in Example IV-11.

First movement: Text, see Example IV-11, first verse. A massive choral and orchestral movement whose intent is to portray the "mighty fortress." It starts full force, without introduction, and takes in turn each phrase of the chorale melody in embellished form as the subject for an imitative exposition. At the conclusion of each exposition (*fugato* is the technical term for this kind of treatment), the high trumpet sounds the chorale phrase above the choral-instrumental mass, and is answered canonically one measure later by the bass instruments and organ.

Second movement: Text, see Example IV-11, sung by soprano as duet with bass: the latter sings the following words not derived from the chorale verse.

> Every soul by God created, has by Christ been liberated. They whose Jesus' standard bear, to His service dedicated, all will in His victory share.

In the orchestral accompaniment of this movement, according to Schweitzer, we hear the tumult of battle and the sound of horses' hooves. The bass "interpreter" of the soprano text asserts his message of hope against the background much as decorative elements are superposed in baroque architectural ornament.

Third movement. Bass Recitative and Arioso (not chorale text).

> Text: Thou child of God, consider what complete devotion the Saviour showed for you in His supreme atonement, whereby He rose triumphant over Satan's horde, and human sin and error and all things base. Let not, then in your being, the Evil One have a place. Let not your sins convert the heaven there within you into a desert! Repent now of your guilt in tears *(here arioso begins)* that Christ the Lord to you be fast united.

This is recitative typical of Bach in its melodiousness and expressiveness, following lyrically the voice inflections of speech.

Fourth movement. Soprano Aria.

> Text: (not from chorale)
> Come dwell within my heart; Lord Jesus I adore Thee. Bid evil all depart and let Thine image ever shine before me. Away sin, how base thou art!

This lovely aria is accompanied simply by the basso continuo, and is of the *da capo* type of construction. The poetry of the text belongs to the pietistic movement current in the Lutheran church of Bach's time.

Fifth movement. Chorus: Chorale text and melody. (Example IV-11)

In this exciting movement in concerto style, the symbolism of the pilgrim band withstanding the power of Evil is vividly pictured by the massing of the chorus in unison on the chorale melody while the orchestra seethes around them.

Sixth movement. Tenor Recitative and Arioso (free text: see Example IV-10). This movement matches the Bass recitative, III, both in the fact that it is recitative, and that it concludes in arioso style.

Seventh movement. Duet for Alto and Tenor (not chorale text).

> Text: Blessed he who praises God, whose Words will sanctify him; more blessed still is he who bears Him in his heart. With him will grace abound nor can the foe come nigh him; at last will he be crowned when death shall set him free.

This is a so-called Italian chamber duet, with oboe *obbligato* (or decorative part) really creating a trio. Note the imitative passages, and the occasional parallel movement between the voices, giving a sweetness and grace to the texture. The predominantly tranquil mood is broken momentarily near the end of the movement, where the words "and death shall set him free" *(wenn es den Tod erlegt)* are set to a rather grotesque chromatic figure.

Eighth movement: Chorus, orchestra and congregation.

A harmonized version of the chorale, using the text appearing in Example IV-11. As in painting and architecture of this period, this final music invites the listener to enter its world, bring into a close relationship the Christian and the message of the chorale text.

Most of the church cantatas which are based upon chorale melodies conclude with a performance of the chorale in its original hymn version.

It is notable that Bach's few secular cantatas, the *Coffee Cantata* and the *Peasant Cantata* for example, are written in exactly the same style as his sacred ones, the only difference being in the text.

Solo Song

Although we hear few solo songs from this period nowadays, they were extremely popular, especially in Germany where the *lied* enjoyed a prominence not rivaled until the nineteenth century. The Italian song was modeled largely upon those of the opera, and in France, the *airs de cour* (court songs), originally intended to accompany dancing, became popular in their own right and affected the English *ayres*. The latter had an honorable heritage from the lute songs of John Dowland (1562-1626) and Thomas Campion (1567-1620) in the preceding century. Purcell added to the list, as did many a lesser composer, either with original compositions or settings of folk songs. Folk tunes with new words became popular enough, in Gay and Pepusch' *Beggar's Opera,* to well-nigh ruin Handel's Italian operatic ventures and turn him to the composition of English oratorios.

The Instrumental Forms

Once composers abandoned the vocal style of the motet, *chanson* and madrigal and began writing idiomatically for instruments, their music ceased resembling transcription and began a rapid development

PLATE XIII: *Facade of the Church of San Carlo alla Fontana, Rome, by Borromini. Here is baroque activity transferred to architecture. Note the play of shadow caused by the outward-bulging structure and the ornamentation. (Photo Alinari, Florence.)*

as a legitimate branch of musical art. This commenced in the Renaissance and early Baroque, flourishing so greatly that by the turn of the eighteenth century, instrumental music equaled vocal music in forms and importance. Since most of the music for instruments sprang from the same ancestors, many parallel forms are to be found when comparing keyboard, small ensemble and orchestral music. The development of the canzona into the sonata, the canzona and ricercar into the fugue, and dances into the suite, combined with variation, is shared among the various performing media. Space does not permit a close examination of the music produced during this development, but the following short description may serve to fill in the gap between the early years of the seventeenth century and the beginning of the fully developed High Baroque in 1680.

Keyboard Music

Music for the harpsichord, clavichord and organ flourished during the early seventeenth century in three centers of importance——England, France and Italy——each of which contributed a technique of especial value to the eventual synthesis of keyboard styles. We already have examined the English keyboard style in the preceding chapter and noted the preference for variations and the skill developed by the virginalist composers in writing them. These tendencies were continued in the keyboard music of Henry Purcell, who showed a distinct preference for the "ground" or passacaglia-chaconne type of variation. These are well illustrated in his *Harpsichord Lessons* and *Suites.*

French keyboard music took as its point of departure the lute music which was so popular. This consisted at first of transcriptions of polyphonic music, later compositions which employed the devices learned from such transcriptions. Essentially, this is a free style using chords, arpeggios and quasi-imitative passages in lieu of consistent polyphony in a specified number of parts, simply because this polyphony was impossible to play upon the lute. Ornaments too, as in the English style, were necessary to provide accents or sustaining quality to the tones. Jacques Champion de Chambonnieres (1602-1672) transferred this "broken," or "free" style of the lute to the harpsichord, establishing a variety of texture which has been characteristic of music for keyboard instruments ever since. He also adopted the lutenist fashion of giving descriptive or whimsical titles to his compositions, which were, actually, mostly dance movements. This, too, became a tradition in French music for the harpsichord.

In Italy, the fount of composition and performance of keyboard music was the organist at St. Peter's in Rome, Girolamo Frescobaldi (1583-1643). His approach was thoroughly polyphonic, although he was a daring harmonist in the use of chromaticism, and a virtuoso performer who wrote technically difficult and imaginatively expressive passages in his organ music. In the collection of music which he published in 1635, the *Fiori Musicali,* he advised the performer to "find out the affection of the passage" before playing it, to articulate rapid passages by phrasing them in the manner of a singer, to slow down at the approaches to cadences, and to vary the tempo throughout a composition after the manner of madrigal performance in order to enhance the expressivity of the music. His style, then, was noted for its harmonic daring as well as this romantic, non-Doctrine of Affections attitude.

The Netherlands composer, Jan Pieterszoon Sweelinck (1562-1621), affected a large group of later North German organists with his variations, toccatas, fantasies and chorale settings. He was closely allied with English virginalist composers in technique and sympathy, so much so that some of his works are included in the Fitzwilliam Virginal Book. Sweelinck's variations on chorale melodies established the foundation of this technique, which culminated in the work of Bach. In his treatment, the plainly-heard chorale melody is surrounded with rhythmic motives, unceasing in their repetition, often gaining motion and tension up to the climactic and brilliantly improvisatory coda which closes the piece. The Fantasies of this composer were highly important in the early development of the fugue. They were based upon a single subject of abstract, rather than affective, design, which was used in a number of imitative passages, each with new countermelodies, treated to enlargement or diminution of its time values, combined in stretto and surrounded with increasingly active rhythmic figuration, finally arriving at an exciting closing climax. Other so-called "echo" fantasies transfer the polychoral technique of the Venetian composers to the two manuals of the organ, registered in soft and loud dynamic levels. Sweelinck's inspired yet logical treatment of the formal and rhythmic aspects of these compositions rank him as one of the most important composers of the early Baroque.

The German keyboard style began to develop only during the middle Baroque period. The most notable keyboard composer of that region was Johann Jacob Froberger (1616-1667), a student of Frescobaldi, and a widely travelled musician who assimilated the variation technique of the English, the free style and ornamentation of the French and the bold harmony of the Italians. While he wrote toccatas, canzonas and ricercare, he is most noted for his suites of dances, patterned after the French style of Chambonnieres. These works move toward the standardization later accepted by the composers of the high Baroque, of basing the suite on the German *Allemand,* the French *Courante* and the Spanish *Saraband.* Later, the Irish-French *Gigue* (jig) became the fourth member.

Of passing importance because of his composition of keyboard sonatas, the first transfer of the Italian *sonatas da camera* and *da chiesa* to the keyboard instruments, is Johann Kuhnau (1660-1722), Bach's predecessor at the St. Thomas Church in Leipzig.

The important keyboard composers of the high Baroque are Francois Couperin (1668-1733), Johann Sebastian Bach (1685-1750), Domenico Scarlatti (1685-1757), the son of Allessandro Scarlatti, and George Frederick Handel (1685-1759). As might be expected, Handel represents the Italian style combined with a certain German harmonic depth, while in Bach's music for the harpsichord and organ we find the culmination of the style of the period, drawing from all of his predecessors and contemporaries the most important aspects of their compositions and fusing these in a superb synthesis that signifies "Baroque" to many people. Couperin and Scarlatti represent more national and individual approaches, affected as they were by the cultural climates of the French and Spanish courts, respectively. Their music, together with that of George Phillip Telemann (1681-1757), music director at Hamburg for many years, represents a late phase of the Baroque that we classify as Rococo. The Rococo characteristics are essentially a use of small scale musical structures, an inclination toward intimate persuasion rather than theatricality, a reserve and delicacy of melody and harmony, a variety of mood in one movement (Scarlatti), and considerable use of ornamentation, whether applied to a melodic line or integral in it. Nevertheless, the music of these composers uses the essential Baroque concepts of bass-soprano melodic tension, tonality and structure, and functional harmony. Now let us turn to the music.

The Suite

The Suite is one of the most important of the compound forms used in the Baroque. It passes essentially unchanged from those written for keyboard instruments to the orchestral medium, although the latter usually begins with an imposing French Overture. The French, who called such groups of dances *Ordres,* and the English, who named them *Lessons,* were apt to show great flexibility in the number, order and kind of dances which they used. The Germans, however, tended to make the first dance an Allemande, followed by Courante, Sarabande and Gigue, often placing optional rococo dances, called *Galantieren,* between the last two. Occasionally, the German suites are entitled *Ouverture* or *Partita* in the late Baroque, although the latter term originally meant a set of variations. Frequently a prelude, otherwise called *Ouverture, Sinfonia* or *Fantasie* opens the Partita. The dances are in binary form (p. 126), usually of the rounded variety, and each may be followed by an ornamented variation called a *double.* In some cases, two dances of the same kind (*e.g.* Menuet I and Menuet II) may be found, in which case the first one is repeated after the second, creating a compound ternary form (Menuet I: Menuet II: Menuet I, usually without its internal binary-form repeats). In addition to those dances inherited from the Renaissance (see p. 106), the Allemande, Courante and Gigue, the following ones frequently are found. All but the Sarabande were classed by the German composers as *Galantieren.*

Sarabande: triple meter, slow, with a typical rhythm which pauses on the second beat of the measure. Usually the third dance in a suite.

Air: not a dance, but an instrumental piece in song style in which melodic replaces rhythmic interest. Usually in binary form.

Bourée: duple meter, brisk tempo, usually begins with an upbeat.

Gavotte: quadruple meter, fairly quick tempo. Made popular by Lully in the operatic ballet, this dance has a rather dignified air even when gay. Often followed by a second Gavotte entitled *Musette* because it has a sustained tone or drone throughout, similar to music of the small bagpipe known as the musette.

Loure: duple-compound meter, moderate tempo with a typical dotted rhythm which emphasizes the strong beats of the measure.

Menuet: triple meter, moderate tempo, graceful yet courtly and dignified in style. Usually slower than the menuets found in the symphonies of the Classic Period. Often appears in pairs, in which case the second has thinner or lighter instrumentation, often that of a trio of instruments.

Passepied: triple or duple-compound meter, quick and spirited tempo.

Polonaise: triple meter, moderate tempo emphasizing the characteristic rhythm which may be read: One-te-ta Two te Three te.

Rondeau: a form, not a dance, consisting of the plan A B A C A, in which A is the refrain and the other letters represent *couplets.* All are clear formal units of eight or sixteen measures. There may be an optional number of sections, but the final one must be A.

From time to time a set of variations may appear as one of the *Galantieren,* and usually is identified by name as a chaconne or pasacaglia.

The following suites are representative of their composer's style and technique of keyboard writing. All are well played on easily available recordings.

Handel: *Suite V, Set 1,* in E Major. Includes the famous "Harmonious Blacksmith Variations." Essentially Italian style.

Couperin: *Ordre No. 8* in b-minor. Notice the "free-style" of writing, the profuse but necessary ornamentation, and the descriptive titles and music. This Ordre contains the beautiful "Passacaille," a set of variations in rondeau form.

Scarlatti: Any of the 600 sonatas will illustrate this composer's style, although more than one is necessary for a full picture. Each is a binary movement, some with distinctly different themes in the tonic and dominant areas. Others are more monothematic, but variety of figuration weakens such a description. The style is free, nonpolyphonic, with sometimes extremely daring dissonant harmony. Sometimes Spanish and Moorish melodic or rhythmic influences.

J. S. Bach: *French Suite No. 5,* in G Major. The style is a synthesis of the French and Italian styles, and consists of a basso-continuo kind of structure with less free addition or omission of voices than found in the other works above. The rich harmonic movement, the use of nonfinal cadences to enhance the movement, the flow of rhythmic figures and the motivic interplay are all most characteristic of this composer. Bach usually is more economical of his thematic material and uses it also in developmental ways to a greater extent than the other composers, a characteristic which is to become highly important in the ensuing centuries.

The Orchestral Suite

Although primarily we are interested at this point in keyboard music, the orchestral counterpart to the keyboard suite is so closely related that it can be understood most easily in the light of the music which we have just heard.

The French opera under Lully opened with an Ouverture and a set of dances, and this sequence was adopted by German composers generally, and entitled simply *Ouverture*. The most famous works in this category are the four by Bach, now generally called the *Orchestral Suites*. The first, in C-major, opens with a typical French overture in which the second section has concerto-like solo passages for the oboes and bassoon.

The second suite is scored for solo flute and string orchestra with continuo, thus creating the atmosphere of a flute concerto. The French overture is massive and impressive sounding, despite these relatively slight forces, and the flute has ample solo work during the rapid section. The dances which follow show Bach's attempt to write in the *style galant*, the new French Rococo style which was so popular. However, he has not the knack for turning out a slick and rather superficial product, and as *Rococo* music, the experiment is not an unqualified success.

The third and fourth of the suites are written for "festival orchestra," with three trumpets and timpani, in addition to oboes, bassoon (in No. IV) and strings. The overtures are correspondingly splendid in sonority: the Third uses little concerto-principle, but the Fourth employs the three oboes and bassoon in opposition to the strings. The *Third Suite* contains the famous "Air," a long-breathed, tension-filled melodic line of great beauty over a "walking bass." It is suggested that the listener sing, or at least breathe with the melodic phrases, in order to participate in this composition; this will reveal more fully Bach's mastery of the long vocal line.

Free Forms with Fugue

We have mentioned before the frequent occurrence of two-movement forms of which the first is variously entitled Prelude, Toccata, Fantasy, or Capriccio, and the second is a fugue. The opening music is improvisatory in nature, consisting of flourishes of virtuoso passage-work, or perhaps arpeggiation of a chord progression, sometimes polyphonic, or dance-like, or even a set of variations. The fugue which follows is not of an improvisatory nature, that is, an expression of the emotion of the moment, but rather "experience recollected in tranquillity," ordered and given shape according to certain traditional techniques. While fugues seldom are alike, since they are each fashioned from different materials, they do have certain things in common. First, the fugue is polyphonic and imitative in its texture and technique. It abides by the tonal conception of structure. It generally is monothematic, although fugues with two or three themes do occur. And finally, it is of no specified length, nor does it have any hard and fast requirements in regard to the manipulation of the thematic material, other than the use of imitation.

Before we examine an example of the fugue, let us note some things about its structure. Following the simplest tonal requirements of form, we may divide the structure into three sections: *Exposition,* in which the key and material out of which the composition is to be fashioned are presented to the listener in the clearest way possible; *Development,* in which the possibilities of this material are explored in several ways; and *Recapitulation,* essentially the return to the tonic key, but fashioned out of the thematic material in some way.

The Exposition, then, will consist of a section essentially in the tonic key, closed by a cadence; it presents the fugue *subject* (the technical term for the theme) in imitation at least once in each of the voices or parts. Some fugues have two or more expositions, going through the procedure a number of times to thoroughly expose the subject, or to present a number of subjects which are usually developed and combined later in the composition. Such fugues with multiple subjects are accordingly called double or triple fugues, and are quite lengthy. Accompanying the fugue subject, after it has been introduced alone, is a melodic phrase called the *countersubject,* which subsequently may or may not be important. The cadence closing the exposition is usually weakened, even though it is of the final type, by the continuity of the polyphony driving through it, and/or by the fact that the tonic chord is not in its most stable inversion.

The Development often consists of short modulatory sections called *episodes,* usually constructed out of rhythmic and melodic motives from the subject or countersubject, and usually involving the device of sequence. When the episode reaches a new key, the subject is stated in that key, resembling the ritornello procedure. The subject may be imitated, subjected to stretto, elongation of the time values of its notes *(augmentation),* or the reverse, shortening of these values *(diminution),* sometimes even turning the subject upside-down *(inversion)* or backwards *(retrograde),* or combinations of several of these. Generally, the episodes and statements of the subject alternate, but certain fugues may be designed to exploit only one characteristic of the subject, perhaps its capability of stretto imitation at various distances. In such fugues, modulation usually plays only a small part, and the episodes are correspondingly less important.

The Recapitulation has the prime function of emphasizing the return to the tonic key. It too, is fashioned out of episode and subject, treated in such a way as to prepare the final cadence. It also may contain tension and emphasis techniques, such as stretto and organ-point, perhaps faster motion through the use of smaller note values, and often harmony which reaches a climax on a dissonant version of the dominant chord before the final resolution. Frequently, fugues which are preceded by toccatas have improvisatory-sounding passages near the close, as though to remind us of the association. Now let us examine a "simple" fugue.

For our first example we shall choose the second prelude and fugue in Bach's *Well-Tempered Clavier* (Example IV-12). The music appears on page 166 with the important sections and thematic elements identified.

We hear first the prelude, a kind of warm-up improvisatory composition, in which one basic melodic pattern is repeated many times. Pay particular attention to its harmonic significance which consists of a long chord progression enlivened by the melodic motive. When the climax has been accumulated by motion and harmonic tension, it explodes in an improvisational passage of broken chords, after which, over an organpoint sustained in the bass, two parts move in canon at a faster tempo for two phrases. The intensified excitement then reaches a different kind of climax in the slow recitative-like measure after which broken chords over a tonic organpoint bring the piece to a close.

The fugue which follows is a representative one—at least in the regularity of its structure. Bach seldom wrote two fugues exactly alike, since he regarded the fugue as a procedure rather than an invariable form. All of his fugal compositions have points in common, but differ widely in mood and methods of exploiting the material. Before we go further, let us examine the materials used and exposed here. First of all, notice that the subject consists of repetitions of a rhythmic motive —two short notes followed by three notes twice the duration of the short ones—a rhythmic motive which is easily recognizable. Next look at the scale line of rapid notes which occurs in the first voice at the point where the answer enters. Here we have the precedent for many of the scales to be used later in the fugue. Now let us examine the fugue more closely:

EXPOSITION

Measure 1, 2   Announcement of the subject in the tonic.
      3, 4   Answer by soprano.
      5, 6   Episode based on motive A.
      7, 8   Announcement of subject by the tenor.

DEVELOPMENT

Measure 9, 10   Episode, modulating new keys, uses motive and scale.
      11, 12   Subject in new key, soprano, accompanied by D.
      13, 14   Episode, modulating, uses C and D.

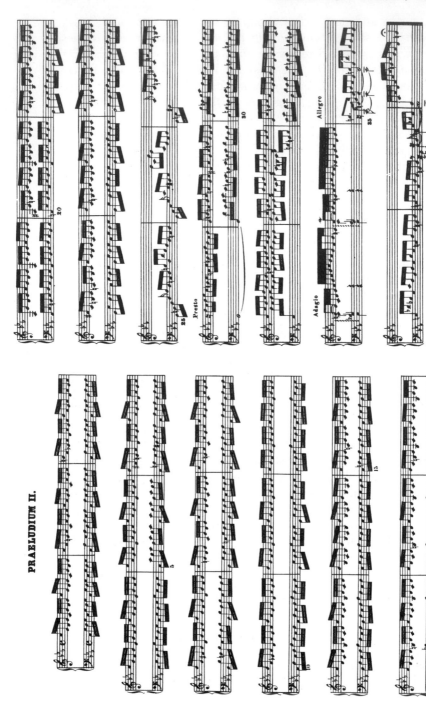

EXAMPLE IV-12: Bach, Prelude and Fugue in C Minor, No. 2, *Well-Tempered Clavier.*

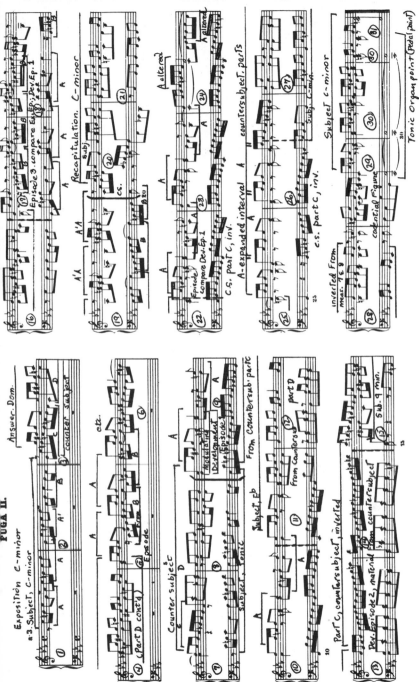

EXAMPLE IV-12 (Continued)

15, 16   Subject in new key, alto, accompanied by C, later by D.
17, 18, 19   Episode, modulating back to tonic key; composed of two sections, the second of which interchanges the tenor and alto parts of the first.

RECAPITULATION

Measure 20, 21   Subject in soprano accompanied by D, tonic key.
22, 23, 24   Episode, non-modulatory, extending material of measures 9, 10.
25, 26   Subject in soprano with expanded intervals, accompanied by C.
26, 27, 28   Subject in tenor, low register, lending to climatic pause.
29   Firm cadence figure leading to held note in tenor (organ-point),
29, 30, 31   Coda, subject in soprano, leading to strong final cadence.

An equally interesting prelude and fugue is the one which opens the first volume of the *Well-Tempered Clavier* (Example IV-13). Here the prelude consists entirely of chord patterns in an improvisatory manner such as a continuo player might use in an orchestral piece. It is entirely homophonic, with cunningly devised chord progressions which lead to climactic sections just as might happen in melodic compositions. In the fugue the emphasis is on the stretto process, with non-thematic material at a minimum, and no consistent use of the same accompaniment ideas.

EXAMPLE IV-13: Bach, Prelude and Fugue No. 1, *Well-Tempered Clavier.*

Prelude

Fugue

While other composers of the Baroque wrote fugues, it is to Bach that we turn for the final mastery of this technique. Not only did he write two sets of preludes and fugues in each of the major and minor keys, the *Well-Tempered Clavier,* in order to demonstrate the possibilities of the new tempered system of tuning which was coming into practice because of the modulatory demands of the tonal system, but also numerous other such compositions for harpischord and organ, closing his career with the monumental, unfinished *Art of Fugue,* a series of fugues and canons, all based on the same subject treated in all possible ways.

Among the most popular organ works containing fugues, and deservedly so, are the *"Little" Fugue in G Minor,* the magnificent *Toccata in D Minor,* which contains as one of its sections a fugue based upon a common violin idiom, the *"Wedge" Fugue in E Minor,* whose subject skips back and forth in ever-widening intervals, and the masterly *Passacaglia and Fugue in C Minor,* a true passacaglia with twenty variations of the eight-measure theme, followed by a double fugue, one of whose subjects is based upon the passacaglia theme. (Example IV-14).

But the fugue is not confined to the keyboard instruments. We already have heard fugal techniques in the church cantata and it abounds in choral music of the period. Again Bach is outstanding, although Handel also wrote some magnificent examples in his oratorios. The Italian style of the fugues in the *Messiah* makes them less monumental than those of Bach, but this is not a disadvantage. The chorus, "For unto us a Child is born," exhibits this light touch, as does "His yoke is easy," at the close of Part I. Handel tends to gather his voices together from time to time in purely chordal and rhythmic pas-

EXAMPLE IV-14: Bach, *Passacaglia and Fugue in C Minor.*

THEMA FUGATUM

sages, weakening the sense of polyphonic continuity, but adding drama and contrast. More serious fugues in the *Messiah* are: "Behold the Lamb of God," "And with His stripes" and "He trusted in God." Let us compare the tightly-knit fugue that forms the second Kyrie in Bach's *B-Minor Mass* with one of similar seriousness, "He trusted in God" from the *Messiah*. (Examples IV-15 a and b.) The Bach example uses a chromatic subject, exposed in regular fashion, combined in two strettos later during the movement. The subject enters in the development from time to time, but the really noteworthy effects appear in the cascading imitations of episode material. This movement illustrates Bach's technique of "grandeur through accumulation" rather than by dramatic procedures, for it is like an overwhelming argument in its effect. The fugue from the *Messiah* is one of Handel's most thoroughgoing choral fugues, but has quite a different effect from the Bach Kyrie. It is less flowing, with rather emphatic cadences at the close of many phrases, and the simpler, less tense harmony generated by the polyphony creates correspondingly less harmonic urgency. It is also not as massive, this Italian openwork counterpoint, with its profusion of sequences, and certainly not overwhelming in effect. But it moves easily, with assurance, uses the materials well, and makes clear the text——the latter not always an achievement of Bach's stringent polyphony.

There also are a number of fugues in the chamber and orchestral literature, but the tendency is to mix them with concerto elements or to treat fugally such dances as the gigue rather than to write orchestral

EXAMPLE IV-15a: Bach, Kyrie II, *Mass in B Minor.*

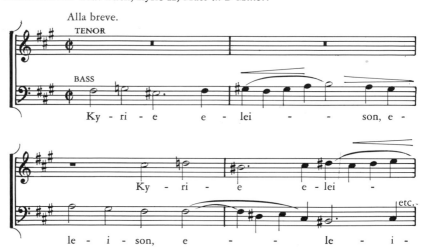

EXAMPLE IV-15b: Handel, "He trusted in God," *Messiah.*

preludes and fugues. Thus, these movements are parts of compound forms such as the concerto or the suite. Those in the concerto we shall encounter shortly.

Variation

We have already encountered a large number of variations in various situations: the Purcell arias over a strophic bass (passacaglia), the chaconne treatment used by Handel in the "Air" of the *Suite No. 5,* the *Passacaille* in rondeau form of Couperin, and the *C-minor Passacaglia and Fugue* of Bach. Let us add two more to this passacaglia-chaconne family before examining other variation types.

The first is the agonized "Crucifixus" (Crucified) movement of the *B Minor Mass.* To gain the greatest dramatic effect, however, this movement must be heard preceded by the "et incarnatus" ("and was made man") and followed by the "et resurrexit" ("and rose again"). The first of these three opens with a short introduction by the orchestra, subdued, grieving, with a drooping affective motive whose meaning is immediately clear. The five-part chorus enters in imitation with a skipwise descending figure, which perhaps symbolizes the descent of the Holy Ghost as the words unfold—"et incarnatus est de Spiritu

Sancto ex Maria Virgine" ("and was incarnate by the Holy Spirit of
Mary the Virgin"). There is a short ritornello by the orchestra alone
after the chorus has sung this, then the text is repeated to the same
melodic designs. Again the ritornello, and in hushed tones of wonder,
while the orchestra foreshadows the tragic eventual death, the chorus
intones "et homo factus est" ("and was made man").

The "Crucifixus" movement (Example IV-16) consists of polyphonic variations on a ground of four measures repeated 12 times. The
orchestral accompaniment consists only of the expansion of the continuo
chords appearing on the main beats of the measure. The single word
"crucifixus" and its drooping melodic motive are repeated imitatively
twice in each of the four voice parts before the sentence "etiam pro
nobis sub Pontio Pilato" ("and was crucified for us under Pontius
Pilate") enters, also in imitation. A cadence is reached at the end of

EXAMPLE IV-16: Bach, "Crucifixus," from *B Minor Mass*.

the phrase "passus et sepultus est" ("died and was buried"). The next section repeats the text of the first part, but with a chromatic version of the first motive used in order to create tension, and to picture the anguish of the Christian soul in contemplating these words.

There follows one of the most staggering dramatic blows, not only of all baroque music, but also of all music since Bach. The exultant shout of the five-part chorus, together with the festival orchestra, trumpets, woodwinds, timpani and strings, proclaims the resurrection in a fugal-concerto movement of rapid tempo and brilliant figuration.

The second important set of variations is that masterly work for harpsichord, the *Aria with Thirty Variations,* the so-called *Goldberg Variations* written by Bach for a virtuoso pupil of that name to please his patron, Baron Kaiserling. The general procedure is that of the chaconne, with the harmony and variation length essentially the same throughout. However, each variation is of a different type. The list includes canons at various intervals, fugues, inventions, overtures, pastorales, toccata-like movements and a quodlibet or mixture of popular songs of the day with the aria chosen for the theme.

The Chorale-Variation and Chorale-Prelude

The church organists of Bach's time often used familiar hymn tunes as the bases for their preludes to the service, or to introduce the congregational singing. Often such movements were improvised, but Bach and other organists have left us written-out examples of this form. The melody of the chorale is used frequently as a *cantus firmus,* and is surrounded by counterpoint or accompaniment which interprets the words. Such a chorale-prelude is *Durch Adam's Fall ist ganz verderbt* (By Adam's fall is all destroyed). The melody is in the upper part, the "fall" is symbolized by large downward skips of a 7th in the pedal part ——and, because the "fall" was into sin, and sin's affective quality was chromatic——the 7ths move in half-step sequences. As if this were not enough, Bach represents the serpent referred to in the text by the snaky convolutions of a middle part! Once introduced, these patterns are continued throughout the piece. Not all of the chorale-preludes use this type of treatment; in some, the hymn melody is treated abstractly, while in others it is difficult to interpret the affective motives. We have already heard the opening of the cantata *Ein feste Burg* and the use of the chorale as a fugal subject. A more extensive set of chorale-variations appearing in a cantata is the Easter cantata, *Christ lag in Todesbanden* (Christ lay in the bonds of Death), No. 4 in the list of these compositions, in which each movement is a variation of the chorale.

Chamber and Orchestral Music

During the first three-quarters of the seventeenth century, we find the instrumental canzona drawing farther and farther away from its vocal models, in that the number of sections were reduced and those remaining were correspondingly lengthened. This development led to two varieties of sonata——a term which is merely a shortening of the earlier *canzona per sonar*, a canzona for playing. The first of these was the *sonata da camera* (chamber sonata), consisting of four or five movements following the tempo plan of Fast-Slow-Fast-Slow, in which the opening movement might be fugal, while the others were dances or dance types, thus approaching the suite. The second was the *Sonata da chiesa* (church sonata), intended to be played during religious ceremonies, which had the opposite tempo plan, Slow-Fast-Slow-Fast, of which the last two movements retained a dance-like character, usually that of the sarabande and the gigue, and the first two were homophonic and polyphonic respectively. These develoments were brought about mainly by a group of composers at Venice, of whom Legrenzi (1626-1690) was foremost, and later by Vitali (1644-1692), Torelli (c. 1650-1702) and especially Arcangelo Corelli (1653-1713) working in Bologna. The latter composer is largely responsible for the "standardization" of the *Sonata da chiesa* as the early form of both the trio sonata and its orchestral counterpart, the concerto. The conservative composers of the Italian school retained this format for a long time, even after the more progressive three-movement, Fast-Slow-Fast plan had been adopted by Vivaldi and the German composers.

The sonatas may be classified according to the number of parts for which they were written. The solo sonata, excluding Scarlatti's *Essercizi*, found its most notable representative in Bach, who composed six for the unaccompanied violin and six for the unaccompanied cello. Remarkably, they are conceived in a polyphonic style, including fugal techniques, for instruments whose technique is usually thought of as essentially melodic, certainly not harmonic, still less contrapuntal. But Bach's adroit use of harmonic and polyphonic suggestion, as well as the strong sense of functional harmony, makes these works masterpieces in the literature of music, not merely curiosities for the violin and cello. The reader is invited to prove this for himself by listening to the *First Violin Sonata*, which follows the *sonata da chiesa* plan of movements, or the remarkable "Chaconne" from the *Violin Partita No. 2* (so-called because it follows the dance plan of the suite), if only to prove that the violin *can* play polyphony! The cello suites are equally worthy, for they, like the violin works, are valuable as music, not merely virtuoso exercises.

The sonatas in two parts usually employ a solo, most popularly the violin or flute (both the transverse variety and the recorder), plus the basso continuo pair, although in many cases, the keyboard instrument may do double duty, providing the bass line and harmony, especially when an instrument of lighter tone quality, such as the flute, is used for the solo. Many of these sonatas were written so that they could be played by any of the three instruments, insuring them a wider circulation than if they were restricted to only one.

The most popular chamber music was, however, the trio-sonata, consisting usually of two violins, cello and keyboard——four performers, since the basso continuo pair is reckoned as one unit in the ensemble, although the cello frequently departs from a strictly harmonic bass function and takes part in the polyphonic and melodic interplay with the two upper parts.

The sonatas for four and five parts were written for what we would now call a chamber orchestra, probably with two or three instruments playing each of the four parts, and were frequently called *Sinfonias,* a term which was also used for the introductory music in the Italian opera, particularly that of Alessandro Scarlatti. As such, it connotes orchestral performance. These works, with their contrasting movements, become the so-called "orchestral concertos," providing the only important instrumental ensemble music other than the suite during this period. The concerto element, however, infiltrated the purely orchestral style, and as early as 1623, we find works entitled *Sonate in Sinfonie* (Bernardi) as well as *Canzoni, overe Sonate, concertate per chiesa* (Merula, 1637) (Canzonas, or Sonatas, in concerto style, for church use). These become the solo and group concertos of the Baroque after 1680, although at that time, the types are not always clearly separate.

The Trio Sonata

The literature is rich in examples of this form, but all have certain qualities which are well illustrated in the short and sober *Sonata da chiesa in E Minor, Op. 3 No. 7* by Corelli to be found in Masterpieces of Music before 1750, Vol. III, side 1. Note how clearly the key is established, the squareness of the phrasing, the use of imitations, the chains of suspensions and the use of sequence patterns in the melody. These are stable characteristics of Corelli's style.

The sonatas of Corelli excited international admiration and emulation among composers. Couperin began writing his ensemble works in the style of the Italian master, gradually achieving a fusion of the Corellian style with his personal and French style. Besides this compliment, Couperin wrote an explicit compliment in his *Apothéose de Corelli* (Apotheosis of Corelli), a work descriptive of Corelli's reception at Mount Parnassus, home of the Muses. The formal plan of this work is that of the *sonata da chiesa* with interpolated movements, and represents Couperin's highest achievement in the sonata field.

Purcell, with the English tradition of the "fancy" for viols behind him, created in his late period a number of sonatas for three and four parts. The best known of these is probably the so-called *"Golden"* *Sonata*, again influenced by Corelli, but full of fresh and surprising melodic and harmonic turns.

Neither of the two prolific giants of the late Baroque, Handel and Vivaldi, produced significant trio sonatas, although they did write them. This leaves those works of Bach to be considered. In addition to six trio sonatas for the two keyboards and pedal of the organ, he wrote only four instrumental trio sonatas, one of which is included in *The Musical Offering*. They are all in the 4-movement *sonata da chiesa* pattern, and employ flute and violin, or two violins or two flutes, together with the continuo.

Bach: "Trio Sonata in C Minor" from *The Musical Offering*, for Flute, Violin and Basso Continuo

Concerning the origin of *The Musical Offering*, Johann Forkel (1749-1818), the first biographer of Bach, writes:

His (Bach's) second son, Carl Philip Emanuel (Bach), entered the service of Frederick the Great in 1740. The reputation of the all-surpassing skill of Johann Sebastian (Bach) was at this time so extended that the King often heard it mentioned and praised. This made him curious to hear and meet so great an artist. . . . But the King's expressions being repeated in several of his son's letters, he (Bach) at length, in 1747, prepared to take this journey, in company with his eldest son, Wilhelm Friedemann. At this time the King used to have every evening a private concert, in which he himself generally performed some concertos on the flute. One evening (Sunday, May 7, 1747), just as he was getting his flute ready and his musicians were assembled, an officer brought him the written list of the strangers, who had arrived. With his flute in his hand, he ran over the list, but immediately turned to the assembled musicians and said, with a kind of agitation: "Gentlemen, old Bach is come." The flute was laid aside, and old Bach, who had alighted at his son's lodgings, was immediately summoned to the palace. . . . But what is more important than this is that the King gave up his concert for this evening and invited Bach . . . to try his fortepianos, made by Silbermann, which stood in several rooms of the Palace. . . . Bach was invited everywhere to try them and to play unpremeditated compositions. After he had gone on for some time, he asked the King to give him a subject for a fugue in order to execute it immediately without any preparation. The King admired the learned manner in which his subject was thus executed extempore; and, probably to see how far such art could be carried, expressed a wish to hear also a fugue with six obbligato parts. But as not every subject is fit for such full harmony, Bach chose one himself and immediately executed it to the astonishment of all present in the same magnificent and learned manner as he had done that of the King. . . . After his return to Leipzig, he composed the subject which he had received from the King in three and six parts, added several intricate pieces in strict canon on the subject, had it engraved under the title *Musikalisches Opfer* (Musical Offering), and dedicated it to the inventor.[1]

The subject which the King gave to "old Bach" is shown in Example IV-17. Bach used it as the thematic basis, in *The Musical Offering*, for two ricercare in three and six voices, eight canons and a perpetual canon, a canonic fugue and trio sonata. We do not know what

EXAMPLE IV-17:

reception this "learned" work received; no more is heard of it at the Palace. In a sense, the entire *Offering* is a set of variations on the King's theme, which, incidentally, is a good one, designed after Bach's own heart. The three elements which constitute it (the opening triad, the large downward skip, and the descending chromatic scale) are rich in thematic elements. As usual, Bach makes the most of them, either in their original state, decorated, with the skips filled in, or inverted. The first and third movements of the trio sonata are binary in form, while the second is fugal and concerto-like, and the fourth is a fugue. Bach's technique of continuous, flowing polyphony is well-illustrated here, and the use of expressive chromaticism, while not overtly affective, is most effective. After hearing the Corelli sonata, there hardly is any need to point out the distance both the form and technique have

---

[1] Johann Forkel, ON JOHANN SEBASTIAN BACH'S LIFE, GENIUS AND WORKS, 1802. Translated by Mr. Stephenson, 1808. David and Mendel, THE BACH READER, W. W. Norton & Co. Inc. 1945. New York.

traveled on their way to Bach's summation. We shall discover a similar development in the concerto.

While Bach and Handel were reaching the consummation of the grand Baroque style in their two individual syntheses, that style was already on the way out, gradually and increasingly being replaced in the courts and theaters by a simpler, more charming homophonic fashion rising out of the French Rococo. Perhaps the most famous exponent of the new taste in music was Georg Philipp Telemann (1681-1767), universally admired, even by Handel and Bach, to the point that the latter chose Telemann to be godfather to his son, Carl Philipp Emanuel Bach. Telemann was a prolific composer, who, said Handel, "could write an eight-voice motet faster than one could pen a letter," but this facility did not always prevent his compositions from being superficial. He admitted to "swimming with the tide" in order to earn a living, and could easily adopt any style, a faculty which Bach did not possess. Nevertheless, much of his music has a charm of melody and rhythm which is attractive, even if it never plumbs the emotional depths. The reader should listen to a trio sonata by Telemann in order to help bridge the gap between the styles of the High Baroque and the early Classic.

The Concerto

The concerto, developing from the canzona via the *sonate da chiesa* and *da camera*, consists of three main kinds in the High Baroque from the time of Corelli and his Bolognese colleagues onward. The first, called the orchestral concerto, we have discussed on page 177 as the Sinfonia, a form which becomes more important as an ancestor of the Classic symphony than as an example of Baroque music. Pre-eminent are the other types of concerto, the *concerto grosso* and the solo concerto.

The concerto grosso format requires two ensembles, a small one of expert soloists, called the *concertino* (little concert), and a large one, the orchestra, called variously the *concerto* or the *ripieno* (the "remainder," that is, after the soloists have been extracted). The orchestra consists of strings and continuo, while the constitution of the concertino may vary. Corelli and his followers, among whom was Handel, used the trio sonata grouping for the concertino, but Bach and Vivaldi often employed wind and stringed instruments. Corelli tended toward the *sonata da chiesa* form with additions and variations, while

Vivaldi and Bach wrote three movements in the tempo pattern of Fast-Slow-Fast. Handel followed the Corelli model, but employed more formal variety than the Italian master.

Corelli: *Concerto grosso No. 8* ("Christmas Concerto")

The final movement of the "*Christmas*" *Concerto* is said to be a musical rendering of Botticelli's painting, *The Nativity*. The movements consist of sections of contrasting tempos and textures, and might be outlined thus:

I. *Vivace* (very fast): a short introduction of 7 measures by whole ensemble (tutti).
   Grave (very slowly): an imitative section for the tutti.
   Allegro (fast): a binary movement using the concerto principle.
II. *Adagio* (very slowly): a ritornello form in which the ripieno doubles the concertino from time to time.
   Allegro: a curious movement for the tutti, consisting wholly of chord-diffusion of the harmonic progressions.
   Adagio: return of the former material, with a new coda.
III. *Vivace:* a short, fast dancelike movement in binary form. Some contrast between the ripieno and concertino as well as the use of the orchestra as an accompanying medium.
   Allegro: an imitative ritornello form, binary in structure, which makes some use of the echo effect. It flows directly into the next movement.
   Largo pastorale (slowly, suggesting a graceful rustic dance): a slow dance movement in quadruple compound meter, of the type called the Siciliano. Binary in form with ritornellos, and uses the echo effect. Unlike the preceding movements which have been in minor or related "flat" keys, this one is in G-major, and provides a luminous contrast in the string sound and a pleasant conclusion to the work.

Handel: *Concerto grosso, Opus 6, No. 3, in E Minor*

The concertino is formed on the trio sonata group, and the ripieno is the usual string orchestra. Frequently, as in the entire second movement, the two are combined in tutti (full orchestra) passages. The plan is similar to the *sonata da chiesa*, although the first movement is a French overture.

I. *Larghetto:* triple meter, e-minor, alternating tutti and concertino.
Movement closes on a half-cadence. (Example IV-18a).
Andante: quadruple-compound meter, e-minor, an orchestral
fugue in which the striking subject has a counter-subject of
such importance that the movement might qualify as a double
fugue. Short return of the slow tempo for final cadence. (Example IV-18b).

II. *Allegro:* quadruple meter, e-minor, a typical ritornello-form,
with alternations of the bold theme with idiomatic passage-
work in the concertino.

EXAMPLE IV-18: Handel, *Concerto grosso in E Minor.*

III. *Polonaise, Andante:* triple meter, G-major large rounded binary
form, an example of a dance treated in concerto style.

IV. *Allegro ma non troppo:* duple compound meter, e-minor, alternations of concertino and ripieno, a sort of "reversed echo"
effect, since the smaller sound precedes the larger. Binary form,
with very short first section.

Vivaldi: *Concerto grosso, Op. 3, No. 8 in A Minor*

"*Il prete rosso,*" or the "red priest," as Antonio Vivaldi (c. 1678-
1741) was known to his fellow Venetians because of the color of his

EXAMPLE IV-19: Vivaldi, *Concerto grosso, Op. 3, No. 8.*

hair, was the prolific composer of 49 operas, 540 instrumental works and many large vocal and choral compositions. He wrote much of this music in the concerto style and cultivated especially the solo concerto, featuring in most of these the violin, although there are works in which other instruments, especially winds, are important. He was a composer of an original and experimental turn of mind, and explored the possibilities of musical description in some of his concertos. His cycle, *The Seasons,* and the individual concertos entitled variously *The Tempest on the Sea, The Hunt* and *The Night* feature original and interesting effects, mostly achieved through the use of idiomatic figuration for the ripieno as well as the solo violin.

The concerto grosso we have selected is typical of this composer's general attitude toward the form, whether solo or grosso, and the materials. There are three movements, marked *Allegro, Larghetto* and *Allegro* (fast, rather slowly and fast). These are clearly ritornello forms in which the string concertino does little to develop the orchestral themes, but rather indulges in brilliant idiomatic violin figures. The rapid movements have the motoric rhythm characteristic of the concerto, and the slow movement uses a striding orchestral theme much like some of Handel's. The first movement opens with a clear statement of the tonic key by means of what has been called "hammerstrokes"— full, decisive block chords on I-V-I (Example IV-19). The texture is mostly homophonic, even when the concertino is playing, although there is a little imitative work between the solo violins in the slow movement.

Perhaps the most important aspect of this and the Corelli concerto is the idiomatic character of the string writing, both for the ripieno as well as the concertino. Indeed, in addition to bringing the instrument itself to a high degree of perfection, the Italians developed most of the string figures used during the following centuries and laid the foundation for subsequent string technique in these and similar works.

Bach: *Brandenburg Concerto No. 2, in F Major*

The six examples of concerto grosso which Bach composed in 1721 sum up, in their diversity and perfection, the various aspects of that form in its most brilliant era. They were written as a compliment to the Margrave of Brandenburg and presented to that nobleman with a fulsome dedicatory letter by Bach. We have no record of their ever having been performed by him, and the manuscripts, still tied in the original package, were sold after the Margrave's death for a ridiculously low sum. Fortunately, a former student of Bach's, Johann Kirnberger, purchased them and thus preserved them for posterity.

The first Brandenburg concerto has four movements—the usual three plus a combined Menuetto and Polacca——but all the rest have the usual Fast-Slow-Fast trio of movements. The third concerto is missing a slow movement, but this was intended to be improvised by the harpsichordist, according to the best authority. Of the six, numbers 1 and 2, 4 and 5 are concerti grossi, although in the latter two, the violin and harpsichord have the lion's share of the concertino playing, making them rather close to being solo concerti. Numbers 3 and 5 are essentially orchestral concertos, with sections of that ensemble standing out from time to time in contrast. We have chosen the second concerto since it is quite typical and a most beautiful work.

The concertino consists of a high trumpet, flute, oboe and violin, with the usual string orchestra and continuo furnishing the ripieno.

I. (No tempo marking), duple meter, F major. (Example IV-20a.) The tutti states the strongly tonal and extended melodic material, after which each of the concertino instruments, violin, oboe, flute and trumpet, enter in that order with new material, each accompanied by the one immediately preceding, and each entrance separated from the other by a ritornello of the first two measures of the opening tutti, now in the dominant. When all of the solos have taken their bows, the closing tutti takes up the material beginning at measure 3 of the opening and finishes the statement, still in the dominant. During the course of the movement, Bach integrates the two ensembles from time to time, rather than always playing one off against the other. Notable are two areas of highly unstable harmony, and one later in the recapitulation, and the strong cadence and pause which indicate the close of the development.

II. *Andante*, triple meter, d minor. A piece of chamber music employing only the flute, oboe, violin, two cellos and the harpsichord. This, like the *Suite in B Minor*, is a quasi-rococo composition, imitative in nature, in which all of the possibilities of the subject and its "sighing" countersubject are explored. The last third of the movement is devoted largely to harmonizations of the "sigh" which are subtly shaded by

EXAMPLE IV-20: Bach, *Brandenburg Concerto No. 2.*
a. I
THEME AND BASSO CONTINUO

b. III
Allegro assai

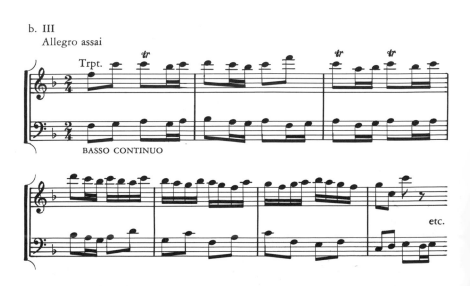

the choice and relative positions of the instruments. The quiet yet inexorable march of the basso continuo is also very characteristic.

III. *Allegro assai:* duple meter, F major. (Example IV-20b.) This movement is a rollicking fugue, the exposition of which is devoted to the concertino. In matter of fact, the orchestra other than the basso continuo has very little to do except accompany the concertino from time to time. The basso continuo occasionally shares thematically in the gaiety, and the movement ends excitingly with a quotation of the subject.

The *Concerto in the Italian Style* by Bach is an unusual example of the transfer of the concerto grosso concept to a single keyboard instrument, employing the free style to represent the chordal tutti as well as the more melodic solo.

The Solo Concerto

In this type of concerto, the essential technique is the same as in the concerto grosso, with the exception that there is only one solo instead of a group, and therefore there is more opportunity for virtuoso passages than before. The solo concerto was exceedingly popular, especially with violinist-composers such as Vivaldi, although, to do him justice, he wrote concertos for every instrument capable of solo performance. Bach contributed to the list also, with concertos for violin, harpsichord, and multiple concertos for two violins and for two and three harpsichords. Notable are the violin concertos in A minor and E major, the concerto for two violins in D minor and the harpsichord concerto in D minor.

SUMMARY

During the one hundred and fifty years of the Baroque period, perhaps the most important single development was the replacement of the modal scales by the tonal system. This made possible the characteristic tonally controlled forms which were representative of the age: the opera and its aria forms, the binary dances of the suite, and the continuously developing but tonally structured procedures of the fugue and the concerto. The new importance of melody and bass, after the Renaissance concept of equal interest divided among polyphonic voices, together with the strongly functional supporting harmony, were forces that shaped all of the music. The dramatic tension, reflected by the concerto style and the use of instruments, and the aesthetic theory of the Doctrine of the Affections made the musical communication to the listener both vivid and comprehensible. It was, more than any preceding time, an age of music in the grand manner.

THE BAROQUE SPIRIT IN THE OTHER ARTS

We repeatedly have encountered the coupling together of free and strict forms in our examination of Baroque music. The prelude and fugue, recitative and aria and other such pairings illustrate the Baroque fondness for the contrast of improvisation and fantasy with thoroughly worked-out intellectual pieces. We find the same qualities illustrated in the art of the period. Parallel to the fantasy was a vein of rationalism which controlled and, paradoxically, enhanced the enthusiasm without rendering it academic or cold. These qualities may be seen in our illustrations: St. Theresa in Ecstasy by Bernini (Plate X), the facade of the Church of San Carlo alla Fontana (Plate XII) designed by Borromini, and Rembrandt's The Night Watch (Plate XIV). In all of them the carefully planned design, when one realizes it, is in high contrast to the imaginative use of line, color, perspective and space to appeal to the senses of the beholder and to draw him into a closer contact with the art-work.

First in importance, and most obvious to the eye, is the passion for large and noble subjects, whether these be long musical works like the St. Matthew Passion of Bach, or Handel's Messiah, the great canvases of Rembrandt, Rubens and Tiepolo, or the large buildings of Borromini. In the opera of the time, only demigods, princes and kings were allowed to be the heroes, and in the same way Rembrandt dignified the honest burghers of Amsterdam with apparent nobility in his painting. The subjects and situations are generally larger than life and more intense.

The force of the exuberant imagination may be found in many details and techniques of these art-works. Dramatic contrast is one

PLATE XIV: *"The Night Watch" by Rembrandt. Note the dramatic use of dark and light, the impression of space extending far down the street and the various motivic repetitions of parallel lines. The sense of activity and motion is typically baroque. (Courtesy of the Netherlands Information Service.)*

of them. The love of contrasting tone colors and sharp changes in intensity so frequent in the music has parallels in painting. Here the masses of bright and dark colors provide comparison to the terrace dynamics of the orchestra, and to the tone colors of the winds, especially the trumpet, against the monochromatic string background. In architecture, a play of light and shadow is created by the projecting and receding portions of the building. The love of continuity and motion already has been remarked upon in the music; now examine the garments of St. Theresa, the activity of the figures of *The Night Watch* and the movement implicit in the buildings. In the latter, motion is created by the inward or outward bulging of facades and stairways, the twisting of columns, the profusion of decoration and the curved moldings and carvings which lead the eye from one part to another.

Along with nobility of subject, richness of effect was desired by these artists. This was often created by the colors used—many times shades of the same color—the amount of detail, and the depth of perspective, or in music, the richness of harmony, which bears a close resemblance to pictorial perspective. St. Theresa seems suspended in limitless space, for example, and the many folds of her robe add to the impressive effect. The multitude of figures in *The Night Watch* creates the same effect of richness, and the avenue behind the soldiers stretches away to the limits of the imagination. The detail of the architecture already has been mentioned, and it is hardly necessary to point out the immense importance of perspective in this art. Now listen again to the first movement of the cantata *Ein' Feste Burg* with these qualities in mind!

The sum of all these techniques is the communication of emotion. Of course, this is less so in the case of architecture, for such communications is not its prime function. But like the musical episodes whose feeling is ruled by the Doctrine of the Affections, both Rembrandt and Bernini have caught in their works an intense moment of drama which is emphasized by every detail of the composition, just as it is in music. Rational enthusiasm and exuberance then, an all encompassing imagination, and the deployment of every artistic technique in order to impart emotion to the beholder are the ideals and methods, so often successful, of baroque art.

LIST OF IMPORTANT TERMS

Forms
aria
arioso
binary, rounded binary
cantata, chorale cantata,
    chamber cantata
canzona, *canzona per sonar*
chaconne
chorale, chorale prelude
compound form
concerto: grosso; solo; orchestral
double
fantasie, fancy
French overture
fugue, double fugue
Galantieren
monody

movement
opera: seria, buffa
oratorio
Ouverture
passacaglia, *passacaille*
Passion music
recitative: secco, accompanied
ricercar
rondeau
Sinfonia
single form
sonata: *da chiesa, da camera, trio*
suite
ternary form,
    compound ternary form
toccata
variation

Techniques, Materials
  affective motives
  augmentation
  basso continuo
  bass, figured
  bass: ground, strophic
  cadenza
  chromaticism
  coda
  concerto principle, style
  continuo polyphony
  countersubject
  da capo: al fine; dal segno
  Development section
  diminution
  echo effect
  embellishment
  episode
  Exposition section
  free style
  functional harmony
  idiomatic writing
  imitation
  improvisation
  inversion, chord
  modulation
  motoric rhythm
  organpoint, pedalpoint
  ornamentation
  Recapitulation section
  resolution (of dissonance)
  ritornello
  sequence
  stretto
  subject
  terrace dynamics
  text-painting
  tonal system, structure
  transition

Orchestration
  concertino
  concerto, ripieno
  festival orchestra
  keyboard instruments, clavier
    harpsichord, clavichord, organ
  lute
  recorder
  trumpet, natural, valveless
  tutti
  violin family
  viol family

Miscellaneous
  Doctrine of the Affections
  virtuosity of performance

Composers
  Bach, Johann Sebastian
    (1685-1750)
  Corelli, Arcangelo (1653-1713)
  Couperin, Francois "Le Grand"
    (1668-1733)
  Frescobaldi, Girolamo
    (1583-1643)
  Froberger, Johann Jacob
    (1616-1667)
  Handel, George Frederick
    (1685-1759)
  Kuhnau, Johann (1660-1722)
  Lully, Jean-Baptiste (1632-1687)
  Purcell, Henry (1659-1695)
  Scarlatti, Alessandro (1659-1725)
  Scarlatti, Domenico (1685-1757)
  Sweelinck, Jan Pieterszoon
    (1562-1621)
  Telemann, Georg Philipp
    (1681-1767)
  Vivaldi, Antonio (c. 1675-8-1741)

BIBLIOGRAPHY

Biographies:

David, H. and Mendel, A., eds., *The Bach Reader*. New York: Norton, 1945.

Geiringer, Karl, *Johann Sebastian Bach, The Culmination of an Era*. New York: Oxford, 1966.

Miles, R. H., *Johann Sebastian Bach*. New Jersey: Prentice-Hall, 1962.

Spitta, P., *Johann Sebastian Bach*. New York: Dover, 1951.

Terry, C. S., *J. S. Bach*. New York: Oxford, 1933.

Deutsch, O., *Handel: A Documentary Biography*. New York: Norton, 1955.

Flower, N. H., *George Frederick Handel*. New York: C. Scribners, Cassell & Co., 1923.

Weinstock, H., *Handel*. New York: Knopf, 1946.

Holland, A. K., *Henry Purcell: The English Musical Tradition*. London: Penguin Books, 1949.

Holst, Imogene, *Henry Purcell: The Story of His Life and Works*. London: Boosey & Hawkes, 1961.

Westrup, J. A., *Purcell*. New York: Pellegrini & Cudahy, 1949.

Mellers, W., *Francois Couperin and the French Classical Tradition*. London: Dobson Ltd., 1950.

Pincherle, M., *Corelli, His Life, His Music*. New York: Norton, 1956.

Kirkpatrick, Ralph, *Domenico Scarlatti*. Princeton: Princeton University Press, 1953.

Pincherle, M., *Vivaldi*. New York: Norton, 1957.

General:

Artz, F. B., *From the Renaissance to Romanticism*. Chicago: University of Chicago Press, 1962.

Bukofzer, M., *Music in the Baroque Era*. New York: Norton, 1947.

Dorian, F., *The History of Music in Performance*. New York: Norton, 1965.

Fleming, W., *Arts and Ideas*. New York: Holt, 1955.

Hutchings, A. J. B., *The Baroque Concerto*. New York: Norton, 1965.

Kerman, J., *Opera as Drama*. New York: Vintage Book K88.

Pevsner, N., *An Outline of European Architecture*. Baltimore, Md.: Penguin Book A 109.

Sachs, C., *The Commonwealth of Art*. New York: Norton, 1946.

ADDITIONAL LISTENING

Because of the widespread interest in 17th century music, there is no need to present a discography; a search through the record catalogues easily will provide many choices of works by the following composers. In a few cases the author has recommended a particular recording which he feels is notable for the performance.

Bach, J.S.

B Minor Mass
St. Matthew Passion
Cantata No. 4, Christ lag in Todesbanden
Concerto for Violin and Orchestra in E Major
Concerto for Two Violins and Orchestra in D Minor
Brandenburg Concertos
Partita in Bb Major, for harpsichord
Concerto in the Italian Style, for harpsichord
Toccata and Fugue in D Minor, for organ
"The Little" G Minor Fugue, for organ
Chorale Preludes for Organ: *Jesu, Joy of Man's Desiring,*
        By the Waters of Babylon, A Mighty Fortress

Corelli

Concerti Grossi, Opp. 5 and 6
Sonatas, Opp. 1, 2, 3 and 4

Couperin

Pièces de Clavecin·(the *Ordres*)
Le Parnasse (Apothéose de Corelli)
Pièces en Concert·
Les Concerts Royaux
Leçons de Ténèbres

Frescobaldi

Fiori Musicali
Canzoni per Sonar

Froberger

Suites de Clavecin

Handel

Alcina: London A-4361
Messiah
Israel in Egypt
Concerti grossi, Opp. 3 (Oboe) and 6
Concerti for Organ
Royal Fireworks Music
Sonatas for Flute, Oboe
Suites for Harpsichord
Water Music
Xerxes, opera

Kuhnau

Biblical Sonatas for Harpsichord

Lully

Bourgeois gentilhomme, ballet suite
Carrouzels pour Monseigneur
Dies Irae, Motet for double chorus and orchestra

Purcell

Anthems
The Faery Queen, opera
Fantasies for 3, 4, 5, 6 and 7 Viole da gamba
Ode for St. Cecelia's Day
The Indian Queen, opera
Music for the Funeral of Queen Mary
Sonata for Trumpet
Sonatas in III, IV parts
Suites for Harpsichord, Bach Guild 570/71
Te Deum and Jubilate (chorus and orchestra)

Scarlatti, Alessandro

Cantatas: Floro e Tirsi; Clori e Lisa; Infirmata vulnerata; Il Giardino di
    amore, opera
Concertos, sonatas

Scarlatti, Domenico

Sonatas (Essercizi) for Harpsichord

Sweelinck

Organ music
Psalms
Variations on Popular Songs

Telemann

Cantatas
Concerti for various instruments and combinations
Musique de Table (Suites)
Sonatas of various kinds

Vivaldi

Concerti: The Seasons *(Gli Stagioni); La Cetra,* Op. 9; *Cimento dell'
armonia e dell' invenzione,* Op. 8; *L'estro armonico,* Op. 3 (These are
all collections of violin concertos); Concertos for diverse instruments,
such as bassoon, cello, flute, guitar, harp, mandolin, oboe, clarinet,
trumpet, horn, etc., alone or in various combinations.
Gloria, in D major, Chorus and orchestra
Juditha triumphans, oratorio

V THE CLASSIC
PERIOD, 1750-1827

HISTORICAL PERSPECTIVE

THE EIGHTEENTH CENTURY is the last act in the political and humanistic drama whose tensions began in the Renaissance and whose accumulated power exploded in the American and French revolutions. This century must be viewed as a continuation of the growth of humanistic and scientific thought which began in the sixteenth century, and one which enriched the parade of man's intellectual and social progress with the achievements of Lavoisier and Priestley, Watt, Jenner, Kant, Voltaire, Rousseau, Lessing, Hume, Adam Smith and Goethe. Enthusiastically bearing the banner of reason, men of this time ever more confidently stormed the barriers of religion, superstition and ignorance, attempting a rationalistic interpretation of the universe and man, an undertaking impossible of failure in their eyes. They realized with increasing clearness the tyrannical, frivolous and vicious aspects of their political and social organization and criticized them in plays, novels, pamphlets and essays which ranged in tone from vitriol to ironic wit. They believed that intelligence could set men free of the old bonds, mentally as well as physically, and they strove mightily to attain this freedom.

If the guiding word for the Baroque was *power*, that of the succeeding era was *freedom*. It was in the name of liberty that social thinkers such as J. J. Rousseau (1712-1778) opposed the oppressive absolutism of monarch, church and social class. Voltaire (1694-1778) became the most influential spokesman for the new order, opposing with his biting scepticism the dogmas of an authoritarian church, intoxicated with the discoveries in the natural sciences, and proposing a concept of a new enlightened world. Not Rousseau's idealistic world of "noble savages" and "back to nature,"——he was too sceptical and civilized to believe in that dream——but a world in which freedom of thought and action, regulated by the ideal of the common good, was possible.

The great *Encyclopedia* (1751-1776) of Diderot and his colleagues was also a force in this struggle for freedom, for it was not an encyclopedia in the modern sense, objective and factual, but rather the expression of the opinions as well as the knowledge of its contributors. They too were instrumental in setting up the new religion of science, a belief that total knowledge of the world and universe was attainable, given time and research, a view that has fallen only in the second half of the twentieth century. This new religion opposed the old in a violent struggle, one which is still joined.

The scene of the drama of the eighteenth century is France, with the surrounding countries as vitally interested spectators. The weight of the monarchy upon the common people of France had become almost unsupportable at the time of the death of Louis XIV in 1715. The Duke of Orleans, regent for the five-year-old Louis XV, allowed the pleasure-loving court to amuse itself with increasing frivolity and corruption at the expense of the multitude of overtaxed poor. The precious and exquisite art which reflected the taste of the French aristocracy of this time was the Rococo, the *style galant*. Miniature, refined, decorative in nature; gold, white and pastel in tint; pleasantly formal, sensitive to nuance, presenting a perpetually smiling face, the amoral aristocratic culture of Paris and Versaille set the tempo to which all of the "civilized" capitals of Europe danced. Life was no longer a grand design but a series of exquisite miniatures, and the arts reflected that existence. Too shallow to continue under the pressures of disastrous and costly wars, the erosion of acid criticism by the social philosophers, and the opposition to the corrupt and dogmatic religious system, the pretense of government fell with the stones of the Bastille in 1789. But the cultural effects, the *style galant,* had so penetrated the artistic sensibilities of Europe that they survived to color the architecture, decoration, painting, music and formal manners for some time to come.

During the prelude to revolution in France, a less bloody but equally significant movement gathered headway in Germany. Marked by a desire for freedom of expression, emotion and thought in literature, the first eddy in the current which was to become predominant in the next century appeared in the decade following 1770 as *Sturm und Drang* ("Storm and Stress"), the title of a play by Maximilian von Klinger. Primarily a literary movement influenced by Lessing and Rousseau, this colored other forms of artistic expression, becoming the seed of the nineteenth century Romantic movement. Numbered among its rebels were Schiller (1759-1805) with his play *Die Räuber,* and young Goethe (1749-1832), who, in *Werther's Leiden* ("The Sorrows of Werther") produced a study of neurosis which caused a wave of suicides among the susceptible lovesick youth of Germany. More familiar to us are the poetic rebels of England, Byron (1788-1824), Shelley (1792-1822) and Keats (1795-1821), as well as the less rebellious but equally influential Wordsworth (1770-1850), Scott (1771-1832) and Coleridge (1772-1834). Romantic emotion was to penetrate music increasingly as the turn of the century approached, in that of such composers as Haydn, Mozart and especially Beethoven, whose entire art is founded upon the paradox of controlled freedom.

Meanwhile, England fought for the American colonies and for supremacy of the seas, exporting the products of her industrial revolution (1750-1850) to colonies in India newly-won by Clive (1751-1761), and expanding her colonial influence to the South Seas through the voyages (1767-1779) of Captain Cook.

With the dissolution of the First Republic of France in 1804, the Napoleonic era ushered in a new, neo-Roman revival, strong in France, but also romantically appealing to other countries, although most of them subsequently had little money to expend on the construction of arches, temples and the like since they were busy defending themselves from the instigator of this Romanism, Napoleon Bonaparte. And when in June of 1815, the Battle of Waterloo reversed the tide of French conquest, the cult of antiquity assumed less dangerous forms, one of which was the establishment of the sciences of archeology and anthropology. Nevertheless, this classicism influenced the arts to a greater or lesser degree—greater in the official painting of Jacques David (1748-1825), an example of whose art appears in Plate XXII, and lesser in the music of any composer of the time. Of course, this may have been partially due to the lack of Classical models; but if the term is applied in its essential meaning of poise, suitability of form to content, and spirit, much of the music of this time merits the name of classic. But some of it, often the most valued works, are tinged with a certain romantic coloration which we find attractive in that it reveals the human spirit more satisfyingly——a factor important because of our own romanticism.

So, the century of freedom achieved many of its aims, building in the process the foundation for the civilization of our own time, and erecting new restrictions which we, in our search for freedom, find it necessary or desirable to demolish. New let us see how the music of the eighteenth century reflects, when it does, the period which saw its birth.

DEVELOPMENT OF THE CLASSIC STYLE

The music of the first part of the Classic Era, up to the turn of the nineteenth century, was a variable mixture of traits stemming from opera, the rococo and nationalistic translations of the rococo, chiefly into German and Austrian dialects, and the romantic tendencies toward stronger emotional expression.

The Rococo style in music was light, elegant, decorative, playful and aristocratic, as typified by the compositions of the French harpsichord composers of the time. Chief among these was Couperin, whose allegiance to the Baroque we explored in the preceding chapter. But, the grandeur of expression we found there is not always characteristic of his music, for there are many dainty trifles with fanciful titles which belong to the intimate and delicate *style galant,* as the rococo was often called. The short phrases, simple harmony and excessive ornamentation have their counterpart in wall decorations of shell-figures, delicate scroll and leaf designs, all executed with the utmost refinement. Couperin is not alone, but accompanied by a host of lesser composers as well as by the great figure of eighteenth century French music, Jean-Philippe Rameau (1683-1764).

In northern Germany, Carl Philipp Emanuel Bach (1714-1788), the third son of Johann Sebastian, strongly influenced the music of the period by the insistence upon an emotional content in his music, restrained to rather subtle nuances and shading which appealed to the emotional sensitivity of the performer and listener. Not entirely abandoning the Doctrine of the Affections, he made it less rigid in application, favoring the rapid change from one emotional state to another by means of frequent shifts in tempo, dynamics and key. The music was intended to sound spontaneous——"artless and nautral"—— thus implying a certain simplicity and directness, avoiding the excessive ornamentation of the *style galant.* While intended to convey emotion, this music remained within the bounds of "good taste," making no theatrical gestures nor sweeping the listener into a cosmos of sound as the Baroque had done. This was the *empfindsamer Stil,* the style of sensibility.

The more forceful expression of feelings was related to the romantic literary movement, and was designated by the same name, *Sturm und Drang.* In 1756, Edmund Burke wrote in his *Essay on the Sublime and the Beautiful* that in art there is an element which transcends beauty: "Whatever is fitted in any sort to excite the ideas of pain and danger, whatever is in any sort terrible, or conversant about terrible objects, is the source of the Sublime." In short, composers sought for the sublime in a romantic style which featured dynamic outbursts in minor keys, agitated and syncopated accompaniments, passages of dissonance, and broken or distorted melodic fragments. The full effect of these techniques was attained by juxtaposing such passages with others of milder nature, probably in the *empfindsamer Stil.* While *Sturm und Drang* passages occur in the music of Haydn and Mozart, they are relatively infrequent, finding their greatest exponent in Beethoven, the great transition composer who ushered in the era of nineteenth century romanticism.

The Italian version of the rococo became established in the comic opera, the *opera buffa.* It is often recognizable by its spirit and verve, its piquant and appealing lyricism and a certain witty objectivity, as though the composer were saying, "This is just makebelieve——but isn't it delightful!" This manner was Mozart's natural language, expressed most freely in his stage works, but always present to some degree in other compositions.

With the derision of the militant modernist, the baroque polyphonic style was named the "learned style," and was felt to be suited only for church music, conservative as always. But the art of Bach and Palestrina as well—came to be valued highly by the great composers of this era. The middle and late periods in the creative lives of Haydn, Mozart and Beethoven were times when these men immersed themselves in the study of counterpoint, immeasurably enriching the works which followed with their interpretations of fugue and the devices produced by polyphonic writing.

So we see that the music which we so glibly term "classical" is compounded of many different, even opposing styles. The various composers use different proportions of each of these styles combined in a purely personal manner to achieve the particular synthesis which we recognize as typical of Haydn or Mozart, Beethoven or Schubert. But the *manner* of classicism is important too. Ideally, the Classic artist retains an objectivity toward his materials, carefully controlling the balance of form and content, while expressing his ideas clearly.

He creates *absolute music,* for the most part, abstract designs in sound. He presents his material straightforwardly and affirmatively, raising no philosophical questionings. The degree to which such feelings appear indicates the amount of admixture with romanticism, an element which is never wholly absent. Generally, the Classic composer works well within a tradition, seeking no surprises or innovations for their own sakes. He may, by the constant practice of his art, broaden and gradually expand the tradition in which he began, bringing it to new heights hitherto unsuspected and unappreciated by his contemporaries. But this, we must remember, represents the evolution developed during a lifetime of music. The materials with which he chooses to work are usually simple and clear, the basic realities of his art, and he desires no more than that these qualities inform the result. This is the ideal situation, attainable most completely by an IBM machine. In practice it turns out that composers are flesh-and-blood beings who have sorrows, joys and the multitude of experiences common to all mankind. Overtly or not, these experiences color the composer's attitude toward the ultimate realities which he imparts in his music, making it meaningful through shared experience. No classic composition of any merit is free of these elements—indeed, the "impurities," like the strength-giving alloys of steel, give the works their unique value. In the music of Haydn and Mozart we sense the personalities of the composers, a restrained (by good taste) view of their attitudes toward life and its problems—the spirit of sensitive human beings.

COMPOSERS OF THE CLASSIC ERA

The work of Haydn, Mozart and Beethoven, the "Viennese Classics," spans the entire period and shows the growth of the style from its roots in the rococo phase of the baroque to its final flowering in the compositions of Beethoven. Let us first meet these composers and examine the circumstances under which they worked, then attempt to show their relationship to one another.

Franz Joseph Haydn, 1732-1809

This man, the first outstanding composer of the classic style, was born in a poor peasant hut in the little village of Rohrau in Austria. His native musical talent was noticed at an early age, and after some local

PLATE XV. *Franz Joseph Haydn. Portrait by Thomas Hardy, 1792. (A. C. K. Ware, Ltd., London.)*

musical instruction he was sent to Vienna, where he received further training and sang in the choir of the Church of St. Stephen. He was an assiduous pupil, and, while learning all that the meager instruction at the church afforded, studied compositions by other composers as well as theoretical works on harmony and counterpoint. He was turned out of the choir to fend for himself when his voice changed and he managed to earn a pittance by giving lessons, accompanying, and playing in cafes and theaters. After some years he was able to secure a position in a nobleman's establishment, where he composed and directed the small musical organization. One of the great patrons of music in Vienna, Prince Esterhazy, became favorably impressed with Haydn's efforts, and secured his services for the rather large musical establishment at the castle of Esterhaza, some eighty miles from Vienna. Here Haydn had an orchestra with which to experiment, and experiment he did for the next twenty-nine years. Not only did Haydn conduct the orchestra at the numerous balls and concerts, but also he composed most of the music played, repaired and tuned the instruments, supervised the clothing, food and shelter of the musicians, and, withal, kept an even temper and sunny disposition. Almost all of his compositions produced at this time were the property of Prince Esterhazy, but upon the death of that prince and the accession of one not so interested in music, Haydn, then fifty-eight years of age, decided to retire from his post and release his works for wider public performance. He was aided in this by the London impresario, Salomon, under whose auspices Haydn made two highly successful trips to England. For those voyages he wrote two sets of six symphonies each, now called the "London Symphonies," the last compositions in that form he was to create, numbering from Symphony No. 93 through 104. Haydn and Mozart were fast friends who admired each other's music greatly. While in England, Haydn was therefore shaken upon hearing of his friend's death at the early age of thirty-five. Haydn himself remained alive for two more decades during which he composed little, and that slowly. That little was pure gold, however, for to those declining years we owe the two great oratorios, *The Creation* and *The Seasons*.

Wolfgang Amadeus Mozart, 1756-1791

This man, an incomparable musical genius, was born in the town of Salzburg, evinced exceptional performing and composing talent at an early age, and when he was six years old was taken on a concert tour of Europe by his father. During the next ten years other tours were made which served as a liberal education to Mozart in musical styles as well as in the ways of the world. With his phenomenal memory for music and extraordinary musical powers, he assimilated the diverse elements of the Italian, French and German styles, and blended them in his own personality to a perfection seldom realized in any age. Mozart's father was an excellent musician and parent, and trained his son to the best of his abilities in both roles. Clearly, such a talented and trained musician as Wolfgang, who knew the outstanding musical figures of all Europe, might well expect success to fall into his lap when he decided to venture forth on his own. This happened all too rarely during his short life. There are many reasons for Mozart's lack of worldly success, not the least of which was the general feeling that his music was too complicated. This opinion seems well-nigh incredible to us today, but it had the effect of limiting performances of his works. Secondly, he was unable, or disinclined to become a musical servant in the houses of the nobility, as Haydn had done. As a matter of fact, this system of patronage was beginning to totter, so that his luck with it might not have been too great. Then too, Mozart was somewhat impractical and con-

PLATE XVI. *Wolfgang Amadeus Mozart. Unfinished portrait by Lange, 1782. (Courtesy of the Austrian Information Service.)*

siderably too generous in financial affairs, often depleting his own resources in order to help out a friend. So he was obliged to eke out a comparatively poverty-stricken existence in Vienna by teaching, giving concerts, composing and borrowing money. During the last ten years of his life, one jump ahead of his creditors, and physically exhausted, he wrote some of his greatest music.

Mozart composed some 600 complete works, including 22 operas, 52 symphonies, 25 piano concertos, 12 violin concertos, 14 concertos for other instruments, 24 string quartets, 60 solo works for piano, and 27 choral works. These were first numbered in chonological order by the Viennese botanist and Mozart enthusiast, Köchel, and later revised by the Mozart scholar, Alfred Einstein. The Köchel number, abbreviated K. or K.V. (for *Köchel Verzeichnis*) always is used officially to identify a composition by Mozart.

Ludwig van Beethoven, 1770-1827

Ludwig van Beethoven was born into the family of a ne'er do well musician in Bonn, Germany. The father, a drunkard, saw that he had talent, and, with dreams of producing another *Wunderkind* like Mozart, drove the boy to music. How narrow an escape, in the light of modern child psychology, did the world of music have then; it would have seemed most logical that the boy would hate music, and resolve to learn a trade or profession as far from music as possible! But the genius that lay half-awake in young Ludwig seems to have reversed the usual process, and, by the time he was ten—no child prodigy—he was proficient enough on the piano, viola and organ to support his mother and brothers (and probably spare a coin or two for his father) certainly not in a lavish style, but one that was somewhat removed from poverty. Beethoven's schooling was quite inadequate in academic subjects, and probably aroused in him his lifelong interest in self-education. Bonn offered many opportunities to hear good music and see operas and of these we may be sure Beethoven took advantage, often playing in the orchestras. In 1779 an experienced and well-trained musician, Neefe, was appointed court organist, and, under his influence, Beethoven exhibited such talent and progress as to cause Neefe to predict that his pupil would be Mozart's successor. Also during this period, through the friendship of Franz Wegeler, a young medical student, Beethoven made the acquaintance of the von Breuning family, in whose home he tasted the joys of appreciation and association with refinement.

In 1792 Beethoven set out to conquer musical and aristocratic Vienna. His piano playing and brilliant improvisations made him famous among the music lovers of the nobility, who soon took him under their protection, just as they had Haydn and, to a lesser extent, Mozart. But there was a great difference. The older composers had almost the status of servants, obliged, in the case of Haydn, to wear the uniform of the prince who employed them; Beethoven was accepted on an equal footing—indeed, he arrogantly insisted upon it, and through the force of his personality and musicianship succeeded. But his aristocratic friends, the Lichnowskys, Brunswicks, Lobkowitzes, and Liechtensteins soon perceived that the composer in Beethoven should be encouraged over the virtuoso, and made it possible for him to write and experiment with instrumental groups. The string quartet employed by Prince Lichnowsky was placed at his disposal, and Prince Lobkowitz even provided him with an orchestra from time to time!

PLATE XVII. *Beethoven during his first Vienna years. Painting by W. J. Mohler, c. 1804. (The Bettmann Archive.)*

Beethoven's genius, now free from monetary considerations, soared beyond the aristocratic circle which fostered it. His compositions were not "social music," but addressed to a larger audience, an audience of middle-class music lovers who immediately understood him, even if the critics did not. For these worthy gentlemen, expecting compositions which followed the strictly classical trend, were often outraged at the "novelty," sometimes "barbarism," of this powerful music.

Occasionally these qualities arose in Beethoven's social behavior, shocking and momentarily outraging his friends. But so often was Beethoven aware of man's shortcomings when compared with the ideal man he envisioned, that the disparity could not but enrage him, and cause him to utter a "hearty free word," as he put it.

Another factor tended to increase his irritability. During his late twenties he had been bothered by a buzzing in his ears, and by 1802 he realized that in spite of all the doctors could do, he was becoming deaf. The realization of this loss, so obviously fatal to his music, brought on a crisis which nearly ended in suicide. But the indomitable will-power which he had developed from his difficult childhood, and the equally unconquerable force of his genius conspired to keep him alive. Little by little he realized that his life was not ruined, but an inexorable change accompanied this truce with his affliction. A deaf musician, he felt, would seem ridiculous to most people, and this attitude his pride would not suffer. No longer could he meet humanity on his previous terms, and Beethoven withdrew to semi-seclusion, having converse with only a small circle of true friends. Meanwhile, during the years from 1802 to 1812 the music poured from his pen, undoubtedly a result of his gradually becoming aware of the indomitable creative force within him. At this time he became familiar with a number of outstanding literary works, as well as some of their authors. The Greek classics, as well as the works of Goethe (whom he met personally), Schiller and Klopstock opened new horizons. Some of these works provided occasions for music, such as the incidental music to Goethe's play *Egmont*, and Kotzebue's *Ruins of Athens*.

As time went on, Beethoven withdrew more and more from the world. His increasing deafness, and the realization that he could not marry or lead a normal life, were deciding factors. Then too, his preoccupation with the pure and spiritual realms of tonal expression, the translation of experiences too profound for the traditional syntax of music, effectively removed him from earthly worries and desire to mingle on equal footing with his fellow men. Then, in 1827, his fifty-seventh year, he succumbed to his final illness.

Beethoven's creative life usually is divided into three periods. The first, regarded as rather imitative of the style of Haydn and Mozart, embraces the years 1782-1800. The second includes most of the well-known compositions and extends from 1801-1814. The third period works include the *Ninth Symphony*, the *Missa Solemnis*, the last five string quartets and the last five piano sonatas. William S. Newman, in his exhaustive study of the sonata idea, has proposed a five part division which seems more in keeping with the nature of the compositions and with Beethoven's growth as a composer.

1782-1794: Student period. Includes the last ten years in Bonn and the first two in Vienna. No works with opus numbers.

1794-1800: Virtuoso period. Young Beethoven out to conquer Vienna with his playing. Opus No. 1 through about No. 27, although some later opus numbers were written during this time also, such as the *Third Piano Concerto, Op. 37.*

1801-1808: "Appassionata" period. Period of despair over increasing deafness, the "Heiligenstadt Testament" and the greatest influence of the *"Sturm und Drang"* style upon his music.

1809-1814: "Invasion" period, so-called because it extends from the siege of Vienna by the French to their withdrawal and the Congress of Vienna. This period is marked by "a more intensified, personal, deliberate approach to composition."

1815-1826: "Sublimation" period of the last great works, in which the alienation between Beethoven's musical expression and the world in which he had to exist reaches its greatest degree.

STYLISTIC RELATIONS AMONG THE VIENNESE CLASSICS

To Haydn principally, although a host of lesser composers contributed to the result, we may attribute the consolidation of the Classic style out of the diverse elements of the disintegrating late Baroque style and the experiments of such men as C. P. E. Bach. It was Haydn who first realized most successfully the dramatic elements of the new homophonic, polythematic developmental style and the structures which were organically necessary to it. Mozart not only assimilated what elements he needed from Haydn's creative thinking, but also from the style of the Italian opera buffa and from Johann Christian Bach, another son of the Leipzig cantor. Yet Mozart's mature style was not eclectic, but a very personal synthesis, perhaps most influenced by Italian music, and, like Italian music generally, melodious in a vocal sense, with an ease and refinement so often to be found in the "classic sound." Formally, Mozart was not experimental. "He took over and made use of current forms . . . with such ease that if he had had to invent his own forms he would hardly have been able to find any better suited to his thought."[1]

Beethoven was the heir to the work of Haydn and Mozart, but from his earliest available compositions there is a strong individuality which is not content merely to accept the legacy without expanding and extending it. Like Haydn, Beethoven experimented with the structural procedures of the style, but whereas Haydn was in the process of discovering them, Beethoven's task was to fulfill them. Thus his dynamic and organic structures are far larger quantitatively and qualitatively than those of the other two masters. In part this is due to musical expansion, but the advent of the heroic Napoleonic era and the increasing romantic fever had created a culture, ideal and audience different from that which the two older masters had addressed. Beethoven was the musical spokesman of the new time, and worked out a language which the time understood.

FORMAL AND GENERATIVE PRINCIPLES

Aesthetic Ideals

The main motivating factor of music in this era is entertainment and pleasure, not spiritual exaltation or the sense of intellectual adventure in abstract musical constructions. "Learned" or serious works generally were regarded with disfavor during the times of Haydn and Mozart, although the grandiose pretensions of the Napoleonic era and the romantic cult of the genius, together with Beethoven's force and directness, made such compositions highly acceptable to audiences in the second and third decades of the nineteenth century.

The Doctrine of the Affections, while living on in some of the affective melodic *clichés*, had lost its authority over the formal aspect of music. In the works of C. P. E. Bach and the *empfindsamer Stil*, the ideal now was to present a kaleidoscope of emotional changes through the use of different affective motives, thus breaking into fragments the baroque unity and continuity of material in a movement. Indeed, one of the problems faced by the late eighteenth century composer was the welding of such fragments into a unified and coherent whole.

---

[1] Girdlestone, C., *Mozart and His Piano Concertos*. New York, Dover, 1964.

In the works of Haydn and Mozart there is a containment of emotion within the formal bounds of the good taste of the period. The outward display of strong feelings was regarded by society as being impolite, and the arts of the time followed suit. But such contained emotion is often more poignant to the spectator than an overwhelming flood would be, and in this aspect the music of Haydn at times and particularly that of Mozart reaches its most profound moments. This is also true of many passages in Beethoven's works, sometimes strongly contrasted with the more extroverted emotions presented in surrounding sections. This attitude might generally be defined as expression of feeling enhanced by restraint.

Tonality

The constructive forces of tonality were used in the Classic Period in much the same way as in the seventeenth century——that is, by statement of key, departure and return. Indeed, the tonal forces were strengthened by a simplification of the harmony, replacing, in the German style at least, the chromatically altered chords through which Bach achieved some of his finest effects with the basic I, IV and V chords, together with a few seventh chords which smoothed modulation or harmonic motion toward the dominant. This simplification caused greater contrast between neighboring areas in different tonalities, an effect which became highly important in the forms of the period. The emphatic cadence, made so by repetition or a following pause, was used as a strong key-defining device to set off the separated structural sections of a work. This separation, with clearly defined limits, is a characteristic of classic styles in general, and may be compared to the opposite tendency toward continuity and fusion of boundaries which is representative of romantic style.

In baroque music, the departures in key from an established area are usually not very striking nor very distant. In the music of Haydn, Mozart and Beethoven, the contrast between tonic key and dominant key is emphasized during the first two-thirds of the period, while in the last portion, the strong contrast of tonic to a key a third away becomes favored. The predominant homophonic texture and the profusion of strong key-defining cadences make these tonal contrasts most effective in outlining the form of the composition or in projecting the emotional tone of sections or movements.

The Sonata Principle

We have seen how, in the preceding style, the fugal and concerto principles created important forms as technical procedures working within the confines of tonality. In the eighteenth century, however, the disintegration of the baroque aesthetic, including the spinning out of affective motives, the tendency toward long melodic lines and the preference for continuo polyphony all made the development of new forms a necessity. The rococo and *empfindsamer Stil* with their fragmentary themes and rapid changes of feeling, the simplified harmonic vocabulary, the aesthetic which demanded nothing too obviously serious or profound or complex gradually solved the problem by evolving what we shall call the sonata principle. Perhaps it should really be called the sonata-allegro principle, for it is in the first movement of the sonata, the *allegro,* that this structure is best exemplified.

The sonata principle is a concept of structure embodying the *opposition* of two key areas, each characterized by dramatically contrasting thematic material and the development of some of the thematic material, usually in an area of constantly modulating tonality. The texture is homophonic, with polyphony occasionally used as a developmental procedure. The themes themselves are usually short, easily remembered patterns which may also embody a rhythmic motive. They are made to grow organically in the development areas by repetition, extension, imitation, fragmentation, inversion, and any of the other manipulations which the composer finds applicable to them. But, as in all tonal forms, the underlying concept of key establishment, departure and return provides the structural framework.

Contributory Styles

As we have noted, three substyles were more or less assimilated to form the basis of the main eighteenth century style. These were the Rococo, of French origin, the opera buffa style from Italy, and the German *empfindsamer Stil.* One could read pages of words attempting to describe each of these, but their essential nature may be picked up more easily and pleasurably by listening to examples of them. The Rococo element in the Classic style is well illustrated by the third movement of the *Divertimento in D Major, K. 334,* by Mozart, and the opera buffa style by the overture and opening scene of the same master's opera, *The Marriage of Figaro.* For examples of the *empfinds-*

amer Stil one may go to its greatest exponent, C. P. E. Bach, and listen to any of his works for keyboard, particularly the slow movements of the Wurttemberg or Prussian Sonatas.

THE MUSICAL STYLE OF THE CLASSIC PERIOD

Melody

Melody in this style usually is not extended, but rather short, often consisting of two-measure patterns which are symmetrically balanced against each other in a question-answer relationship. These patterns often contain rhythmic or melodic motives which later may be used for development. The melodic patterns often are composed of more-or-less decorated triad structures of a disjunct instrumental nature. Lyric melodic ideas, of course, are more conjunct, but they too may reveal an inner structure of triad tones. The harmonic implications of these melodic phrases usually are very clear, partly from their triadic construction and partly because of their symmetrical nature which often swings back and forth between I and V. The vigor or lyricism of such themes is due in part to the tempo prescribed as much as to the design of them. Coming from the Rococo or the more expressive *empfindsamer* styles, they often contain *clichés* resembling in expression and shape the baroque affective motives. Other such patterns were derived from operatic music, such as the stereotyped formula for stag royalty that opens Mozart's *Symphony No. 41*. When chromaticism is used in the Classic theme it almost always is decoration added to heighten the expressive quality and is harmonized with nonchromatic chords.

Harmony

We already have discussed the simplification of harmony characteristic of this style and the importance of cadences in the tonal plan. Now let us address ourselves to the practical task of seeing how the harmony was used. Renaissance music produced harmony as a by-product of the polyphony, and Baroque style expressed the harmonic content through the basso continuo. In the middle eighteenth century, the basso continuo parts gradually were being written out in orchestral and chamber music, either making them harmonic filler played by orchestral instruments such as the bassoons, horns, violas and second violins, or, if for keyboard (as in sonatas), by making them quasi-independent parts of the ensemble with thematic rights equal to those of the other instruments. But in all music, figuration had to be devised to create the harmonic accompaniment and to provide an undercurrent of motion. This was accomplished by the use broken chord figures, the most common of which was named the *Alberti bass,* after an obscure Italian composer (Example I-9, diffused). The bass line now made no pretensions toward melodic beauty, but became purely functional and harmonic.

The treatment of dissonance was entirely traditional, with the dissonant figures developed during the seventeenth century assimilated into the style. Certain composers, however, devised new-sounding situations for these dissonances which were not always understood by their contemporaries. Such is the opening of Mozart's *Quartet in C Major, K. 465.*

Rhythm

In the music of Haydn and Mozart, the rhythmic life, while present and interesting is not a major factor. It tends to be continuous, as in the Baroque, but light and unaccented. Like the phrasing of the melodic materials it is symmetrical and square. In the hands of Beethoven, however, rhythm and its manipulations becomes an expressive device of great power. His use of syncopations, cross accents and accents upon unexpected beats of the measure give vigor and drama to his music.

Texture

Polyphony is rather infrequent in the eighteenth century, other than in conservation works for the church——and not always there! ——and in developmental practices within forms. Haydn, Mozart and Beethoven all wrote fugues during their careers, sometimes very important ones, but they were usually for connoisseurs and appear in string quartets or, again, religious music. The eighteenth century fugue is rather different from its Baroque ancestor, probably because of the different world in which it was born and the strongly different musical style and methods of the classic period.

Sonority—The Classic Orchestra

Any discussion of the classic style must take into consideration the classic orchestra. This graceful and flexible instrument developed from the basic string orchestra of the Baroque with the routine addition of a few woodwind instruments, first oboes and bassoons, then flutes, horns, trumpets and timpani for emphatic effects, and finally the clarinets and still later the trombones. The woodwind instruments were usually used in pairs, as were the horn and trumpet. These latter were the so-called "natural" instruments without valves, and were therefore capable of playing only the notes of a particular harmonic series. By this time, the fashion, and quite possibly the technique, of the high "Bach" trumpet had disappeared, and the brass instruments were limited in function to playing held notes around which the harmony revolved, or simple bugle-call themes. One of the *clichés* of the period is the hunting-horn call, either for solo horn, or more often for a pair of horns in two-part harmony. The trumpet is seldom a solo instrument, but is used for dynamic weight. The trombones, soon to enter the orchestra in the music of Beethoven, were employed by Haydn and Mozart only in church and operatic music.

The flexibility of this new classic orchestra was used in different ways by the composers, each according to his own "sound ideal." Haydn's sonorities are apt to be thinner and somewhat harsher than those of Mozart, more transparent, less rich and full-sounding. He relied more heavily upon the strings, whereas Mozart showed a typical Teutonic fondness for passages in which the woodwinds play without string support. The late "London" symphonies of Haydn, however, exhibit a somewhat different approach to the use of winds, coming closer to the Mozartian sound than is usual in the earlier works.

Beethoven's scoring, often for powerful dynamic effects, usually is not so transparent as that of Haydn and Mozart. In his search for new sounds to project his heroic ideas, he added the trombones to the orchestra, and expanded its outer ranges by using the piccolo and the contrabassoon. With the orchestra of Beethoven we arrive at essentially the ensemble we use today.

One of the important orchestral devices to be developed in the eighteenth century was the *crescendo* and *diminuendo*——the gradual increase and decrease of the intensity of sound. Seemingly developed by Johann and Carl Stamitz with the court orchestra at Mannheim, it soon replaced the older terrace dynamics, and was marked in the music of most of the progressive composers of the time.

FORMAL STRUCTURES

The forms of the Classic Period are a part of the style, just as those of the Baroque were. But in the earlier period, the important structures of fugue and concerto depended upon the continuous expansion of the material until the desired length of composition was achieved. There were no rules, even general ones, which specified how many ritornelli might appear in a concerto, or how many expositions or recurrences of the subject a fugue might have. There are types of *open forms*. But in the eighteenth century, the forms tended to be *closed*, with more or less definite sequences of events within them. When these were completed, the form was concluded. The most important of these structures were those derived from the binary form by evolution or addition. These *single forms* then were combined in groups into *compound forms* of which three types may be recognized.

The Sonata

This highly important sequence of movements has a rather definite pattern which can be described in terms of possible single forms and tempos as follows:

I. First Movement: *Allegro* (fast); almost always sonata-allegro form, with or without introduction and/or coda.

II. Second Movement: *Andante* (somewhat slowly); sonata-allegro form with lyric themes, expanded sections; sonatina; theme and variations; ternary form.

III. Third Movement: *Moderato* (medium speed); always a compound ternary form composed of two menuets, A and B, each of which is a complete binary form in itself. The entire movement consists of A-B-A. This movement is omitted in the occasional three-movement symphonies.

IV. Fourth Movement: *Allegro* to *Presto* (fast to very fast); sonata-allegro form; sonata-rondo form; rondo; occasionally theme and variations.

Such a compound form written for one or two instruments is called a sonata; written for three or more instruments, it is named from the kind of instruments and the number, *e.g.*, a string trio, a woodwind quintet, etc. A sonata for orchestra is called a symphony. The most important sonata for a single instrument of this period is the piano sonata. The combination of piano and violin provides the predominant duo sonata. The chamber sonata most popular is the string quartet made up of two violins, viola and cello. Other ensembles will be encountered, but their names will usually be self-explanatory.

The Divertimento

These works, including their close relatives the *serenata* (serenade) and *cassation,* were written for small groups of instruments, the composition of which depended upon whether the music was to be played indoors or outdoors. If the former, strings were the basis, with brass or woodwinds added, whereas if outdoor performance was intended, only the brass and woodwinds were used. There is a variable number of movements, usually from five to seven, usually including an opening sonata-allegro, two menuets, one or two slow movements and a concluding rapid finale, often in rondo form. The style is light and obviously intended for entertainment, although the great *Serenade for Wind Instruments in B♭, K. 361,* by Mozart contains more serious music than one would expect from the title.

The Concerto

Certain features of the Baroque concerto were retained in the Classic period. For one thing, the concerto principle was still valid and was used in these works. The three movement plan with a fast-slow-fast sequence of movements, favored by Vivaldi, also was retained. And, the opening tutti, which established the key and presented the thematic material, became a part of the later concerto. But the larger aspects of the form were essentially those guided by the sonata-allegro principle:

I. First Movement: *Allegro;* almost always a concerto-allegro form, sometimes with certain modifications.

II. Second Movement: *Andante;* lyric sonata-allegro; sonatina, theme and variations; ternary form.

III. Third Movement: *Allegro* to *Presto;* sonata-rondo; rondo; sonata-allegro; rarely theme and variations.

Now let us examine the single forms used as movements in the above compound forms. The most important of them derive from the rounded binary form studied on page 126, in Chapter IV. The steps in the evolution are shown in Example V-1, in which lines connect related parts of the structures. In the rounded binary, the themes appear in the tonic key (Theme and Key Area I) before modulating (transition), and cadencing, usually on the dominant. If the composition is in a minor key, the cadence usually is made in the related major key three half steps above the minor tonic. In general, the modulation moves *away* from the tonic to another key. Section I immediately is repeated, which, however, does not affect the formal structure. Section II begins *away* from the tonic, often with the key or chord at the conclusion of Section I, and frequently with a quotation of Theme I; modulates back to the tonic (Key Area I), repeats the thematic material and cadences in the tonic. Normally, this section then is repeated.

To this basic structure, the sonatina form adds an area after the transition (Key II) characterized by new and usually contrasting themes (Theme II), instead of stopping with the cadence. The retransition may be of the same length as in the binary, and it performs the same function, returning to a quotation of Thematic Material I in Key I. But the strong feeling for symmetry of form now acts, bringing back a version of the transition which returns to the tonic instead of modulating (circular transition), and the form closes with the repeat of Thematic Material II in the tonic key (Key I).

The sonata-allegro expands the beginning material of Section II into a development of any of the thematic material which moves through several keys, rarely touching the tonic, and closes on the dominant so that the retransition may take place. Of course, as the forms evolve, the character of the thematic material becomes more suitable to the large form, and certain refinements are added such as closing sections just before the end of the exposition to round off that section with repeated decorative cadences. Of course, symmetry demands that this subsection be repeated at the end of the recapitulation.

The sonata-allegro may be prefaced with an introduction, usually in a slower tempo, which strongly establishes the tonic key of the movement, and may throw into stronger relief the following thematic material, epecially if that material is unassuming in character or lyric. In some cases, the introduction may be fashioned out of the important thematic motives to be more formally presented here.

The sonata-allegro and sonatina may have a section called the *coda* added to the end of the recapitulation for the purpose of reinforcing the feeling of tonic key by repeated cadences. In Beethoven's music, the

EXAMPLE V-1: *Evolution of Forms from the Rounded Binary.*

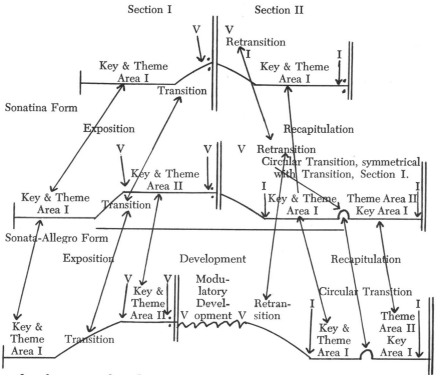

coda often is exploited as a second development section and is correspondingly long.

Having examined the theory of these forms, let us see how they are put into practice. We shall use the *Symphony No. 39, K. 543,* by Mozart as our example since it clearly illustrates these forms without the often confusing experimental tendences of Haydn to bother us. But we shall not hear the movements in order, but rather begin with the "Menuet and Trio" (III), a pair of binary forms, followed by the second movement, an expansive sonatina, then the first movement which is a sonata-allegro prefaced by an imposing introduction. The finale, another sonata-allegro, will, interestingly enough, come last.

Example V-2a shows, first, a piano transcription of the Menuet and Trio with a running commentary on the form. The example then does the same for the sonatina form of the second movement, and also for

EXAMPLE V-2a: *Mozart, Symphony No. 39*, in E♭, Movements III, II and I.

Edition Peters.
6556

6556

the final movement. This music may be played on the piano, or followed with a recording. In the latter case, one may keep the place by counting the meter and thus moving from measure to measure. Or, the instructor may call out the measure number as the music is being played. Follow the note patterns as you would a graph, for that is what music notation is. The structure will be much plainer if the score is used than without it.

The finale of the 39th Symphony of Mozart is a monothematic sonata-allegro without introduction and a short coda. The important motive of the first theme, heard at the very beginning serves also as the principal member of the second theme and bears the brunt of the development. The brusque beginning of the development is always something of a surprise in this opera buffa movement. The transition, consisting mostly of broken chord figures, is rather typical of many such passages in other sonata-allegros in its harmonic character and also in loudness. The themes are shown in Example V-2b.

The reader should now reassemble the movements of this symphony in their proper order and listen to it as Mozart intended. One should always try to be aware of the form as well as the more obvious features of symphonic movements; only by analytical listening will the full appreciation of the music be gained.

THE SYMPHONIES OF MOZART

Of the forty-one extant symphonies of this composer, only the last six (omitting No. 37, which is by Michael Haydn) are played with any frequency. The 34th Symphony deserves to be played more frequently, as do some of the others, but for the most part they are less individual to us, more members of a class, and therefore less interesting. The last six, however, are strongly individual and of lasting interest. About half of the forty-one symphonies omit the minuet, as do Numbers 34 and 38, leaving three movements in the symmetrical Fast-Slow-Fast sequence.

EXAMPLE V-2b: Mozart, *Symphony No. 39, in E♭*, Finale

The general style of the symphonies essentially is based upon the opera buffa style, but with more harmonic richness, beauty of detail and depth of feeling than is encountered in other opera composers of this time. Mozart's music sometimes was criticized by contemporaries as "having too many notes in it," for they expected the usual shallowness of style; today we tend to agree with him "that there are exactly the right number." Indeed, it would be difficult to find where any notes or passages could be removed without upsetting the delicate balance of the music. Mozart even dared to affront the critics with finales in the tonic minor key of the symphony, even to closing on a minor chord. He felt that dramatic truth was preferable to the spurious happy ending dictated by his pleasure-loving aristocratic listeners. He, himself, was only too aware of the darker side of life. He had the courage to be bold with grace, honest with elegance, profound with beauty.

The *Symphony No. 40, K. 550*, in G-minor is a dark and defiant work, more overtly emotional in quality, but impeccable in craftsmanship. The first movement, a sonata-allegro, as are II and IV, is tightly knit with the use of the opening rhythmic motive. The desperation of the opening of the development is shocking, echoed later in the finale at the same location. The lyric second movement employs imitations, rich and sometimes chromatic harmony and a quick two-note figure which appears throughout the movement as a unifying motive. The Menuet certainly is not of the usual ballroom variety, for it abounds in vigor with striking syncopations and dissonances which must have shocked ears tuned to the usual polite dances. The Trio is an example of lovely chamber music sounds, with the typical golden tones of the French horns alternating with the string orchestra. The Finale recaptures the mood of the first movement, beginning with an ascending arpeggio known as the "Mannheim skyrocket," an invention of the Stamitz brothers. It is an uncomplicated sonata-allegro whose dimensions are calculated so nicely that it needs no coda to balance it.

The last symphony, *No. 41, K. 551*, in C Major, turns away from the introspection of the 39th and 40th, and reveals a spirit poised, serene and confident, feelings not expected to be associated with Mozart's later life. This work, in a sense is, more representative of the late eighteenth century than are the others. Again, I, II and IV are in sonata-allegro form, and the form of the first movement is quite regular although expanded somewhat in size. This expansion is due to the use of an opera buffa theme of melodic proportions for the closing section instead of short, cadential patterns. The fact that the development is in two sections also adds to the length of the movement.

The second movement is in *empfindsamer* style, rather quiet, almost neutral in character. A winding scale passage becomes an important unifying device, rather like the two-note motive of No. 40, II. The transition passage is in a more agitated variety of the *empfindsamer* style, with restless syncopations and mild dissonances. The Menuet is a rather regal movement employing a chromatic theme; the trio has an interesting touch at the beginning, since it repeats the cadence of the last part of the menuet, thus charmingly providing continuity. The finale is the largest jewel in this symphony, however, for it reveals a fusion of the opera buffa and the serious styles such as no other composer had attempted and few since have been able to bring off with the apparent ease of Mozart. The several members of the first thematic group are presented in normal fashion the first time, then in a more contrapuntal setting the second time, leading into the transition. The second key area is filled with polyphony made up of several motives.

The development is made up largely of imitative sections featuring the opening, long-note theme of the first key area and the rhythm followed by a scale of the second. In the coda, little by little all of the thematic motives of both areas are combined in five part polyphony, and the movement ends with joyous and vigorous chords.

In the music of Mozart we may expect few experiments with form; everything is mastered, assured, polished; no pioneering is necessary. But in the symphonies, quartets and sonatas of Haydn experimental irregularity is to be expected, and one somehow feels uneasy if the structure follows the usual plan. For this reason we have broken our usual chronological order to examine the work of Mozart first. Having, we hope, a firm grasp on the established forms, let us see what surprises Haydn has in store.

THE SYMPHONIES OF HAYDN

Haydn wrote 104 symphonies during his long lifetime, and they provide a history of the form, from the earliest works, written for a small group of strings and continuo with perhaps an oboe or horn, to the twelve "London Symphonies"——the ripest products of his artistic maturity——scored for the typical classic orchestra. Haydn's themes usually are devised with an eye to developmental possibilities and therefore are usually less lyric. His orchestration, often lovely in sound, has quite a different sonority from Mozart's, and the scoring of developmental passages, where everything must be heard, may be rather intellectual. In the London Symphonies Haydn addressed a larger audience than he was used to at Esterhaza, and therefore exerted himself to be expressive, forceful, full of sentiment or wit, and above all, coherent. In these things he shows himself to be a true son of the Enlightenment.

Because of the nature of Haydn's style, we shall present a somewhat fuller analysis of the movements of *Symphony No. 92,* in G-major, subtitled "The Oxford Symphony," than with the later Mozart works.

I. The movement opens with an adagio introduction (a frequent practice with Haydn) which suggests at least one of the important motives of the exposition (Example V-3). The opening of the EXPOSITION, allegro, presents immediately the most important group of motives in the entire movement. These are numbered in the example. The organization of the first key-area is A-B-A, where B consists of motive 4 followed by broken

chord figures and scales. The transition also is formed of this
material and modulates, pausing on the dominant of the new
key (V of V). The second key area utilizes the material of A,
especially the rhythmic motive of 2, and leads to the jaunty
closing figure plus cadentially oriented scales and chords.

EXAMPLE V-3 I: Haydn, *Symphony No. 92*, First Movement

FIRST MOVEMENT: Adagio-Allegro spiritoso

INTRODUCTION Adagio

DEVELOPMENT: there are four subsections.

1. Repetition of the closing theme in a new key and more
    forceful dynamic; modulation.
2. Motive 1 developed in diverging and converging patterns
    in the oboes and bassoons.
3. Stretto imitation, with syncopation, of motive 1; combina-
    tion with closing theme. Expansion of the five note scale of
    1 into seven or nine note scales in imitation.

4. Motive 4 in bassoons, combined with chords in the winds based on the rhythm of 2, harmonic passage-work in the violins. Resembles section B of the first key area in the Exposition. Modulates, pausing on V^7 of the dominant; this resolves to the V^7 of the tonic, which is the unstable chord over which the main thematic material begins.

RECAPITULATION: this section is irregular, compared with the sequence of events in the exposition. It is characteristic of Haydn to treat the recapitulation in the broadest manner, regarding it less as a return of themes than as a reaffirmation of the tonic key. This is what happens:

1. Return of the A-B, now using imitation, followed by the closing theme as part of B.
2. Return of A, now in g-minor (same tonic tone, but now expansion into the unexplored minor realm is opened up).
3. Motive 4 developed over sliding harmonies, later in imitation.
4. Development of closing theme in overlapping imitative dialogue between first violin and flute. This expands into——
5. Thematic group A, with diverging scales in the woodwinds, repetition of the skip (related to 4, but now downward and a third rather than a tenth), later motive 1 in diverging and converging patterns.
6. Passage-work similar to B, including a quotation of the closing theme (cellos and bassoons), and strong cadential movement.
7. Closing theme, followed by scales, cadence.

CODA: this is based upon the A theme complex, the sudden shift to a new key (E-flat), the chord passages based upon rhythmic motive 2 ending with a deceptive cadence, the A theme in its second theme role, and finally the closing theme, decorated with scales, and the closing cadential chords.

II. *Adagio*, D-major (dominant key), compound ternary form. The A section (Example V-3 II), an expression of tender sentiment in the *empfindsamer* style, is organized as a binary form, but with the sectional repetitions written out as variations rather than literal repeats. The B section, in d-minor, employs the agitated syncopations and strong dynamics of the "Storm and Stress" style. It is also in a written-out binary form, but with no repetition of Section II. Rather, this section develops

EXAMPLE V-3 II: Haydn, *Symphony No. 92*, Second Movement

SECOND MOVEMENT: Adagio

FIRST SECTION: A

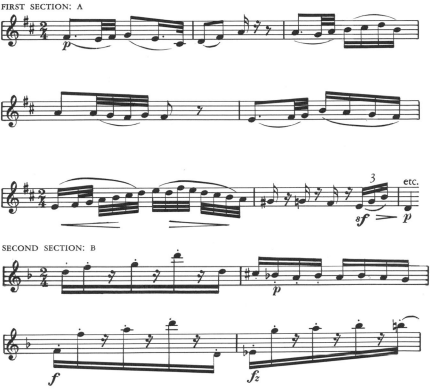

SECOND SECTION: B

some of the motives in rather extended fashion, and upon the return of its first thematic material adjusts the harmony toward the V chord, thus making a smooth entry into the returning A section. The latter begins in the same way as before, but with somewhat fuller orchestration. Its course is turned smoothly toward the coda with development and extension of some of the melodic motives. There are characteristic rhetorical pauses on unstable harmony, a Haydn mannerism, which add to the gentle emotion of this section.

III. *Menuetto and Trio: allegretto,* G-major, compound ternary form (Example V-3 III). Both the minuet and trio are in rounded binary form, somewhat extended by development in the retransition. The minuet has rather heavy accents, a Haydn characteristic, and an unexpected and interesting pause near the beginning of its second section. The trio is an essay in syncopation: the first note, in the horns, is on the third beat of the measure, but tends to sound like the first beat. It is amazing to note how Haydn later squares the phrase off so that it will end on the first beat of the measure.

EXAMPLE V-3 III: Haydn, *Symphony No. 92*, Third Movement

IV. *Presto*, G-major, sonata-allegro form. (Example V-3 IV).

EXPOSITION: first Key Area: this consists of a charming little melody with some unexpected chromaticisms, repeated three times. Transition: fuller orchestration, louder dynamic level, more motion, with the motive 1b repeated. The previous first theme appears in the low strings during the course of the modulation. Second Key Area: orchestration lightens, second theme played by first violins. Closing section: fashioned out of clearly recognizable motives from the first theme.

DEVELOPMENT: the following sections readily are noticeable——
  1. Introductory section in which the first theme is quoted in minor, followed by a pause; the first part of the theme is now played starting on different pitch levels and separated by pauses.

EXAMPLE V-3 IV: Haydn, *Symphony No. 92*, Fourth Movement

FINALE: Presto,   FIRST SUBJECT

SECOND SUBJECT

2. Imitative, between violins and upper winds followed by cellos, and lower winds. Thins out to modulating versions of the first theme accompanied by a chromatically descending scale line which breaks into a motive from the first theme from time to time. The section ends with a chromatically rising and falling motive derived from the same first theme, now used cadentially.

3. The tension of the previous section disappears as the second theme is played by the first violins over a simple accompaniment. It modulates by the simple process of repetition on ascending scale steps (sequence). Imitative dialogue based upon a motive from this theme is used to gradually increase the tension, and at the climax the opening motive of the main theme appears in forceful octaves by the whole orchestra. These broad gestures relax into a dominant preparation, still quoting the opening of the first theme, which leads to the recapitulation after a pause.

RECAPITULATION: this section is much like the exposition, but not so repetitive since the development section was so clearly based upon these themes.

CODA: this is almost a small development section in itself, adapting motives from the first theme and transitions themes to cadential purposes. Near the end the strings have an amusing extended version of the first theme. Here, pauses appear on unexpected and unstable notes. The usual emphatic closing cadences follow.

Symphony No. 94, in G major ("Surprise" Symphony)

This work is one of the most frequently performed of the "London Symphonies." It receives its name from the loud chord in the second movement which Haydn said would "wake up the ladies in the audience." (Evidently concert-goers in his time were not so different from those of today!)

I. The first movement begins with a slow introduction to set off the slightness of the beginning theme of the allegro, which is of much the same motivic kind as in the 92nd, but not so rich in motives: the upward skip of a fourth followed by a descending scale, the rhythm of these, and the following scale and arpeggio figuration. The first key and theme area is fairly extensive and besides the themes mentioned, introduces a short upward chromatic scale which prepares for the main thematic motive. The second thematic elements are vague of outline, possibly to concentrate attention on the motives of the first theme, and the closing section consists of scales, chords and references to the first theme. The development deals principally with this theme also, plus scales and broken chord figures resembling those from the transition. The recapitulation is apt to begin without one's noticing it if he is not careful! It becomes shortened and uses a new passage for the circular transition, if such may be said to exist here, for the process grows organically through the section, with little correspondence to the exposition; the main theme is further developed, as is the closing theme to a small degree.

II. The most famous movement of the symphony is the set of variations on a simple theme that slightly resembles "Twinkle, twinkle little star." The usual *variation theme* in the Classic period is a *binary form*, not just a melodic fragment of the kind we have been referring to by this word. The sequence of harmonies contained in the two sections of the binary form are repeated almost exactly in each variation, and each is the same number of measures as the theme except when it is in the opposite mode (i.e., major to minor, or vice-versa). Thus, the Classic variation belongs to the chaconne type. But unlike the Baroque chaconne, one usually can find the original melody of the theme quite plainly stated in each variation, embellished perhaps, but recognizable. This set by Haydn is quite typical. The melody, a little exercise in tonic and dominant triads, modulates to the dominant and cadences in eight measures; the repeat is written out, and the instrumentation altered slightly. Then comes the bang on the V chord. Section two brings back a reference to the theme and is not repeated. There is little to remark about in the variations, so easily recognizable are they. The second one is in minor, which involves a little musical engineering and more variety and length than the others. In some cases, the repeats of the binary sections are rewritten and re-orchestrated. A short coda ends the movement.

Haydn was fond of variations and wrote many in his symphonies and chamber music. Mozart did not use them in his symphonies, and only occasionally elsewhere, although there are a number of interesting sets for piano; the finale of his great *Piano Concerto in C-minor,* K. 491, consists of variations on two themes, arranged in ternary form. A less profound set closes the fine *Sinfonia Concertante in E♭* for winds and orchestra, and the first movement of the *Piano Sonata in A-major,* K. 331, is a pleasant series. The variation form appealed strongly to Beethoven, and we shall remark upon his work in this field when we discuss the *Symphony No. 3.*

III. The Minuet and Trio is, as expected, in compound ternary form. The minuet is rounded binary with perhaps a little more development in the retransition than one usually expects, while the Trio, as if to make up for it, is rather short.

IV. The Finale introduces us to another as yet unfamiliar form, the sonata-rondo. A study of Example V-4 will reveal the outline of this structure. The main differences from the sonata-allegro consist in (1) stating the main thematic idea in the tonic key at the beginning of the development, and (2) bringing the same theme back after the closing group in the recapitulation. The diagram indicates the relationship to the sonata-allegro (*cf.* Example V-1), and the letters below show the alternation of

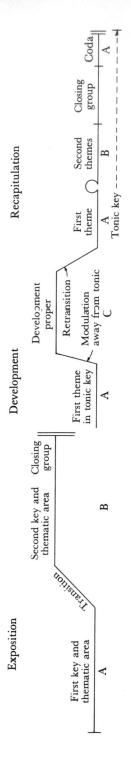

EXAMPLE V-4: *Sonata rondo form.*

the main key and section, A, with the others, B and C. This form is very popular for finales, and is sometimes called merely Rondo, from its resemblance to the Third Rondo form. The presence of a development section which modulates and a recapitulation all in the tonic key, however, make the term sonata-rondo more accurate.

The first thematic and key area states its material immediately, or rather, understates it, as Section I of a binary form. This is repeated loudly in a reorchestrated form, after which a rounded Section II appears. This is not repeated, but plunges into a transition which develops motives from the main theme as it modulates. It is quite vigorous and long. The second theme uses a broken chord as its main feature, and is mostly noticeable from the thinning and quieting of the orchestration. A short closing passage leads to an emphatic cadence which immediately is contradicted, bringing the key back to the tonic and a quotation of the eight measures of the main theme, after which ensues a vigorous development of the rhythmic motive of that theme. This closes on a seemingly foreign chord, but the relation to the beginning of the main theme is revealed by changing one tone of the arpeggio, and the recapitulation begins. As in the first movement, this is full of development, both in thematic work and in modulation, although the tonic key repeatedly is affirmed. The CODA enters abruptly in a completely new key and develops the thematic motives again, finally closing wittily and emphatically in the tonic key.

As was mentioned earlier, the symphonies of Haydn for all their individuality belong strongly to one type, and when one has grown to expect the kinds of themes used and the extensive development (the *empfindsamer* slow movements and the rather heavy minuets) he is free to seek out the differences in detail, the witticisms and the delightful other small features that distinguish one work from another. Haydn is a good example of the classic composer's working consummately well within the style; this is particularly true of his orchestral works, for his chamber and solo music is more audacious.

THE SYMPHONIES OF BEETHOVEN

While Beethoven received the fully formed classic symphony from the hands of both Haydn and Mozart, he seems to have felt more akin to the procedures and concepts of the older master. Thus, we find

Beethoven emphasizing thematic development, *empfindsamer* and "*Sturm und Drang*" expressiveness, symphonic economy in obtaining the greatest extension from the smallest amount of material and formal experiments of the most far-reaching kind. To Mozart, Beethoven's debt is obscure for he used almost none of the opera buffa style and his art is less olympian. That Beethoven admired Mozart's music we know, but we must strongly suspect that he realized that the Salzburg master had so completely summed up his portion of the style that there remained nothing left upon which to improve.

The first two symphonies of Beethoven, while original and new, show plainly their relationship to those of Haydn. But when we arrive at the Third Symphony, we immediately realize that a new voice and concept of the symphony have appeared. This new concept involves an extension of the time scale through which each movement moves, for they become longer because of larger areas in each key, slower harmonic changes and the dynamic and rhythmic yet repetitive development of motivic material. Beethoven's time scale is the largest possible in which the dramatic form of the sonata-allegro can function, for, with more complicated tonal changes or more themes (both used by later Romantic composers), the listener's memory cannot retain the feeling of the tonic key and its return becomes meaningless because unrecognized. The form, then, becomes incoherent and the whole aesthetic system upon which it was based is violated. One of the most serious problems faced by the nineteenth century composers after Beethoven was that of the symphony for just these reasons.

The classic symphony of Haydn and Mozart was, as Tovey points out,[2] a new kind of suite in which the inner tensions of each movement were on a scale which allowed them to be resolved *within* the movement. But in the case of the sonatas and symphonies of Beethoven, the emotional issues raised cannot be resolved within the movement, long and formally complete as these may be. The succeeding movements of the compound form must round them out. The comparison with the acts——or movements——of a play is revealing, especially since Beethoven would seem to be dramatizing human existence. The separate movements of such works thus are made parts of a whole by means of what we might term psychological or emotional unity, supplementing the purely musical unity which Beethoven was often at pains to establish.

The Beethoven concept of theme is important. These musical ideas usually are quite simple and often are rather uninteresting in them-

---

[2] Tovey, Donald Francis, *The Forms of Music*. New York, Meridian Book M36, 1956.

selves in the way that a brick is uninteresting. They require development and amplification to reveal the possibilities for building structures which they contain. Some seem immediately profound and symbolic, despite their simplicity, while others take on significance through interaction with other elements of the music.

Drama requires tension, and Beethoven's musical dramas reveal his mastery of ways of achieving this, his timing of tension and relaxation, his purposive use of this necessary element. Instability of rhythm and harmony are employed in highly imaginative ways, and the careful use of gradual or sudden dynamic changes imbues his music with shock and power. The sudden change of key to give the material a new and fresh sound frequently is invoked, and the contrast of keys in general is used most effectively. Aside from these, there is the gratuitous inspiration, the irrational stroke of genius which we feel to be exactly right after it has happened, but which no one could foresee. Such a place is the oboe recitative in the recapitulation of the first movement of the *Fifth Symphony,* for example, or the horn entrance at the recapitulation of the *Third Symphony.* In an art as rational as Beethoven's, these inspirations are the more exciting.

Haydn's music had revealed wit and humor, but not in the broad, humanistic way that Beethoven exhibits. His humor ranges from the obvious——as in the introduction to the finale of the *First Symphony*——to more subtle kinds, of which the *Eighth Symphony* has a liberal share. Do not listen to Beethoven always as a superhuman, but enjoy him as a fellow man when he speaks as a man. For above all, Beethoven's music reveals to us a great human being in whom we may recognize ourselves.

Symphony No. 1, C Major, Opus 26

Our experience with the symphonies of Haydn and Mozart should prepare us well for this work, for the forms of the movements are quite clear, and only the style has a new quality (but one related, nevertheless, to the previous composers). The first movement is a concise sonata-allegro with an interesting introduction which begins in the subdominant, moves to the dominant, and finally resolves to the tonic at the beginning of the *allegro con brio.* The composer was taken to task by the critics after the first performance for such an outlandish beginning to a symphony, but its structure is clear to us now without explanation. Notice the importance of the rhythmic motive, and the simplicity of the lyric second theme, the use of syncopation and the different-sounding orchestration.

The second movement, *Andante cantabile con moto* (with motion, lyrically), is a sonata-allegro form which is quite Haydnesque in spirit. The second thematic material is similar to the first, and the secondary ideas are distinctly subordinate and almost episodic in nature.

The third movement, while marked *Menuetto e Trio,* also is indicated to be played *Allegro molto e vivace* (Very fast and lively). Certainly this is no sedate or elegant minuet, but rather a *scherzo.* This name was given to such movements first by Haydn and generally is adopted by Beethoven. The form is the same as that of the minuet and trio——compound ternary—— but it is more than a speeded-up minuet. The composition is engineered to be played rapidly, with a different rate of chord change, more agile themes, etc,——a sportscar rather than family stationwagon.

The finale is preceded by an *adagio* introduction which, despite the tempo indication, is a delightful bit of fooling. The sonata allegro is quite straightforward, and the coda balances the introduction in humor.

Symphony No. 3, in E , Opus 55 ("Eroica")

This work is an essay on heroism, as the nickname might indicate. The subject of the work is probably not Napoleon, to whom at first it was dedicated, but rather Beethoven himself, who had struggled with the demon of his deafness and all it signified to him, and finally emerged victorious. That the composer consciously imagined himself the hero of the work, as Richard Strauss was later to do in *Ein Heldenleben,* one doubts strongly. But whatever the riddle's answer, this powerful work continues to impress us as the musical image of a great man.

I. *Allegro con brio;* sonata-allegro form with long coda.

The meaning of the first movement is summed up for us at its inception: the two crashing chords proclaim anything but serenity, and the harmonic instability which arrives so surprisingly during the first statement of the bugle-call theme presages a struggle to come (Example V-5a). Now comes the usual restatement of this principal idea on a grander scale. The simplicity of this noble theme is particularly noteworthy, and the fact that it is a broken chord figure makes it usable in many situations. The rushing impetus is made even more stormy by the exciting syncopations that occur during this main section. Now Beethoven presents three separate transitional themes in succession, all basically motivic. It is significant that the devel-

EXAMPLE V-5 I: Beethoven, *Symphony No. 3.*

FIRST MOVEMENT: Allegro con brio

a. FIRST SUBJECT

b. TRANSITION 1.

c. TRANSITION 2.

d. TRANSITION 3.

SECOND SUBJECT

e.

CLOSING MATERIAL

opment section is concerned mostly with these themes and the first theme (Example V-5b,c,d). The reason is made plain when we hear the second theme (Example V-5e): lyric, although not melodic, it contains no motives and is static, calm, immobile. It provides a moment of rest among the torrents of sound which have preceded it. These resume with a striking crescendo passage, and the closing material, recalling the main theme and containing passages of rhythmic shocks and dissonances energetically brings the exposition to a forceful close.

Development: There are some eleven sections here, rather clearly distinguishable from each other, although smoothly interconnected for the most part. Mainly as a "roadmap" which will emphasize Beethoven's developmental techniques, we shall list these sections below. Of significance is the fact that the essentially static second theme never appears, since it would restrain the forward motion of the development. Beethoven instead presents us with a lyric substitute, a "new" theme (probably derived from the counterpoint to the opening theme, or from the first transition theme) which brings dramatic relief from the agitated development of the first and third transition themes. It is interesting to note that this substitute second theme is never broken up or extended in the same way that the other themes are treated, but always occurs intact, its two phrases firmly planted in a key.

1. A phrase from the last part of the second thematic area, serving to lead into the development.
2. Quiet appearance of first Transition Theme——note its motivic character.
3. First Theme, bodily lifted one-half step higher upon each repetition: a tension device, especially when accompanied by a rise in dynamics.
4. Motive from Transition Theme No. 3, accompanied by syncopated and offbalance patterns in the winds and strings; increased motion and agitation. Later broken chord patterns in the low strings, then similar but faster patterns in the first violins, leading to a climax and resolution of the modulation in a new key.
5. First Transition Theme, quietly beginning in a manner similar to Section 2, but extended, leading into the next section.
6. Fugal development of a phrase whose main rhythmic motive is derived from the first transition theme, with later a motive from the third one. This gains in strength, and moves into the next section.
7. A long series of syncopated chords, massive and forceful, linked to the preceding section by the shorter syncopation of the first Transition Theme. Actually, this may be called a development of the syncopations heard in the exposition. The motion within the long-held chords is maintained by the Transition Theme rhythm. The chords increase in dissonance at the end of the passage, but not resolve immediately. In an intensely dramatic passage, the strings mass together, as it were, in a phalanx, wheel and march off to a new tonal region. These passages represent the highest climax of the development.
8. The coolness, stability and lyricism of the "new" theme (Example V-5g), which now appears in the oboes and strings, affords a welcome relief from the high drama of conflict which has developed. It is repeated four times, twice on each key level.
9. Abruptly, with a very short connecting phrase, the first theme returns, now with its broken chord pattern expanded upward in a fanfare of spiritual elation. Again, the whole pattern is repeated at increasingly higher levels of pitch. At the high point, the "new" theme returns.
10. After one appearance of the lyric theme Beethoven follows

it with the short phrase derived from the first Transition Theme, as though to make clear their relationship. This is passed down through the orchestra, landing on the dominant of E-flat, which is the tonic key of the symphony.

11. The function of this last section is to prepare for the entrance of the tonic recapitulation by emphasizing harmony of dominant quality. There are three subsections, the first of which is devoted to striding bass arpeggios based upon the first theme, accompanied by similarly derived figures in the winds. The second section thins out the orchestral sonority, and consists of a chord progression which emphasizes the dominant harmony. The third part is very quiet, the calm before the storm, and increases tension and anticipation to such a point that the first horn can wait no longer, but comes in prematurely with the tonic first theme against the dominant harmony in the strings. This was thought frequently to be a mistake in the horn part, but upon such a suggestion at one of the rehearsals by Ries, Beethoven's pupil, the master made clear his intent by boxing Ries's ears! It must have been infinitely more telling in those days of unjaded hearing than now, when our ears are accustomed to much stronger dissonance.

RECAPITULATION: This is a reasonably exact counterpart of the exposition, but the element of conflict and the excitement connected with it is much relaxed. The dissonant C sharp which occurred during the first presentation of the main theme is now treated in a new, more quickly resolved way, the orchestration is changed, and the lyric element of the themes is emphasized. The conflict is over, and the air has cleared.

CODA: The coda which follows dwarfs every other symphonic coda written up to this time in length and function, for it acts as a second development section, balancing and opposing the first. The development here is relaxed, full of good humor, with markedly stable harmony and rhythm——the antitheses of the former section. The material used is principally the main theme, now with a counterpoint added, and the "new" theme. Worthy of mention is the short downward flight of steps—— E-flat, D-flat, C——by means of which we enter the coda, a Beethoven structural device. In this movement the drama and balance of the sonata-allegro form have been expanded to heroic size, but with a sensitive regard for the beauty of the proportions——the regard of a classically-minded composer.

II. *Marcia funebre: Adagio assai.* C minor, expanded and developed compound ternary form.

The second movement is the famous "Funeral March," set in the key that seemed to have the blackest connotations for Beethoven—C-minor. Now, the fact that this is a march has certain formal implications to Beethoven, and, in general, he follows them. A march is a stylized dance; to create a longer composition than just the eight or sixteen measures that a dance form (binary structure) comprises, a trio is added, as with the minuet and a three-part form consisting of march-trio-march results. This is what Beethoven uses, but there is a difference.

The hushed, somber march theme (Example V-5h) with which he begins was arrived at after numerous versions were sketched and discarded, reshaped and recomposed. The decorated triad, supported by the deep notes of the double basses calls up in the imagination all of the tragedy and solemnity that would attend the death of a hero. The oboe proclaims the second period of the theme, after which it cadences on its related major key. A more consoling theme in the strings enters (i), giving way, after two mild climaxes, to the return of the main theme. But only the beginning of it is quoted, and the major theme appears now in the winds supported by the strings. A codetta follows, which contains as its high point an astringently dissonant chord in the winds, and the first march section ends.

The second section, the trio, is in the parallel major key, and exhibits a little more motion as a result of the chord-diffusion patterns in the string accompaniment (j). The high points are the two fanfares, quite war-like in nature, employing full orchestra with emphasis on the trumpets and timpani. After the second of these, a strong descending phrase brings the harmonic movement to a half-cadence, and we are now ready for the return of the march. The normal procedure would now be to recapitulate the first section with some changes in scoring, probably shortening the repeated sections, add a brief coda—the movement is already as long as most slow movements—and move on to the next movement, the scherzo. Let us see what Beethoven does.

The somber main theme begins just as we remember it, at least for the first phrase; but the second, that upward, questioning scale line which ends on a dissonant note, is repeated,

EXAMPLE V-5 II and III: Beethoven, *Symphony No. 3.*

SECOND MOVEMENT: Adagio assai
PRINCIPAL SUBJECT

THIRD MOVEMENT: Allegro vivace
SCHERZO

and we make a cadence in a new key. Now *that,* in itself, is not too surprising—but on the cadence note a fugal passage of great tension and gripping dramatic power begins, and grows by imitative addition until the whole orchestra is involved. Finally, the fugue is spent, and the movement quiets down to what surely will be the last repetition of the main idea. But it has no sooner begun than it trails off on a high note. A forceful return of the "battle" passage of the trio ensues, here developed at length, and in the harsh minor tonality, possibly reminding us with its crushing force that this was a hero. Subsequent to this, the "consoling" theme referred to above returns so we see now that a developmental section, full of drama and surprise (more than one would expect in a funeral march), was inserted between the main march theme and its major key follower. The remainder of the recapitulation of the march is regular, but is rescored almost completely, giving more important parts to the wind instruments, and fuller, more rhythmic accompaniment to the strings. Instead of the expected final cadence, a deceptive one is used, and this chord immediately is treated as the tonic of a new key with moving results. Beethoven reveals to us at this point his overwhelming humanity and sympathy: only a few measures, but how poor this already meaningful work would be without them. In the final measures the music seems to be moving forward toward a cadence glimpsed in the distance. Beethoven has one more thing to say. The main theme begins in the first violins, accompanied only by the *pizzicato* cellos and basses. But it is slightly changed, and then it breaks into fragments, gasping, trying to convey, for the last time, its unutterable grief.

This has been a long movement, but notice how Beethoven realizes *when*——*exactly* when——to jar us, to arouse our attention and interest by variation, polyphony, or orchestration. The "Funeral March" must be listened to with the realization that Beethoven is here saying immensely profound things about despair, tragedy and death. That is, it must be listened to seriously and intensely with participation in each event.

III. *Scherzo: Allegro vivace,* E-flat major, compound ternary form.

The scherzo reaffirms the life impulse, and the upsurging creativity of a heroic spirit. "Oh, life is so beautiful—to live it a thousand times!" said Beethoven. This movement is one of the two most masterly scherzos in all of the nine symphonies, and it is significant that the other one occurs in the *Ninth Symphony,* which runs a rather parallel course in meaning and ethical idea to the "Eroica."

The form is regular—scherzo-trio-scherzo with coda. The first measures, which of course are quoted repeatedly during the piece, consist of the rapid alternation of two chords, setting up a kind of duple "harmonic rhythm" (Example V-5k). This is contained in a triple meter, and the conflict between the two creates a nervous tension which Beethoven emphasizes by directing that these measures be played in a very soft and *staccato* manner. Such tension eventually must explode, and Beethoven allows it to do so, but not too soon—only when he has aroused our expectations to the breaking point. There is a forceful descending broken chord passage in syncopated rhythm which is worth taking note of, for upon its return Beethoven changes meter to duple for four measures in order to intensify the instability. Needless to remark, this procedure is very rare in the eighteenth and early nineteenth centuries, and demonstrates the manner in which Beethoven will break with tradition if such action heightens the expressiveness of his music. The trio is based upon an elaborate fanfare, first stated by the horns and repeated several times during the section (1). It is not just another fanfare, however, but puts the virtuosity of the players to a severe test. Beethoven takes the first horn up almost to the top of its range, while the low horn of the group has rapid notes to play in its lower register where such action is not only difficult but also precarious. But no matter! This is a heaven-storming passage, and, as Beethoven probably knew, when instrumentalists are confronted with difficult passages, they soon learn to perform them, and the erstwhile impossible enters the literature as not only possible, but even probable! So it is with these horn passages, although even with modern instruments they offer a challenge. One wonders how they sounded in Beethoven's day.

IV. *Finale: Allegro molto,* E Flat Major, theme and variations with coda.

The last movement storms in with a rushing introduction, not in the expected E♭ major tonic of the symphony, but in a kind of G minor. By the time the introduction is ended, however, the tonality has settled down to the expected key, and

EXAMPLE V-5 IV: Beethoven, *Symphony No. 3.*

FOURTH MOVEMENT Allegro molto

m. THEME, PART 1.

the introduction concludes with a half-cadence. The theme of the variations to follow (Example V-5m) is now ticked off by the *pizzicato* strings, punctuated by a few loud and assertive chords in the wind instruments (m). If you listen carefully you will hear that this theme is a small rounded binary form with both sections repeated. But whoever heard of understating a theme so completely? We shall find this skeleton underlying or within—sometimes even used as melody

—all of the variations of this large movement. According to Sullivan,[3] Beethoven here chooses the variation form to show the varieties of achievement possible to him after triumphing over his difficulties. But these are no mere "character" variations. While some of them stay rather close to the theme, or to the gay, dance-like melody (n) that combines with the theme and reappears from time to time, the best description of the procedure is *developmental*. Indeed, this developmental variation technique is one of the achievements of Beethoven, not to be matched by Romantic composers until we reach Brahms, at the farther end of the century. Let us also keep in mind that Beethoven probably knew this theme quite well, after having used it in a ballet, and after having written fifteen piano variations on it!

A series of variations obviously has unity, but Beethoven has sought here not only to emphasize this quality, but also to provide variety of a kind not usually encountered in variations, by subjecting these to a larger formal plan. The movement, after the introduction and the statement of the theme, is organized as follows:

Tonic Key:
> Var. 1: Theme in middle register, played by the strings, surrounded by simple two-part broken polyphony.
> Var. 2: Theme in higher register, played by the strings with running scale accompaniment, changing at times to repeated chords.
> Var. 3: Theme in bass, higher upon repetition: dance-like melody (n) in upper parts, often running passagework in strings.

Transition to Other Keys:
> Var. 4: Fugal development of first four notes of theme (o).
> Var. 5: Dance-like melody, "flute" variation, beginning with few instruments, finishing with all strings and woodwinds. Cadence repetition.
> Var. 6: March, using first four notes of theme as *ostinato* accompaniment. Codetta spins out cadence figure.
> Var. 7: Transitional variation, first four notes of theme as *ostinato* accompaniment to dance-like melody which appears first in major, than minor, then developed, modulating simply to Var. 8.

---

[3] Sullivan, J. W. N., *Beethoven: His Spiritual Development.* New York, Vintage Books, 1927.

Tonic Key:

> Var. 8: Development of inverted version of first four notes of theme as double fugue; other subject is scale figure. Dance-like melody appears once above the polyphony. Much attention toward end to theme notes; long variation (p).
>
> Var. 9: Dramatic tempo change; slow variation of dance-like melody, new harmonization; instrumentation grows to Var. 10.
>
> Var. 10: Twin of preceding, but on larger scale; winds have dance-like melody, now sounding more important because of emphasis (horns especially) and tempo; remainder of orchestra plays repeated chords or broken chord figuration.

Coda:

> Tonic key: various lyric sections which make one suspect variation, but if so, very developed. Return of introduction, now in right key, followed by motives from dance-like melody: growing jubilation to the end.

The innovations in this symphony are many, too many to discuss here. The important ones for the development of the symphony are those of size and unity. It is longer than any previous symphony, but measured by subjective time, it is exactly the right length, testifying to the perfection of Beethoven's sense of timing in the succession of musical events, both within each movement and from movement to movement. The unity of this work, so necessary in a large structure, is largely that of style, although the sense of psychological unity——it is about one subject throughout——usually is present. Some analysts have made a case for the derivation of all of the principal themes from the triad pattern of the "buglecall" of the first movement. The ambiguity of the situation is intriguing, for many symphonic themes in the classic era are based upon triad patterns. Did Beethoven have this in mind, or didn't he? We shall probably never know for certain, but the fact remains that the themes all match in breadth, constructive potential and dramatic appropriateness.

Symphony No. 5, C Minor, Opus 67.

The "Eroica" reveals Beethoven to have been an idealist; let us now show his defiant and optimistic spirit. The Fifth Symphony is unified by the progression through its movements from darkness and struggle to light and triumph, sometimes wavering, as in life, but eventually reaching the goal. This psychological unity is dramatized and magnified by the use of a strong rhythmic motive throughout the series of movements at moments when it is most telling. The feeling of progression is intensified before the climactic finale by a connecting passage from the previous movement which dramatically summarizes the progress of the whole symphony.

We will call the rhythmic motive of this symphony a *motto theme* since, like a verbal motto, it is quoted without change at every appearance. A second type of theme is the *germ theme*, which usually has a melodic pattern of importance. It may be incorporated into other melodic shapes, be inverted, given different rhythmic values or otherwise expanded or contracted to form new-sounding themes. While it may be associated at times with strong rhythmic patterns, these must give way to the organic growth which is its most valuable quality. We shall make considerable use of these two thematic concepts in the next chapter.

I. *Allegro con brio*, sonata-allegro form

This first movement is one of the most concentrated musical creations in existence, dominated by the motto theme hammered out defiantly by the orchestra at the very beginning (Example V-6a,b,c,). It is an example of the form stripped of all unnecessary detail; the transition is shortened drastically, the second theme occupies a definitely subordinate role, and the closing materal is fashioned out of the main theme. With our previous experience it is extremely easy to follow formally,

EXAMPLE V-6: Beethoven, *Symphony No. 5.*

FIRST MOVEMENT: Allegro con brio

a. PRINCIPAL SUBJECT

b. SECOND SUBJECT

SECOND MOVEMENT: Andante con moto

c. THEME A

and this is the reason for Beethoven's drastic simplification: he wants nothing to stand in the way of direct communication of his ideas. He undoubtedly is successful!

II. *Andante con moto,* Theme and variations.

This movement is rather complicated to explain in words, so we shall refer to the diagram of its form for clarity (see pages 264-265). As can be seen, it consists of a two-part theme, the first section in A♭ and the second in C, joined by a transitional passage which is the same fanfare as the C major part to which it modulates. There are two peculiarities about the music apparent here: the first is the interruption of the lyric melody of theme A by repeated cadence figures, and the second is the questioning way in which theme B ends, or rather dissolves into the mysterious bridge passage to the first variation. Formally, Beethoven has discarded the binary structure as the basis for the theme, although in some other later works he continues its use. Here, the dramatic necessity of the nature of this movement evidently made him favor a freer organization. Variation 1 is very much like the theme, but only the A section is really varied. The motto theme of the symphony may be heard in the low strings during the transition. Variation 2 treats theme A at length and develops the transition, but theme B, while beginning triumphantly, is left hanging in the air with a sense of anticlimax. The bridge passage also is extended, including a little march in the woodwinds, after which theme A appears in canon between the violins and high woodwinds. The coda begins at a slightly faster tempo with a bassoon solo, and the multiple cadences heard in theme A are used to bring the movement to a close.

III. *Allegro*, Scherzo and Trio

This Scherzo has been compared by some writers to a depiction of a grotesque dream——and it must certainly have seemed so to the double-bass players who had to cope with the treacherously rapid passages in the Trio. The forms of the scherzo and trio are traditional, that is, binary, but the first sections are very brief and the second sections extremely long by comparison. The Scherzo is made up of two elements: the shadowy, rising arpeggio which opens the movement, and the motto theme which follows it, hurled forth by the horns like some elemental force. The Trio uses only the scalar theme given first to the double-basses, extending it by repetition and development. The return of the scherzo is rewritten and somewhat shorter. But the astonishing aspect of this reprise is the ghostly quietness and the dry sounds of the softly plucked strings. Ghostly indeed is the motto in the solo woodwinds, hushed with premonitions. The music drops down to a deceptive cadence, beginning the transition to the finale. Little by little motion begins, instruments are added and the intensity increases until the music has built up an enormous dominant chord in C major which is sustained to the last moment before resolving on the brilliant tonic harmony which opens the final movement.

IV. *Allegro*, Sonata-allegro form.

The last movement is a broad sonata-allegro, a hymn of exultant power and triumph. The fanfare-like main theme is attended by several other subordinate themes, the most

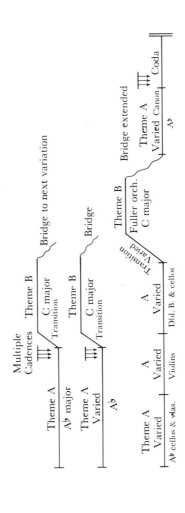

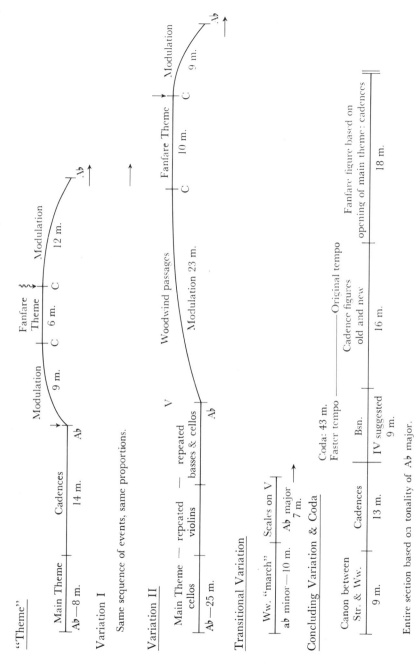

Diagram of Second Movement, Symphony No. 5 by Beethoven

"Theme"

Main Theme   Modulation   Fanfare
                                     Theme   Modulation
Ab —8 m.   Cadences   9 m. C 6 m. C   12 m.
             14 m.   Ab

Variation I

Same sequence of events, same proportions.

Variation II

Main Theme — repeated — repeated   V   Woodwind passages   Fanfare Theme   Modulation
cellos   violins   basses & cellos
Ab —25 m.   Ab   Modulation 23 m.   C   10 m. C   9 m.

Transitional Variation

Ww. "march"   Scales on V
ab minor—10 m.   Ab major
                 7 m.

Concluding Variation & Coda

                                 Coda: 43 m.
                                 Faster tempo ———— Original tempo
Canon between   Cadence figures   Fanfare figure based on
Str. & Ww.   Cadences   Bsn.   old and new   opening of main theme: cadences
9 m.   13 m.   IV suggested 16 m.   18 m.
                         9 m.

Entire section based on tonality of Ab major.

Diagram of Second Movement, *Symphony No. 5* (Beethoven).

important of which are the chorale theme of the transition and the second subject, which incorporates the rhythm of the motto in its scale-line movement. Beethoven still has one surprise before the long concluding coda. Just before the recapitulation, when the dominant has duly prepared for the return of the main theme in tonic, Beethoven inserted a passage like that of the scherzo which is made up of the motto theme. After this grim reminder, the movement concludes joyously.

Other Beethoven Symphonies

Time and space do not permit a detailed examination of the remaining four symphonies, but a few words concerning them are necessary. The Sixth, Op. 68, called the "Pastoral" Symphony, was written at about the same time as the Fifth, and represents the alternation between heroic and lyric symphonies that marks the work of Beethoven in this form. Symphonies numbered 1, 3, 5, 7, and 9 tend toward the heroic, while numbers 2, 4, 6, and 8 are more lyric and personal. As we have mentioned, it is to this *Sixth Symphony* that the programmatically inclined Romantic composers point in justification for their descriptive symphonies. But Beethoven is more inclined here to the description of feelings rather than imitation of natural sounds, although these do occur in the second and fourth movements of the work. The *Seventh Symphony, Op. 92*, is a large essay on rhythm. Each of the movements has a distinct rhythmic idea which furnishes the basis for the structure. Themes are almost unimportant, especially in the two outer movements, and consist of simple patterns such as broken chords and scale sections. The unifying factor here is rhythm and its manipulation, which provides an inner and more subtle coherence to the separate movements than program or theme quotation. It is a predominantly cheerful work, easily accessible to the listener. The *Eighth Symphony* is an idealization of the earlier classic symphony, and for this reason was misunderstood and criticized by concertgoers from Beethoven's time through the first half of the Romantic period. It is short and economical of material, but not terse and serious. Rather it represents Beethoven in a good humor and contains some of his most witty writing.

To sum up briefly the gigantic *Ninth Symphony*—the symphonic work representing Beethoven's third creative period—is an impossible task, so we shall content ourselves here with only a few remarks about it. It is written in the traditional four movements, but with the scherzo as the second and the slow movement as the third in the sequence. Each of the first three movements proposes a philosophy of life to oppose the antagonist of Beethoven's—and every man's—life: Fate. In the first movement, the inexorable problem is stated; in the second, energy, the creative force of life; in the third, sublime contemplation, mysticism; in the fourth these are summed up one by one in the intro- duction and rejected; the wonderful theme symbolizing joy, the answer to Fate, is chosen, and the chorus and soloists sing a variegated hymn to joy in the words of Schiller.

It is in this last symphony that Richard Wagner will find his justi- fication for the combination of voice with orchestra in a symphonic manner. It was—and still is—a monument to classicism, for Beethoven explored and inhabited the forms and ideals of classicism completely, leaving no further development possible. In a sense he precipitated the Romantic movement in music, for none could surpass him, and weaker personalities could only imitate—except for his Viennese compatriot Schubert, who was too profoundly original in his own way to merely copy. Beethoven wrote "The End" to an era.

THE CONCERT OVERTURES OF BEETHOVEN

Beethoven was one of the first master composers to write music for the spoken drama. Overtures to operas were common, and seldom were detached from the stage presentation at this time; but the over- ture to a play is apt to be performed in the concert hall without the play, giving rise to what we now call the *concert overture.* Soon com- posers of the Romantic era wrote descriptive overtures not intended to preface stage works, but to exist on their own merits. In this they followed Beethoven's lead. He composed four overtures to plays, of which the ones to *Coriolanus* by von Collin and *Egmont* by Goethe are the most moving. In them he sums up the central idea of each play. One need only hear *Coriolanus* to know that the play is concerned with heroism and tragedy.

In form, these works are all sonata-allegro, strongly resembling the first movement of a symphony in their sense of compressed drama. Indeed, the *Overture to Coriolanus* might well serve as the first move- ment of the *Fifth Symphony* insofar as emotional attitude and key are concerned.

The four overtures to Beethoven's opera, *Fidelio,* are heard fre- quently, especially the *Leonore No. 3 Overture.* This was one of three overtures written for the opera before its name was changed, and represents Beethoven's dissatisfaction with them for various reasons. These compositions, while not approved by Beethoven for opening music to the opera, are excellent works in themselves, more so than the overture which he finally accepted for this purpose, entitled *Fidelio*. Still other overtures, such as *The Consecration of the House,* were written to celebrate some special occasion and may be regarded as abstract compositions.

THE CONCERTO

The solo concerto emerged from the experimentation characteristic of the transition from Baroque to Classic style as the preferred kind of combination of skilled player with orchestra. The concerto grosso, in its eighteenth century version, has few examples, and, of course the orchestral concerto was replaced by the symphony. Among the composers who contributed to the development of the classical concerto, two names stand out, composers whom we have met before: C. P. E. Bach and Johann Christian Bach of London. The latter had the most decisive influence upon Mozart, who brought the form to its classical point of perfection. We have mentioned the compound form of the concerto on page 217; let us examine the only movement different from the symphonic forms, the first, to see what the product of Mozart's genius was.

The old baroque concertos began with a tutti section which strongly stated the tonic key and the important thematic material of the movement; in the classical concerto, this opening tutti by the orchestra does the same thing, now as a sonata exposition, or rather, closer to the recapitulation, since it is all in the tonic key (see Example V-7). Here, except for occasional ritornelli and the exercise of the concerto principle, resemblance to the baroque concerto ends. After this opening tutti, the movement proceeds formally as a sonata-allegro with the material shared in some manner between the orchestra and the soloist until the moment at which the coda would begin. Here the orchestra drives rhythmically and dynamically to an emphatic incomplete cadence (*e.g.,* IV-V, but no resolution), whereupon the soloist plays an ornamental and brilliant passage concluding with a trill on the dominant chord which signals the conductor that the cadenza is finished and that the orchestra may conclude the movement with the coda. Such a signal is necessary, for the cadenzas of this

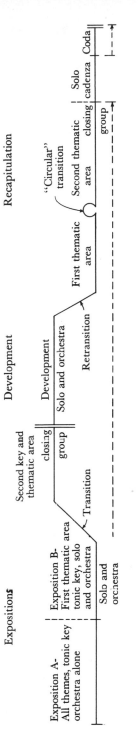

EXAMPLE V-7: *Concerto-allegro form.*

period were improvised, not written out in the conductor's score, and therefore were of variable length. We are fortunate in having a few cadenzas which Mozart wrote out for the use of his students; and Beethoven, fearing perhaps the bad taste that virtuosi who are not composers sometimes exhibit in their cadenzas, carefully wrote out cadenzas for the use of performers of his concerti. Other movements of the classical concerto may have cadenzas also, as indicated in the score. In some works in which the solo part is highly decorative by nature, as for example Mozart's great *Clarinet Concerto (K. 622)*, all indications of cadenzas may be omitted. Other changes in the concerto-allegro plan involve the occasional omission of the opening orchestral tutti or the use of a short introduction to the tutti by the solo instrument alone (Mozart's *Piano Concerto in E-flat (K. 271)*, which sets the precedent for the Beethoven Fourth and Fifth Piano Concerti where more is made of this introduction).

The first movements of the Mozart concerti are apt to abound with themes, some of which may be the personal property of the orchestra or the solo, and never shared. Other themes, once heard, may disappear for the remainder of the movement. Despite this seeming waywardness, the effect is one of clear organization and organic unity. Beethoven simplified the whole process, making it more symphonic and in accordance with his usual style.

Mozart writes one of three types for the slow movements of his concerti, which are almost always marked *andante* rather than the slow *adagio,* and are set in the quiet and reposeful subdominant key. One type is the *galant,* elegant, rococo movement, graceful and quite objective, often in minuet meter and tempo. The second abandons the rococo element in favor of a singing, flowing manner, more subjective in nature, often with deeply-felt melancholy passages. The third style is tragic with a depth of resignation and poignancy hardly found in the works of any other composer. Yet one is left with no feeling of heaviness or depression after hearing such movements, for they transcend as pure art the suffering and bitterness of experience which called them into being. We feel consoled and strengthened by them, as by any great work of art.

The final movement sometimes is shocking after a tragic slow movement, for it is almost always a fast and gay sonata-rondo. But when we realize that the serious mood cannot be prolonged, that the composer has used just enough time to say everything, that nothing more remains, we begin to comprehend the reason for the abrupt change of mood. The solution of the problem is consistent with the eighteenth century aesthetic attitude, also, for only in a few highly personal works does Mozart write a serious finale such as that of the G minor Symphony or the C minor *Piano Concerto (K. 491).* Beethoven solves the problem in a different way by dissolving the close of the slow movement into a transition which musically and emotionally bridges the gap between the two contrasting movements.

The problem of balance and interaction between solo and orchestra is the essential one of the classic concerto. Mozart, and after him Beethoven, solved the problem in many ways. The simplest answer, and one used by many shallower concerto writers before and after Mozart, was to make the orchestra a subservient accompanist to the dazzling display of the soloist. A more subtle method is to reverse the roles, giving the solo interesting accompaniment to the orchestral voices. The third and most fruitful answer is that of dialogue, interplay and symphonic collaboration between them. Most concertos will at one point or another use all three methods.

It is difficult to choose, out of the riches of Mozart's concertos, any one for special comment. For first acquaintance, perhaps the Piano Concertos in C Major (K. 467) and A Major (K. 488), might be suggested, followed later by the two more subjective ones, K. 466 in D Minor and K. 491 in C Minor. Among the five violin concertos, all written in 1775, the last three (K. 216, 218, 219) are well worth hearing. Of the concertos for wind instruments the great *Clarinet Concerto in A-Major* (K. 662) stands high above the rest. *The Concerto for Bassoon* (K. 191) and the *Fourth French Horn Concerto* (K. 364) are filled with charm, while the flute concertos for the most part are rather empty in their *galanterie.* Two survivors of the concerto grosso, standing midway between the concerto and the symphony, are the *Sinfonie Concertante* (K. 364) for violin, viola and orchestra, and K. 297b, for oboe, clarinet, bassoon, horn and orchestra. Both are in E flat, and both contain some of this composer's finest music.

Only two of Haydn's concertos are in the common repertoire, the *Concerto for Trumpet,* and that for cello. Since Haydn was not a performer he had neither the need nor inclination to pour into the concerto his most significant ideas. The trumpet work is pleasant and is played mostly because of the dearth of concerti for that instrument. The *Cello Concerto,* however, ranks with the best of those composed for this instrument, pleasing to the listener and grateful and brilliant for the soloist.

In the concertos of Beethoven we find the typical expansion of form, the symphonic development of thematic material shared between the solo and orchestra as equals, and the grand manner which set the style for the coming century. They are more obviously *virtuoso* concertos than those of Mozart, for the soloist plainly has to work harder! Yet this is not empty display, but genuine music which is difficult because it has to be——there is no easier way to project the composer's thoughts.

The important concertos of Beethoven are the five written for the piano and the one written for the violin. The first two piano concerti acknowledge his debt to Mozart, but the Third, in C Minor, Op. 37, the Fourth, Op. 58, in G Major, and the Fifth, Op. 73 in E Flat (the "Emperor") are more characteristic. The C Minor concerto is most noteworthy for the advance in symphonic writing and orchestral craftsmanship, but it is forthright, rugged and witty and an excellent vehicle for the pianist. The G Major work is feminine in its lyricism, opening with a short introduction of the main theme by the piano alone before the orchestral tutti. Its slow movement pits the power of the orchestra against the tranquil persuasiveness of the solo, and there is a transition to the spirited finale. The great E flat concerto opens with a magnificent introduction, cadenza-like, for the piano and orchestra, which recurs in the movement. The slow movement is one of Beethoven's most prayerful adagios, and there again appears a transition to the syncopated first theme of the finale. The *Violin Concerto in D Major,* Op. 61, is one of the greatest works in the literature of that instrument. It is not dazzling, but requires the utmost in taste and musicianship as well as technique to play well. More lyric and decorative than one expects in Beethoven's music, it still shows the strong organizing hand of this classic composer.

THE PIANO SONATA

To the instruments already existing and popular in the Baroque was added the piano, or fortepiano, as it was usually known, invented by the Italian harpsichord maker Cristofori about 1710. Designated by him as "harpsichords which could play both loud *(forte)* and soft *(piano),*" these instruments in continuously improved form superseded the dynamically inexpressive harpsichord from about the 1780's until by the turn of the century the older instrument had almost disappeared. This change was not without struggle on the part of harpsichord makers, however, who invented various devices to control the volume of sound at the desire of the player. None of them worked so well, however, as the direct control of the fortepiano player over the force with which he pressed the keys of that instrument. The old clavichord, which could produce sounds of varied dynamic range at the will of the performer, retained its popularity for home use, but in the end finally gave up to the less delicate and more sonorous tone of the piano. The composers of the *empfindsamer* school exploited the expressive capabilities of the clavichord to the fullest extent before its demise, particularly Carl Philipp Emanuel Bach (1714-1788). His sonatas, intended especially for this instrument or the early piano, were highly expressive and effective compositions of the *empfindsamer* and *Sturm und Drang* styles which influenced Haydn and Beethoven profoundly in their approaches to writing for the keyboard.

Essentially, the change in style from the Baroque harpsichord idiom to that of the piano is representative of the shift from the formality, precision, clarity and reason of the early eighteenth century to the moody, individual, shifting emotional states characteristic of nineteenth century Romanticism. The Classic might even be defined as that short time in which the expressive elements were in equilibrium with the older concepts of clarity and formality, although these were embodied in new structures, most important of which was the sonata-allegro. Technically, the discursive development and extension of a few motives in Baroque music, together with the static aesthetics of the Doctrine of the Affections, was replaced by the short, simple and varied melodic phrases of the rococo, supported by simple, unobtrusive (and usually thematically unimportant) accompaniment. One important writer on the sonata, William S. Newman (see bibliography), points out that the rococo really exists in two phases: the early one, characterized by much of the music of Couperin, with its high degree of ornamentation, and the second one in which the ornamentation is reduced and the simpler phrase style has replaced the continuously expanding motivic work of the Baroque. It is this second style, combined with expressive elements derived from the opera buffa and the *empfindsamer* and *Sturm und Drang* schools that characterize what we call the Classic sonata.

The typical three or four movement structure of the sonata was the work of a great many lesser-known composers who used a great degree of freedom in the structure of the single forms and in their deployment as movements. The tempo sequence of the movements was usually Fast-Slow-Fast, with a minuet of moderate pace inserted between the second and third movements if a four-movement work was desired. Although there are a few sonatas whose first movement consists of a theme and variations in moderato tempo, the sonata-allegro form usually occupies this position. If the sonata has three movements, the last is sometimes the minuet and trio, otherwise the forms are those given as possible for the symphony on page 216. The relationship of the sonatas of Haydn and Mozart, with their individual movements to the "fused" compound form of Beethoven, also is comparable to the symphonies of these masters.

The choice of examples for analysis is difficult because of the wide range of style and organization of the sonatas for piano of the three Viennese masters. The following are offered, however, as showing the more important features of their writing.

Haydn: *Sonata in C Sharp Minor*, Hoboken Catalogue XVI/No. 36 (Composed before 1780) (Example V-8).

Of the 52 sonatas of Haydn, 21 fall into the three movement (F-S-F) category, while there are only 8 in two movements and 3 in four movements. Of the 52, 18 include a minuet as the second or third movement, and slow movements cast in variation form are quite frequent. The three movement sonata we have chosen exhibits Haydn's experimental approach to both the single forms of the movement and to the compound form. The style is the free idiomatic writing characteristic of the *empfindsamer* manner, and the music abounds in dynamic contrasts, abrupt shifts of key and expressive melodic elements. It is, perhaps, more effective upon the piano than it would be on either the harpsichord or the clavichord, at least to modern ears.

I. *Moderato, C Sharp Minor.* The first movement is an economical sonata-allegro form in which almost every motive of the first six measures receives some sort of development during the course of the movement. The development proceeds in two sections, separated by a dramatic pause, and further development takes place in the recapitulation. This aspect of the work is Haydn's, of course, but the debt to C. P. E. Bach is apparent in the *empfindsamer* style of the movement.

II. *Scherzando:* Allegro con brio. Theme and Variation form. Haydn's experimental attitude is displayed in here placing a fast set of variations (a rather unusual tempo for such a form) between two moderately-paced movements. Furthermore, there are two complete binary-form themes, one in A major, the other in A minor. The variations follow the form and harmony of the themes quite closely, and the first four measures of the A major theme reappear from time to time, rather in the manner of the French rondeau we heard in Couperin's *Passacaille*.

EXAMPLE V-8: Haydn: *Sonata No. 36, C Sharp Minor.*

III. *Menuetto:* Moderato. The rather severe yet elegant Menuet is in rounded binary form in C sharp minor, while the warmer and more relaxed Trio is binary and in the rather unusual key, for this period, of C sharp major.

Other samplings of the various moods and styles to be found in the Haydn sonatas might include the almost Beethovenian power of No. 52, matching it against the more rococo elegance of Nos. 35 and 37. But all exhibit the experimental, youthfully inquiring spirit of this master, just as the symphonies and chamber music do.

Mozart: *Sonata in B Flat Major,* K. 333 (Composed in 1778) (Example V-9).

If we grant the influence of C. P. E. Bach on the keyboard music of Haydn, we must grant the similar effect of the music and friendship of Johann Christian Bach (1735-1782) on Mozart's compositions. This man, the "London Bach," had worked out his personal style in Italy, a keyboard treatment *par excellence* based upon the vocal music of opera and the facile idioms of minor Italian masters. Mozart met him in London in 1765. But the influence of J. C. Bach on Mozart is more subtle than his brother's on Haydn, mainly because the Italian style which Mozart had assimilated already had none of the eccentricities of the *empfindsamer* aesthetic, none of the sharp contrasts, the almost arbitrary wrenches in the music upon which its particular expressivity

EXAMPLE V-9: Mozart, *Sonata in B Flat Major,* K. 333.

depends. The J. C. Bach and Mozart styles seek to move the listener by pure beauty of melody, restrained yet effective harmony and idiomatic keyboard writing that "lies under the hand." The romantic passages are rather few, although it must be admitted that the great *Fantasia* and the *Sonata in C-minor (K. 475 and 457)* are works which lie closer to the expression of Beethoven than is usual with Mozart. But it is this *seeming* simplicity that has so often led the unwary listener to undervalue Mozart's piano music. Even the pianist thinks "this will be easy to play"——until he tries to cope with it. The notes *are* easy, but this is only the beginning of the problem, for one is led by them into depths in which only the most sensitive and able musicianship can comprehend and recreate the musical image.

I. *Allegro*, B-flat major. Sonata-allegro form.

    Fifteen out of Mozart's sixteen piano sonatas are cast in three movement form, of which this is an example. The profusion of thematic material, once it is examined analytically, is rather bewildering, but one is not conscious of the luxuriance upon hearing the movement, so organically are the parts related. The closing section occupies a rather large space proportionately, and concludes with a typical trill on the dominant and short cadence figures. The development includes a section which is not thematically derived, and the circular transition is much extended; otherwise, the movement follows Mozart's usual procedures.

II. *Andante cantabile*, E-flat major. Sonata-allegro form.

    Four expressive and lyric themes occupy the exposition, the second belonging to the transition and the fourth to the closing section. The development is short but concentrated—— more so than that of the first movement where development is expected. But the important quality is the singing nature of Mozart's melodic line, straight from the opera.

III. *Allegretto grazioso*, B-flat major. Rondo, with cadenza.

    The rondo is a sectional form, with alternations of new material and a principal theme, often symbolized as A-B-A-C-A (five-part rondo). This form frequently is encountered in final movements, particularly those of concertos. History does not tell us whether this particular movement was intended by Mozart to conclude a concerto which was never finished, or whether it is an experiment in the sonata form. Be that as it may, the movement includes a written-out cadenza in concerto-style, together with the typical orchestral preparation for such a display passage.

The A theme is first understated (in the concerto, by the solo alone), then presented loudly, as though the orchestra has taken it up. B is an opera buffa theme and closes with a long trill. The C section begins in minor but moves later to a warmer section in major, and is characterized by a theme with wide leaps. Between these sections is transitional material, often dominant in harmony which arouses expectation of the tonic key and the A theme. The cadenza is prepared concerto fashion, and develops some of the material briefly before exploding into scales and trills. A short coda finishes after the A theme has returned, somewhat reinforced in sonority.

It is clear from this and other sonatas by this composer, that he is not overly concerned with thematic development or the projection of moods of struggle or high elation. Rather, he seeks to place before us mildly contrasting or interrelated musical events which somehow are organically cohesive, although the way that this is accomplished often defies analysis. The piano style is more adept and fluid than Haydn's, difficult in its simplicity and full of pitfalls for the unwary player. Like the calm water over great depths, the serenity and olympian beauty of this music may cause the casual listener to miss the significance of what Mozart has to say.

The Beethoven Piano Sonatas

The thirty-two piano sonatas of Beethoven form a more important portion of his musical production than do those of either Haydn or Mozart when compared to their symphonies, string quartets or operas. The piano had become, by Beethoven's time and partly through his exploitation of it, the vehicle for the most profound and intimate expression of the individual. The resources of the instrument had been developed gradually until by the second decade of the nineteenth century it was only a little less sonorous than the grand piano of today. The rapidity of the repeating action had been improved, and the possibility of dynamics from a sonorous fortissimo to the merest whisper could be realized by a skillful player. Beethoven took full advantage of this instrument, exploiting the full range of tone, introducing rapid dynamic contrasts, inventing new accompaniments and creating a new style of writing for the piano. His piano works parallel the symphonies in their expressive aims and in comparative size, although some of the formal experiments seem to be made first in the keyboard works, later in the ensemble music.

The first piano sonata is a good counterpart to the First Symphony. Here as there, we find the same originality, the same formal mastery and the same debt to previous composers, particularly to Haydn. But in the subjectivity of the Adagio movement and at places in the vigorous *prestissimo* finale the rugged composer of the later sonatas is forecast.

Sonata No. 8, Op. 13, in C minor ("Pathetique") (Example V-10).

 I. *Grave: Allegro di molto e con brio,* C minor. Sonata-allegro.

  Note the intense dramatic expression from the very beginning, the thicker and darker sonority, the bold use of chord masses, colors and dissonance, dynamic contrasts and the expression throughout of forward-driving energy. The sonata-allegro form is dislocated for expressive purposes by the return of the dramatic introductory material and the changes of tempo. The key relationships are now those of the third away, together with the usual dominant.

 II. *Adagio cantabile,* A flat major (third relationship to C minor). Rondo form.

  This is a typically subjective slow movement by this composer, richly and satisfyingly harmonized. It offers relief from the energy of the first movement and an expressive foil to it. The form is A-B-A-C-A, rondo.

 III. *Allegro,* C minor. Rondo (A-B-A-C-A-B-A-coda).

  Somewhat more "classical" in treatment of the piano than the first movement, but suitably energetic and headlong despite the thinner sonority. The return of the B section is merged with the preceding A, making that section a little shorter than before. Note the tension aroused by the transitions preceding the A section and how Beethoven employs this for the coda.

Sonata No. 23, F Minor, Op. 57 ("Appassionata") (Example V-11).

 I. *Allegro assai,* F minor, sonata-allegro.

  This demonic movement employs three important themes of mutually contrasting character, the second of which, more lyric and "noble" in character, is symbolically broken off before reaching its cadence. Other subsidiary ideas also are important, not only as "cement" between major sections, but also as motives capable of bearing development. There is much highly inventive accompaniment and passage work. Note the motive of the Fifth Symphony.

EXAMPLE V-10: Beethoven, *Sonata No. 8*, Op. 13.

FIRST MOVEMENT: Introduction

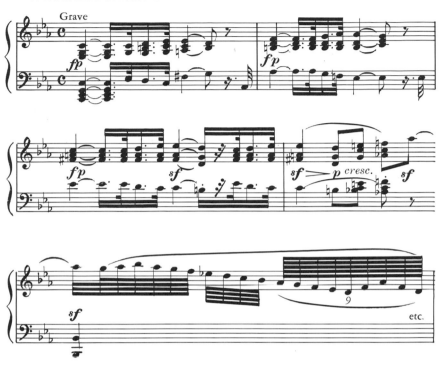

(BEGINNING OF THE BODY OF THE MOVEMENT)

SECOND MOVEMENT

THIRD MOVEMENT

EXAMPLE V-11: Beethoven, *Piano Sonata No. 23*, Op. 57.

FIRST MOVEMENT

Allegro assai

II. *Andante con moto,* D flat major, theme and variations.

   Again a static movement as in No. 13, but more pro-
nounced due to the slowly moving chords and the small harmonic vocabulary used. The note-value of the moving parts of
each variation is twice as fast as that of the preceding one, and
each begins in a higher region of the keyboard, returning to
the low, dark range near the end of the movement. Note the
dramatic use of the deceptive cadence *(cf., Symphony No. 5)*
which forms the harmony for the bridge to the final movement.

SECOND MOVEMENT

THIRD MOVEMENT
Allegro ma non troppo
theme

III. *Allegro ma non troppo*, F minor, sonata-allegro form.

The rushing arpeggio-scale theme, together with the short chords which combine with it form the basic material of this movement. The contrasts of key and theme are almost obliterated, and the sectional boundaries of the form are for the most part erased in favor of the almost insensate energy. Even short sections of polyphony do not impede the motion but are forced to submit to it. The rise and fall of the dynamic level within wide limits make this movement resemble the tension and momentarily harnessed energy of a volcano ready to erupt. Note that while this movement counterbalances the first in many ways, one senses that it is not finished but rather moves out of hearing as darkly energetic as ever.

Sonata No. 28, A Major, Op. 101 (Example V-12).

I. *Etwas lebhaft, und mit der innigsten Empfindung.* (Allegretto, ma non troppo), A major, sonata-allegro form.

What a contrast between the preceding work and this one! This lyric, deceptively simple-sounding movement would seem to predate the "Appassionata" until we examine the depth of its simplicity and the subtlety of its form. And yet we must remember that not all of the works of the middle period years are heaven-storming, and that there are also moments of peace, meditation and quiet movement. Note in this third period sonata the economy of material, the play of sonority resulting from unusual chord spacings and opposed registers of the keyboard, and the fusion of the sections of the form into a gentle continuity.

II. *Lebhaft, Marschmässig* (Vivace, alla Marcia), March and Trio.

This is a jaunty, somewhat humorous march using dotted rhythms and subtle syncopations. Despite the fact that it is a march, the mood is intimate, not martial or brilliant. Idiomatic piano style, but it requires very careful playing and attention to dynamics and outlining of the phrases of uneven lengths. Note the frequent wide spacings between the hands. The Trio uses canon, but in a very discreet manner.

III. *Langsam und sehnsuchtsvoll* (Adagio, ma non troppo, con affetto), Free.

The first measure of this section——really not a *formal* movement——provides the melodic pattern which the following measures develop expressively, reaching a cadenza finally which concludes with a reminiscence of the opening of the first movement. Essentially a slow movement, this section resembles

EXAMPLE V-12: Beethoven, *Sonata No. 28*, Op. 101.

FIRST MOVEMENT

SECOND MOVEMENT

THIRD MOVEMENT

INTRODUCTION AND FOURTH MOVEMENT

Zeitmaass des ersten Stückes.

Tempo del primo pezzo; tutto il Cembalo ma piano

Alle Saiten

Geschwind, doch nicht zu sehr, und mit Entschlossenheit

the typical Beethoven meditations of other sonatas and symphonies, full of feeling and seriousness.

IV. *Geschwind, doch nicht zu sehr, und mit Entschlossenheit.* (Allegro, with decision), Sonata-allegro.

As we might expect, the boundaries of this sonata-allegro are smoothed over in the interests of continuity. The first motive of the main theme is developed fugally in rather unidiomatic piano writing. This is one of the indications that in the coming sonatas, Beethoven is going to write what the music demands, not necessarily what the player can play easily! The recapitulation is partly rewritten, and the movement ends with a quietly humorous coda, again exploiting widely separated sonorities. The whole sonata uses the now familiar key relation of thirds. Not all of the last sonatas are of the gentle lyricism and happiness of this one; it was chosen partly for its brevity, partly because it is an accessible introduction to the third period style, and partly to correct any notion that may have arisen which pictures Beethoven constantly storming and struggling against Fate in his music.

CHAMBER MUSIC

The Classic era was the heyday of chamber music. Widespread musical culture and the rise of the devoted amateur performer contributed in a large measure to the creation of hundreds of compositions for various small ensembles of strings and winds with or without piano. This music has been compared to the conversation of friends, an intimate give-and-take of thematic material and a sharing of accompaniment duties. It was not always so, for in the growth of chamber music from the early eighteenth century models, the interest first centered in the upper part, with accompaniment drudgery assigned to the middle instruments and a harmonic bass holding up the entire structure. The string quartet, which owes its ancestry to these works for string orchestra, reached a crisis in the 1750's, particularly illustrated in the quartets of Haydn. This pioneer sought to break the hold of the first violin on the ensemble by writing movements in fugal style, reverting to the polyphony inherited from the Baroque as a means of equalizing the duties of all members of the group. This led to further development in breaking down the strictness of the continuous four-voice counterpoint into what we might call dialogue polyphony, the conversation spoken of earlier. This "broken-work" texture was, of course, used in his orchestral writing as well, and was adopted by other composers, becoming the characteristic technique of the period.

Of the various combinations of instruments used in chamber music, the string quartet came to be most favored. It offered a challenge to composers, for within the limited possibilities of such a group, reliance had to be placed upon the quality of the music itself, regardless of technical tricks. It was not a miniature orchestra, and bad music could not be made attractive by colorful instrumentation or large masses of sound. Everything was transparently audible, and mistakes——at least by the composer——were not to be tolerated!

Haydn wrote string quartets throughout his life, finding the medium responsive to some of his most advanced ideas. Mozart studied the quartets of the older master and, by his own admission, learned to write in this medium by following the examples. Beethoven, born into the already accomplished high Classic style, created what are undoubtedly the finest and most profound compositions in the literature, unequaled until those of Béla Bartók appeared in the twentieth century.

All three of the Viennese masters wrote for other combinations of instruments as well as the string quartet. Most notable of these are the four fine string quintets, the marvelous clarinet quintet and the two piano quartets written by Mozart.

Haydn: *String Quartet in D Major, Op. 64, No. 5,* ("The Lark") (Example V-13).

I. *Allegro moderato,* sonata-allegro form.

Haydn has constructed two complementary themes, the first of which appears alone, then as accompaniment for the other, which soars above it like the lark for which the quartet is named. The development section uses all of the important themes from the exposition, and this process is continued in the first section of the recapitulation, while the second section more closely resembles the treatment in the exposition.

EXAMPLE V-13: Haydn, *String Quartet, Op. 64, No. 5.*

II. *Adagio cantabile,* ternary form.

The first (A) section is in binary form, and the second (B) develops one of the motives of the A section in the parallel minor. When A returns, the melody is rather highly ornamented.

II. Adagio cantabile

III. *Menuetto* and *Trio.*

The Minuet is a rounded binary form with rather odd proportions (I-8 meas., II-18 meas., coda—16 meas.), but Haydn manages to make them sound balanced. The Trio is in the parallel minor key (A minor), is not rounded, and derives its opening theme from the last scale figure of the minuet.

IV. Finale: *Vivace,* Ternary form.

This is a "perpetual motion" movement, with rapidly running scale patterns throughout. The B section is based upon the imitation of a syncopated subject combined with the rapid notes, and which is used in a clever stretto passage. The energy increases with the return of the A section and the combination of all the instruments in the rapid scale work.

IV. Vivace

Mozart: *Quartet in A Major, K. 464.* Example (V-14).

The six quartets which Mozart dedicated to Haydn, of which this is one, show his assimilation of the development techniques and their combination with his opera buffa style. These six quartets represent the apex of his achievements in the medium, and the one chosen here reveals clearly how well he understood Haydn's "new and special manner" and even found ways to improve upon his model.

I. *Allegro*, Sonata-allegro form.

As usual, the form is crystal-clear, but more space than usual is devoted to the development of the first theme and its rhythmic motive and especially toward the end of the development imitative work with the second theme.

EXAMPLE V-14: Mozart, *String Quartet*, K. 464.

II. *Menuetto* and *Trio,* Compound ternary form.

    The Minuet is fashioned out of two simple ideas: the first appears twice at the beginning of the movement, and the second is the rhythmic figure which follows. These become charmingly involved with each other as the movement progresses. For contrast, the Trio is neither polyphonic nor developmental.

II. Menuetto

III. *Andante,* Theme and seven variations.

    These are more complex variations than one usually expects from Mozart. Although the harmony of the theme is largely retained in each variation, the melody tends to disappear, leaving only fragmentary traces. The fourth variation is in the parallel minor key.

III.   Andante

IV. *Allegro non troppo,* Sonata-allegro.

    This movement is an essay in symphonic economy, making as much out of as little material as possible. Like the first movement, it uses a great deal of imitative polyphony. The opening chromatic scale fragment and the rhythmic motive which appears twice after it (*cf.* rhythmic motive of the first movement) permeate the entire movement, relieved by nonthematic broken chords, repeated notes, and short cadence figures. The fusion of the "learned" and *galant* styles in this movement point

the way to the magnificent integration of them in the finale of
the "Jupiter" *Symphony No. 41.*

Beethoven: *Quartet in E-Flat Major, Op. 74,* ("The Harp")
(Example V-15).

This work was composed in 1809, the year of the siege of Vienna by
Napoleon. More important to music lovers, it was the year of three
great creations in the key of E flat by Beethoven: the *Fifth Piano Concerto, Op. 73,* the *Piano Sonata, Op. 81a* ("Les Adieux") and this
quartet. It also represents the beginning of the transition from the
desperate years after 1801 during which Beethoven faced his growing
deafness with anger, despair and thoughts of suicide. But in 1809 he
finally had realized that while his affliction separated him from humanity, it did not hinder the composition of music. He had transcended his
deafness and looked with assurance to the future. Indeed, assurance
and more is the tonality of the "Egmont" music, the *Seventh* and
Eighth Symphonies, the *String Quartet, Op. 95* and the works in E flat
already mentioned. And there are moments——the introduction and
parts of the Adagio of the E flat quartet, for example——when something else shows through, a glimpse of the ecstatic calm and mystic
experience out of which the great last works were written. Janus-like,
then, this string quartet is a summation of the past and a portent of
the future.

I. Introduction: *Poco adagio. Allegro.* Sonata-allegro with introduction.

The lyric introduction emphasizes the subdominant key,
and by this instability makes the arrival of the tonic most satisfactory. The thematic material consists of four ideas noted as
A, B, C and D in Example V-16, which are developed consistently in the central section of the movement and in the coda.

The A motive gives rise to the more extended arpeggios from which the work gets its nickname.

EXAMPLE V-15: Beethoven, *String Quartet*, Op. 74.

II. *Adagio, ma non troppo.* Variation-rondo form.

This is one of the movements in which the techniques and expression of Beethoven's last period compositions are forecast. The music is purified of the *clichés* of the *empfindsamer* style, and is more classically poised and interwoven in texture. The form is one which Haydn had used, a rondo——

A-B-A'-C-A"-Coda——in which each appearance of the main
section is a variation of it. The movement increases in complexity of accompaniment and melodic embellishment, but the
coda returns to a simpler texture and melodic state.

III. *Presto*. Scherzo and Trio, extended by repetition.

The principal thematic idea in the construction of this
movement is the rhythmic motto of the *Fifth Symphony* to
which accompaniment and harmonic figures are added. The
proportions of Section I to II are 8 to 68 measures! The Trio
is played faster and is more linear in its technique. The alternations of exact repetitions of the Scherzo and Trio are:
S-T-S-T-S-Coda. The coda is entered by a deceptive cadence
and builds through repeated notes to a dominant seventh chord
(V^7) which, according to Beethoven's directions to the players,
leads directly to the last movement without pause.

IV. *Allegretto con Variazioni*. Theme and Variations.

There are six variations in this movement, plus a long coda
which accelerates near the end. The theme is made up almost
entirely of a dotted-note figure, which, contrary to expectations, Beethoven does not develop. Each variation except the
sixth is founded firmly upon the harmonic progression of the

theme, but new melodic figures are evolved from the theme melody in each variation. The sixth one abandons even that! These, then, are *developmental variations*, comparable to those in the finale of the *Third Symphony* in technique.

IV. Allegretto con variazioni

Vln. I p cresc.

cresc. f

VOCAL MUSIC OF THE CLASSIC PERIOD

Opera

At the beginning of the eighteenth century, Italian opera held sway over the theaters of all Europe excepting France. The *opera seria* had become somewhat more serious through the elimination of all irrelevancies, including the occasional comic scenes, by the reforming zeal of Apostolo Zeno (1668-1750) and Pietro Metastasio (1698-1782), both court poets in Vienna. The latter was the most famous writer of opera *libretti* during the period, and composers repeatedly set his works to music. The comedy, now expelled from the opera itself, appeared as *intermezzi* between the acts of the opera, resulting in two simultaneous productions. The comic interludes were first patterned after the Renaissance *commedia dell' arte*, with improvised situations and dialogue, both taken from common life, and songs of a popular nature. They became popular enough to become independent of the serious opera, and, with dialogue set to recitative, became known as *opera buffa*, or comic operas. While the *opera seria* continued the practice of the Doctrine of the Affections in limiting each aria to a single emotion, the comic works quickly adopted the techniques of the rococo style, adapted them to the rapidly changing situations of comedy and eventually perfected the style into a means of depicting not only comedy, but also more serious and tender emotions. The influence of the sonata was felt, also, and the rigid *da capo* aria, while sometimes used, more often was replaced by the flexible and dramatic forms which were simultaneously evolving in instrumental music. The *opera buffa* style is an integration, then, and the debt cannot be assigned to either instrumental or operatic music alone. Important composers who helped to perfect the *opera buffa* were Pergolesi (1710-1736), who wrote the delightful intermezzo *La serva padrona* (1733), Galuppi (1706-1785), who, with the dramatist Goldoni removed the improvisatory nature of the early intermezzi, Paisiello (1740-1816), whose setting of *The Barber of Seville* (1782) Rossini had to contend with in 1816, Cimarosa (1749-1801) the composer of *Il matrimonio segreto*, and, of course, the crowning composer of the genre, Mozart, among whose *opere buffe* may be singled out such masterpieces as *The Marriage of Figaro* (1786), *Così fan tutte* ("Thus Do They All," 1790) and *Don Giovanni* (1787).

Let us examine some of the opening scene of *The Marriage of Figaro* in order to learn how the *opera buffa* style is used. As we have remarked, the baroque opera technique is rigid, while that of the classic *opera buffa* is flexible. The older style might be compared to the telling of a story with the use of photographic slides, while the *opera buffa* is that of the motion picture. The new style accomplished in one movement of binary or sonata form what would have required several arias in the opera seria. The main plot of *The Marriage of Figaro* is concerned with the intrigues surrounding the marriage of Figaro and Susanna, valet and maid respectively to the Count and Countess Almaviva. The Count, notorious for his extramarital love affairs, has his eye on Susanna, as she is well aware. The adolescent page, Cherubino, has a typical crush on the Countess, and shows a positive genius for being discovered in the wrong places by the Count, who, despite his affairs, is extremely jealous and suspicious of his wife. The main part of the opera is devoted to the outwitting of the Count by Figaro, Susanna and the Countess, all pursuing rather different plans. The sub-plot concerns Dr. Bartolo, a busybody musician who abets the Count, and Marcellina, an elderly spinster who has matrimonial designs on Figaro.

In our analysis of the opening scene, we shall use the usual Roman numerals to signify the keys of sections, the capital letters A, B, C, etc. for themes, and *mod.* for modulation to a new key. These symbols will parallel the text, which is not intended for singing, but as a more literal translation of the original Italian than is usually possible for performance purposes. The music may be followed in a vocal score if desired.

Le Nozze di Figaro ("The Marriage of Figaro"), Libretto by Da Ponte,
  Music by Mozart

OVERTURE: Sonatina form, musical idioms in the opera buffa style,
  which, by their mobility, symphonic character and dynamic fluctuations clearly forecast that the opera to follow is a comedy of
  intrigue. This movement is one of the clearest sonatinas in the
  Classic literature, showing three thematic groups (First, Second
  and Closing Themes), as well as the rapid retransition to the Recapitulation typical of the sonatina.

ACT I

No. 1: Duet between Figaro and Susanna (Example V-16). The Count
  has given them the room in which we find them, and Figaro is pac-
  ing it off while Susanna tries on a hat before a mirror. Note how
  Figaro's "measuring theme" (A) gradually is replaced by Susanna's
  lyric theme (B) as she gains his attention, and how their affection
  is symbolized in the latter sections of the movement by their singing together in harmony.

I, A,B:
  Introduction by the orchestra
I, A:
  Figaro:
    Five . . . ten . . . twenty . . . thirty . . . thirty-six . . . forty-
    three . . .
I, B:
  Susanna:
    Yes, I'm pleased with that,
    It seems just made for me.
I, A&B:
  Susanna:
    Do look here, dear Figaro *(repeat four times)*
Mod. V
  Figaro:
    Five . . . ten . . . twenty . . . thirty . . . thirty-six . . . forty-three.
  Susanna:
    Look at my hat, dear Figaro; don't you think it's lovely?
V, B:
  Figaro:
    Yes, my dearest, it's very pretty;
    It looks just made for you
V:
  Susanna:
    Do look here
  Figaro:
    Yes, my dear
    (This is repeated until she really does get his attention)

V *mod.* I:

> Figaro and Susanna:
>> Yes, I think it suits you (me) nicely,
>> It looks just made for you (me).

I, B:

> Susanna and Figaro:
>> On this morning of our wedding
>> How delightful to your (my) dear one
>> Is this charming little hat
>> Which Susanna made herself.

The form of this duet, then, resolves itself into a binary structure in which Section I takes two forms: first, the variety which does not modulate, and second, the variety which does. The orchestral introduction may be disregarded, although musically, it is the same as the first sung section. Note how the climax, both musically and emotionally, is reached at the retransition, with the tension of the dominant waiting to resolve. Here we have a clever musical parallel with the dramatic situation.

EXAMPLE V-16: Diagram of No. 1, Duet, Figaro and Susanna.

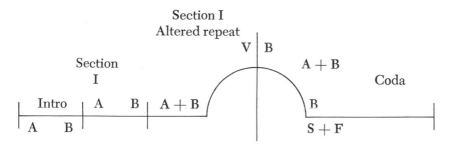

No. 2: Recitative (secco) and Duet. Susanna asks what Figaro is doing, and he informs her that the Count has generously given them this room for their bedroom. Susanna says that if this is so, he can sleep there alone. Upon Figaro's questioning, Susanna replies that she has her reasons, whereupon he tries to prove that it's the ideal place for them, in the following aria.

This aria, of true symphonic unity, cannot be tied down to any strict structural formula, since it not only characterizes Figaro and Susanna, but also, by its changing keys and themes, shows alternate possibilities which the situation of the room has suggested to the quick-witted feminine instincts of Susanna, (Example V-17).

I, A:

> Introduction by the orchestra
>
> Figaro:
>> Supposing one evening
>> My lady should want you,
>> *(repeat preceding line)*
>> Din, din! Din, Din!

Mod. to V:

> What a long way you found it before!
>> *(Figaro, taking every situation at face value, then thinks of the obvious alternate possibility, set in the simple contrasting key)*

V, B:

> Figaro:
>> Or else, if I'm summoned
>> To go to his lordship
>> *(Repeat)*
>> Din, din! Din, din!

Mod. to I:

> In three leaps I'm there at his door.

(The music immediately modulates to VI, the related minor, showing not only the contrast of Susanna's grasp of the situation, but also the difference between her character and that of Figaro).

VI, A¹:

> Susanna:
>> Supposing one morning
>> The dear Count should ring,
>> *(Repeat)*
>> Din, din! Din, din!
>> And send you three miles away,
>> Din, din! Din, din!

Mod. to I,A:

>> Din, din, and the devil
>> Should lead him to my door
>> In three leaps . . .
>
> Figaro:
>> Susanna, No more!
>> *(Repeat)*

> ⌈Susanna:
> ⎨   And here, in three leaps! Din, din! Din, din!
> ⎪Figaro:
> ⌊   No more! No more!

I: Recitative

> Susanna:
>> Now listen . . .
>
> Figaro:
>> Quick, tell me!

I, C:

> Susanna:

> If you want to hear the rest, *(repeat)*
> Forget your suspicions which do me wrong.

I, C: *(Repetition of the preceding)*

> Figaro:
>> Tell me the rest, *(repeat)*
>> Doubts and suspicions freeze me . . .

Coda: IV, D:

> Susanna:
>> Dismiss your suspicions
>> Figaro:
>> Doubts and suspicions freeze me
>> *(Repetition of the above in duet)*

I: *(Continuing repetition)*

I, A: *(Closing cadences, to the above words)*

The following formal diagram of this duet may assist in following the close cooperation of situation, character and music.

EXAMPLE V-17

Recitative: Susanna reveals to the almost incredulous Figaro that the Count, with the help of Don Basilio, the music master, is wooing her. Figaro resolves in the next recitative and aria to outwit the Count.

Recitative: Figaro. This is not a secco, but an accompanied recitative, which adds to its expressiveness.

> Bravo, my noble master! Now I begin to understand the secret, and to see your whole scheme clearly; to London you go as minister, I as courier, and Susanna . . . confidential attachée . . .
> It shall not be! Figaro has said it!

Aria, Figaro. Rounded Binary, with an insertion of a new section between the Retransition and the Recapitulation.

I, A:

> If, my dear Count, You feel like dancing, *(repeat)*
> You may go dancing, but I'll play the tune *(repeat)*

Mod. V:

> If you'll attend my school,
> I'll teach you how to caper!

V, B: *(repeat of above two lines)*

Mod. V⁷:

　　I'll know how *(repeat four times)*

Mod. VI:

　　But wait . . . *(repeat)*

(Pause, then the inserted section in new (duple) meter, faster tempo, reflecting an outburst of anger)

I:

　　By dissembling, by pretending, by mocking, by stinging——

　　I'll reverse the mechanism of this little joke! *(repeat)*

I, A: As at the beginning.

　　If, my dear Count, you feel like dancing *(repeat)*

　　You may go dancing, but I'll play the tune, yes, I'll play the tune.

Codetta, presto, orchestra alone.

　　The following diagram traces the course of Figaro's resolve, here resembling somewhat the *da capo* aria, but with more freedom.

EXAMPLE V-18

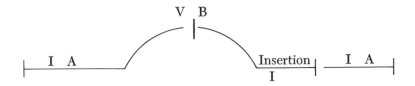

　　In these three musical numbers, then, we see the adaptability of the classic binary forms to the changing situations called for in comedy. This is reflected throughout this charming opera, sometimes being used for the construction of large, continuous and coherent sections of music, such as the trio of No. 7, where a full-fledged sonata-allegro appears, the two sonata-allegro forms of the finale to Act II, before Figaro enters, the marvelous sextet later in this act, and the moralizing conclusion to Act III. The whole opera abounds in illustrations of the aptness of music and form to the expression of the words at any moment.

　　The French, however, with the strong tradition of Lully and Rameau still active, refused to accept entirely the new Italian opera, and a performance of Pergolesi's *La serva padrona* in Paris by a touring Italian troupe *(Bouffons)* in 1752 set off a lively argument concerning the relative merits of the Italian and French styles. In this "War of the Bouffons," the queen and the intellectuals held that the naturalness and charm of the Italian opera were superior to the stilted and artificial situations of the French, while the king and Mme. Pompadour stood with tradition. As has been pointed out, the comparison was not really valid, since *comic* opera was being compared with opera *seria,* but the quarrels had the effect of stimulating interest in the composition of a new popular French style.

A similar outburst attended the arrival of Gluck (1714-1787) in Paris in 1773, when he was pitted against an Italian composer, Piccinni (1728-1800), in the arena of the *opera seria.* This was essentially a contest of the old against the new, for Gluck, together with his gifted librettist had created in 1762 a really classical opera, *Orféo ed Euridice,* on the same subject as Monteverdi's path-breaking work. He continued this style in *Alceste* (1768), *Armide* (1777) and his masterpiece, *Iphigenie en Aulide* (1779). When he published the score to *Alceste,* Gluck prefaced the music with a dedication which includes this summary of his aims:

When I undertook to write the music for *Alceste,* I resolved to divest it entirely of all those abuses, introduced into it either by the mistaken vanity of singers or by the too great complaisance of composers, which have so long disfigured Italian opera and made of the most splendid and most beautiful of spectacles the most ridiculous and wearisome. I have striven to restrict music to its true office of serving poetry by means of expression and by following the situations of the story, without interrupting the action or stifling it with a useless superfluity of ornaments; . . . I have felt that the

PLATE XVIII. *Bust of Gluck by Houdon. This sculptor excelled in the portrait bust. (Courtesy of Service de Documentation Photographique des Musées Nationaux.)*

overture ought to apprise the spectators of the nature of the action that is to be represented, and to form, so to speak, its argument; that the concerted instruments should be introduced in proportion to the interest and intensity of the words, and not leave that sharp contrast between the aria and the recitative in the dialogue, so as not to break a period unreasonably nor wantonly disturb the force and heat of the action.

Furthermore, I believed that my greatest labor should be devoted to seeking a beautiful simplicity, and I have avoided making displays of difficulty at the expense of clearness; nor did I judge it desirable to discover novelties if it was not naturally suggested by the situation and the expression; and there is no rule which I have not thought it right to set aside willingly for the sake of an intended effect.

Gluck's adherence to these principles in the main created an operatic style of classic purity, perhaps the only really classic style in the Classic Period! One need only listen to the famous aria *"Che faró senza Euridice"* in *Orféo* to understand what Gluck was striving for. The noble simplicity and clarity, and the poignancy of the lament are all the more effective for being restrained. The interruption by recitative only heightens the effectiveness of the song. Other arias in the work, however, such as that one which closes the first act, while effective, hark back to the older style. Almost all of the recitative is melodious and accompanied by the orchestra, in contrast to the usual *buffa* and *seria secco* style. The use of the orchestra in commenting upon the action and in tone painting is, in its classic poise, far different from either *opera seria* or *buffa,* and led Berlioz to extol it in his treatise on orchestration in the nineteenth century.

Church Music, Secular Oratorio

What we have discovered about the use of style and forms in opera applies equally well to the music composed for the mass or oratorio, even though the situations do not change in these with the mercurial rapidity of opera buffa. There is no essential difference in musical style between the sacred and secular works of Haydn, Mozart and Beethoven, except that they reffect a seriousness of purpose and an elevation of the stylistic devices in proportion to the subject which they serve. Thus, we find arias, duets and other ensemble combinations in the masses and oratorios, combined with much homophonic and some polyphonic choral writing. Preeminent among such compositions are the two secular oratorios of Haydn, *The Creation* and *The Seasons,* and the various sacred compositions of Mozart, such as the *Mass in C Minor,* K. 427, the *Requiem Mass,* K. 626, the *Vesperae solemnes de confessore,* K. 339 and the motets *Exsultate, Jubilate,* K. 165 and *"Ave, verum corpus,"* K. 618. Beethoven's *Missa solemnis,* Op. 123, while showing the individual stylistic characteristics of this culminating composer of the Classic period, essentially without reference to the Italian operatic style, reflects the continuation of the tradition on a grand scale.

MUSIC AND THE OTHER ARTS

The artificial society of the Rococo produced only a few artists, and these were better than we might expect. Watteau and Fragonard owe a considerable debt to Rembrandt and Rubens, although they nowhere approach the passion and truth of either of those giants. The methods and organization of paintings of this time reflect those of the Baroque, but are miniaturized, refined and less vigorous. More detail, slightly less diffusion of line, fragmentation of masses into short, curved lines, more closed spatial suggestion and less action appear when we compare these paintings to those of the preceding period. But the difference is mostly one of degree, not of kind, and the choice of subject matter exerts a dominating influence similar to the importance of the melodic line in the music. When we examine paintings of these artists, such as Watteau's *L'Amour Paisable* (Plate XIX) we find scenes reflecting courtly sentiment, artificial manners, and an almost static quality. The fervor and tension of the Baroque is gone, and in its place we have delicate and restrained lyricism. The art of Boucher reveals even more clearly the elegance and formalism of the day. This artist was a favorite of Madame de Pompadour and painted many portraits of her. Chardin illustrates the bourgeois style with his genre paintings (Plate XX).

Few sculptors worth mentioning appear at this time. The only one in whom interest has survived is Houdon, whose works show strong classical tendencies. He is preeminently known for his portrait busts, and has transmitted to us the expressive likenesses of Gluck (Plate XVIII), Voltaire, Rameau, Frederick the Great and others.

Examples of rococo architecture are numerous: the salons of Louis XV, Mme. de Pompadour and Marie Antoinette; the Sans Souci Palace of Frederick the Great in Potsdam; the Great Gallery of the Schönbrunn Palace in Vienna (Plate XXI). All of these exhibit the delicacy and grace of ornament, the elegance of color associated with the dying days of the French monarchy.

PLATE XIX. "L'Amour Paisable" *by Watteau. A picnic portrayed in the typically elegant style of the French rococo. (Courtesy of the Archive-German Information Center.)*

The classic element in art of this day turned to rather cold and lifeless copies of Greek and Roman architecture and sculpture. There was no vital impulse in this dubious art, and it remained academic and sterile. In this style of painting the tendency is toward realism in that the lines are sharper and more angular, and there is severe use of light and shade. All unnecessary purely decorative elements are eliminated, and the subjects usually are taken from classic Greek or Roman history. Jacques Louis David represents this style in his *Oath of the Horatii* (Plate XXII) and other similar works.

If we are to make instructive comparisons between the music of the eighteenth century and the other arts of the period, we must realize constantly that the musical style in all cases is the result of a synthesis of the many modes of expression characteristic of the various subcultures of the time. We must also make allowance for the changes in the rococo style when practiced by a German and in the *opera buffa* style when employed by an Austrian. While it is seldom that an entire work is written in one single style, we may find movements or sections of works in which one style is so predominant as to render the comparison with the other arts on a more nearly equal basis.

PLATE XX. "The Blessing," *by Chardin. A typical genre painting extolling the pleasures of middle class life—the "bourgeois style" in art. (Courtesy of the French Cultural Services.)*

Such a movement, for example, is the first minuet of Mozart's *Divertimento in D-major for Horns and Strings,* K. 334. This music is almost a parody of the *style galant* and is comparable to paintings by Watteau (Plate XIX), Pater, Boucher, Lancret and Fragonard. The first and last movements belong to much the same category of popular "music for conversation" which the aristocratic patrons of these composers required. And many a finale of Haydn's sparkles with the verve and wit which have come to be the legendary qualities (possibly mythical too!) of these conversations between the intellectual elite and their princely patrons.

Mozart's *opera buffa* style has no parallel in the other arts except perhaps one of mood. Certain literary works of the time, especially plays in the comic vein, might, in the hands of accomplished actors, approach the rapid give and take of this style.

The *empfindsamer* style, less elegant than the rococo and *buffa,* appears in the music of Haydn, usually in slow movements of symphonies, sonatas and chamber music, and in some songs, such as his setting of "She Never Told Her Love" from Shakespeare's *Twelfth Night.* In Beethoven this style becomes the basis of two rather opposed emotional states—one of humor, as exhibited in the Sixth and Eighth

Symphonies, and the other a mood of mystic exaltation appearing in the slow movements of such works as the *Violin Concerto*, the *"Emperor" Concerto*, the *Ninth Symphony* and the *Bb String Quartet*, Op. 130.

The bourgeois style in the other arts, while it was not new to them, becomes of increasing importance in the time of growing social con-

PLATE XXI. *The Great Gallery in Schönbrunn Palace, Vienna. The relation of this charming rococo salon to the baroque style is plain but the heaviness, tension and architectural grandeur of the baroque is replaced by elegance, classical symmetry and lightness, both in color and in style. (Courtesy of the Austrian Information Service.)*

sciousness, and, while it sometimes takes on over-sentimental, coarse or erotic tones, must still be included in the productions of the period. It ranges from the biting satire of Hogarth to the cheap lechery of Greuze, passing along the way the purer sentiments of Chardin and Boilly whose paintings may be used as comparable to the musical examples, although often without the depth of feeling present in the music. Works by some of the earlier Dutch genre painters as well as some by Rembrandt seem to contain more comparable expressiveness.

PLATE XXII: *"The Oath of the Horatii" by Jacques David. A typical painting of the classic revival in France. Note the severe, balanced treatment, the noble theme and the emotional restraint. This type of classicism is very seldom found in the music of the Classic Period. (Courtesy of Service de Documentation Photographique des Musées Nationaux.)*

And the literary works of Voltaire, Rousseau, Richardson, Fielding, Goldsmith, Diderot and Lessing all sought middle-class readers through subject matter and style.

For examples of the "storm and stress" style in painting and sculpture we must look ahead to the Romantic era, to the works of Géricault, Delacroix, Ingres and their followers—free artists not controlled by the wishes of their princely patrons. But in the literature of the eighteenth century, in addition to some minor figures, we find the poets Herder and Schiller, and the young Goethe, all of whom produced stirring works which combined social revolt with tremendous imaginative force and agitation.

When we turn to Beethoven, the comparison with the other arts becomes more difficult, for no genius equivalent to the giant of Bonn appeared upon the contemporary scene in the plastic arts. If we make allowances, certain of the paintings of David show points for comparison (Plate XXII). In these pictures the subject matter is of distinction, the spatial organization is clear and forceful, and the statement of the "theme" is direct: all that is lacking is the genius to breathe life into the work. One of the great forces which helped to mold Beethoven's view of life was the revival of interest in the heritage of ideals from ancient Greece. These ideals he adopted wholeheartedly and tried to make his music express them: heroism, freedom and lofty moral tone. Beethoven had to enlarge the forms and sonorities of the traditional classic symphony in order for it to contain these large ideas. In the "Eroica" we find the elevation of the heroic ideal to unprecedented heights; and in the Ninth Symphony a total view of the life of man and his battle with fate. Possibly the only other creative figure of the times to bear comparison with Beethoven is the creator of Faust—Johann Wolfgang von Goethe. Both encompassed a world view and both struggled with the demon within themselves in order to present that view with classic clarity.

LIST OF TERMS

Rococo, *style galant*
Sturm und Drang
    (Storm and Stress)
Empfindsamer Stil
    (Sensibility style)
Opera buffa style
Learned style
thematic development
theme
Alberti bass, broken chord
    accompaniment
sonata principle
tension devices
formal symmetry
closed forms
Sonata, Symphony
transition, retransition
"circular" transition
codetta

parallel, relative minor keys
pianoforte
virtuoso performer
dialogue polyphony
developmental variations
fugato
motto theme
germ theme
symphonic economy
symphonic unity
psychological unity
programmatic unity
quotational unity
germinal unity
concert overture
developmental coda
Köchel Catalogue
divertimento
dominant preparation

BIBLIOGRAPHY

Haydn

Brevet, M., *Haydn*, London 1926.
Geiringer, K., *Haydn, A Creative Life in Music*, Norton, N.Y., 1946.

Mozart

Biancolli, L., *Mozart Handbook*. World, Cleveland, 1954.
Blom, Eric, *Mozart's Letters*. Pelican Book A239, Baltimore, Md., 1956.
Burk, John N., *Mozart and His Music*. Random House, N.Y., 1959.
Dent, E. J., *Mozart's Operas*. London, 1963.
Einstein, A., *Mozart, His Character, His Work*. Oxford, N.Y., 1951.
Girdlestone, C., *Mozart and His Piano Concertos*. Dover, N.Y., 1964.
Turner, W. J., *Mozart, The Man and His Works*. Doubleday Anchor Book A24, N.Y., 1955.

Beethoven

Burk, J. N., *The Life and Works of Beethoven*. Modern Library, N.Y., 1948.
Hamburger, ed. *Beethoven, Letters, Journals and Conversations*. Doubleday A 206, N.Y., 1960.
Sullivan, J. W. N., *Beethoven, His Spiritual Development*. Mentor Books, N.Y., 1947.
Turner, W. J., *Beethoven: The Search for Reality*. Dent, London, 1933.

General Information

Artz, F. B., *From the Renaissance to Romanticism*. University of Chicago Press, Chicago, 1962.
Einstein, Alfred, *Gluck*, in The Great Composers Series, Collier Books AS377X, New York, 1962.
Grout, Donald, *A Short History of Opera*, Columbia University Press, New York, 1965.
Kerman, J., *Opera as Drama*. Vintage Books, N.Y., 1959.
Loesser, A., *Men, Women and Pianos*. Simon & Schuster, N.Y., 1954.
Newman, W. S., *The Sonata in the Classic Era*. University of North Carolina Press, Chapel Hill, 1963.
Pauly, R., *Music in the Classic Era*, Prentice-Hall, New Jersey, 1965.
Strunk, O. ed., *Source Readings in Music History: The Classical Era*. Norton, N.Y., 1965.

ADDITIONAL LISTENING

The literature of these composers is so full of treasures that choices are difficult. Those below are only a few possible ones.

HAYDN

Symphonies
   No. 98, E♭
   No. 100 ("Military")
   No. 101 ("Clock")
   No. 102
   No. 103
   No. 104 ("London")

Concertos
   Trumpet Concerto
   Cello Concerto

Chamber Music
   String Quartets:
     Op. 33, Nos. 1-6
     Op. 54, Nos. 1-3
     Op. 64, Nos. 1-6
     Op. 71, Nos. 1-3
     Op. 74, Nos. 1-3
     Op. 76, Nos. 1-6
     Op. 77, Nos. 1, 2

Choral Music
   The Creation, Oratorio
   Lord Nelson Mass

MOZART

Symphonies
   No. 29, A Major, K. 201
   No. 34, C Major, K. 338
   No. 35, D Major ("Haffner")
     K. 385
   No. 36, C Major ("Linz"), K. 425
   No. 38, in D Major ("Prague")
     K. 504

Concertos
   Piano Concerto No. 9, E♭, K. 271
   Piano Concerto No. 14, E♭, K. 449
   Piano Concerto No. 20, D Minor,
     K. 466
   Piano Concerto No. 21, C., K. 467
   Piano Concerto No. 23, A, K. 488
   Piano Concerto No. 24, C Minor,
     K. 491
   Violin Concerto No. 4, D, K. 218
   Violin Concerto No. 5, A, K. 219
   Sinfonia Concertante for Violin and
     Viola, E♭, K. 364
   Sinfonia Concertante for Winds, E♭
     K. 297b
   Concerto for Bassoon, B♭, K. 191
   Concertos for Flute, K. 313, 314,
     315
   Concerto for French Horn, E♭, K.
     495
   Concerto for Clarinet, A, K. 622

Chamber Music
   String Quartet No. 15, D Minor, K.
     421
   String Quartet No. 19, C, K. 465
   String Quartet No. 20, D, K. 499
   String Quintet G Minor, K. 516
   Sonata for Two Pianos, D, K. 488
   Sonata for Violin and Piano, B♭, K.
     454

BEETHOVEN (in addition to any of the symphonies and string quartets):

"Kreutzer" Sonata for Violin and Piano, Op. 47
Septet for Violin, Viola, Cello, Double bass, Horn, Clarinet and Bassoon,
    Op. 20
"Waldstein" Sonata, piano, Op. 53
Piano Concertos No. 3 and 4, Opp. 58 and 73
Violin Concerto, Op. 61
Overtures to *Coriolanus,* Op. 62, *Egmont,* Op. 84, and *Leonore* No. 3,
    Op. 72
Fidelio, opera, Op. 72
Trio ("Archduke"), Op. 97
Two Trios, Op. 70
"Diabelli" Variations, Op. 120
Missa Solemnis in D, Op. 123

VI THE
ROMANTIC
PERIOD, 1827-1900

HISTORICAL PERSPECTIVE

THERE WERE FOUR principal forces at work in the nineteenth century which will aid in understanding the material and intellectual achievements of that period. The first of these was the industrial revolution. The growth of machine industry from 1800 to to 1900 was phenomenal, not solely due to the invention of new machinery, but rather to the new and increasingly efficient uses of power. Steam power (derived from the burning of coal) was first, followed in the 1870's by the use of petroleum and electricity. And the efficient use of power led to Power, as was demonstrated to all the world by the American Civil War (1861-1865), the first major conflict in which the railway was important and in which the industrial might of a nation concentrated upon the production of weapons. The factory system created greater urbanization, and with it the division of society into the capitalists and the working class. Trade unions sprang up for the protection of the proletariat and Marx and Engels urged them to throw off their oppressors in the Communist Manifesto of 1848. The rise of a strongly materialistic philosophy coincided with the increasing number of scientific discoveries, and the combination of these with the "profit motive" created a rapidly accelerating technology, runaway by the close of the century, which remains one of the major problems of the twentieth century. But, lest we overemphasize the bad side of the industrial revolution, let us remember that it also brought about improvements in public health, state accident insurance, improved social justice and the beginnings of European constitutional government.

The second force with which we must reckon was the doctrine of evolution. This was presented in a systematized and documented fashion by Charles Darwin in 1859, but had been preceded by more than half a century of speculation by other natural philosophers. Called by one historian "the outstanding intellectual achievement of the nineteenth century,"[1] the concept was applied to every phase of human knowledge by Herbert Spencer in his *System of Synthetic Philosophy*.[2] It became an issue of contention between the clergy and the scientist, of course, for Darwin applied the doctrine to all biological evolution, including man, thus opposing the biblical idea of creation. But the continuing discoveries in the natural sciences all supported the theory of evolution, and indeed, pointed toward the mechanistic explanation of man, his world and the universe as the correct one. Materialism and mechanism: no wonder that someone remarked that "the opposite of poetry is not prose, but science."

That the bases for almost all of the modern work in physics, chemistry, astronomy, biology, mathematics and medicine were laid in this century is a matter to be remarked upon. The names of Cauchy, Abel and Gauss in mathematics; Thompson, Davy, Joule and Helmholtz in thermodynamics; Oersted, Ampere, Ohm and Faraday in electricity; Maxwell and Hertz in electromagnetic waves; Dalton, Gay-Lussac, Avogadro, Berzelius, Mendeleev, Curie and Gibbs in chemistry; Mendel, Schwann and Schleiden, Pasteur and Koch in biology and bacteriology; Huxley, Hall, Wm. James, Spencer and Freud in psychology and psychiatry; and Jenner, Morton, Simpson, Lister, Semmelweiss, Osler, Metchnikov in medicine: these are names with which to conjure. By the end of the century the laws of thermodynamics and conservation of energy were established, leading with advanced metallurgy to the internal combustion engine and the steam turbine. The work in electricity had made possible the telegraph, the telephone, the electric light, the dynamo and electric motor and all of the associated equipment these imply. The investigations in chemistry brought new medicines,

---

[1] *An Intellectual and Cultural History of the Western World*, Vol. 3. Dover, N.Y., H. E. Barnes, 1965.
[2] Spencer, Herbert, *Collected Works*. New York, Adler, 1966.

compounds for war or farming, dyes, techniques to purify metals for photography and a thousand other uses. The advances in psychology and psychiatry abolished the lingering belief in diabolism as a cause of insanity, studied the sane and improved, among other things, the educational processes. The work of Freud allowed man to peer within his own mind to discover its secrets. Surgery was now made not only painless by anesthesia, but also safer by the use of antiseptics, and immunization against many communicable diseases was introduced. The discovery of the germ theory of disease, the cellular nature of organic life, the nature of protoplasm and the bacteria causing tuberculosis, leprosy and anthrax were all products of this century.

Technology and industry were not slow to apply the discoveries in the sciences, and one practical application after another followed in an ever increasing flood. They helped to build the Panama and Suez Canals, establish transatlantic cable service, perfect the repeating rifle and erect the great bridges, skyscrapers and towers of the late nineteenth century.

This was an era of strong nationalism devoted either to establishing or preserving the nation state. France weathered the Second Republic and the Second Empire before becoming stable. Germany became an empire on the way to domination in 1870, and Italy was united into a nation in 1861. Greece established her independence in 1825, but her northern neighbors in the Balkans had to wait for the end of World War I for autonomy. At the same time, the great powers were extending their colonial empires until by 1900 the climax of five centuries of colonization was reached, and European civilization, for better and for worse, overshadowed the world. The Near and Far East became outposts of British, French, Dutch and German influence. Japan was opened to the world in 1853-54, and set about becoming a modern state with amazing rapidity. And America, with a gold rush in '49, and a civil war in 1861-65, was slowly recovering and advancing until, by 1900 she had outstripped both Germany and Great Britain in the industrial race and was on the way to becoming one of the superpowers of the world.

Now that we have some idea of the material and intellectual achievements of this country, let us examine the world of the arts and try to find out the attitudes and ideals which prevailed among the poets and writers, the painters, architects and musicians.

The Romantic movement of the late eighteenth century began as a rebellion against the rationalism and formalism of the times, and expressed itself first in literature of the *Sturm und Drang* type, as we have seen. It remained a strongly literary movement throughout the century, but its ideals of freedom, idealism, and individuality appealed to painters, sculptors, musicians and architects as well as poets and novelists, and these expressed the romantic spirit in their work. Music, because of the highly abstract yet powerful nature of its materials was regarded as the highest Romantic art, yet it owed much to literature for new formal concepts and for the perfection of the marriage of words and melody in the art song and opera. But perhaps we should take a closer look at the phenomenon of romanticism before getting too deeply involved in its manifestations.

First and foremost, romanticism is the presentation of the highly individual reaction of the artist to experience. It is an emotional interpretation, for the Romantic artist only uses as material the experiences which have affected him deeply and which rise to the surface of his unconscious as inspirations. These he endeavors to present in his work with all of the thrilling immediacy with which they have affected him. He believes firmly in the power of his imagination to accomplish this; he lives by faith in it, and is distrustful of any constraint or convention which would seem to limit his creative freedom. His experiences, transformed into his art, often create an intuitive form, quite satisfying in itself, but apt to be miniature, for the sustaining of an inspiration requires a structure to support it. In some cases, a not too restrictive traditional form may serviceably *hold* the inspiration without becoming organic with it, like a pudding mold. And certainly, in some cases, the artist is too bound to tradition to escape some of its conventions, although he may not be aware of his bondage. But "romanticism is not a question of figures and forms, but of the composer's being a poet," said Robert Schumann, one of the standard-bearers of the musical part of the movement.

What moved the creative spirit of the artist in the early nineteenth century, when romanticism was most genuine? The earliest writers sought new and interesting material in stories of the Middle Ages, *Romantisch* being their term for Romanesque. This interest in the past, actually more Gothic than Romanesque, was expressed in the novels of Sir Walter Scott, the plays and poems of Schiller and Victor Hugo, the architecture of Cologne Cathedral and the British Houses of Parliament, and in pictures of ruined castles and monasteries which became popular. Someone has said that the Gothic was to romanticism as the Classicism of the Greeks was to the Enlightenment. But not only Europe of the Middle ages, but all times and places appealed to the romantic temperament. The Near and Far East also were irresistibly attractive, as evidenced by Fitzgerald's translation of the *Rubaiyat of Omar Khayyam,* Goethe's *Divans,* Delacroix' harem scenes and lion

PLATE XXIII. *"The Bewitched" by Goya. The supernatural and fantastic element in romantic art is extended here to an almost expressionistic degee. (Courtesy of the Trustees, The National Gallery, London.)*

hunts and even the "turkish music" of otherwise classically minded composers as Mozart, Gluck and Beethoven. Operas on exotic subjects were also popular, as they still are. Whatever the time and place, the romantic artist recreates it nearer his heart's desire than it could be in reality. His idealism makes it a better world in which all kings are noble and all ladies fair.

Thus, there is an aspect of dreaming, a yearning for unreality in romanticism. This manifested itself in other ways, in supernatural fantasies not often on the level of Goethe's *Faust,* but more frequently resembling *Dracula, Frankenstein's Monster, Robert le Diable, Der Vampyr* and *The Bleeding Nun.* Morbid and fantastic, brooding on death, Young's *Night Thoughts* reveals in its text "thrilling mortuary images":

> The knell, the shroud, the mattock and the grave;
> The deep damp vault, the darkness and the worm.

So some of Chopin's *Nocturnes* reflect some of this feeling, and Goya's *Caprichos* (Plate XXIII). On the healthier side, but not less fantastic in purpose, are the many death dances and witches' orgies of the orchestral music.

Nature affected the Romantic strongly, whether from the ruggedness and wildness of scenery or weather, uncontrollable by man (Plate XXIV), or from the tender serenity of the pastoral landscapes as painted by Constable and the French Barbizon School (Plate XXXIII). The wonder of childhood and its purity, the state of love and its idealism, and the security offered by religion to troubled minds were all attractive to the romantic and brought forth appropriate artistic works ranging from the monumentally passionate *Tristan und Isolde* and the *Symphonie fantastique* to the sentimental, banal and insipid French popular songs of the period.

Beginning in rebellion against the rationality of the enlightenment, romanticism soon took arms against the drabness of existence in the factory town, the philistinism of the comfortable bourgeoisie, the political injustices of the times and the overwhelming certainty of science that everything could be explained by the action of cause and effect and natural laws. The romantic felt as Matthew Arnold did, when he wrote:[3]

> We admire with awe
> The exulting thunder of your race;
> You give the universe your law,
> You triumph over time and space!
> Your pride of life, your tireless powers,
> We laud them, but they are not ours. .

---

[3] *From Stanzas from the Grande Chartreuse,* in *The Poetical Works of Matthew Arnold,* ed. Tinker and Lowry. New York, Oxford Univ. Press, 1950.

PLATE XXIV. "The Falls of the Rhine at Schaffhausen" by Turner. A typical romantic landscape emphasizing the forces of nature—a more picturesque version of the revolt against the Enlightenment. (Courtesy of The Museum of Fine Arts, Boston.)

Romanticism preferred the mystery surrounding natural happenings, whether these were changes in the weather or changes in the hearts of men. It longed for a return of faith, but alas, this was not to come in the increasingly scientific world.

Almost from its beginning, this was a period of "art for art's sake," for not only would the unruly personality of the artist not submit to convention and order, but, more practically, the time of patronage was past. In only a few rather astonishing cases was an artist supported by a patron. Moreover the strong individuality of the artist insisted that his works be accepted on *his* terms, not necessarily those of the public or the critics, certainly not of a patron. In doing this the artist removed himself somewhat from his audience, and the audience, in turn, often felt that his painting, music or sculpture was obscure, difficult. Often the artist took no pains to explain his meaning, preferring the mystification. During the century, the gap between the creator and his public widened, and it did not stop with the turn of the century; we still are confronted with the paradoxical problem of art of our time which is not understood by its contemporaries.

Toward the end of the century, romanticism gave way to realism, a sometimes harsh and brutal portrayal of life and existence as it really was. Zola, Flaubert and Whitman are realistic writers. Painters like Courbet, Manet, sculptors like Rodin, composers such as Mascagni, Leoncavallo, Charpentier, Puccini and Richard Strauss took part in this aspect of romanticism.

In summation, then, we realize that romanticism is ardently emotional, often seemingly irrational, fantastic and ambiguous——all reactions of the individual to the shocks of existence. It is revolutionary and demands freedom of utterance and manner, but paradoxically seeks the reassurances of love, friendship and religion. It yearns for the distantly unattainable, the exotic, the novel sensation, and touches upon death, the supernatural and the diabolical. It opposes commonness, formality, rigid conventions, conservatism and the humdrum and monotony of life. And it escapes from these through its fantasies and imaginative flights to times and places that never were in the world.

ROMANTIC MUSICAL STYLE

The first and most important aim of the Romantic composer was to communicate emotion through music in as intense and immediate way as possible. To accomplish this he bent all the resources of melody, harmony, rhythm, tone-color and form to his purpose, frequently to the detriment of traditional structures. To supplant these, he altered them in various ways, evolving new forms: or, he discarded them—— or thought he did——in favor of new intuitive or literary patterns which provided an axis about which the music could revolve. But the greatest innovation came through the expansion of the resources of the tonal system through chromaticism.

Melody

Romantic composers realized that perhaps the most potent musical element for the communication of feeling was melody——not the short, epigrammatic musical idea we have called the theme, but rather the *complete* statement of a musical thought, lyric and explicit in its emotional connotations. The short piano compositions of the period often were based upon a single melody of this type, and the structural sections of larger forms frequently were characterized by melody rather than any marked contrast of key, particularly the second thematic area of the sonata-allegro form. This preference for melody was at odds with the sonata-allegro and other developmental forms, for these sprang essentially from the concept of the theme as a small, incomplete idea, and thus these large forms posed a dilemma for the romantic composer. He solved it in two ways.

The first way was through the use of a *germ theme*, a short pattern of tones whose melodic shape was composed of a few well-defined intervals. This germ theme served as a major constructive element in larger melodies, sometimes repeated within them several times. For development, the pattern was extracted; or, looking at it from the point of view of the melody, the melody was fragmented and these fragments used in the same way that themes had been employed before. We shall find this method particularly in the music of Schubert and Brahms.

The other way used a process called *theme transformation* and was similar except that the germ theme was exposed as a fragment, essentially melodic, but with a rhythmic structure, at the beginning of the composition. It was then manipulated rhythmically, inverted, decorated and extended, often serving as part of a larger melody. Thus, it is in a sense the reverse of the process explained in the previous paragraph; it is synthesis, while the other is analysis. The synthetic approach was used particularly by Liszt, Wagner and Strauss while Schumann and Berlioz used both methods.

In contrast to the irregular melodic line of the Baroque and the "straight line" of the late Classic period, Romantic melody often is sinuous in profile, rather like some of those found in the rococo music, but on a larger scale, usually moving more slowly, not obviously decorative but sensuously curved. It usually is extremely vocal in character, and the listener tends to empathize with it, "singing" it in his mind and unconsciously in his throat. We shall encounter it frequently in orchestral music, and will characterize it there as instrumental lyricism. The postromantic composers, Strauss particularly, were successful in employing wide leaps in their melodies without sacrificing the vocal quality while adding to the expressiveness of the line. Melodic chromaticism was also employed throughout the nineteenth century more freely than before, often together with chromatic harmony, but sometimes as "sliding" passing tones between diatonic chords which gave the melody a more sensuous expression.

Among the devices used to organize and direct the melodic line, the sequence remained highly important and was often over-used. Moreover, it became a factor by means of which the tension of the line could be increased to a climactic point, creating a species of form called the "dynamic curve." The Prelude to *Tristan und Isolde* by Wagner illustrates the concept. From a soft beginning which exposes a few motives, the dynamic level of the piece increases with ascending sequences of the material, sometimes interwoven so that simultaneous sequences on several levels are apparent until a climax is reached, after which the excitement quickly dies down.

Suspensions also appear in Romantic melody, although they may be weakened in their effect by the complex or chromatic harmony which surrounds them. Applied ornamentation of the Baroque-Classic variety is almost nonexistent in instrumental music except for that of the piano where the coloraturas of the opera were elaborated in dazzling cascades of rapid notes. We find these particularly in the music of Chopin and Liszt. Of course, Italian opera did not forsake the liberty of improvised embellishment, and the works of Bellini, especially, include written-in decorations of the melody.

Tonality and Harmony

While some composers of the nineteenth century continued to employ the functional harmony of the tonal system with only a small amount of chromaticism, the gradually increasing use of this variety of unstable harmony had strongly affected the music of most composers by the close of the century. The development of chromatic harmony is, in fact, one of the outstanding achievements of the period. The freedom-seeking departure from the familiar ground of diatonic harmony into the uncharted possibilities of chromaticism brought with it two useful and sometimes startling effects: distortion and ambiguity.

Distortion of familiar material for the intensification of emotional communication has always been used in the various arts. We need only look at the paintings of El Greco (Plate IX), the churches of Borromini (Plate XIII) and Fischer von Erlach, the sculptures of Michelangelo and the music of Gesualdo and J. S. Bach (Cantata No. 80, mov't. 7) to note how effective the device is. The normal state of tonal harmony always had been based upon the major-minor scale system expressed in triads which defined the key center or tonic. Previous harmonic distortion contrasted sharply with the "normal" harmony in which it was imbedded, but in some romantic music the distortion was so consistent that we are not always aware of it as a strong factor. This romantic distortion consisted of the chromatic alteration of one or more notes of diatonic triads and 7th chords until their functional, key-defining quality was weakened or destroyed. The more chromaticism which appeared in a passage, the more closely the scale being used approached the twelve-tone chromatic scale which, as we saw in Chapter I, does not possess a tonic tone or keynote. This ambiguity of key was not troublesome if the passage were short, but over long spans of time the structural plan of the music, if cast in the traditional forms depending upon the contrast of tonality, was weakened or destroyed. New forms and techniques had to be devised which were based upon the *chromatic*, not the tonal, scale. This dilemma was reached at the close of the century, with the full realization of the implications of Wagner's *Tristan* harmony. It remained for the twentieth century to find a solution.

Both cadences and modulation also became distorted through the Romantic desire for continuity, fusion of structural boundaries and the desire for that apparent profundity of expression which accompanies ambiguity. Cadences were pillars of tonality in the seventeenth and eighteenth centuries, and modulation quite simply was the process of changing key in accordance with the structural design of the music. In the nineteenth century cadences often became deceptive, and resolved ambiguously on a chromatically altered rather than a diatonic and functional chord. This process enhanced the flow, for the harmonic movement was not halted, but only turned in another direction. This new direction implied modulation——often not at a crucial point in the structure, but merely at a phrase ending——and modulation occurred so frequently that all sense of key and structure were confused or lost. It was effective in communicating certain kinds of feeling, as Wagner demonstrated in *Tristan* by using the moving, resolution-seeking chromatic harmony to depict the unfulfilled yearning of the lovers. These distortions and ambiguities represent the seeking spirit of romanticism, its irrationality and its desire to capture new and more intense emotion. They represent a twilight state of individuality far removed from the rational daylight of the preceding two centuries, a movement toward an inner region of subjective fantasy and mystic vision.

Rhythm and Tempo

No particular virtuosity in the handling of rhythm is to be noticed in Romantic music. To be sure, both Schumann and Brahms are masters of unstable rhythmic devices, and these strongly affect the totality of their music. But most other composers use the rhythmic *clichés* and devices inherited from the past.

The rhythm of harmonic change——the so-called *harmonic rhythm*——is quite slow in most Romantic music, and the rapidity of the notes seems to have little effect upon it. Much of this music gives the effect of thoughtful, somewhat solemn motion in contrast to the rapidity of movement in works of the Classic Period. Indeed, in some cases the movement stops altogether, as in the static harmony of the Prelude to *Das Rheingold*, by Wagner, where a single E♭ chord is sustained for some thirty-two measures of moderate tempo. Similar shorter passages occur in the works of Bruckner, Liszt and Brahms, a preoccupation with a single sonority which has been called by some writers a "mysticism of the chord." It leads to Schönberg's *Klangfarbenmelodie* in the early twentieth century, a variation in tone color within the context of a single chord.

One of the most striking aspects of tempo in Romantic music is the frequency with which the tempo changes, continually slowing down or speeding up in order to reflect the irrational welling-up and subsiding of emotions. The *discontinuity* of tempo may occur anywhere, but is found most frequently at the beginning of a composition where the music seemingly rises, uncertain and groping, from the depths of the unconscious. Later, in many works in sonata-allegro form, the tempo is retarded for the lyric second theme in order to make it more effective. Thus, lyricism affects the formal structure not only in the characterization but also in the rhythm of its parts.

Despite the fluctuations of tempo, there is to be felt a strong continuity and flow in most Romantic works. It is achieved by the ambiguity of the harmony, the long-line span of the melody and the presence, especially at formal boundaries, of unstable rhythm. The rhythm of the succession of movements in the compound forms is also blurred by transitions and bridges between them, as well as within the forms themselves. The continuum of life experience is suggested by these long stretches of music, waking as well as dreaming moments.

Of especial importance in the rhythm of form to the Romantic composer are the beginning and ending of a composition. We are likely to find, then, introductions prefacing the main material of a movement, introductions which may seem to come from nowhere, stealing into our consciousness and transporting us by magic into the dream world of the music. In many cases, however poetic they may sound, these preludes have the very realistic function of presenting germ motives which will be elaborated later. Having coaxed us into the music, the Romantic composer often brings us gently back to reality in the same way, lingering over the final cadences, multiplying them with deceptive and plagal endings, and often bringing into view for the last time an important germ theme or cyclic motive. Highly poetic, these codas are also often practical, for they may balance the movement, enforce the cyclic quality, or psychologically resolve tensions created within the piece particularly if it is dramatic or operatic in nature.

Texture

Corresponding to the intense interest in harmony, the texture of most romantic music is homophonic, often with elaborate accompaniment figures which upon casual listening resemble polyphony, but which in reality are firmly based upon the chord of the moment. These figures contribute to the rhythmic life and motion and replace the old Alberti-bass and similar patterns used by the eighteenth century composers. Some real polyphony is to be found in the works of Schumann, Berlioz and Brahms, often employed for developmental purposes or in traditional fugal movements for chorus. It tends to sound, however, harmonic in conception, without the balance and freedom between harmony and melodic line to be found in the works of Bach or his renaissance predecessors.

Improvisation

While the art of improvisation did not die out entirely, for the most part it became a virtuoso trick, exploited by the sensational pianists and violinists of the period. There was no lack of these, and often sincere artists were forced to compete with them on their own terms. The two towering virtuosi of the day, Franz Liszt, the pianist, and Niccolo Paganini (1782-1840) provide us with examples of performers who, while often genuine in their musical attainments did stoop to meretricious practices on the platform. Much of Liszt's music, such as the *Hungarian Rhapsodies*, reflects his dazzling showmanship, abetted by his practice of lowering the lights and placing the piano sidewise to the audience so that his noble profile might be admired! Paganini's music is more problematical, for we must balance somehow the rather plain music of the printed page against the rapturous accounts of his performances of it by such trustworthy critics as Schumann, Berlioz and Liszt. The fact of the matter seems to be that Paganini, fearful that other violinists might steal his thunder if he wrote down exactly what he played, notated merely the plainest skeleton of the movement and relied upon improvisation to lend it glitter and fire. His technique was all but unbelievable, from all accounts, and he inspired Liszt to emulation.

Discontinunity of tempo often lends to the music a feeling of improvisation. Another manipulation of rhythm was used by romantic performers, particularly pianists, to create a flexible, improvisatory and expressive motion in the melodic line. This was called *tempo rubato*. It consisted of holding back or moving forward in the melody against a strictly measured and even accompaniment exactly in the way that a good jazz singer does today. Such flexibility is a necessary part of the music of Chopin, for example, just as it is of popular music of the twentieth century. Other composers of the nineteenth century do not require tempo rubato in their works, nor should it be always used in Chopin's; the sensitivity of the artist must decide.

Sonority

Music of the Romantic period is notable for the variety of color it employs as well as richness of sonority. Melody and harmony were conceived for particular instruments by composers, and color became to them one of the fundamental elements of music. One may compare the piano transcription of a work by Mozart or Beethoven with a similar reduction of a Berlioz or Liszt composition. The Classical works sound best on the monochromatic piano because the abstract qualities of the music are foremost, and the blend of melody and harmony is intellectually good. But the Romantic works, because they depend so much upon the color of the instruments, the effects of spacing of individual parts and the blend of certain sonorities, sound weak and unsatisfying. These composers were writing music *for the orchestra,* not just writing music which could be played by the orchestra.

To achieve the contrasts in tone color and to expand the resources of the Beethoven orchestra, new instruments were added, old ones improved and the numbers in each section increased until there were usually three of each woodwind, four to six horns, three trumpets, three trombones, tuba, enlarged percussion, harp, and enough strings to balance the wind instruments. These numbers were increased as the century moved on, resulting in the gargantuan orchestras of Strauss, Mahler and early Schönberg.

Among the new instruments added as regular members of the orchestra were the improved harp, various kinds of clarinet such as the small, shrill E-flat instrument, the English horn, the contrabassoon, various percussion in addition to the timpani, the Wagner tubas, which were really a species of bass French horn, and at the close of the century the newly-invented saxophone and the bass flute. For the most part these new members contributed distinctively colored solo sounds, but often also filled out the already existing section of the ensemble so that a four or five tone chord could be scored in one instrumental color.

The most important advances were made in the improvement of the old instruments, particularly the wood and brass winds. Theobald Boehm (1794-1881), after much experimentation, devised a new design and key system for the flute which improved its ability to play in tune and to execute difficult passages with greater ease. His theories and designs were applied to the other woodwinds with excellent results. Similar investigations created the valve systems of the brass instruments, whereby they were enabled to play chromatic scale passages through the addition, by means of valves, of lengths of tubing which lowered the pitch by half-step degrees, and which could be combined to fill chromatically the gaps between the rather distant lower members of the harmonic series. Thus were developed the modern French horn, trumpet, cornet and tuba; the trombone needed no such improvement, but better manufacturing methods raised its quality.

Despite the large size of the orchestra, the music frequently was more notable for variety and delicacy of color than for volume of sound, which, of course was easily available when desired. This variety often was achieved by using the single instruments as solos, analogous to a painter's use of pure, unmixed color. Just as in painting, it is possible to mix tone colors by duplicating one part in another, either at the same pitch, octaves higher or lower, or at some more colorful interval such as the third or sixth. This device was called *doubling*, and had been used by Haydn, Mozart and Beethoven for the same reason, as well as to strengthen the sound of a weak solo instrument. The technique became highly developed and refined as the nineteenth century moved onward, reaching its climax in the music of Richard Strauss, and creating a reactionary return to the use of pure tone color in the music of Mahler, Debussy and succeeding twentieth century composers. It is of interest to note that the composers of program music were spurred by their imaginations to explore the field of tone color more extensively than were the more conservative writers, although Brahms achieved notable results in the darker shades of orchestral sound.

THE MUSIC OF THE ROMANTIC PERIOD

For convenience we may classify most of the composers of the nineteenth century into three general categories. The first consists of *evolutionary* composers such as Brahms, Schubert and, to an extent, Schumann, who found the traditional forms and techniques adequate for what they wanted to express, but who expanded or organically changed these structures during their creative lives. The *revolutionary* composers felt that their new ideas and their new musical language could not be contained legitimately within the confines of the inherited symphonic structures, and therefore sought new shapes for their music. They often depended upon literary programs to dictate the sequence of musical events of a composition, or relied upon their intuition for coherence. Instead of the *abstract* music of the evolutionists, they preferred *descriptive* and *program* music which related a story or interpreted a poem in tones. The main composers of this group were Berlioz, Liszt and Wagner, but Schumann and Mendelssohn also had some sympathies in this direction. Bruckner was adopted by the revolutionary group but really belongs in the evolutionary camp. The third classification is that of *nationalistic* composer. In a sense, all composers of the time were nationalistic, for Brahms and Wagner are as typically German as Berlioz is French and Schubert Viennese. Yet these were in the main stream of Romantic musical culture, and establish, as it were, the norm. Composers such as Smetana and Dvořák from Bohemia, Grieg from Norway, and Moussorgsky, Borodin and Rimsky-Korsakov from Russia are impressive as strongly nationalistic composers because they employed folk idioms and patriotic programs in their music which were new to European listeners and which contrasted freshly with the central styles of Germany and France. The Italians were concerned almost entirely with opera, and the English imported all of their music until the late nineteenth century produced Edward Elgar; thus, these two countries stand outside of our classification, although for different reasons.

The Romantic Symphony and Symphonic Poem

In the nineteenth century, the grand symphony, written along the lines seemingly indicated by Beethoven, was regarded by many composers as the epitome of musical composition. Since almost all of the important composers wrote orchestral works in symphonic form, an examination of these will reveal style tendencies and changes characteristic of the times, and provide an insight into smaller works in which these tendencies also prevail.

For the more conservative composers, Beethoven's Third, Fifth, Seventh and Ninth Symphonies provided a point of departure. The perfection of abstract musical structure, the use of unifying devices and the clear individuality of these works appealed to those who sought the future in the past. Others, more adventurous or clear-sighted, regarded as significant the use of programmatic indications in the Sixth, the loosening of the classic sonata format by the inclusion of a funeral march in the Third, the highly individual and romantically forceful spirit and spiritual program of the Fifth, and, finally, the use of the voice and chorus in the Ninth. The Beethoven concert overture, too, appealed to some who saw in it the possibilities of expansion to major proportions with the inclusion of descriptive devices which related a story. Others merely made the overture more picturesque, a painting of scenes and moods. The Romantic tendency toward fusion of structural sections and the necessity of a high degree of unity prompted experiments such as the Schumann Fourth Symphony in which the movements are intended to follow one another without pause and in which the thematic elements are also highly interrelated.

The significant new departure which resulted from such experimentation was the one-movement symphonic poem, usually a composition
which sought to relate a story or follow in some way a literary program. A few basic themes were stated near the beginning of such a
work, and all other themes were derived from them by the process of
melodic variation known as *theme transformation*. In this way, the
symphonic economy of previous composers was attained. As we have
intimated, these processes filtered down through all Romantic music,
and we find them in piano pieces, songs, chamber music, and
highly significantly, in the opera and the music drama. To some composers, such as Brahms, the use of descriptive programs seemed to
disregard the legacy of the past, the responsibility of which he felt
keenly. Thus, two streams of musical thought exist in the second half
of the century: abstract music and programmatic music. Brahms was
almost the only composer of first rank in the conservative group,
although Schumann also felt the weight of the past but was too adventurous to remain with it and too modest to risk comparison with the
great works of Haydn, Mozart, Beethoven and Schubert. Berlioz, Liszt
and Wagner were the progressive composers who sought in program
music and the music drama, which used the same techniques, an
escape from the past, a reaching out into musical regions as yet unexplored. "The music of the future," Wagner proclaimed it, but as it
turned out, he was wrong and the aesthetic was mistaken; for, music
does nothing outside of expressing itself——sounding form, relations
between tones as abstract as any mathematical proposition. But the
mistake was fruitful and brought forth many beautiful works without
which the world would be much poorer.

Let us begin with an early Romantic composer, one who, in his
music written at the same time Beethoven was composing the last
great works of his time, served to make the transition in a different
way into the romantic age.

Franz Schubert (1797-1828)

Schubert essentially was a lyricist, as his many great songs would
testify, but one with a strong sense of musical form due to his admiration for the music of Mozart. Realizing the inherent unsuitability of
full-blown melody for the construction of large works of the sonata
type, he worked unceasingly to find techniques which would allow
him to retain his melody and also build upon it. He accomplished this
by the use of motivic fragments incorporated in the lyric substance
which could be isolated for developmental purposes.

Schubert had a highly developed harmonic sense, romantic in its feeling for the exact sonority, change of chord quality or shift in key. Some of the most beautiful passages in this composer's music result from the modulation, gradual or abrupt, to a key a third away from the preceding tonality. We shall find some striking examples of this in the works which we examine.

The orchestration of this composer is also colorful, romantically expressive and highly suitable to his lyric temperament. Schubert was not essentially an aggressive and optimistic composer such as Beethoven, and, while some full orchestra passages may be loud, somehow the forceful quality found in similar passages of Beethoven is not present. Schubert's most effective moments are tender, subjective, romantically yearning and lyric.

Symphony No. 8 in B Minor (The "Unfinished Symphony")

This, the first truly romantic lyric symphony, consists of two movements only: a moderately rapid first movement in sonata-allegro form, and an *andante* second movement in sonatina form. The remaining two movements were sketched in part, but never completed. Schubert may have felt that the first two movements expressed completely what he had to say, and that the others would prove superfluous. Judging from the sketches, he was quite right, for these are not his best work and would certainly shatter the poetic mood of the first two with anticlimactic effects. Perhaps he could not sustain the mood, or perhaps other matters claimed his attention. Certainly he did not intend it to be a two-movement work, quite unthinkable by the Classic standards to which he more or less adhered. For the second movement, instead of preserving the unity of key, as it would if planned to be the conclusion of the symphony, is, instead, in the "proper" tonality for a second movement, the subdominant. So unfinished it is, and we may be thankful for it.

It is easily understood, even upon casual listening, for the lyricism and attractive orchestral colors are appealing. This is the consummate art which conceals art, for it is most tightly organized throughout; perhaps the effort of accomplishing this is related to the lack of the two final movements.

The aesthetic program is a Romantic one: struggle——Romantic because of the defeat which finally comes, instead of the Classic triumph, or even false gaiety. We find in the two movements a program

EXAMPLE VI-1A: Schubert, *Symphony in B Minor*.

FIRST MOVEMENT: Allegro moderato

a. GERM THEME

b. PRINCIPAL SUBJECT

c. SECOND SUBJECT

d. DEVELOPMENT

e.

EXAMPLE VI-1B: Diagram of First Movement.

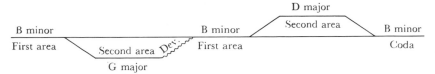

typical of Schubert which appears frequently in his songs. It was first noted by Alfred Einstein, and concerns what had long been thought of as Schubert's somewhat irresponsible use of the major and minor tonalities, seemingly shifting from one to the other with no reason other than the search for variety. Einstein pointed out that for the song texts which expressed reality——almost always situations of defeat, pessimism and unhappiness——the tonality chosen was minor. When the words expressed the yearned-for happiness, all too seldom attained, the major tonality was used, frequently with a transformation of the same melodic material of the previous minor section. This happens so frequently in the songs that it cannot be accidental; by extension to works without words, we may gain some insight into Schubert's intent. Thus, not only does the beautiful second thematic idea of the first movement express the ideal world, but also the main subjects of the second movement. The orchestration reinforces the feeling in every case.

I. *Allegro moderato*, B Minor. Sonata-allegro form. (Example VI-1A).

We already have spoken of the lyric quality of this symphony as well as its tight organization. Let us see how these two rather incompatible characteristics are combined. The opening of the movement consists of a melodic phrase in the deep register of the orchestra, scored for cellos and double-basses, somber and resigned in expression. It begins on the tonic tone and wends its way to a melodic cadence on the dominant. Upon examination it is seen to contain short scale lines or skips in the first four measures which outline the interval of a 3rd. The next two significant skips consist of the interval of the 4th. If we examine the principal themes of this and the second movement, we cannot but be struck by how many times similar scalar or skipwise 3rds are used, and how frequently the interval of the 4th, or its inversion, the 5th, is incorporated into the melodies. These, then, are germ motives, and subtly unify the two movements by their frequent appearance. The use of motto themes seems crude by comparison! It is also significant that Schubert chooses to develop this opening theme rather than either the first or second group of themes when he reaches the development section. The second theme, most familiar of all in this work, receives some beautiful extension to form the closing material, but it is never fragmented and developed in the usual way. Of course, in developing the opening theme, all of the other themes are being developed too, since they are formed from the motives contained in it.

The form is very clear, especially since Schubert has reduced the number of thematic ideas in each section to a single subject. The most striking point in the exposition is perhaps the transition, which is shortened drastically. The tone retained by the horns, the third of the tonic chord, serves as a kind of pivot upon which the harmony turns toward the new key of G major, a 3rd below the B minor tonic. Here again, the interval of the 3rd is at work! In the recapitulation, similar pivoting occurs, but now it moves upward to the more usual key of D major, again a 3rd away. These key relationships result in a tonal design for this movement which are not entirely classical, for the second theme in the recapitulation is *not* in the tonic key. Such a key plan, shown graphically in Example VI-1B, revolves, as it were, upon the axis of B minor, and the downward 3rd of the exposition is answered by an upward 3rd in the recapitulation. The second theme and closing themes in the recapitulation must therefore modulate to reach the tonic for the beginning of the coda; this is accomplished by extending the melody of the second theme a few more measures, and is hardly noticeable unless one is looking for it. The coda is a development section of sorts, concentrating upon the resigned and pathetic qualities of the introductory theme.

II. *Andante con moto,* E Major, sonatina form with development within the main sections.

Example VI-1C shows the principal themes, again employing the germ motives of 3rd or 4th, and Example VI-1D indicates the formal plan of the movement, not quite as regular an axis arrangement as the first movement. It will be noted that each of the main key areas of both exposition and recapitulation are ternary in design, and that the central section of each is devoted to development of the material. Again, the transition is pivotal; a single harmony is outlined melodically which almost magically changes in quality upon its arrival at the new key. The modulation which occurs in measures 6-9 of the second theme, under the sustained tone in the solo instrument, also is quite magical in effect, for the tone quality of the solo seems to change iridescently as the shifting har-

EXAMPLE VI-1C: Schubert, *Symphony in B Minor.*

SECOND MOVEMENT: Andante con moto

PRINCIPAL SECTION

EXAMPLE VI-1D: Diagram of Second Movement.

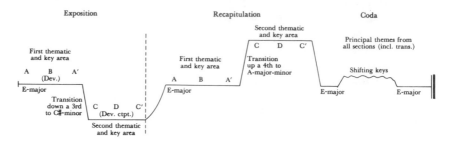

monies move to the new key. The tolling horns of the recapitulation, indeed, the poetic use of these Romantic instruments
throughout the movement, is noteworthy. The singing quality
of the solo instruments is typical of this composer's felicitous
orchestration. The coda combines elements of each of the main
sections with the transition figure, and is, in a musical as well
as a poetic sense, a summation of the work. The Romantic
withdrawal from the world of sound and imagination is the
function of this beautiful coda; one is left with a feeling of
nostalgia for Schubert's dream world as the vision evaporates.

Robert Schumann (1810-1856)

Schumann, like Schubert, was a lyric composer, but did not share
his predecessor's pessimism, although he might well have done so,
for he fell ill with schizophrenia during the latter part of his short life.
His early work was almost entirely for piano, and it is possible that
from the percussive nature and the clear articulation of this instrument he derived his fondness for crisp dotted rhythms and vigorous
motives. His orchestration also reveals the grouping of chord tones in
patterns reminiscent of those which fit the pianists' hand.

Possibly at his best in smaller works such as songs and piano
pieces where formal organization is not so crucial, Schumann nevertheless essayed larger works with some success. In them, however, one
is apt to find a succession of intimate moods more suited for the salon
rather than the large frescoes needed for the concert hall. In support
of the short mood pieces, he developed a highly individual melodic

and harmonic style characteristic of one of his alter egos, the romanticist Eusebius. The counterpart, Florestan, was vigorous and assertive, while Dr. Raro personified the classic element of moderation and learned technique. Schumann carried on imaginary conversations among these three in his critical articles in the *Neue Zeitschrift für Musik,* a critical paper which he founded and for which he was almost the sole writer.

The most creatively and thoroughly organized orchestral work to come from his pen is the *Symphony in D Minor,* Op. 120, which, however, was composed second in the series of four, but withdrawn due to his dissatisfaction with it, reworked, and later issued with the larger number. Here is a related though somewhat different solution to the romantic symphony from Schubert's, and an attempt through new devices to attain an even greater unity among four movements.

Symphony No. 4, in D Minor, Op. 120

There are five movements to this work, by Schumann's count: Introduction, Allegro, Romanze, Scherzo and Finale. The fact that the Introduction is honored as a movement is indicative of its importance even though it is no longer than one would expect such an introduction to be. The movements are directed by the composer to be played without pause between them. Beethoven had used such indications and provided musical links between movements as we have seen, but this is one of the first symphonies to use this device throughout. This procedure also supports another unifying element of the work: the delay of the recapitulation of the thematic material until near the end of the work——the bridge between the Scherzo and the Finale, to be exact. The boundaries between movements also are weakened or bridged over so as to give the impression of continuous flow from beginning to end, although tempo changes do tend to give a degree of separation. Certain movements or sections of them are related to later ones, again bringing separate elements into closer connection with each other (see the diagram in Example Vl-2A). Despite the complexity of the procedures, the result is not dry, pedantic and uninteresting, but a vigorous and poetic work of art.

Introduction: *Ziemlich langsam:* The function of this section is to bring to the attention of the listener the germ themes which the composer employs. Two of these appear as the section progresses (Example Vl-2B, 1 and 2). The third is the chord progression in D minor, I-IV-I. The tempo increases as the Allegro is approached, and the first theme is made up of germs 1 and 2. Note the procedure of

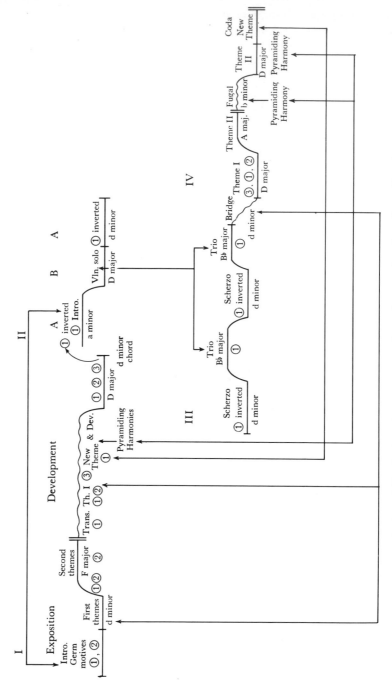

EXAMPLE VI-2A: Schumann, interrelationships within *Symphony No. 4.*

EXAMPLE VI-2B: Schumann, *Symphony No. 4.*

MIDDLE SECTION: VARIANT OF THE FOREGOING

III. SCHERZO: Lebhaft
(note harmony)   1. INVERTED

TRIO

(See middle section of Romanze, above.)

TRANSITION:
Langsam

IV. FINALE: Lebhaft 3   IMPORTANT MOTIVE

TRANSITION

SECOND THEME (note resemblance to B theme of Romanze, Trio of Scherzo)

entering the development section and the "pyramiding" of the trombones. While the sonata-allegro form of this movement is quite continuous, especially in regard to second key area and themes, the opening of the development and the return in less fragmented form of earlier themes will provide guideposts. Note, at the close of the movement, how the rhythmic pulse is maneuvered so as to make the final chord sound rhythmically weak. This leads us to expect another one, but instead, the first chord of the Romanze is sounded. Similar techniques of weak ending or actual transitions link the other movements. Perhaps the least satisfactory part of the entire work is the coda, quite plainly an effort to whip up excitement and energy for a bang-up finish. It does not come off, however, and usually merely sounds noisy and nervous. Perhaps if Schumann had peered farther ahead, he might have ended with a grand peroration of the germ theme, or something more symphonically economical and appropriate.

Schumann's other symphonies use some of the devices we have found in the Fourth, but none is so thoroughly worked out. The First and the Third have titles of "Spring" and "Rhenish," respectively. In the latter the composer said that he seemed to see a religious celebration as the "subject" of the finale, but, as in most of his other compositions with names, the titles are more apt to be suggestions to stir the imagination of the listener rather than musical description and explicit tone painting.

PLATE XXV. *Robert Schumann. Daguerreotype taken in the early 1850's. (The Bettmann Archive.)*

Hector Berlioz (1803-1869)

One of the greatest of the Romantic composers, one whose originality and worth has come to be realized only at mid-twentieth
century, originally was intended for the medical profession. But the
hold of music was too great to resist, and like Schumann and the study
of law, Berlioz spent his time in the concert hall rather than the dis-
secting room. Playing no instrument except for some strumming on
the guitar, he learned the colors and capabilities of each so well that
he became the first great Romantic master of the orchestra. The modern student of orchestration may well read his *Treatise on Orchestration* for inspiration and penetrating observations, if not for information
on the instruments, which is now a little out of date although revised
by Richard Strauss in 1904. Like Schumann, Berlioz was an excellent
critic and essayist, and many of his articles may still be read for information and pleasure.

Berlioz, like other nonacademically trained composers had the
advantage of not being weighed down by the burden of the past; but

PLATE XXVI: *Berlioz and Liszt. Drawing by Kriehuber, Vienna, 1846. A
gathering at Liszt's which includes, from left to right: Kriehuber, Berlioz, Czerny,
Liszt and Ernst. (New York Public Library.)*

he also had the disadvantage of not clearly understanding the gifts of the past which would have been useful to him. His view of the sonata-allegro form essentially was that of thematic contrast without a deep comprehension of the tonal motivations beneath the themes. His procedure often carries the day, for it is romantically impetuous and bears the listener along on a tide of emotion and sonority, leaving him little time to locate his geographical position. But this is Berlioz with both his virtues and faults, like many another composer.

There are three immediately arresting characteristics of his style: the orchestral sonority and the varied hues which he is able to command; the long-line melody unlike that of any other composer, and more individual and peculiar (in the original sense of that word) than one would expect; and last, his unerring sense of drama in deploying color and melody in his music.

Nevertheless, being in the *avant-garde* of his time, he sought ways to help the public understand his work, and, being literary to begin with, put forth the concept of the *program symphony*, a musical work which follows the events in a story and pictures them in music. To be sure, he later withdrew the scenario of the *Symphonie fantastique,* insisting that the music was capable of existing without the words, as it is; but the damage was done. His best programmatic works either use a few words of suggestive description without detailing the story step by step *(Harold in Italy),* or they incorporate the text into the work as vocal or choral music, explaining and commenting upon the story as it progresses. Such a composition is one of his greatest, the dramatic symphony *Roméo et Juliette.*

Symphonie Fantastique

The literary plan of this work revolves around the love of a young musician, and, egocentrically, the effects of his disappointments upon him. The pervading character in the plot is the beloved woman, and to her is assigned a theme—— more than a theme, a complete melody some forty measures long. This is the *idée fixe, the* obsession which is the axis around which the scenes and their emotions revolve. The first seven measures (Example VI-3) are quoted in appropriate places in each movement, thereby serving the purpose of a motto theme. Other portions of it (germ theme fragments), as well as the first measures, are changed into new-sounding themes for use in the various movements by *theme transformation.* Each movement of the symphony represents a complete scene, or chapter in the story, and the whole is presented as a series of opium dreams in the mind of the hypersensitive narrator. Here is the situation in a translation of Berlioz' own words:

A young musician of extraordinary sensibility and overflowing imagination in a paroxysm of despair caused by unhappy love has poisoned himself with opium. The drug is too feeble to kill him, but plunges him into a heavy sleep accompanied by the weirdest visions. His sensations, emotions, and memories, as they pass through his diseased brain, are transformed into musical images and ideas. The beloved one herself becomes to him a melody, a recurrent theme *(idée fixe)* which haunts him everywhere.

First Movement: "Reveries, Passions: First he remembers that weariness of the soul, that indefinable· longing, that somber melancholia and those objectless joys which he experienced before meeting his beloved. Then, the volcanic love with which she at once inspired him, his delirious suffering, his return to tenderness, his religious consolation."

The opening music materializes out of thin air, introducing the listener into the private world of the young musician. This introduction consists of a series of contrasting variations representing the reveries and passions mentioned in the program, and employs some interesting orchestral effects. The movement proper begins with the announcement of the *idée fixe* in the tonic key, followed by transitional and modulatory material which leads to the dominant key and the statement of the second theme, a transformation of the opening measures of the *idée fixe*. The material which follows smoothly joins the closing section, if such can be said to exist, with the development. Here the *idée fixe* is repeated in its entirety in the dominant key——a rudimentary development device, but perhaps Berlioz wants to impress it upon our memories so that we will recognize it in later movements. Further development in sections contrasting in orchestration, mood, tension and key follow this restatement, even including a fugal working-out of the second theme. Very often the accompaniment figures as well as the leading melodic material are derived from the *idée fixe*. The recapitulation of the first theme occurs at the height of a climax, after which the section is entirely recomposed, with all previous formal sections, including the second theme, dissolved. The coda is also a reassembly of thematic fragments, ending in a plagal cadence reminiscent of the "religious consolation" mentioned in the program. The discontinuous motion, the brilliance of the orchestral contrasts, and the impetuosity of many of the sections lends a nervous intensity to the movement, quite characteristic of Berlioz' personality.

Second movement: "A Ball: At a ball, in the midst of a noisy, brilliant fête, he finds the loved one again"

EXAMPLE VI-3: Berlioz, *Symphonie fantastique.*

I. IDÉE FIXE-PRINCIPAL THEME: Allegro

II. VALSE: Allegro non troppo

IDÉE FIXE

Entire *IDEE FIXE* quoted, as above, 3/8 meter.

III. Adagio

OPENING DUET

b. Vl. & Fl.

cresc. poco a poco

IDÉE FIXE

c. Fl. & Ob.

(Example VI-3 II). This is a French waltz, rather fast, elegant, and graceful. The introduction is one of the earliest symphonic compositions to use the harp, and, as might be expected, Berlioz employs it brilliantly. The *idée fixe* does not appear until the trio, and is later brought back in the coda. The waltz section flows into the trio without a break, and, similarly, there is no pause between the trio and the resumption of the waltz.

> *Third movement:* "In the Country: On a summer's evening in the country he hears two herders who call each other with their shepherd's melodies. The pastoral duet in such surroundings, the gentle rustle of the trees softly swayed by the wind, some reasons for hope that had lately come to his knowledge, all unite to fill his heart with long-missed tranquility, and lend brighter colors to his fancies. But SHE appears anew, spasms contract his heart, dark premonitions appear to him. What if she proved faithless? One of the shepherds resumes his rustic tune, the other does not follow. The sun sets—far away there is rumbling thunder —solitude—silence."

This third movement, more or less the offspring of the nature scenes in the Beethoven Sixth Symphony, is the crown of this work and one of the most beautiful and successful of the Romantic "nature pieces." The statement of the theme of this set of variations is preceded by an introduction, a conversation between the male voice of the English horn and the female tones of the oboe. (Example VI-3 IIIa). The symbolism is plain and the melancholy and pensive mood is established. Now the theme appears (IIIb) introduced by the first violins and a flute in unison. It is approximately thirteen measures in length, and consists of transformed motives from the *idée fixe*. The variations which follow are free and developmental in nature, often relying upon the use of particular orchestral combinations and color for their effect. After an agitated climax, the image of the beloved appears, interrupted by expressive passages in the low strings. There are four discernable variations in all, the *idée fixe* occurring between the third and fourth, all joined by transitional passages of different kinds which often obscure the beginning of the variation. The coda brings back the introduction, but now the English horn calls in vain, answered only by the thunderous rumbling of four timpani played with sticks whose heads are made out of sponge to give the proper quality of sound. These, and the closing sigh of the strings effectively produce the mood of melancholy solitude suggested by the program.

Fourth Movement: "March to the Scaffold: he dreams he has killed his loved one, that he is condemned to death and led to the execution. A march, now gloomy and ferocious, now solemn and brilliant accompanies the procession. Noisy outbursts are followed without pause by the heavy sound of measured footsteps. Finally, the *idée fixe*, like a last thought of love appears for a moment, to be cut off by the fall of the axe."

In the opinion of this writer, we have here the most realistic piece of music ever penned which is still susceptible to the title "music." The orchestration abounds in new and amazing effects, like the sneering of the muted horns in the few introductory measures, the ghostly gibbering of the bassoon as a countermelody to the gloom-laden, dragging footsteps of the main march theme, or the incisive chord which interrupts the *idée fixe*, followed by the low string pizzicato which brings irresistibly to mind the picture of the severed head falling into the basket. And during the "brass band" trio sections, one can easily visualize Madame LaFarge imperturbably knitting as the tumbril rolls by (Example VI-3, IV).

Fifth Movement: "Dream of a Witches' Sabbath: he sees himself at a Witches' Sabbath surrounded by a fearful crowd of spectres, sorcerers and monsters of every kind, united for his burial. Unearthly sounds, groans, shrieks of laughter, distant cries, to which others seem to respond! The melody of his beloved is heard, but it has lost its character of nobleness and timidity. Instead, it is now an ignoble dance tune, trivial and grotesque. It is SHE who comes to the Sabbath! A howl of joy greets her arrival. She joins the diabolical orgy. The funeral knell, burlesque of the *Dies Irae*, Dance of the Witches. The dance and the *Dies Irae* combined."

In this movement, Berlioz shows that without a doubt—if one existed before—that he is a Romantic composer. The unholy rites celebrated by evil and supernatural beings was a favorite subject of the Romantic era. Numerous musical compositions—Moussorgsky's *Night on Bald Mountain,* and Saint-Saen's *Danse Macabre,* to name only two—together with stories such as *Frankenstein's Monster, Dracula,* and, of course, the grandfather of them all, *Faust,* demonstrate this penchant. Musically, too, the audacious combination of a witches' dance with the Latin chant for the dead from the Requiem Mass— "*Dies Irae, Dies Illa* . . ." "Day of wrath, day of judgment"—here is another romantic trait. Formally, as we have noted, this is a large fantasy and fugue—actually a double fugue, since it has two subjects, the witches' dance and the *Dies Irae,* which are combined in the latter part. The introduction establishes the eerie mood in a fine piece of tone painting—establishes it so well that the burlesque of the *idée fixe* sometimes comes as a considerable shock (IVa). The fantasy section proper is devoted to the exposition and development of this theme. Then a foreboding descending passage by the bassoons, cellos, and double-basses ushers in the funeral knell and the grim tune of the Latin mass (IVb). It is stated in long note values by the tubas and bassoons first, a version twice as fast in block chords by the brass follows, and then the *pizzicato* strings parody the theme in a typical rapid 6/8 rhythmic pattern. The next section is devoted to the exposition of the witches' theme, (IVc), which under different circumstances might pass as a rather guileless Italian *tarantella*. It is introduced fugally, after which a contrasting episode drawn from the introduction appears, and this in turn is followed by another fugal exposition of a chromatic version of the dance theme. Then the *Dies Irae* is combined with it, the two are loosely developed, along with some previous material, and the movement ends with an orthodox authentic cadence.

The orchestra which Berlioz employs in this composition is large, calling for, in addition to the double woodwinds and four horns, two cornets, two trumpets, three trombones, two tubas, two bassoons in addition to those usually employed, bells, bass drum, four timpani, and "extras" such as piccolo, clarinet in E♭ and English horn. Only in the final movement are all used, but the augmented brass section functions as a "band" in the "March to the Scaffold."

Now what is epoch-making about this work? First of all, the mere sound of it. It was performed in 1830, only three years after Beethoven's death, and represents a view of the orchestra undreamed of by the older master, for in it tone-color supplants purely thematic logic in a way comparable to the replacement of draftsmanship by color in the work of many Romantic and Modern painters. Were one to play this symphony on the piano, he would get an entirely distorted view of the work. It was *written for the orchestra* and it must be heard in the orchestra. The tone-colors of the instruments, and the ways in which the orchestra functions are of the utmost importance. This is *color orchestration*—type-casting, if you will, suiting the role exactly to the instrument.

Secondly, the audacity and originality of this conception of the orchestra, and the functions of its parts—soloistic, opposed, *en masse*, the exploration of mutings of the brass, the materials of drumsticks, the use of the string effects such as *pizzicato* and *col legno*—these point forward toward the techniques of the modern symphony orchestra.

Thirdly, the use of motto and germ themes in the most thorough and dramatically appropriate way, creating unity and coherence out of rather disparate parts. Liszt is usually given the credit for this technique, but Berlioz employed it first, adapting the technique to fit the various situations encountered in the different types of compositions he wrote. Thus we find similar uses of identifying and germ themes in *Harold in Italy* and *Roméo et Juliette* which are dramatically appropriate to the individual stylistic characteristics of each work.

Fourthly, the use of a definitely stated literary program which presumably dictates the episodes of the form. In this work, literary "accident" and musical logic approach, so that no violence is done to the classic format, although, to be sure, this is far from a classic symphony in form as well as content! The "fantastic" nature of the program is also an innovation of some importance, opening the door to this aspect of romanticism. Did someone say "Is the program necessary—cannot we listen to this music without knowing in advance what it tries to portray?" The answer? Listen to it—and decide for yourself.

Berlioz wrote many other works well worth hearing and which now are being performed with increasing frequency. We may oppose the lovely and expressive *Romeo and Juliet* dramatic symphony with the mighty *Requiem,* with its four brass bands, symphony orchestra and large choruses, or the *Damnation of Faust* with the pellucid *L'Enfance du Christ.* One day we may hope to hear some of the operatic works, for the reputation of Berlioz among present-day listeners is rapidly growing. And as our reaction against the nineteenth century wanes, we may come to appreciate the truly original and worthwhile qualities of this full-blooded Romantic of the first generation of his century.

Franz Liszt, 1811-1886

Liszt is, in many respects, the Byron of music. He revealed in his compositions a temperament fiery and bold, a pioneer spirit in that movement called the "music of the future" which opposed the conservatism of Brahms so violently. He was the foremost pianist of his day, and the friend and benefactor of many of his colleagues, among them Berlioz, Chopin and Wagner. Himself a none too stable union of opposing tendencies, he typifies the best in progressive romanticism, as well as the worst in oversentimental and gaudy vulgarity. It is unfortunate that many of his weaker compositions have gained popularity through their shallowness and superficial brilliance, for Liszt also composed many sensitive and expressive works. He realized, like Schumann, but more keenly, that the new music needed new forms, and during his career sought solutions for this problem. He adopted the technique of *theme transformation,* making it generally applicable to the development of thematic material, whether the composition was programmatic or not. Thus, we frequently find in the music of Liszt a series of sections, each devoted to a particular mood and using as thematic material a transformation of the basic theme suited to the prevailing sentiment. This kind of sectionalism replaces the classic idea of development so firmly held and exploited by Brahms. In essence, theme transformation is a kind of melodic variation rather than development, although in the music of Liszt and others development occurs as well. He was a superlative performer of Beethoven's piano works, by all accounts, and undoubtedly had delved deeply into that master's formal procedures, adapting those which suited his style, theme transformation among them.

Liszt was fully equipped to carry the Romantic banner to new heights except for one element which was lacking: genius of the searching and universal kind, the variety possessed by Beethoven, Mozart and Bach. These were whole men whereas Liszt was not. The fatal Romantic ambivalence divided him between worldliness and religion. Repeatedly Liszt announced his retirement from the concert stage and his retreat to meditation and institutional security. This ambivalence is found in his music, some of which reflects the vulgarity of the concert showman; in other works we find a musical subjectivism of the most refined kind.

In the most famous of his tone poems, *Les Préludes,* Liszt employs a basic germ motive out of which most of the other themes and melodies are derived. The discontinuous motion, chromatic harmony and virtuoso technique are all present, now transported into the richer and more varied colors of the orchestra.

Les Préludes is typical of the sometimes vacillating attitude of even the most progressive Romantics in regard to their descriptive music. Perhaps as musicians they did not really believe that it was completely legitimate, and certainly they all realized, as attested by their words on the subject, that the music had to stand on its own in the final analysis. This particular tone poem was intended to be one of a series of movements of a larger work which never materialized. It had nothing to do with Lamartine's poem *Les Préludes* at the time of its composition, but adopted it as a program later. Certainly the poem fits the music, episode by episode, but the suspicious fact remains that the music is formed after the plan of a Romantic sonata-allegro, using theme transformation and development, key relations a 3rd apart and discernible exposition, development and recapitulation sections. The episodes of the poem which are reflected in the music may be characterized by the following excerpts:

> "What is life but a series of preludes to that unknown song the first solemn note of which is sounded by death? Love is the magic dawn of every existence, but where is the life in which the first enjoyment of bliss is not dispelled by some tempest? . . . Yet no man is content to resign himself for long to the mild beneficent charms of Nature; when the trumpet gives the alarm, he hastens to the post of danger, so that he may find in action full consciousness of himself, and the possession of all his powers."

The succession of episodes and their formal functions in *Les Préludes* is as follows:

Introduction: Improvisatory beginning, with discontinuous motion: presentation of the primary and secondary germ themes (Example VI-4). Long preparation on the dominant chord for the beginning of the movement proper.

Exposition: *Section I. Andante maestoso,* C major. Germ themes in simple transformations in the trombones against string arpeggios, chords in wind instruments (b).
Section II. Lyric section with theme transformation in the strings (c), acting as modulatory passage to next part.
Section III. E major. Formally, a second thematic area, presenting a melody in the horns which uses the principal germ theme as the framework (d). Builds up to a climax which subsides on a few questioning chords based on the germ theme in the upper winds.

Development: *Section IV* the "tempest". *Allegro ma non troppo.* The germ theme, followed by a short chromatic scale section (e) is sounded ominously in the low strings, followed by an agitated development which uses the chromatic scales, a new martial rhythm and increased tempo (f). This reaches a climax after which the tempo and dynamics relax.
Section V. A lyric, pastoral section, lightly scored. Inversions and other less easily recognized transformations of the germ motives provide the material (g). Structurally, this and the following section provide the necessary contrast to Section IV and the coming agitation.

Recapitulation: *Section IV.* The "love music" of *Section III* reappears, but is disturbed by the "trumpet alarm," leading directly to——
Section VII. Allegro marziale. This last section transforms the germ motives rhythmically into a series of military calls (h). The long dominant preparation returns, leading to——

Coda: *Section VIII*

EXAMPLE VI-4: Liszt, *Les Préludes.*

This tone poem is not descriptively realistic, as was the "March to the Scaffold" of the *Symphonie fantastique,* but in using a more abstract germ theme, which by this very quality renders it free to be transformed according to the varying emotonal sequences of the program, Liszt achieves a more tightly unified yet agreeably varied composition. The music refers to the sections of the poem in a very clear fashion, sometimes using what have since become *clichés.* They are poetic and bombastic by turns, religious and sentimental: here we find the man mirrored in his music.

From the 1850's onward, Liszt wrote considerable music for orchestra, most of which employed the theme transformation technique, whether the work was avowedly programmatic or not. Many piano compositions before this, as well as the two piano concertos, similarly are constructed of episodes unified by this practice. His *Faust Symphony* is really a set of three symphonic poems, each devoted to the main characters of Faust (the hero himself), Marguerite and Mephistopheles. The final movement employs all three themes, and concludes with a choral setting of a text drawn from Goethe's drama.

The Tone Poem in Nationalistic and Postromantic Music

Many nationalistic composers chose the tone poem as the medium for telling the legends of their native lands, painting pictures in tones of the countryside or exalting their national heroes. One of the best known of these is *The Moldau,* one of a series entitled *Ma Vlast* (My Homeland) by the Bohemian composer Bedrich Smetana (1824-1884). In the nature of a rondo, the theme of the River Moldau recurs in increasingly forceful and developed style as the music traces its course from the rise of the brooklet in the mountains past villages celebrating folk festivals, through forests and meadows, rapids and waterfalls, to the battlemented city of Prague, where the past glories of the nation resound in the music.

The Russian nationalist composers produced a great many pieces of programmatic music, among which may be found Moussorgsky's barbaric orchestral celebration of a witches' orgy, *Night on the Bare Mountain,* Liadov's *Baba Yaga,* Rimsky-Korsakov's sophisticated orientalisms in *Scheherazade,* after the *Arabian Nights,* and Borodin's *On the Steppes of Central Asia.* Such works not only relied in many cases upon the literary program for their formal structure, but also afforded the composers opportunities for brilliant orchestration, a technique in which they were extremely skillful. Tchaikovsky, while genuinely Russian in his music, usually is classed as an international composer rather than a nationalist one. Perhaps the best of his programmatic works is the *Overture-Fantasy "Romeo and Juliet."* Rather than letting the events of the story provide the structure of the music, Tchaikovsky chose to present in the sections of a sonata-allegro form the themes which represent the characters of the story. We shall find the same plan of the sonata-allegro in the non-programmatic first movement of his *Symphony No. 6.*

A number of French composers of the late nineteenth century wrote symphonic poems of the Lisztian sort, the best known of whom are Saint-Saens, with his *Danse Macabre* in which Death plays an out-of-tune fiddle for ghosts and sprites in a graveyard, and Paul Dukas' *The Sorcerer's Apprentice,* after a tale by Goethe and made famous by Walt Disney in *Fantasia.*

Of the composers following the Romantic idiom and techniques in the twentieth century——post-Romantic composers, that is——the names of the Finnish nationalist Jan Sibelius (1864-1957) and the German Richard Strauss (1864-1949) stand out. The former imbued the tone poem with the epic grandeur of the Finnish national poem, the *Kalevala,* taking from this episodes concerned with the legendary heroes and gods of the northland. *Lemminkäinen's Return, Pohjola's Daughter* and the poetic *Swan of Tuonela* are played with fair frequency. His best known orchestral work, *Finlandia,* while not a tone poem of the kind we have been discussing, is a nationalistic work based on folk-tunes from the province of Karelia.

Richard Strauss was the son of a famous French-horn virtuoso, and was musically precocious. His musical training was conservatively oriented, but as he developed he discovered the dazzling music of Liszt and Wagner and immediately espoused "the music of the future," without, however, abandoning certain stylistic procedures which he had learned from the music of Brahms, his previous idol. The first works which brought him into prominence were a series of tone poems written during the years 1886-1903, several of which are still popular as showpieces for orchestra, so brilliantly are they scored. Among these are *Don Juan, Tod und Verklärung* ("Death and Transfiguration"), *Till Eulenspiegel's lustige Streiche* ("Till Eulenspiegel's Merry Pranks"), *Also sprach Zarathustra* ("Thus Spake Zarathustra") and *Don Quixote.*

The tone poem *Till Eulenspiegel's lustige Streiche* clearly shows Strauss' adoption of theme transformation technique as a thoroughgoing principle, for hardly a motive in the work is not derived from one or both of the two themes shown in Example VI-5. The work is based upon tales of a medieval German scamp whose escapades are

EXAMPLE VI-5: Strauss, *Till Eulenspiegel.*

pictured in the various episodes of the music. Strauss gave no explicit program for these, but allowed a critic to make one and gave it laughing approval. The distinctive rhythmic energy and melodic style of this composer are illustrated well by this work, as is his characteristically rich and colorful orchestration. Strauss often keeps the instruments busy by giving them little thematic scraps as accompaniment figures, a technique which adds to the general effect of pseudo-polyphony. The themes of the example are presented in an introduction which is balanced by an epilogue after Till's dramatic execution.

The other tone poems are similar, although they employ different kinds of scoring. *Don Quixote,* for example, is a set of variations on a "knightly theme" for cello, viola and orchestra, while *Also sprach Zarathustra* adds an organ to the already large orchestra.

In the music of Gustav Mahler (1860-1911), less post-Romantic in length of life than the others, we find no avowed programs to any great extent. However, the suggestive melody and orchestration would seem to indicate that the composer often used a programmatic basis for his symphonic movements, but did not reveal them to the world. Some information about this subject may be found in his letters.

Johannes Brahms, 1833-1897

Certain composers, inclined by nature or training to a more sober view of the art of music, decried what they felt was the gaudy and meretricious debasement of Beethoven's heritage. Not for them were

PLATE XXVII: *Johannes Brahms. Photograph about 1895, previously unpublished. (From the author's collection.)*

the easy virtues of program music, but rather the abstract symphonic path, difficult and overshadowed by the giants of the past. One composer of the nineteenth century stands as a solid monument to this conservative and responsible point of view, and that is Johannes Brahms. This intensely self-critical composer filled the most truly classic forms of his time with a Romantic language of lyric and constructive character. He understood that one of the perils which beset the Romantic artist was that of the loss of form. Rather than fill the empty classic shell with his music, or endeavor to create new forms, Brahms, like the sturdy peasant stock from which he sprang, began with the tradition and exerted himself to continue it in the same direction, applying evolution instead of revolution. He felt the responsibility of tradition: his first symphony was finally completed only after he was forty years old. But he also felt the responsibility to himself, and rigorously criticized, discarded and rewrote his works until they satisfied him. It would not be going too far to say that in point of technique, no composer of the Romantic era rivals him. But this is exactly what his contemporaries objected to. "All technique and no invention, no melodies" they cried. We find this hard to understand, for to modern ears, Brahms' music is full of satisfying lyricism, balanced with enough development to give depth, and combined with a sober, yet rich orchestration.

Brahms is a lyric composer with a certain kinship to Schubert, and therefore faced similar problems in creating large works. These he worked out in the same way as the earlier composer, using fragments of melodies or including germ motives in melodies. Certain of these reappear in a great many of Brahms's compositions: those noted at the beginning of Example VI-6A, for instance, are used in other works, especially the first one which the composer used as the musical translation of his motto, *Frei aber Froh* (F-A-F: Free but Joyful). Many melodies not employing this motive, however, are of similar span; others revolve about one tone, using the other motives noted.

This composer's harmonic style uses a rather wide vocabulary of chords, but they give a strong feeling of functional movement within a clearly stated tonality, and are not especially chromatic in the way the Liszt's harmonies often are, or his son-in-law's, Richard Wagner.

The rhythm is unstable and subtle, for the most part, but with little of the shock of Beethoven's syncopation. Rather, the instability urges the music onward, and often contributes to phrases of uneven length, which may begin on an odd beat of the measure and end in a similar way. Frequently the technique is to be found of substituting three notes where two occurred before in the same span of time, giving the music a different impetus and character.

Brahms favored the darker orchestral and solo colors, and often deepened these by the doublings of other instruments playing the same melodic line a third or sixth away from the leading one. Chords, too, are apt to have the thirds emphasized, giving them an unusual richness.

Of all of the Romantic composers, Brahms was the most skilled polyphonist. Yet the power of the chordal combinations is so strong in his music that even fugal writing seems to derive from the chord progressions rather than the emergence of harmony from the strongly linear melodic combinations, as in "pure" polyphony. Nevertheless, the polyphonic aspect gives Brahms's music depth and subordinate detail, a sense of "things going on" which invites rehearing.

The general mood of Brahms's earlier works——for piano or chamber or choral combinations, before his first essay into orchestral music ——was a buoyant, energetic romanticism tinged with darker colors. The orchestral music, however, is seldom really gay, for it moves too ponderously and is really too serious for genuine lightheartedness. It

is at times monumentally exciting, or serene, or profound, always on a
large scale. Brahms reserved most of his humor for his songs and piano
works. But such seriousness was quite characteristic of the period,
which took its art seriously, and especially during the second half of
the century, in which Brahms worked.

More than any other composer of the period, Brahms excelled in
the art of thematic development, not just theme transformation,
although he used that, too. One of his favorite developmental methods
is to extend a thematic fragment, growing a new-sounding melodic
idea organically from the old one. And he does not confine development to the section of that name in the sonata-allegro; many expositions contain development, if not on the surface of the music, under-
neath as accompaniment figurations. Sometimes a theme will be accompanied by itself in a rhythmically changed version! Such techniques
are, of course, eminently symphonic.

Symphony No. 3, in F Major, Op. 90.

This work is the shortest of Brahms's four symphonies, and, in some
ways, perhaps the most approachable. It consists of the usual number
of movements, but the second and third, instead of being a slow and a
dance movement respectively, are two lyric movements of somewhat
lighter nature than the outside ones. One commentator has used the
term "intermezzi" for such movements, a favorite, noncommittal title of
the composer himself for short piano pieces. All of the movements share
in the use of the germ themes; the motto is not always obvious to the
listener, although it may be found in the printed score.

I. *Allegro con brio.* Sonata-allegro (Example VI-6)
The first movement opens with the motto theme in a broad
gesture leading to the main part of the theme. The motto may
be heard in the bass accompanying the melodic material. New
rhythmic and melodic materials are used in the transition which
moves to a key a 3rd away from the tonic. The graceful second
theme is in triple compound meter and leads to a marchlike
figure. Development follows, first of the second theme, later of
the first theme in inversion and fragmentation combined with
the motto and a rapid version of the second theme. The exposition does not cadence, but flows directly into the development
section proper, which has many beautiful moments——the
surging first phase of the second theme in minor, the gradual
shortening of the marchlike theme, or the noble fanfare of the

EXAMPLE VI-6A: Brahms, *Symphony No. 3.*

II. PRINCIPAL SUBJECT: Andante

horns playing the motto against the string background. The rest of the movement is formally regular, and the coda is devoted to development of the first theme and quotation of the motto, which closes the movement.

II. *Andante*. Evolved sonata-allegro form

This lyric movement uses a relatively small amount of thematic material, much of which is interrelated through germ themes, all promoting a strong feeling of unity throughout. The form apparently is a sonata-allegro, but the recapitulation is rewritten and makes only passing reference to the second theme, while the melodic-rhythmic pattern of the transitions is employed to accompany the first theme. It is an example of Brahms technique of continuous variation, of always changing a theme in some way upon its reappearance so as to seem fresh and different. Of especial interest is the way he treats the repetitions of the motto theme, which in this movement are used as part of a cadential figure. The analytical listener will find much to interest him in this movement, which seems so simple on the first few hearings.

III. *Poco allegretto*. Ternary form.

This elegiac movement employs the three-tone scale figure (A) as a thematic motive as well as a unifying figure. Brahms's subtle use of rhythmic instability is especially interesting in the hesitant beginning of the B section.

IV. *Allegro*. Sonatina form

This movement opens with the understatement of a theme which makes extensive use of Motives A and B as the chorale theme does later in the transition. Motive A is prominent also in the second theme and the closing material. There is much internal development of the various themes and rhythms within the exposition, together with references to the first theme of the opening movement. The recapitulation is an enormously expanded version of the exposition, including development and transient changes of key which return shortly to the tonic or dominant. The first theme is both augmented and diminished in its metric values, often in triplets, to provide accompaniment to the normal version of the theme. The coda begins with a curiously winding variation of the first theme in triplet rhythms, played by the violas. Little by little the strings are muted and play wavering figures related to the B motive of the first theme, while above them we hear variations of that theme, then the motto theme, and finally, in slow and solemn tones, the chorale. The tonality gradually turns from F minor to F Major. Near the end, the motto returns, combined polyphonically with the motive from the first theme, and finally, during the last, long drawn out F Major chord, the upper strings echo the first theme of the opening movement, closing the circle of movements and bringing the work to a tranquil conclusion.

Peter Ilyitch Tchaikovsky, 1840-1893

The professional life in music of this composer began late, at the age of twenty-two. Previously he had had several music teachers, but none of these discerned any signs of genius in their pupil. Upon making the decision to be a musician, Tchaikovsky applied himself to the study of musical theory with such good effect that after three years Nicholas Rubenstein engaged him as professor of harmony at the newly established Conservatory in Moscow. From this time on his musical career progressed rapidly. In 1876 there began a strange friendship with Nadejda von Meck, the widow of a wealthy railroad magnate, who found great emotional satisfaction in Tchaikovsky's music. She began by commissioning works from him at generous fees, and in 1877 settled on him an annuity of 6,000 rubles. In spite of their warm friendship as evidenced in their letters to each other, the two met only twice and by accident, and never shared each other's company. In 1878 he resigned his teaching position, and used his time to compose and travel. From 1887 on he began conducting concerts of his own works, although he was extremely shy and nervous, and, in 1891, came to America, where he conducted concerts in connection with the dedication of Carnegie Hall in New York, as well as others in Baltimore and Philadelphia. In the last year of his life he composed his Sixth Symphony, the "Pathetique," and shortly after conducting the premiere of that work in St. Petersburg, drank a glass of unpurified water and fell victim to a cholera epidemic then prevalent.

Tchaikovsky's music mirrors the man. Shy, irritable, neurotically emotional and pessimistic on one hand, and yet exhibiting a childlike delight in the ballet and fantasy pieces, this composer reveals again the typical dual personality of the Romantic composer. Sometimes the traits mingle, as in the second movement of the Sixth Symphony, and the contrast is heightened but not resolved. His music is highly emotional, relying for communication of these states upon rich and appealing melody, usually with simple harmonization, strong and colorful orchestration, frequent tremendous climaxes and simple form. His sense of unity is strong in the Sixth Symphony, which employs motto and germ themes, but the formal structures are broken down into sections, each of which exists rather independently of the others, and usually is characterized by a single strong melody with subordinate attending

PLATE XXVIII: *Peter Ilyitch Tchaikovsky. Painting by Kusnezoff. (Courtesy of The Tretiakov Gallery, Moscow.)*

themes. Little real polyphony exists in his music, and the developmental procedures, while adequate to his purpose, tend to follow the same pattern in each work. The scale used as counterpoint or decoration, which we shall find in the Sixth Symphony, is common to his other orchestral compositions also, and often seems too simple a device to be really effective. Tchaikovsky probably is the least intellectual composer of the century, and possibly the most emotional in his music; it does not always wear well, for it gives itself too easily.

Despite a number of compositions for other media, Tchaikovsky's real habitat is the orchestra. Here he ceases sounding like a salon composer of pretty dainties, and reaches his full stature. Of the six symphonies which he composed, the last three are standard concert fare; the first three are played infrequently. His concerto for the violin is a standard in the literature of that instrument, as is his first piano concerto in B♭ minor. The second and third piano concertos seldom are played. He composed a number of symphonic poems and overtures inspired by literature and history, among which the favorites are *Francesca da Rimini* (after Dante), *Romeo and Juliet* (a so-called "fantasy-overture"), and the *1812 Overture,* based upon the defeat of Napoleon in Russia that year. A *Marche Slave,* and the *Capriccio Italien* are often heard, as are movements from the *Serenade* for string orchestra. He composed seven operas but the only one performed with any frequency outside of Russia is *Eugen Onegin,* after a story by Pushkin. Occasionally an aria, *"Adieu forets"* from *Jeanne d'Arc* appears on recital programs as does his song *"Nur wer die Sehnsucht kennt"* ("None but the Lonely Heart") on words by Goethe. The ballets *Swan Lake, The Sleeping Beauty* and *The Nutcracker* are in the repertory of practically every professional company the world over.

Symphony No. 6, in B Minor, Op. 74.

The symphony uses a number of germ motives, shown in Example VI-7. Motive A is a "pathetic" *cliché* used in Baroque and Classic music which we encountered in the introduction to Beethoven's *Pathetique Sonata,* Op. 13. Tchaikovsky uses both version A as well as the fragments *a* and *a'* as motive material.

I. Introduction: *Adagio.* Sonata-allegro form: Allegro (Example VI-7).

The motive A is introduced in the darkest and deepest tones of the orchestra, setting the melancholy mood as well as exposing the unifying germ theme. The movement which follows the clear conclusion of the introduction is typical of Tchaikovsky's concept of the sonata-allegro form. Rather complete and independent sections are devoted to the first and second principal themes and their keys, each of which reaches a considerable climax through sequence and increasing dynamics and tempo. The development begins excitingly enough, with a savage statement of A, followed by a quasi-polyphonic involvement of this theme. Scales spanning a fourth (see germ motives) appear, a quiet section ensues which increases to a climax on the crest of which the recapitulation enters. This climax does not subside until the entrance of the second theme, which, like the first theme, is shortened in this restatement. The movement concludes as it began, with a dark and quiet coda.

EXAMPLE VI-7: Tchaikovsky, *Symphony No. 6.*

III. PRINCIPAL SUBJECT-PART 1: Allegro molto vivace

j.

p Str.

DECORATED SCALE

Ww.   Str.   Cl.   etc.

HARMONIZED SCALE

PART 2

k.

Str.

p

a   a   a   etc.

f   SCALE   etc.

IMPORTANT MOTIVES

4TH   + SCALE

SECOND SUBJECT

l.

Cl.   4TH   4TH   4TH   4TH   4TH   4TH

p

4TH   4TH

etc.

IV. PRINCIPAL SUBJECT: Adagio lamentoso

SPAN OF 4TH

m.

Str.   *f*

mf   *p*

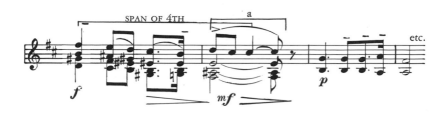

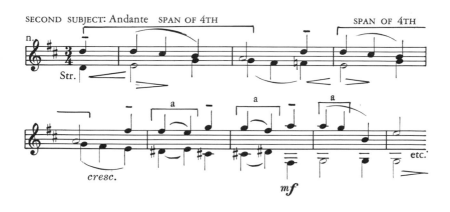

II. *Allegro con grazia*, 5/4 meter. Ternary form with coda.

The meter of this graceful movement is compounded of two-plus-three beats per measure, giving it the effect of a waltz melody with two up-beats. Indeed, casual listening may lead one to mistake it for a waltz! The A sections have a balletic quality, but the B part is devoted to a wailing transformation of the germ theme A.

III. *Allegro molto vivace*. Intuitive form unified by the interval of a 4th.

This is a combination of scherzo and march, the sections of which are juxtaposed for the greatest effect. If one were to force it into a Classical mold, that of the sonatina comes nearest, but it is clearly not a regular one. Motive A may be found in this movement, but it is not nearly so important as the interval of the fourth and the scale. At one point, scales run riot as Tchaikovsky uses them to maintain a high pitch of excitement before the triumphal return of the march. The movement is rather fantastic, and, other than serving as a foil for the final movement, seems a little out of place in this symphony.

IV. *Adagio lamentoso,* Sonata-allegro form.

The opening theme is a cry of despair whose strange and passionate color is due to the crossing of the string parts in such a way that the first and second violins alternate in playing the descending scale. A short transition leads to the second theme, noble, resigned and melancholy in tone, which is derived from the main theme by giving the tones slower rhythmic values. Dynamics and tempo increase until the growing climax is halted abruptly by a percussive chord. The recapitulation is quite regular, apart from reorchestration, and the second theme, now in the tonic minor key, has lost its noble quality and is only despairing. The music descends into the dark colors of the orchestra, and concludes in the region where the symphony began.

Other Romantic Symphonists

Revealing certain conservative tendencies in his symphonies was the nationalist composer Antonin Dvořák (1841-1904), best remembered by his *Symphony No. 9,* subtitled "From the New World." Though it was largely composed during a visit to this country, it contains little that is native American: the subtitle is correct, for it is a composition *from* the New World, not *of* it. The other popular symphonies, as well as works in other forms by this composer, are filled with folkloric and nationalistic elements, and are often very attractive. Dvorák was a *protegé* of Brahms, and adopted some of his cyclic and unifying procedures, a trait clearly evident in his Ninth Symphony.

Alexander Borodin (1834-1887), by profession a chemist, wrote three symphonies of nationalistic Russian character, although less overtly so than some of his other music. The second, in B minor, has proved to be most popular, and is unified by motto and germ theme procedures. Rimsky-Korsakov (1844-1908), the only one of the nationalistic group called "The Mighty Five" who became a professional musician, wrote a number of programmatic works which he called symphonies, but which lie closer to the methods of the revolutionary school, and to the far eastern element of Russian culture in melody and harmony than the more Slavic spirit of Russian folk song.

Anton Bruckner (1824-1896) carried on the spirit of Beethoven in teutonically massive and mystic symphonies sharing some of the Wagnerian techniques of harmony and orchestration. He was a virtuoso organist, a trait which shows in his music, but also a composer whose genuinely mystic Catholic spirit manifested itself strongly in his music.

He wrote nine symphonies, of which the most often performed is the Fourth. His choral music is more frequently heard, including three masses, a *Te Deum* and a setting of the 150th Psalm.

French composers seem to have devoted themselves to opera, operetta, ballet and song composition; it therefore remained for the Belgian organist and composer, César Franck (1822-1890) to found the French school of symphonic composition. He began as a disciple of Liszt, with designs upon the concert stage, but finally turned to organ-playing and became an outstanding performer and improviser, organist at the great church of Ste. Clotilde from 1858 to the end of his life. He wrote, among other works, a single symphony which seems destined to hold its own. It is perhaps the last word in theme transformation and cyclicism, for all of its themes are derived from a few germ themes of the first movement. It breathes a spiritual and striving quality characteristic of the best of this master's organ music. Franck's pupil and friend, Vincent D'Indy, carried on his master's concepts with certain individual differences.

Gustav Mahler (1860-1911): A Post-Romantic Symphonist

"Imagine a work so great that the whole world is actually reflected therein—one is, so to speak, only an instrument upon which the universe plays . . . All Nature is endowed with a voice there, and tells secrets so profound that we can perhaps imagine them only in dreams!"

So wrote Mahler to one of his friends, offering a partial key to his music. By "nature" he meant not only the natural world and the universe, but also the inner nature, his own and that of mankind, and he set out to write music that expressed the romantic love and fear of the natural world, the ecstasies and paroxysms of his spirit, the sense of sin of mankind and the longing for redemption, and the guileless and innocent spirit of the children of nature——the country folk. In no other composer's work is gaiety so childlike, is life so bittersweet, is irony so cutting as in the music of this Bohemian Jew turned Catholic in search for the perfect ultimate values he desired so ardently.

His First Symphony is a good introduction, or his Fourth; they abound in bittersweet Viennese melody, almost Schubertian in quality. The orchestration is a marvel of color and appropriateness, ranging in the First Symphony from the rousing dance of the second movement to the eerie and ironic minor setting of *Frère Jacque* in the third. There are moments of great tenderness too, as well as passages of sentimentality and banality; but we must remember that this man was trying to express the whole world of man and nature.

He wrote nine symphonies, with sketches for a tenth which have been completed in two versions and recorded. The Eighth, the so-called "Symphony of a Thousand" because of the large instrumental and choral forces needed to perform it, is a vision of redemption more grandiose than even Berlioz ever dreamed. In addition, many lieder for voice and piano and several cycles for voice and orchestra are in his catalog. The late *Das Lied von der Erde* (The Song of The Earth), a setting of German translations of nostalgic and pessimistic Chinese poems, the *Lieder eines fahrenden Gesellen* (Songs of a Wayfarer) and the *Kindertotenlieder* (Songs on the Death of Children) are outstanding examples of this side of Mahler's art.

THE CONCERTO

It might easily be deduced that the concerto for solo instrument and orchestra with its combination of intimacy and virtuosity would be a favorite form with audiences of the nineteenth century, and so it was. But it suffered from exactly the two qualities for which it was prized. From intimacy—lyrical intimacy—which precluded the dramatic conflict of the sonata-allegro form, and from virtuosity which too often expanded into showmanship and lost its integrity along the way. The great Romantic composers had to cope with both problems, possibly more acute in the concerto than in works for orchestra alone, and their solutions follow two diverging paths—that of the conservatives like Brahms, and that of the revolutionaries whose culmination in the concerto form arrived in the works of Liszt.

The conservative line used the last Beethoven concertos as models, and we find the clearest examples of these in two concertos by Brahms —the *Second Piano Concerto*, in B♭, Op. 83, and the *Double Concerto for Violin and Cello*, Op. 102. These works extend and make thematic the introductory section to the exposition of the first movement which was added by Beethoven to his *Fourth* and *Fifth Piano Concertos*. Brahms' other two concertos—the *Violin Concerto*, Op. 77 and the *First Piano Concerto*, Op. 15 omit this introduction in favor of the more typical classic procedure. The concertos of Paganini, Chopin, Tchaikovsky, Dvořák and Rachmaninoff, despite some small liberal tendencies, are essentially formally conservative, although often filled with the most personal language and feeling.

The progressive Romantic composers, realizing with varying degrees of clarity the problems which confronted them as post-Classical composers, moved generally toward concertos in single extended movements with single expositions in the sonata-allegro sections and functional or assimilated cadenzas. The continuity of sections in these one-movement works varies: in some cases, such as the Mendelssohn concertos, there are clearly three distinct movements linked by bridge passages, while in other works, notably the Schumann *Cello Concerto* and the Liszt *Second Piano Concerto*, the seams between the sections are almost entirely obscured. Mendelssohn was also one of the first composers to suppress the opening orchestral exposition of the first movement of the concerto, thus reducing the form to a clear sonata-allegro structure with cadenza. His example generally was followed by those composers who still revered the sonata-allegro enough to use it for the first movement or section of their concertos. But, we may note, they were not always successful in writing a good sonata-allegro because of the anti-dramatic lyricism which became a consistent feature of their music. Brahms alone seems to have seen and faced this difficulty and effected a solution.

The cadenza was also put to work by Mendelssohn. In the first movement of his *Violin Concerto*, the cadenza is used as the last stage of the retransition to the recapitulation rather than in its non-functional position in the classical design. Other concertos of the period, however, more often absorb the cadenza into the solo episodes either by making all of the solo interludes cadenza-like, or, vice-versa, making the cadenza less showy and more like interlude material. Structurally, these interludes sometimes become rather independent little pieces, drawing away from the thematic interplay in a manner never found in the Mozartian model.

The romantic concerto is often less wide in emotional scope than its classical prototype, and dwells frequently in a shadowy region of melancholy minor tonality from which it emerges from time to time for glittering virtuoso passages. There is little of the interplay of wit, tenderness, pathos and cheer which mark the concertos of Mozart. And only the Brahms concertos approach anything like the heroism and optimism of the Beethoven works in this form, for Liszt is really only pseudo-heroic, and the gentle Schumann incurably pessimistic, but excusably so for the sake of his lyricism.

The virtuoso elements in the Romantic concerto often decided the fate of the work. Because of this, the Schumann and the first Brahms concertos had cool receptions, for the composers made the virtuosity functional and subservient to the purely musical ends. These works require expert technique to perform, particularly those of Brahms, but there is no element of display *for its own sake*. Other concertos, however, designed for immediate popular acceptance, often consisted entirely of shallow brilliance; fortunately these, except for a few written for the violin, have passed into oblivion. Possibly the most dazzling of the virtuoso concertos still played are those of Liszt. In them the display is so much a part of the music, and the concept of the work so clearly one that includes effect, that they are more forgivable than some others. In them, Liszt tried to employ the new and colorful Romantic orchestra to its fullest symphonic extent, thus requiring more sound from the piano to secure its foreground prominence. In order to achieve this, he invented a bold new idiom for the instrument, making it match the orchestra in color and power. We must perforce admire the progressive spirit of this composer in endeavoring to achieve something genuinely new and alive in this medium.

Oddly enough, for all of the era's penchant for descriptive music, almost none of the great concertos are built around programs. The earliest examples of such works would seem to be the concerto-like programmatic symphonies of Ludwig Spohr (1784-1859), as well as his *Gesangsszene*, a violin concerto written in the form of an operatic scene. Karl Maria von Weber's early one-movement *"Konzertstück"* for piano and orchestra and Richard Strauss tone-poem-double-concerto, *Don Quixote* are all that remain. Berlioz' *Harold in Italy* is hardly of this class, being really a programmatic symphony with viola *obbligato*.

In addition to bona-fide concertos, the nineteenth century gave birth to many single-movement works in variation form for solo and orchestra. Strauss' *Don Quixote,* mentioned above, is such a work, as are Liszt's variations on the plainchant *"Dies Irae"* in his *Todtentanz* ("Dance of Death," inspired by a medieval fresco). César Franck's *Symphonic Variations*, Rachmaninoff's *Variations on a Theme of Paganini* and Tchaikovsky's *Variations on a Rococo Theme* for cello and orchestra, to name only a few. There also were written pseudo-concertos which were disguised by misleading names, such as Lalo's *Symphonie Espagnole,* as well as potpourris of folk or operatic tunes arranged for piano (usually, although sometimes the violin was used), of which the most prominent example is perhaps the still-played *Hungarian Fantasy* by Liszt.

The nationalist composers wrote a few concertos which were, for the most part charming and inimitable in content and conservative-to-weak in structure. That this has been no great barrier to public appreciation is attested by the vitality of the Grieg piano and the Dvořák cello concertos.

OPERA IN THE ROMANTIC PERIOD

The Italian tradition continued strongly into the nineteenth century, still a "singer's" operatic style, with the orchestra distinctly subordinate. The French "grand opera" became even grander until, like the dinosaurs, it collapsed under its own weight and was replaced by the more realistic *opéra comique*. The German opera, a newcomer to the century, began in a somewhat Italianate style, but rapidly became symphonic in all of the implications of that word in the hands of Richard Wagner. Let us examine these phenomena more closely.

Perhaps the most instructive comparison may be drawn between the Italian and German operas, particularly since they both sprang from the same stock——the Italian opera of the late Classic period. The opera of the Italian composers Donizetti (1797-1848) and Bellini (1801-1835) employed highly romantic stories, full of murder, madness and supernatural violence, set in a fluid kind of recitative which moved smoothly into the arias and was accompanied orchestrally. In the works of the Italian genius of the period, Giuseppe Verdi (1813-1901), the orchestra took an increasing part in the total ensemble and the recitative became ever more fluid and joined to the aria; but only in the last opera, *Falstaff* (1893), did the fusion become complete. Even then, the scoring cannot be called symphonic; the work is still a singer's opera, and, more important as we shall see, the characters on the stage are real people with whom we may identify.

The German opera, springing first from the play with songs, the *Singspiel*, and particularly Mozart's *Die Zauberflöte* ("The Magic Flute"), resembled the Italian opera in its separation of dialogue and song. Even the work hailed as the first genuine German opera, Karl Maria von Weber's *Der Freischütz* ("The Charmed Bullet"), despite the folksong quality of some of its numbers, still made clear distinctions between dialogue and the formal songs. However folk elements were so mixed with attractively Romantic supernatural happenings, a simple plot pitting good against evil and most appropriate and colorful orchestration, that the work was an instant success and still holds the German stage today. In the early years of Richard Wagner's apprenticeship, he felt the disparity of this stop-and-go opera, and eventually formed theories and wrote operas to demonstrate his new aesthetic which became a major force during the second half of the century. What he eventually arrived at was a symphonic conception of opera, one in which the voice parts were "endless melody" instead of being merely accompanied recitative. The orchestra was elevated from the role of accompanist, and by the power of its affective utterance commented upon the action, reflected the psychological states of the characters in the drama, and even recalled to the listener's mind, if necessary, previous important events. The substance of what the singers sang and the orchestra played was written in the style of the Lisztian symphonic poem, but instead of deriving everything from a single theme, Wagner assigned themes to each character, important object or idea of the libretto. These were called "leading motives" or *Leitmotive*. The music was formed from these *Leitmotive* transformed according to the action on the stage—that is, if one of the characters were joyful, his leading motive would be transformed into a gay-sounding passage. *Leitmotive* were combined polyphonically, if necessary, reflecting various emotions simultaneously which the listener was expected to unravel! So the German opera thus became symphonic, and changed its name to *music drama*.

It also became even more national than the Italian variety, for Wagner used myths, particularly German myths, as universal stories with meaning to all people in all times. In doing so, and in making the gods, goddesses and heroes superhuman he lost personal contact with his audience, and the dramas dealt with symbols and ideals rather than with real people.

Wagner aimed at the ultimate fusion of all of the arts——dance, mime, art, architecture, poetry, dramaturgy and music——in his "art work of the future, his so-called *Gesamtkunstwerk* (total art-work), but in practice he seldom achieved it, for Wagner the aesthetician was a different person from Wagner the composer. He wrote his own libretti, so shaped as to bring out the symbolic meaning of the drama, and was proud enough of them to have them published sometimes long before he set to work on the music.

In setting these texts, Wagner chose a style suited to the story. For example, in *Die Meistersinger von Nürnberg*, a comedy, the prevailing harmony and melody are diatonic and relatively uncomplicated, while in the psychological study of Romantic yearning and unfulfilled desire of *Tristan and Isolde*, the chromatic and dissonant harmonic style exactly reflects the emotional tone of the drama. These two examples are at opposite poles; most of the other works are written in a style somewhere between them.

Despite this formidable apparatus, Wagner often almost persuades us; but he does it with the music, not the cloudy philosophy or high symbolism. His orchestra is unfailingly rich and varied, and his inventions in sonority are still worthy of remark, although immersion in his ocean of harmony for the three or four hours necessary for the performance of one of the music dramas may leave a twentieth century listener a little fatigued with the luxurious sonority.

Three types of opera existed in France during the nineteenth century: the so-called grand opera, the lyric opera, and the *opéra comique*. Grand opera has all but died out in the twentieth century, and presentations of Rossini's *William Tell* or Meyerbeer's *Les Huguenots* are in the nature of revivals of museum pieces, despite some of the worthwhile music which they contain. After the disruption of the monarchy and its state-glorifying operas in the tradition of Lully and Rameau, grand opera became the art work which added splendor to the achievements of the Revolution. It lived up to its name, relying on spectacular effects on a large scale in the form of crowd scenes, choruses, ballets and overpowering stage settings. The plots were chosen to make the most of shocks and contrasts which would stir the audiences to a high pitch of excitement. The musical scores became more complex, the vocal parts more luxuriant, and the mixture of styles from the most artificial of coloratura arias to popular ballads became so prevalent that the result was often a hodgepodge without clear direction, coherence and unity. It satisfied the revolutionary bourgeois, who would not have comprehended the aristocratic restraint of the previous period, indeed, who would have denounced it. Wagner aptly characterized it as a drama of "effects without causes."

The original distinction between grand opera and *opéra comique* lay in the fact that everything was sung in the former, while in the latter the "recitative" was spoken, much as in our present day Broadway shows. In Germany, this kind of musical play was called a *singspiel,* and numbered among its members, in theory at least, such distinguished works as Mozart's *Magic Flute* and Beethoven's *Fidelio. Opéra comique,* starting out in the eighteenth century as a parody of the more ridiculous aspects of *opera seria,* had given rise to two separate attitudes on the part of opera writers by the time of the French Revolution. On the one hand, it was literally comic opera, though in the French rather than the Italian traditions. On the other, the more sentimental and Romantic works with occasional gay moments are best termed lyric operas. A third, more popular and frivolous stage work was known as the operetta; to it belong the timely satires in music of Jacques Offenbach (1819-1880) whose *La Belle Hélène, Orphée aux enfers* ("Orpheus in the Underworld"), *La Perichole* and *La Vie parisienne* still have popular appeal. In Austria, Franz von Suppé (1819-1895: *Poet and Peasant*) and Johann Strauss the Younger (1825-1899: *Die Fledermaus, Der Zigeunerbaron*) afforded the same kind of entertainment, while in England the Savoy operas of Gilbert and Sullivan accomplished the same purpose together with delightful ridicule of the more full-blown aspects of serious music in *The Mikado, Pirates of Penzance, H.M.S. Pinafore* and others.

Many of the lyric operas which were written and acclaimed during the first half of the nineteenth century in France have fallen by the wayside. One, however, has retained a surprising amount of vitality: it is the setting of the drama contained in Part I of Goethe's *Faust* by Charles Gounod (1818-1893). Achieving two thousand performances in Paris by 1934, in addition to performances in twenty-four different languages in forty-five countries, it is undoubtedly one of the outstanding representatives of French Romantic opera. Shortly after its first performance in 1859, the spoken dialogue was converted into recitative, in which form it is always presented.

The outstanding French work of the second half of the century is, of course, Bizet's *Carmen*. Like *Faust*, a nonproblematical work in its relation to tradition, its spoken parts were also set in musical recitative. We shall discuss this work more fully a little later.

While there is not space enough to examine in detail examples of the three operatic styles, we may point out some interesting and significant moments and techniques from each. It is suggested that the reader familiarize himself with the plots and action of the scenes we have chosen, preferably with the aid of an English translation of the libretto. These are often included in the album of an operatic recording.

Rigoletto, Act IV, by Verdi.

This is high Romantic drama, a mixture of love and self-sacrifice, vengeance, murder and morality, a mixture that nineteenth century audiences flocked to the opera to view. It is hardly less effective today.

Note the use of the orchestra in providing scenic effects, such as the storm and its lightning, and in its role as discreet accompaniment ranging anywhere from actual melodic background to the popular oom-pah-pah rhythm of the Duke's *La donna é mobile* ("Woman is fickle"). The famous quartet is in this act, notable for the melodic characterization of the emotions of all the characters at this point in the action. Of course the shuddering moment when Sparafucile gives the sack containing Gilda's body to Rigoletto is pure drama, the more effective because the jester believes that his revenge on the Duke——and on the world——is consummated, and the venom of his soliloquy is matched only by a similar moment in Verdi's *Otello* when Iago sings his *Credo*. But the composer's masterful theatrical stroke comes a moment later, when the voice of the Duke is heard singing *La donna é mobile* from the inn. Though we know the situation, this device still is effective. The ending is a little drawn out for modern audiences, and the trick of having Gilda not yet but almost dead is a little thin. Yet the act——the whole opera——is convincing because of the music and its characterization of the people who move in the drama. There is no profound symbolism here; the orchestra's role is clearly defined as accompanist and scene-painter; the music moves naturally and convincingly, now supporting the action, now shifting subtly to come to the fore in purely musical numbers; this is Italian Romantic opera in the hands of its greatest composer.

Carmen, Act IV, by Bizet.

This act, too, is the crux of the opera, the confrontation of the amoral Carmen with her cast-off lover, Don Jose, and her murder amid the sounds of victory from the bull ring. After the colorful choruses have ushered the bull-fighters and notables into the arena—— crowd scenes quite typical of many French operas——the orchestra sounds a chromatic phrase which was first heard in the overture and which has appeared from time to time during the opera. It is threatening, and is usually interpreted as a sort of *leitmotiv* representing Carmen's fate. The ensuing duet between Don Jose and Carmen reveals several interesting techniques. The dialogue is mostly carried on in *arioso*, or accompanied recitative of a highly melodious kind, and the sections are welded together by means of deceptive cadences. Many of these occur at crucial moments in the text, and reflect the emotional situation. The rising passion of Jose is well-handled and is ably supported by the orchestra. Note the orchestral doublings of the voices at certain moments in order to color the vocal sound. The harmony of the whole scene is characteristically French in its smoothness and attention to sonority, and the instrumentation is ideal in balance with the voice, supporting and audible without overpowering the singers. Bizet's timing is excellent, for Jose might become a little tiresome to the audience with his repeated implorings, but the composer stops this at the right moment. Again, as in *Rigoletto*, we have here a theatrical stroke typical of romantic opera: Carmen's murder as the crowd streams out of the arena acclaiming the victory of her new sweetheart, Escamillo. We should need to hear the remainder of the opera to realize the power of characterization which Bizet possesses; each person of the drama is painted accurately, from the swaggering roughneck, Escamillo, to the too-good-to-be-true Micaela, to say nothing of Carmen herself. Little wonder that Nietsche acclaimed this work as a true opera in opposition to the murky music dramas of his former idol, Wagner. Even such disparate composers as Brahms and Tchaikovsky felt the power of Bizet's masterpiece. It lives today as familiar music, sometimes on Broadway in a tarnished setting, but more genuinely in the opera house.

The Music of Richard Wagner (1813-1883)

The Wagnerian music drama is, as we have noted, essentially a tone poem which relates a story on the stage and in the music by means of several combined artistic disciplines. Heroic voices and singers with great stamina are needed for roles in these works, for the voice must often compete on rather equal terms with the orchestra, and for long periods of time. The music dramas are usually quite long in comparison to French and Italian operas, requiring four to six hours for complete performance. From time to time there occur purely orchestral sections without voice which are tone poems similar to those we have already encountered, but using several *leitmotive*. We shall begin with one of these in order to facilitate our entry into the Wagnerian world.

Our first example, then, is the excerpt for orchestra called "Siegfried's Rhine Journey" from the last music drama, *Die Götterdämmerung* ("The Twilight of the Gods") of the cycle of four entitled *Der Ring des Nibelungen* ("The Ring of the Nibelung"). Siegfried, the hero, is about to depart from his wife, Brünnhilde, a former Valkyrie, to go adventuring. His path will take him to the Rhine River, in which the Rhine maidens live who guarded the gold which was stolen in the first drama of the cycle. This gold, fashioned into a ring, will make the wearer lord of the world if he will renounce love. It is all rather involved to recapitulate so briefly, but since these motives occur in the excerpt, we must account for them here.

The concert version usually performed opens with the Fate motive (Example VI-8a), after which the coming of dawn is depicted in a short section. During this and immediately after it we hear the motive of "Siegfried the Hero" (b) in the brass, followed by that of Brünnhilde (c). The conversation between the two is omitted in the concert version, but in it Brünnhilde sends her husband forth to new deeds of valor. Now the motive of "Siegfried the Hero" reappears in a boisterously syncopated transformation as he sets out. Brünnhilde follows him with her eyes and heart, hears the sound of his horn in the distance (e), and muses on their love (d). The curtain is now lowered, and the music which follows is an introduction to the main portion of the music drama which ensues. We hear the recollection of the "Magic Fire Music" in which the first music is combined with that of Siegfried's horn (f). As the hero approaches the river, the Rhine motive rises sonorously through the orchestra (g) giving way to the cry of the Rhine maidens and the motive of the Rhinegold (i). The motive of "renunciation of love" (h) appears here and a little later, followed by a concert ending based on the motive of Siegfried the hero. In the music drama, the music flows into the first scene.

The plot of the music drama *Tristan und Isolde* may be summed up in this way: Isolde, a young Irish princess unwillingly betrothed to the aged King Mark of Cornwall, determines to commit suicide during the sea voyage to her future home. Tristan, under whose protection she has been placed, is the nephew and trusted henchman of the king; during a previous battle he killed Isolde's lover, and in

PLATE XXIX: *Richard Wagner. (New York Public Library).*

EXAMPLE VI-8: Wagner, *Siegfried's Rhine Journey.*

THE RHINE

RENUNCIATION OF LOVE

RHINE-MAIDENS AND RHINEGOLD

RHINEGOLD

revenge she plans to poison him also. She bids her maid to prepare a
lethal cup of wine, but out of affection the maid disobeys and instead
prepares a love potion which has the expected result. After their
arrival in Cornwall, their guilty love is discovered by King Mark,
Tristan is wounded in the fray which follows and flees to his castle
followed in turn by Isolde and the king. When she arrives, Tristan is
dying. King Mark comes upon the scene and, after hearing of the
love potion, forgives them. In the closing *"Liebestod,"* Isolde imagines
a vision of Tristan, alive and transfigured, and ecstatically vows a
deathless love as her spirit departs to join his.

The predominant emotion of this opera is that of longing—the
desires of love, and the desire for death and union in death—and
Wagner's basic problem was that of transmuting this feeling into music.
He accomplished it by the use of complex chromatic harmony. The
chords are continually seeking resolution, but the cadences, when they
finally arrive, are apt to be deceptive, thus postponing any sense of
finality, and prolonging the motion. The complex chords add richness
of sonority to the music, as well as instability to the harmony. In much
of the opera, orchestral polyphony provides the background for the
voices, using as its material the various *leitmotive.* The sonority of the
orchestra is predominantly dark as befits a tragedy in which night and
death play such a large part. Let us listen to three sections of the
work, the "Prelude to Act I," the love duet of Act II, and the conclusion of the opera, the *"Liebestod"* ("Love-death") of Isolde. The first
is played before the curtain opens, of course, and is woven out of the
motives to be found in Example VI-9a where they are listed in order
of their appearance in the music. There are many points of resemblance

EXAMPLE VI-9: Wagner: Excerpts from *Tristan und Isolde,* Prelude to Act I.

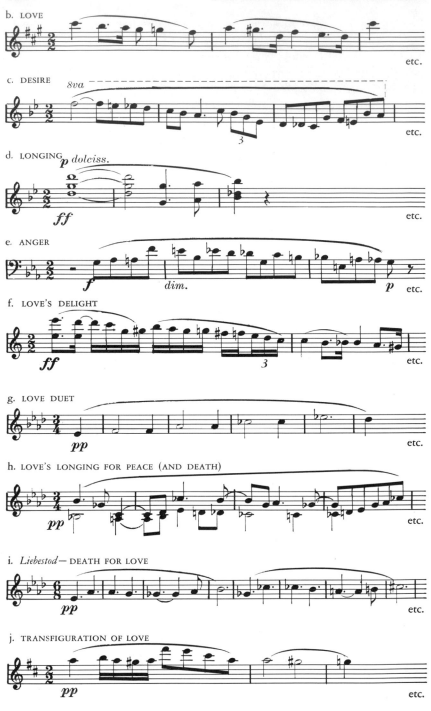

among them, which, weakening their individuality, add to the unity and coherence of the work. Wagner realized this, and by resemblances in motive detail suggests the relations between these ideas and things. Incidentally, it is noteworthy that Isolde and Mark do not possess *leitmotive*, and the sole one for Tristan, "Tristan the hero," appears only in the last scene of the first act, so important are the *psychological forces* and their *symbols*. In this opera perhaps more than in any other, Wagner's orchestra is the psychological interpreter of the stage action; the drama lives more fully in the music than on the stage. In the "Prelude," a structure appears which we have encountered only in its formative stages in other music. This is the *dynamic curve*, a term which will be used to describe the gradual crescendo from a very soft beginning to a loud climax in which the whole orchestra takes part. Such a form is this "Prelude," and our next example, the "*Liebestod.*" Both of these subside rather quickly after the climax, another frequent feature of this formal design.

The love duet constitutes the second scene of Act II. The lovers meet in the palace garden during King Mark's absence. Brangäne keeps watch while they impassionedly sing of their love. Realizing the impossibility of escape from the situation, they sing an apostrophe to night and death, for in death they would be together forever. Brangäne sings a warning, but they pay no heed, reaching in the second duet a climax of ecstasy which presages in themes and dynamic curve the final *Liebestod* of Isolde as she joins the dead Tristan. The important *leitmotive* for the love duet are given in the order of their appearance in Example VI-9b; those which are shared with the *Liebestod* are so marked.

The motives for the *Liebestod* are noted also in Example VI-9b, and include the first two of those given for the Prelude. This excerpt often is played in concert arranged for orchestra alone, but to be appreciated to the fullest extent it should be heard with the voice of Isolde mingling with the magnificent motivic polyphony and sensuous sonorities of Wagner's orchestra.

The *Liebestod* uses the following sequence of the above examples: i-j-i-j-a.

The particular style of harmony used in *Tristan*, with its continual modulation, chromatic chord alterations and deceptive cadences represents the most advanced harmonic technique of the Romantic period. By the use of these devices Wagner was able to achieve musical continuity over a long time span, but at the sacrifice of the form-building principles of tonality. All of the traditional forms, it will be remembered, depend upon the statement-departure-return of a tonal center.

In the case of the love-duet in the second act of *Tristan,* the tonality is highly uncertain over long periods, and only the fluctuation of harmonic tension, the motivic interplay and the rhythm propel the music; its goal, however, is obscure, for no familiar chord progressions indicate a tonal area in which the music may come to rest with a sense of arrival and completion. The questions posed by this work were simply these: when tonality becomes weakened to the vanishing point by chromaticism, how can the music be controlled, how can forms which will give it coherence be created? These implications of *Tristan* were not fully realized until the period 1910-1920, when certain clear-thinking theorists concluded that such works could not employ tonal means since they were not using the seven tone major-minor tonalities, but rather the *chromatic scale* of twelve tones. With this realization, Arnold Schönberg developed a technique which he called "composition with twelve notes related only to each other," *i.e.,* not to a single keynote. We shall examine this development in the next chapter, after first following some other musical issues in the transition period of the early twentieth century.

Other Important Operas

Perhaps the most significant of the operas outside of the German-Italian-French tradition is Moussorgsky's masterpiece, *Boris Godunov* (1874). Truly a national opera in its use of Russian folksong (both genuine and imitated) and the chants of the Russian Orthodox Church, it consists of a series of episodes concerning the relation of a ruler, Czar Boris, to his people, who represent the real hero of the work. Although *Boris* is as crowded with characters as the novel *War and Peace*, Moussorgsky still manages to individualize each of them by some deft stroke. There are many leading motives, but they are not treated symphonically in the Wagner manner and are closer to Verdi's usage. The harmonic language, often atonal as in the great Coronation Scene, affected Claude Debussy by its boldness and novelty. Rimsky-Korsakov, and later Shostakovich, edited the opera and rescored it in order to make performance practicable. We may deprecate their intrusion into some parts of the work, but we must realize that but for Rimsky-Korsakov this opera might not have made its way to the fame which it so certainly deserves.

Of the post-Wagnerian composers to achieve operatic success, Richard Strauss is the most notable. The apparatus is that of Wagner, but the harmonic and melodic style are closely related to the tone poem *Till Eulenspiegel,* which we have already heard. The most Wagnerian of his works is *Elektra,* the most notorious his setting of Oscar Wilde's *Salomé,* and the most popular, the romantic-rococo *Der Rosenkavalier.* Notable works of his which are seldom performed in the United States are *Daphne, Capriccio, Die Frau ohne Schatten* and *Arabella.*

A new movement in Italian opera appeared toward the end of the century known as *verismo,* or realism, similar to the trend known by the same name in literature. It tended to exploit brutal and vivid moments and to depict life as it is, usually among the lower classes or the peasantry. The most famous of the verismo operas are the one-acters *Cavalleria Rusticana* ("Rustic Chivalry") by Mascagni (1863-1945) and *Pagliacci* by Leoncavallo (1858-1919). The popular operas by Puccini (1858-1924), *Madame Butterfly, La Bohème* ("Bohemian Life"), *Manon Lescaut* and *Gianni Schicci,* represent a romanticized *verismo* in which the situations are derived more or less from life, but glazed over with a romantic haze of affecting melody and, for Italian opera of its time, colorful harmony and exquisite orchestration. The twentieth century operas of Gian Carlo Menotti (b. 1911) fall into the same category, except for somewhat more contemporary style and orchestration.

ROMANTIC PIANO MUSIC

The favorite solo instruments of the nineteenth century were the piano and the violin. While the piano literature is quite extensive, that of the violin, except for a few concertos and sonatas, tends toward either sentimentality or gaudy bad taste. The piano became increasingly less expensive and therefore more available to middle class people, and its popularity grew because of its self sufficiency in being able to produce both harmony and melody.

Rather few piano sonatas of real worth appeared during the romantic century, but short lyric compositions were abundant, some of high artistic value, others of the "brilliant but easy" variety for young ladies to strum on the parlor piano. Fortunately, these bushels of polkas, mazurkas, waltzes, quadrilles and variations have mostly vanished or remain as amusing curiosities.

The instrument for which they were written was close to the one of today, with damper and soft pedal, more than one string to each note and of about the same number of keys from bass to treble. In this century of orchestral color, composers learned that the piano tone could be shaded by the use of the damper pedal which, when depressed, raised the felt mutes off the strings and allowed them to vibrate sympathetically with any sounded tone. By careful manipulation of this pedal, they could sustain the tones of a lyric melody in a singing manner, or thunder loudly enough to compete with a full orchestra. The piano always had been the mainstay of composers, but now as never before they explored new chromatic and complex harmonies, more sonorous accompaniment patterns and cascades of rapid notes in the treble that surpassed the most agile coloratura soprano.

Many of the new effects were so intoxicating that virtuoso pianists ——not always the best composers themselves——inundated their works with them in flashy and meretricious effects, dazzling the audience with froth under which there was little substance. Unfortunately, the same kinds of pianists are with us today.

The style of these piano pieces varies from the compositions of Schubert, intended for middle-class *Biedermeier* folks to the most elegant and graceful works of Chopin, whose audiences included the expatriate dukes and duchesses of all Europe. The general style tendencies of songlike melody, modulatory harmony, theme transformation, expressive tempi and dynamics and frequent improvisatory manner were present, just as in the other music which we have examined. Yet each of the great composers for the piano used them in a different way, more individually than in the orchestra, for at the piano, one person was in control of the expression of the music, rather than the multi-headed orchestra.

Of the few sonatas written, a few by Schubert, particularly the last two, those by Schumann, Chopin and Brahms, and the single one-movement work by Liszt are notable and still are performed. But the larger number of works by these composers are the binary and ternary forms which they called Impromptus, Moments Musicales, Nocturnes, Intermezzi and so on, titles which gave no clue to either the form or the content. Of course the dance forms were frequent, especially those of nationalistic origin such as the mazurka, polonaise and especially the more international waltz. And the capriccio and rhapsody appealed by their very titles to the romantic imagination. The suite was now revived, but instead of consisting of dance forms, it was a collection of "characteristic" pieces, descriptive, moody or miniature tone poems.

Rather than attempting to describe the great diversity of compositions by the important keyboard composers, the following list is suggested for listening. One should keep in mind the observations noted above as well as those learned from contact with the orchestral music, for the Romantic style, for all its individuality, has a number of generalized qualities.

SCHUBERT:
Sonata in B♭ Major, from *Three Grand Sonatas, 1828.*
Impromptus, Op. 90
Moments Musicaux, Op. 94
SCHUMANN:
Carnaval Suite, Op. 9 (A set of character pieces all of which are based on the theme ASCH translated via the German scale names into tones as follows: E♭ is *Es*; A♭ is *As*; B-natural is *H*: thus Asch, the name of a small town where a sweetheart of Schumann lived, may become E♭-C-B-A, A♭-C-B, or A-E♭-C-B. When turned backwards, SCHA, the musical notes of Schumann's name appear, and similarly may be rendered into tones. Here, then is the imaginative use of a germ theme.
Fantasiestücke ("Fantasie-pieces"), Op. 12
Kinderscenen ("Scenes of Childhood"), Op. 15
Noveletten (After the singer, Clara Novello), Op. 21
Symphonic Etudes, Op. 13

PLATE XXX. *Frédéric Chopin. A rare daguerreotype made in 1849 shortly before Chopin's death. (The Bettmann Archive.)*

Frédéric François Chopin (1810-1849)

Chopin was the child of a French father and a Polish mother: traits of both nationalities are strong in his music. Chopin himself could be reckoned as French except for the Slavic melancholy and passion in his music. He was one of the great originals of the era, and developed music for the piano in terms of lyricism and sonority far different from those exploited by Beethoven. Chopin's harmony is most unique, offering interesting effects in color and unexpected progressions combined with the most sophisticated melody that ever graced Parisian salons or awakened the pangs of patriotism in a Polish *emigré*. This art of the piano is intimate in the extreme, for the most part, although, as Schumann said, there are often "cannon under the flowers," and certain compositions can roar with the best of the romantic virtuoso pieces. The forms usually are sectional, with contrasting melodies and keys; dances with multiple trios are frequent, as are simple three-part forms. There is much repetition, but it seldom becomes wearisome for Chopin usually adds fascinating and unexpected decorations in the form of dazzling figures in rapid notes, different for each return of the material. *Tempo rubato* is an essential part of this style, lending not only rhythmic flexibility and interest, but also intimacy to the melodic line. These compositions sound, and are intended to sound like improvisations, tossed off on the spur of the moment. They give no hint of the patient polishing process which kept them on the composer's desk sometimes for years after their initial creation. Chopin once wrote to a friend that he felt that he had some small talent for piano composition, and that he would do his best to realize it. Succeeding generations of concert audiences have proved him right. Chopin is at his best in intimate works such as the *Mazurkas, Valses, Nocturnes, Preludes, Impromptus* and *Fantasies*. While some of the *Polonaise* are small works, others are virtuoso concert pieces. The same is true of the *Ballades,* this composer's most successful works in extended form, and the *Scherzos* and *Etudes*. Despite this, there is no attempt to overreach the powers of the instrument and transform it into a veritable orchestra, as Liszt seems to have attempted; it is all *piano* music of the most refined sort.

Liszt

The style of Liszt is closely akin to that found in his orchestral works, but with the addition of the grand virtuoso style, sometimes blatant, but also at times of the most subtle and musicianly kind. The tone-poem concept still obtains, with the chromatic harmony, theme transformation and impulsive movement suggesting improvisation.

Annèes de Pèlerinage: Italie ("Years of Wandering: Italy"). A volume of tone poems in Liszt's best style. It includes *Sposalizio,* an interpretation of a Raphael painting; *Il Penseroso,* ("The Thinker"); *Canzonetta del Salvator Rosa,* (variations on a song by a 17th century poet, painter and musician); interpretations of Petrarch's sonnets nos. 47, 104 and 123; and the *"Fantasia quasi Sonata" Après une lecture du Dante* ("After reading a passage of Dante").

Sonata in B Minor

Perhaps this work is the greatest achievement of Liszt in the realm of piano music. It is multisectional, employing four main thematic ideas which are repeated, transformed and developed to provide the variety of forceful and lyric passages necessary to sustain such a long movement. To be noted are the impulsive and improvisatory nature of the beginning and several passages during the movement; the use of deceptive and unfulfilled cadences which provide continuity; the fluid, unstable chromatic harmony; the occasional cadenza-like passages and rapid ornamentation of the melody; the theme transformations; and the virtuoso style of the piece, calling upon all of the technical resources of the pianist.

Brahms

As might be expected, Brahms' piano music essentially is serious, lyric and structurally well-formed. Surprising is the delicacy of some of the works, the tenderness and the rhythmic subtlety. The improvisational element is quite lacking: Brahms always gives the feeling that he knows exactly where he is going and will proceed without delay. The virtuoso style and ornamentation also is lacking, although the pieces are by no means easy. The virtuoso composer, however, is strongly in evidence if the listener will direct his attention below the surface of the music, for canons, complicated polyrhythms and polyphony frequently are present, often in the most innocent-seeming compositions.

He wrote three sonatas, Op. 1, 2 and 5, all of which are played with reasonable frequency. More often heard are the four *Ballades* of Op. 10, the eight *Intermezzi* and *Cappriccios* of Op. 76 and the seven of Op. 116. The two *Rhapsodies,* Op. 79 and the *Piano Pieces* of Opp. 117, 118 and 119 are the crown jewels of his works for piano, however, revealing the deepest understanding and love of the instrument and the most consummate compositional technique. Op. 118, a set of six pieces, is suggested for first listening.

Other Composers

Of course the field of piano music was cultivated by many other composers. Mendelssohn wrote innumerable short and pleasant works, skillfully composed, which he called *"Songs without Words."* The nationalist composer, Grieg, with *Norwegian Sketches* and *Lyrical Pieces,* and Moussorgsky, with *Pictures at an Exhibition,* provided attractive works for both player and audience. But the keyboard music of Dvořák and Tchaikovsky has little of serious worth to offer, and the less heard of music by Rubinstein, Kalkbrenner, Moscheles and the whole tribe of Romantic virtuosi, the better!

THE ROMANTIC SONG

While the song with keyboard accompaniment had existed from the early seventeenth century onward, no special and continued effort seems to have been made to bring the text and its melody together into a more intimate relationship with the accompaniment. The latter usually consisted of stereotyped harmonic figures which did little else than support the melody, and the latter was often doubled in the keyboard part as though the singer could not be trusted. In the era of budding Romanticism, some song composers such as Loewe (1796-1869) and Zumsteeg (1760-1802) made the first steps toward using the keyboard accompaniment as an equal partner with the voice in creating the mood and transmitting the meaning of the song. Beethoven as well, wrote a few songs in which the piano powerfully supported the emotional content of the words, but it remained for Schubert, in his more than 600 songs, to establish the *lied* (Ger.: song) as an important art form for the century to come.

There are three types of *lied* which may be found throughout the period in the works of Schubert, Schumann, Brahms, Wolf and Mahler, the outstanding composers in this genre. The first concentrates the expressiveness in the melody, relying upon the words to make the mood or situation clear, and employs a more or less abstract piano accompaniment which, other than dynamic and tempo changes, does little to project the song's intent. In a second type, the voice part is almost neutral in expressive quality, serving only to project the words, while the piano part reveals, as it were, the inner emotions of the poet. The third kind lies between the two extremes, and consists of an aesthetic partnership between voice and piano similar to that of a good instrumental sonata, but here aimed at the most complete musical interpretation of the words possible. We shall find examples of all three in the works of the composers which we examine later.

Lieder fall into three general structural classifications: *strophic, altered strophic* and *through-composed* (Ger.: *durchkomponiert*). Let us illustrate these with three songs by Schubert, noting other aesthetic characteristics of the songs and Schubert's style as well.

The strophic form, in which each stanza of the poem is sung to the same music, may be represented thus:

Verses of text: 1 - 2 - 3 - 4 - 5 etc.
Music: A A A A

Such a song is the simple and charming setting of Goethe's poem, *Heidenröslein* ("The Hedge-rose"). The text is as follows:

Strophe I: Sah ein Knab ein Röslein steh'n,
Röslein auf der Heiden,
War so jung und morgenschön
Lief er schnell, es nah' zu sehn.
Sah's mit vielen Freuden.
Röslein, Röslein, Röslein rot,
Röslein auf der Heiden.

Strophe II: Knabe sprach: ich breche dich,
Röslein auf der Heiden,
Röslein sprach: ich steche dich,
Das du ewig denkst an mich,
Und ich will's nicht leiden.
Röslein, Röslein, Röslein rot,
Röslein auf der Heiden.

Strophe III: Und der wilde Knabe brach's
Röslein auf der Heiden,
Röslein wehrte sich und stach,
Half ihr doch kein Weh und Ach,
Musst'es eben leiden.
Röslein, Röslein, Röslein rot,
Röslein auf der Heiden.

(A lad saw a rose-bud on the hedge-rose, and ran to pluck it. He spoke, "I'll pluck thee now," and the rose answered, "If you do, I'll stick you with my thorns so that you'll always remember; and I won't be sorry." The boy broke the rose, the rose mercilessly stuck him, and he will always remember.)

In this little song, the piano part merely supports the voice with a simple harmonic accompaniment. The voice line is folklike and charming. Obviously Schubert did not regard this as a great emotional experience to be set dramatically.

Occasionally a poem containing several stanzas rises to an emotional climax in an intermediate verse, after which the following verses return to normal. When such a poem is set to music, new accompaniment, key and melody often support the climax. Such a form is known as *altered* or *modified* strophic form. The climactic verse is often the third in a set of four, although it may appear anywhere. Using our previous symbols we may indicate it thus:

Verses of text: 1 - 2 - 3 - 4
Music: A   A   B   A

where the climax occurs in the third verse. Sometimes the musical change will occupy only part of a verse, giving an AB or BA arrangement, as in the next song, *Die Forelle* ("The Trout"), by Schubert.

Strophe *I: (A)*	In einem Bächlein helle, Da schoss in froher Eil' Die launische Forelle Vorüber wie ein Pfeil. Ich stand an dem Gestade Und sah in süsser Ruh Des muntern Fischleins Bade Im klaren Bächlein zu! (last two lines repeated)	Within a sparkling streamlet that sang its merry song, I marked a silver trout Like an arrow, speed along. Beside the brook I lingered And watched the playful trout That all among the shadows Was darting in and out.
Strophe *II: (A)*	Ein Fischer mit der Rute Wohl an dem Ufer stand. Und sah's mit kaltem Blute Wie sich das Fischlein wand. So lang dem Wasser Helle, So dacht' ich, nicht gebricht, So fängt er die Forelle Mit seiner Angel nicht. (last two lines repeated)	With rod and line there waited An angler by the brook, All eager, he, to capture The fish upon his hook, While clear the water's flowing, So thought I to myself, His labor will be fruitless: I'm sure the trout is safe.

Strophe
III:
Altered
Section
(B)
	Doch endlich ward dem Diebe
	Die Zeit zu lang,
	Er macht das Bächlein
	   tückisch trübe,
	Und eh' ich es gedacht,
		The angler loses patience,
		He stirs the stream,
		And makes the limpid, shining
		   water
		All dull and muddy seem:
		"I have him," quoth the

(A) RETURN TO MUSIC OF STROPHES I & II:	So zückte seine Rute Das Fischlein zappelt d'ran, Und ich mit regem Blute Sah die Betrog'ne an. (repeat last line)	stranger As swift his line he cast; And heeding not the danger, The trout was caught at last.

In this song, the piano accompaniment pictures faithfully not only the flowing brook and the leaping trout, but also by means of "muddy" sonorities imitates the wily angler's trick. Again, a vignette, not too important, but enjoyable. At the persuasion of one of his friends, Schubert used the first strophe of this song as the basis for a lovely set of variations in his *Quintet* Op. 114, known for this reason as the "Trout Quintet." Obviously, a song in ternary form, A-B-A, might well be classed as an altered strophic form. Even binary form, with the climax near the middle is appropriate for some poems (*Wohin?*), while in *Der Doppelgänger* ("The Phantom Double"), Schubert uses a chaconne type of variation in which the sinister chord progression of four measures is repeated in the accompaniment while the voice declaims expressively and freely above it.

One of the most beautiful of Schubert's altered strophic songs, and one which uses his symbolic significance of major and minor tonalities, is the intensely romantic *Der Lindenbaum* ("The Linden Tree"). Of especial interest is the accompaniment, with its rushing wind-figures, the horn call and its echoes, and the changes in rhythm and sonority which accompany each strophe.

The *durchkomponiert*, or "through-composed" song is the musical setting of a narrative poem in which the action moves continuously forward, or of one concerned with a series of emotions which develop and grow out of each other. There is often no *exact* repetition of previous musical sections, but varied and new music, sometimes in both the voice and the accompaniment, follows the progress of the poem. Usually, however, some unifying device is employed, often rhythmic in nature, in the piano part. This serves to lend musical coherence to the song without interrupting the flow. In the most successful examples, *Der Erlkönig* and *Gretchen am Spinnrade*, this unifying factor not only accomplishes its primary structural purpose, but enhances dramatically the effect of the song in its depiction of action and emotional states. In symbols, then, this kind of form appears thus:

$$1 - 2 - 3 - 4 - 5 - 6 - \text{etc.}$$
$$A \quad B \quad C \quad D \quad E \quad F$$

Unifying Factor: * * * * * *

The "through-composed" song is excellently illustrated by the exciting and dramatic *Erlkönig*, set to words by Goethe. There are four characters in this drama in miniature: the poet, who provides the introduction and coda, the father, the child and the Erlking. This Erlking represents the force of the supernatural, and may be taken to be the devil in one of his many folk guises.

In listening to the song, notice how Schubert creates the mood immediately in the first few measures with the hammering octaves and the foreboding scale figure in the bass. First the poet speaks, melodically, but not too emotionally. Then the father, in the low register, where his part remains until the last, seeks to reassure the child. This reassurance is mirrored in the sturdy leap of a fourth upward with which all his lines except one begin. The rising hysteria of the child is pictured by Schubert's beginning each of the sections in which the child speaks one step higher than the preceding outcry. In addition, the outcries become louder. The wheedling of the Erlking causes a change in the music: the thundering horses' hooves are only suggested, the melody is sweeter, and the dynamic level is lower. At the end the poet returns to relate the outcome. The idea of using the ghostly recitative for the last line was a stroke of genius.

Here is the text of the poem:

Wer reitet so spät durch Nacht und Wind?
Es ist der Vater mit seinem Kind;
er hat den Knaben wohl in dem Arm,
er fasst ihn sicher, er halt ihn warm.
"Mein Sohn, was birgst du so bang dein Gesicht?"
"Siehst, Vater, du den Erlkönig nicht?
den Erlenkönig mit Kron' und Schweif?"
"Mein Sohn, es ist ein Nebelstrief."
"Du liebes Kind, komm, geh' mit mir!
gar schöne Spiele spiel' ich mit, dir;
manch' bunte Blumen sind an dem Strand,
meine Mutter hat manch' gulden Gewand."
"Mein Vater, mein Vater, und hörest du nicht
was Erlenkönig mir leise verspricht?"
"Sei ruhig, bleibe ruhig, mein Kind;
in dürren Blättern saüselt der Wind.
"Willst, feiner Knabe, du mit mir geh'n?
Meine Töchter sollen dich warten schön;

Who rides so late through night and wind?
It is the father with his child.
He holds the boy within his arm,
He clasps him tight, he keeps him warm.
"My son, why hide your face in fear?"
"See, father, the Erlking's near.

The Erlking with crown and wand."
"Dear son, 'tis but a misty cloud."
"Ah, sweet child, come with me!
Such pleasant games I'll play with thee!
Such pleasant flowers bloom in the field,
My mother has many a robe of gold."
"Oh father, father, do you not hear

What the Erlking whispers in my ear?"
"Be still, my child, be calm;
'Tis but the withered leaves in the wind."
"My lovely boy, wilt go with me?
My daughters fair shall wait on thee,

meine Töchter fuhren den nacht-
lichen Reih'n
und wiegen und tanzen und singen
dich ein."
"Mein Vater, mein Vater, und siehst
du nicht dort
Erlkönigs Töchter am düstern Ort?"
"Mein Sohn, mein Sohn, ich seh' es
genau,
Es scheinen die alten Weiden so
grau."
"Ich liebe dich, mich reizt deine
schöne Gestalt;
und bist du nicht willig, so brauch'
ich Gewalt."
"Mein Vater, mein Vater, jetzt fasst
er mich an!
Erlkönig hat mir ein Leids gethan!"
Dem Vater grauset's, er reitet geschwind,
er hält in Armen das ächzende Kind;
erreicht den Hof mit Müh' und
Noth:
in seinen Armen das Kind war todt!

My daughters nightly revels keep,
They'll sing and dance and rock
thee to sleep."
"Oh father, father, see you not
The Erlking's daughters in yon dark
spot?"
"My son, my son, the thing you see

Is only the old gray willow tree."
"I love thee, thy form enflames my
sense;
And art thou not willing, I'll take
thee hence."
"Oh father, father, he grasps my
arm,
The Erlking has done me harm!"
The father shudders, he speeds
ahead,
He clasps to his bosom the sobbing
child,
He reaches home with pain and
dread:
In his arms the child lay dead!

It is plain now that to understand *lieder* one must know the words.
Yet, paradoxically, *lieder* should be sung in the original language, for
translation often is extremely difficult if not impossible. Accents and
vowel placement in the translation should come where they do in the
original, and, of course, the meaning of the text at each point should
be the same. These difficulties often give rise to bad or absurd translations. It is better to listen to the song in the original language, following the translation on the program, or, better still, to do a little home-
work before the recital, looking up the text and listening to the song
on a recording.

Before we leave Schubert, let us recount a little more of his life
and work. He was highly undervalued by his contemporaries, even
by some of the poets whose work he set to music. They felt that he
had talent, but a comfortable, *Biedermeier* talent, not the genius we
now know it to be. Many of his compositions were played or sung
once, then put away; and some, like the great C Major Symphony,
were never played at all. His first successes with songs, at the age of
seventeen, were settings of poems by Goethe, *Der Erlkönig* and
Gretchen am Spinnrade ("Gretchen at the Spinning Wheel"). During
the seventeen years left to him, he composed, in addition to the six
hundred songs already mentioned, nine symphonies, twenty-one piano

sonatas as well as many short piano pieces, thirty-five chamber music works, six masses and seventeen operas.

His *lieder,* and those of composers following him, were often grouped in *song cycles* if all of the poems were written by a single poet as a unified group. Schubert's two song cycles are *Die Schöne Müllerin* ("The Miller's Beautiful Daughter"), and *Die Winterreise* ("The Winter Journey"), both to sets of poems by Wilhelm Müller. The first relates the unhappy love of a young miller, while the second describes the scenes viewed on a coach journey during the bleak season. *Die Winterreise* also contains typically Romantic reflections of nostalgia for lost loves, past happiness and the bitterness of fate. It was appropriate for Schubert to compose, for he wrote it near the end of his life, assailed by illness, poverty and the realization that his genius was only then coming into real maturity. There is an ironic and pitiful attempt at humor in *Die Leiermann* ("The Organ-grinder"), where the poet——Schubert in this case, for the music is the essential thing

PLATE XXXI. *Franz Peter Schubert. Pencil drawing by Kupelweiser, 1821. (Courtesy Austrian Information Service.)*

here——says to the half-frozen, penniless beggar, "Wonderful old fellow! Shall I go with you? Will you, while I'm singing, grind the tune for me?"

Robert Schumann (1810-1856)

Up to the year 1840, Schumann had written exclusively for the piano; in that year he married Clara Wieck after overcoming the disapproval of her father and after a courtship strongly reminiscent of that of Robert Browning and Elizabeth Barrett. His first year of marriage was also his "year of song," for he composed more than one-hundred and thirty songs. While his *lieder* have sensitive and expressive vocal lines, the piano part is often of equal or greater importance in its development of the emotional implications of the poem. There are often important preludes and postludes to a song in which the tones of the piano reveal those things for which there are no words. Many of the accompaniments, if such they can be called, approach independence as purely piano music, so thoroughly does Schumann develop them. Within each song there is usually little effort to use pictorial effects to the extent that may be found in Schubert's songs. Rather the mood is set and the poem is commented upon and interpreted. The *lieder* are made musically coherent by the use of harmonic, melodic and rhythmic figures which recur and often take on symbolic significance through their association with words or emotions of the text.

All of these characteristics are illustrated in the cycle entitled *Frauen-liebe und Leben* ("Woman's Love and Life"), Op. 42, consisting of the settings of eight poems by Adalbert von Chamisso. One of Schumann's masterpieces, this cycle is autobiographical, although Schumann was not aware of this when he wrote it. The songs tell of a young woman's falling in love—I. *Seit ich ihn gesehen* ("Since first I saw him"); II. *Er, der Herrlichste von allen* ("He, the noblest of them all")——her joy at her love being returned; III. *Ich kann's nicht fassen* ("I dare not, I cannot believe it")——a lovely soliloquy on her engagement ring; IV. *Du Ring an meinem Finger* ("Thou, ring on my finger")——the excited preparation for the wedding; V. *Helft mir, ihr Schwestern* ("Help me, sisters")——the announcement to her husband of their coming child; VI. *Süsser Freund, du blickest* ("Dearest one, you look at me in wonder")——the ecstatic outpouring of joy and affection for the child; VII. *An meinem Herzen* ("At my heart"); and finally, the tragic blow of the husband's unexpected death: VIII. *Nun hast du mir den ersten Schmerz getan* ("Now, for the first time, you have given me pain"). Each song is individual, yet through stylistic uniformity a strong sense of unity is to be felt. There is a tender and meditative prelude to the first song, characterized at one point by a lovely deceptive cadence; this music returns as a postlude after the last and tragic song with the most poignant effect, as though the widow were looking back at her past happiness. Musically, the quotation brings the set of songs around full cycle, and poetically it offers the most aesthetically satisfying conclusion conceivable.

Johannes Brahms (1833-1897)

Brahms had no particular year of song, unless it was 1868 when he composed twenty-five of them, but the composition of *lieder* was of considerable interest to him throughout his life. The same painstaking craftsmanship went into the writing of a song as was exerted in composing a symphony. Although a pianist, Brahms's essential point of interest is in the melody, with the piano providing an appropriate background of harmonic figuration which supports the rhythm of the vocal line and establishes the mood of the text. His *lieder* usually have very clear form, often strophic or a version of altered strophic in which a part of the music of each strophe is changed with each repetition to reflect the text more accurately and expressively. More than any of his predecessors, Brahms wrote long, sweeping vocal lines which demand great breath control by the singer and artistry in phrasing. The use of motives to achieve unity is similar to the practice found in Schubert and Schumann.

Brahms wrote only two cycles of lieder, the Romances from Ludwig Tieck's *Magelone (Magelonelieder)*, Op. 33, and the *"Four Serious Songs" (Vier ernste Gesänge)*, Op. 121. The several hundred other songs were usually issued in groups of from three to eight. In addition to the settings and arrangements of German, Czech, and Gypsy folk songs, Brahms also wrote many settings for small chorus, such as the popular *Liebeslieder* ("Lovesong Waltzes"), Op. 52, originally for vocal quartet and piano duet. A cycle rarely heard because it was published for the first time in 1933 and therefore is not included in most complete practical editions, is the melancholy "Songs of Ophelia" from *Hamlet*. In addition to the small choral works mentioned above, Brahms wrote a number of large works for chorus and orchestra, the most important of which is his mighty *Deutsches Requiem* ("German Requiem"), with texts drawn by the composer from the Old and New Testaments. In an age in which the quality of choral music was not usually very high, despite the large amount composed, Brahms's work shines forth like a beacon for its aesthetic worth and appeal.

The following *lieder* are representative of Brahms's production at different periods of his creative life. Through all of them the personality of the composer is to be strongly felt, and only the increasing simplicity and mastery of material attest the growth of the composer.

Op. 19/4: *Der Schmied* ("The Blacksmith"). One of the rather few songs to have a somewhat realistic accompaniment. Strophic.

Op. 32/9, *Wie bist du, meine Königin* ("How art thou, my queen"). A tender love song in altered strophic form, in which the piano frequently doubles the melody an octave higher in small bell-tones. The bass accompaniment consists largely of rather widespread sonorous arpeggios. The altered section is modulatory, beginning in the parallel minor, and returns to major on the refrain word of each stanza, *wonnevoll.*

Op. 43/2, *Die Mainacht* ("The May Night"). The form is A-B-A' with a key change down a 3rd at the beginning of B. The song is harmonically complex, and most beautifully so. The last verse, altered by a pivot modulation at a crucial moment in the text, also has a triplet rather than duplet accompaniment, resulting in a feeling of greater urgency.

Op. 84/4, *Vergebliches Ständchen* ("The Serenade in Vain"). One of Brahms's most delightful and humorous *lieder.* The suitor, serenading his sweetheart beneath her window, begs her to let him in, but the girl stubbornly refuses. We leave to the listener the fun of finding out how clever Brahms's setting is.

Op. 86/2, *Feldeinsamkeit* ("Alone in the fields"). One of Brahms's greatest creations. The deep peace and timelessness expressed in the poem are reflected by the simple accompaniment, with its sustained tones and the motivic countermelody above the voice. Note the long melodic line and the necessity to sing the phrases without a break. There are two strophes, the second of which is altered by a modulation at the words "wie schöne stille Traüme" ("like beautiful, quiet dreams") for greater expressiveness. A similar alteration occurs at *"mir ist, als ob ich längst gestorben bin"* ("it seems as though I long were dead"), leading to the lowest tone of the song, one which is chromatically lowered to move the meaning out of the dream world into another region.

Op. 105/1, *Wie Melodien zieht es mir* ("Like a melody it comes to me"). Widespread bass arpeggios, with occasional doubling of the voice part in thirds, support one of Brahms's most graceful and long-breathed melodies. No strongly expressive modulation occurs until the codetta is reached, when the repetition of the last line is shifted momentarily to a key a 3rd away.

Hugo Wolf (1860-1903)

His birth during the magic decade of the sixties marks Wolf as a post-Romantic of the same generation as Strauss and Mahler. Like them, he often exploited chromatic harmony and was able to invent motives and figures which illustrate his texts to a high degree. In his songs he paid the most minute attention to the speech-melody, mirroring its every nuance in the music. The *lieder* are usually quite short and concentrated, for he was almost psychopathically sensitive to the inner meaning of the poems which he chose and sought to give them the most intense expression of which he was capable. His most important compositions are his *lieder*, although he wrote a successful comic opera, a tone poem and a handful of chamber works. His method of composition was indicative of his morbid sensitivity to poetic texts and foretold the insanity which eventually claimed him. After a long period of depression, he literally would be struck with inspiration for setting some poetry which he had read, and, working at white heat, would set a cycle of poems in as short a time as two weeks. Usually works of a single poet received this concentrated attention, and thus there are the *Mörike Lieder* (53 songs), the *Eichendorff-lieder* (17), the *Goethe-Lieder* (51), the *Spanish Songbook* (44), the *Italian Songbook* (46) and the *Michelangelo-Lieder*. After this frantic purging of melody, another fit of depression would ensue until his musical demon was again aroused.

Each of the songs of this composer is highly individual, for he entered so fully into them that each has its own style. His song in praise of little things, *Auch kleine Dinge*, is seemingly quite simple in words and treatment, but Wolf manages to extract considerable feeling from the text, and poises against the vocal part a descending scale line which moves just after the harmony changes, thereby giving a gentle forward harmonic motion to the entire work. The short introduction and coda give the song an air of casualness and intimacy most appropriate to lieder.

Das Ständchen is not merely another serenade, as its title would indicate, but rather the nostalgic evocation by the poet of bygone days, when he too serenaded his sweetheart like the young man whom he is watching. There are two levels in the song cleverly combined by Wolf into one musical expression. The voice part moves freely to reveal the emotion of the text, while in the background the piano portrays the lute and the song of the serenader. As an added touch, the prelude charmingly illustrates the young man tuning the instrument.

The effort toward psychological interpretation, especially of sadness, which was so characteristic of the post-Romantic composers is well shown by *Das Verlassene Mägdlein* ("The Forsaken Maiden"). Here the sleepy kitchen maid comes down to the kitchen in the cheerless gray dawn to light the fire. She is "sunken in sadness" when she remembers her faithless lover and that she dreamed of him during the night. She weeps. "So begins the day. . . O would it were over." Wolf manages to express real pathos in this short song, using harmonic and sonorous means to make us feel the gray coldness of the kitchen and the heart of the little drudge

A more majestic grief appears in the setting of Michelangelo's second sonnet, *Alles endet, was entstehet* ("Everything must end, that exists"), really an epitaph for Wolf, for the Michelangelo settings of 1897 were the last songs he wrote. Little need be said about this composition, for it explains itself. Despite some of the stereotyped figures, reminiscent of the motive of the Tchaikovsky Sixth Symphony and the "sighing" motives of the Baroque, Wolf expresses without triteness and most powerfully the fatalistic words of the great Renaissance sculptor. Most of the piano part lies in the lower register, nor does the voice rise very high, sonorously in tune with the dark words.

Gustav Mahler and Richard Strauss

Both of these composers were eminent writers of *lieder*. Mahler's have already been mentioned, and it may be repeated here that his song style is very close to that of his symphonies. Strauss' *Lieder*, aside from the characteristic harmonic and melodic style, resemble those of Brahms in the treatment of voice and piano. Perhaps the summit of his achievements in the field is to be found in the *Four Last Songs*, meditations near the end of his life comparable to the *Four Serious Songs* of Brahms. Wagner and Berlioz, as well as Mahler, wrote songs with orchestral accompaniment which are significant contributions to the literature. Berlioz' *Nuits d'été* ("Summer Nights") contains some of his most beautiful inspirations, especially *Le Spectre de la Rose* ("The Apparition of the Rose"). Wagner's *Wesendonck Lieder* were preliminary studies for Tristan, written to the poems of a woman whom he loved during his political exile in Switzerland.

The French Art Song

The French *chanson* is almost the antithesis of the German lied, much as many of the national characteristics of the two people are opposed. Where the late Romantic *Lied*——for the French song appeared during the second half of the century——tends toward introspective sentiments which are idealistic, philosophical, often highly subjective with a degree of emotion which ranges perilously close to sentimentality, the French art song on the other hand is usually more objective, critically observant of the world, yet with sympathy, sometimes vividly realistic and pictorial, often ironic in attitude, restrained in feeling. The French composers carefully avoided the obvious in harmony and melody, sometimes to the point of sounding precious or artificial. One should compare *lieder* and *chanson* by listening to them in juxtaposition.

The best *chanson* composers seldom are represented to any extent by other music, for they were essentially specialists. Gabriel Fauré (1845-1924), the first important master of the genre, wrote many songs which frequently are presented on recitals today. Among these are *Lydia, Après un Rêve, Les Roses d'Ispahan, Clair de Lune, Prison* and the outstanding cycle, *La Bonne Chanson*. Henri Duparc (1848-1933) ceased composing after 1885, but the few songs we have of his are masterpieces. They include *L'Invitation au Voyage*, after Watteau's painting, and *Phidylé, Soupir* and *Chanson Triste*. The next masters of the French song belong to the twentieth century and will be discussed in that chapter.

CHAMBER MUSIC

If we should make a tabulation by composers of chamber music produced during the nineteenth century, we should discover, as might be expected, that the conservative composers lead all the rest—Mendelssohn, Schumann, Brahms and Dvořák. We find a considerable gap between the amount of chamber music produced by them—numbering in the twenties for each—and that produced by the next important composer. Tchaikovsky wrote eight chamber works, followed in descending order by Franck, Smetana, Rimsky-Korsakov, Borodin, Chopin and Bruckner. It is rather interesting to note the number of nationalist composers here. But this list gives no inkling of the importance of the works on the concert stage today. The piano trio and string quartet by Tchaikovsky are occasionally performed, but are certainly not the composer's best and most characteristic works. The well-known violin-piano sonata by Franck still is very popular, but his more ambitious chamber works are played infrequently. The autobiographical string quartet by Smetana, entitled *Aus meinen Leben* ("From My Life"), and the chamber works by Rimsky-Korsakov are heard seldom. The Borodin *Second String Quartet* is reasonably popular, although it sounds rather dated, but the Chopin piano trio and the *Introduction and Polonaise* for piano and cello, along with Bruckner's single string quartet, are almost never played. Those giants of the orchestra, Berlioz, Liszt and Wagner, wrote no chamber music, except perhaps for Wagner's *Siegfried Idyll*, which is scored for chamber orchestra. Moussorgsky was too interested in Russian speech and character to work with anything but song and opera. The romantic urge to create large, powerful and colorful works inclined the composers toward the orchestra, while the appeal of virtuosity attracted them toward the solo piano or the concerto, to the neglect of chamber music.

The desire for harmonic richness in the chamber music of the time is an almost fatal disease, even in the most skillful composers, Brahms and Mendelssohn, although the latter is less at fault since his classical style allows him to move freely in the idiom. Schumann's best works in this difficult medium are generally conceded to be his *Piano Quintet*, Op. 44, and Piano Quartet, Op. 47, although even in these he seems unable to put any trust in the stringed instruments' abilities to carry their parts, and constantly doubles them with the piano, creating a monotonous color which often dulls the senses to the real beauty of the music. Dvořák's chamber music, nationalistic to the core, is perhaps least afflicted by the romantic devotion to harmonic richness, although it is none the less persuasive. The texture is often classical in its transparency, and the music moves comfortably within the smaller framework. This is not always true of the chamber music of Brahms, avowedly the perpetuator of the chamber music tradition, but the music itself is so genuine and meaningful that the imbalance is not troubling. When the size of the ensemble is expanded to include five or six instruments, or when it employs piano, the sonority seems more adequate to the demands of the music. We must not expect the chamber music of this century to possess the lucidity, transparency, elegance and directness of the best works of Mozart and Haydn, much less the personal profundity of the late Beethoven; we must judge and appreciate it on its own merits, for even Brahms, so strongly tradition-oriented, was incapable of expressing ideas which were not part of his time and culture. Only the most blazing geniuses, like Bach and

Beethoven, were able to surmount their time, the first by summing up the music of his age, the second by withdrawing from that of his in order to pursue flights of an ever-developing musical imagination.

Schubert

Schubert, however, so close in many ways to the Viennese Classic masters, moves comfortably within the sphere of chamber music, for it had not yet suffered a decline in popularity, and still formed a part of the music-making to be found in many German and Austrian homes. Schubert composed some of his most beautiful chamber works for just such gatherings, including fifteen string quartets, the two magnificient trios, violin sonatas, and the two quintets, the "Great" C-major, and the "Trout," so-called from the variations on one of Schubert's own songs which forms one of the movements. The *String Quartet in D Minor,* subtitled "Death and the Maiden" because the slow movement consists of variations on the composer's song of this name, uses many of the characteristic procedures we discovered in the B Minor Symphony. The first movement, a sonata-allegro unified by the opening triplet figure, contains a lovely melody for its second subject and a coda which is the summation of the movement. The variations are based upon the chaconne theme of the song, and are essentially of the decorative

PLATE XXXII: *Felix Mendelssohn. (The New York Public Library.)*

type usual in the Classic Period, except that Schubert invents accompaniment patterns which create delightful and new sonorities. The Scherzo is rather brusque, with syncopations, followed by a lyric trio. The last movement exhibits none of Schubert's frequent "finale trouble," but moves surely through its sonatina form and coda. The first theme is rather in the popular "Hungarian" style, followed by a declamatory second theme which contrasts strongly with it. The whole work is more forceful than we might expect, and often makes a larger impression than the B Minor Symphony.

Felix Mendelssohn, 1809-1847

We have not yet said very much about this gifted musician who was born into a wealthy Jewish family in Hamburg and spent his boyhood in Berlin. In a social stratum and an era which presupposed a high degree of general culture, Felix excelled. He was provided with an excellent education, and his musical studies were given the utmost encouragement, even to the provision of an orchestra—small, to be sure, but still an orchestra—for the performance of his early compositions. These included an Octet for strings and the still bewitching music to Shakespeare's *Midsummer Night's Dream,* written in part at the age of seventeen with a most assured hand in the tempered Romantic style that was to stay with him all his life. Through his teacher he developed an interest in the music of Bach, and his revival of the *St. Matthew Passion* in 1829 inspired him to compose his two oratorios, *St. Paul* and *Elijah.* He was highly appreciated in England, but returned to Leipzig to make his home and to found the conservatory as well as to conduct the famous *Gewandhaus* Orchestra which he made one of the best in Europe. Mendelssohn's style is classicistic—that is, it is no longer the genuine classic product, but resembles it closely in technique and form. Indeed, to his contemporaries Mendelssohn seemed to have solved the problem of uniting traditional forms with Romantic contents.

In many compositions, particularly the "Songs Without Words," lyric pieces for the piano, and some of the slow movements of larger works, Mendelssohn's expression become ovensentimental and vapid. With movements in rapid tempo, such as sonata-allegros and scherzos, however, this tendency is avoided, and the music, while not as impetuous as that of Schumann, reveals a refined Romantic temperament coupled with the most skilled craftsmanship. His scherzos, particularly, reveal this quality in their elfin lightness and delicacy and exquisite balance. Mendelssohn's tragedy, however, was that he did not develop as a composer, but wrote in the same polished style at the close of his life as he did at the age of seventeen. His technical mastery and taste advanced, but the creative imagination did not. Perhaps this accounts for his present position as a secondary master who occasionally writes a work of the first rank in which we feel that the ideas and forms are fulfilled. The *Trio in D Minor,* Op. 49, is not one of these, but shows the composer in a more romantic light than many works, has many ingratiating tunes which accounts for its popularity, and exhibits Mendelssohn's technical mastery of the medium and material.

The opening sonata-allegro begins with a fine, impetuous theme which is developed somewhat during its presentation and the transition. The lyric second theme and its accompanying codettas is most characteristic, and may become too sentimental if the tension is allowed to relax. The closing theme returns to the vigor of the first theme, and the development uses the same theme, juxtaposed in a lyric way with the second theme. The balance among the instruments is ideal, all sharing thematic and accompanying material. The development is not dramatic, which is as it should be, for it thus throws into sharp relief the moody and passionate first theme. The recapitulation is altered, made more lyric than the exposition, and closes with a more active coda which brings back both the first and second themes.

The Andante second movement resembles Mendelssohn's lyric piano pieces and is dangerously close to sentimentality if played a little too slowly or with *tempo rubato,* or, in fact, with any license at all! Straightforward performance is needed to save it. The form is clearly ternary, with a darker and more modulatory middle section. A "parting is such sweet sorrow" coda ends the movement.

The Scherzo shows this composer's light touch and finished technique. The form is a large binary structure with extensive development rather than a simple retransition. It is neatly and continuously joined together, so that the motion never stops or pauses, and the joints in the form are cleverly concealed. Obviously, Mendelssohn chose this structure because he wanted continuity rather than the contrast and repetitions of the older tenary scherzo.

The final movement is a variation of the sonata-rondo structure in which the first and second thematic groups employ the same rhythmic motive while melodically different. This makes for a great deal of continuity and vigor in the exposition section, which, other than having a lengthy closing section, is quite normal. The diagram of Example VI-10 indicates the structure. Note that Theme C recurs in the recapitulation in the same key in which it appeared before. This is a rather new formal experiment, but one which is quite successful in Mendelssohn's polished style.

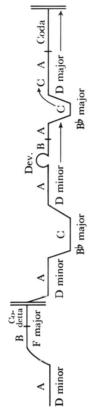

Development takes place within sections and during transitions.

EXAMPLE VI-10: Mendelssohn, Finale of *Trio in D Minor*.

Brahms

One of Brahms's lifelong interests was chamber music, and, although he was not the only composer of this era to cultivate the medium, his efforts are the most noteworthy and most frequently performed nowadays. The clarinet was always a favorite orchestral instrument of Brahms, but, until he met the virtuoso Richard Muhlfeld he had not written any chamber music including this instrument. In 1891, at the age of fifty-eight, he composed the *Clarinet Quintet,* Op. 115 and the *Clarinet Trio,* Op. 114, and later, in 1894, two *Sonatas for Clarinet and Piano,* Op. 120. In each of these, the bittersweet tone-quality of the instrument reflects the autumnal nostalgia and resignation of Brahms's later years. We shall examine the *Clarinet Quintet in B Minor.* The only noteworthy predecessor of this composition is Mozart's work for the same combination, written some one hundred years before. Both works reflect a similar attitude on the parts of the composers and both owe their existence to the happy chance that the composers had come into contact with excellent clarinetists.

The first movement of Brahms's composition opens with a lyric motive in the violins, a sort of revolution around one note (Example VI-11, I-a). This basic shape becomes a unifying motive throughout the work, although Brahms often disguises it rhythmically or by making unessential melodic changes. Another unifying motive, still more basic in design, appears next. It is the descending halfstep, which is immediately inverted, and the combination of the two form the substance of the next two measures. Under them, as though this were a tiny exposition of the most elemental ideas to be used, appears a syncopated rhythm alternately in the viola and cello. While not the only syncopation that the composer uses in the work, it may be taken to suggest the kinds of rhythmic figures to be expected. The sonata-allegro form which follows is an example of Brahms's "artless complexity," for while sounding perfectly natural it employs the most subtle variation and development techniques.

The second movement, Adagio, is in the parallel major key and is ternary in structure. The A section exposes and develops a lovely lyric melody, while the B part is improvisatory in a particularly "Hungarian" way, with emotional tremolos in the strings, cadenza-like passages for the clarinet which include references to the "turn" figure of the first movement. The return of A is rewritten.

The Scherzo is in rondo form, ABACABA, with a slow introduction. The theme of the introduction is a simplified version of the "turn," while that of the A section exploits the step motive from the first movement in a rhythmically compressed form. The fourth movement is a set of five developmental variations with coda. The use of the "turn" from the first movement is fairly obvious throughout the theme and in some of the variations, often rhythmically changed in the latter. The coda is noteworthy, for here Brahms quotes a version of the beginning of the first movement with the thematic germs out in the open. This cyclic procedure is not new to us by now, but still is effective, especially when used so poetically as it is here.

EXAMPLE VI-11: Brahms, *Clarinet Quintet*. The germ themes are indicated by the brackets labeled A and B. A is the "turn" theme, and B is the step motive.

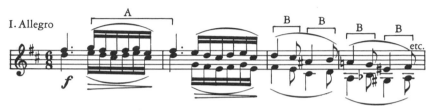

THE ROMANTIC STYLE IN THE OTHER ARTS

Music was preeminently *the* Romantic art because of the directness and power of its appeal to the emotions, but its sisters, literature and painting, were not far behind. In each of the important art media of this period certain similarities may be noted in the use of techniques which emphasize emotional quality. But when the term "emotion" is used, we must not always infer agitation and excitement: quieter moods of tenderness or melancholy are equally genuine. All music was not after the pattern of Berlioz' "March to the Scaffold," not even all of Berlioz' music. Nor was all painting a swirling pattern of motion as in many works of Delacroix, for there was also the calmness of Corot and Turner.

Foremost among the techniques used to heighten the emotional impact of this art was the use of color. We have seen how the Classic composers used it in much the same ways as the Classic artists, such as David, for whom drawing—the clear delineation of forms and their arrangement—was primary, and the use of color secondary. We must realize that color *was* used, however, but that it was not the constructive element which it became in the nineteenth century. One need merely look at black and white reproductions of the paintings of Géricault, Delacroix, Corot and Turner to realize the importance of color in this art. In literature we need only quote the word-music of two outstanding poets of this century to show the importance of the vowel and consonant sounds themselves as well as the imagery in the creation of effects of color in language. The first example is the opening stanza of Byron's poem, *The Destruction of Sennacherib*.

> The Assyrian came down like a wolf on the fold,
> And his cohorts were gleaming in purple and gold:
> The sheen of their spears was like stars on the sea
> When the blue wave rolls nightly on deep Galilee.

The second is from *Ulalume* by Edgar Allen Poe (although *The Raven* might do as well). Notice the difference in color connotations from those of Byron's work.

> The skies they were ashen and sober:
>   The leaves they were crisped and sere—
>   The leaves they were withering and sere:
> It was night in the lonesome October
>   Of my most immemorial year;
> It was hard by the dim lake of Auber,
>   In the misty region of Weir—
> It was down by the dank tarn of Auber.
>   In the ghoul-haunted woodland of Weir.

The tendency of poets to rely increasingly upon verbal music and color led to the "modern" poetic practice of combining words for their sound values alone, disregarding the sense of the result. This verbal "orchestration" at its height is exemplified in poetry in the words of the symbolist poets Mallarmé, Baudelaire and Yeats, and in some of the prose of James Joyce, Paul Valéry, Marcel Proust and Thomas Wolfe. Later, meaning was reintroduced by the use of "color" words associated in such a way as to suggest other levels of meaning impossible to traditional combinations, thus enriching literature by a new dimension.

The reading of the above poetic excerpts suggests another device of Romanticism: the fusion and continuity of parts, here demonstrated by the commas, dashes and semicolons, which allow the flow, urged on by the rhythm, to reach only non-final cadences within the stanza. This weakening of conclusive devices is shared in music, as we have seen. It is reflected in painting by the use of less sharply defined lines and by the use of curves which transfer to one another so that the eye

PLATE XXXIII. *"Oriental Lion Hunt" by Delacroix. Not only the exotic subject, but also the motion, which almost creates an abstract design, proclaim the romanticism of this painting. In color the effect is greatly enhanced. (Courtesy of The Art Institute of Chicago, Potter Palmer Collection.)*

is caught up in continuous motion, excellently illustrated in Delacroix's *Lion Hunt* (Plate XXXIII). Such continuity and diffusion may be compared to the orchestral polyphony of Wagner, in which there is a constant fusion of one *leitmotiv* with another.

There is also a constant play of dynamic values, of loud and soft, light and shadow, assonance and dissonance in these art works. In the music and painting, details are often sacrificed for overall effect—the preference for the broad canvas and the orchestra rather than the miniature and the string quartet. And as we have shown above, poetry linked together unusual and unexpected words in order to form richer total effects than might be secured by more traditional procedures.

The strong projection of the individuality of the artist also is felt by the listener or beholder of this art. The creative artist is the conscious interpreter of the real or dream world which he presents to us, whether he be the Berlioz of the witches' orgy, Constable before

PLATE XXXIV. *"A View of Salisbury Cathedral"* by Constable. An early Romantic, quasi-Impressionistic treatment of landscape. (Courtesy of The National Gallery of Art, Washington, D.C., Mellon Collection.)

Salisbury Cathedral (Plate XXXIV) or Poe and his raven. Most important, he interprets this world in his own images and symbols in highly personal and inimitable forms and arrangements. "The style is the man" was never before more true, for the element of psychology entered the Romantic arts and began shaping the course of music and painting particularly, toward the styles of the twentieth century which are termed *Expressionism* and *Surrealism*. The researches of Freud, it might almost be said, were rendered historically necessary by the Romantic cult of the individual.

Perhaps one of the most obvious unifying threads that ran through all of these artistic endeavors was the choice of subject matter—what the music, poem, novel or painting was "about." As we have seen earlier in the chapter, distance in time or place had great charms for the Romantic. The escape from the world which was becoming "too much with us" became highly important to the romantic individual who saw the death of imagination and fantasy in the realistic world of the industrial revolution. He fled to the opera house to hear Gounod's *Faust,* Wagner's *Tristan und Isolde* or Marschner's *Der Vampyr.* Or, he attended concerts of such works as Berlioz' *Damnation of Faust* or Wagner's *Faust Overture* or Liszt's *Faust Symphony.* Or he mused on German folksong and on Teutonic musical profundity in the symphonies of Brahms or Mahler. Perhaps he picked up a book which spirited him back to the middle ages, such as *Ivanhoe,* or to America with *The Last of the Mohicans,* or chilled his blood with *Macbeth* (for to this century Shakespeare was a supreme Romantic) or with *Dracula* or *Frankenstein's Monster.* He may have gone to an art gallery to see Delacroix's illustrations for *Faust,* or his oriental scenes from North Africa; perhaps he was pleasantly scandalized by Ingre's harem women and *odalisques,* or, at the other extreme, admired the rather sentimental portraits of English beauties by Lawrence and Reynolds, or their French counterparts as pictured by Ingres or Renoir. Or, to get some fresh air, he may have walked to the construction site of a new cathedral—or library, college building, postoffice or railway station—in the genuine Gothic style, such as St. Clotilde in Paris, or St. Patrick's in New York. "Anytime but now, anyplace but here" seemed to be the watchword.

But this was not wholly true, for painters like Daumier, novelists like Zola, dramatists like Ibsen and composers like Mascagni, Leoncavallo and Puccini turned away from these escapes and faced the often ugly reality of their times (Plate XXXV). Some of their observations were real protests, shocking in their truths, while others sugarcoated the unpalatable and turned it into works which appealed to the upper middle class, who were delightfully scandalized at the stage violence and immorality. But in some works the psychological insight penetrated uncomfortably deeply, causing real shock and a moment's glimpse of motives usually hidden within the subconscious.

To sum up, then, we find that the arts of the nineteenth century shared several comparable techniques whose purpose was to induce an emotional response, and that those techniques which accomplished this best became highly developed. We find also that the arts shared subject matter which attempted to escape reality, or which delved into the subconscious; or which faced reality and interpreted it in an emotional way. The arts most cultivated were music, literature and painting, with sculpture and architecture far behind and largely devoted to works in the Gothic revival or the oriental genre, without the marked advancement in techniques which occurred in the other arts. We shall see, in the next chapter, how this advancement and refinement led to the *impasse* out of which the art of the twentieth century slowly emerged.

PLATE XXXV. *"The Third Class Carriage" by Daumier. An example of realism by an artist, like Zola in literature, dedicated to exposing the seamy side of life to the attention of the public in order to hasten social reform. (Courtesy of The Metropolitan Museum of Art, New York, The H. O. Havemeyer Collection.)*

LIST OF TERMS

program music
absolute music
musical distortion
musical ambiguity
instrumental lyricism
theme transformation
tone poem, symphonic poem
symphonic economy
tempo rubato
discontinuous tempo, motion
continuity of flow
tone color
doubling
third relationship

cyclic symphony
leitmotiv, leitmotive
Lied, Lieder
song cycle
strophic
altered strophic
through-composed
     (durchkomponiert)
secco recitative
parlando
music drama
Gesamtkunstwerk
dynamic curve
verismo

BIBLIOGRAPHY

Berlioz

Barzun, Jacques, *Berlioz and the Romantic Century*, (2 vols.) Columbia University Press, N.Y., 1950.
Barzun, Jacques, *Berlioz and His Century*, Meridian Books, Cleveland, Ohio, 1956.
Berlioz, Hector, *Memoirs*, Knopf, N.Y., 1948.
Berlioz, Hector, *Nights in the Orchestra*, ed. Barzun. McClelland, N.Y., 1956.

Brahms

Gal, Hans, *Johannes Brahms, His Work and Personality*, Knopf, N.Y., 1963.
Geiringer, Karl, *Brahms, His Life and Work*, Oxford, N.Y., 1947.
Neimann, W., *Brahms*, Knopf, N.Y., 1947.

Chopin

Hedley, Arthur, *Chopin*, Dent, London, 1947.
Hedley, Arthur, editor and translator, *The Selected Correspondence of Fryderyk Chopin*, Heinemann, London, 1962.
Weinstock, Herbert, *Chopin: The Man and His Music*, Knopf, N.Y., 1949.

Dvořák

Newmarch, Rosa, *The Music of Czechoslovakia*, Oxford, London, 1942.
Robertson, Alec, *Dvořák*, Dent, London, 1945.
Stefan, Paul, *Antonin Dvořák*, Greystone Press, N.Y., 1941.

Liszt

Searle, H., *The Music of Franz Liszt*, Dent, London, 1954.
Huneker, J. G., *Franz Liszt*, Scribner's, N.Y., 1927.

Mahler

Mahler, Alma, *Gustav Mahler: Memories and Letters*, Viking, N.Y., 1946.
Newlin, Dika, *Bruckner, Mahler and Schönberg*, Oxford, N.Y., 1947.
Redlich, Hans F., *Bruckner and Mahler*, Dent, London, 1955.

Mendelssohn

Radcliffe, Philip, *Mendelssohn*, Dent, London, 1954.
Selden-Goth, G. *Mendelssohn's Letters*, Pantheon, N.Y., 1945.
Werner, Eric, *Mendelssohn: A New Image of the Composer and His Age*, Free Press, N.Y., 1963.

Moussorgsky

Calvocoressi, M. D., *Modeste Moussorgsky*, Essential Books, Fair Lawn, N.J., 1956.
Leyda, J. and Bertenssen, S., editors. *The Moussorgsky Reader*, Norton, N.Y., 1947.

Rimsky-Korsakov

Rimsky-Korsakov, N., *My Musical Life*, Knopf, N.Y., 1942.
Serov, V., *The Mighty Five*, Allen, Towne & Heath, N.Y., 1956.

Schubert

Brown, Maurice J. E., *Schubert: A Critical Biography*. St. Martin's Press, N.Y., 1958.
Deutsch, Otto E., *The Schubert Reader*, Norton, N.Y., 1947.
Flower, N. H., *Franz Schubert, The Man and His Circle*, Tudor, N.Y., 1928.
Einstein, Alfred, *Schubert, A Musical Portrait*, Oxford, 1951.

Schumann

Abraham, Gerald, ed., *Schumann, A Symposium*, Oxford, London, 1952.
Chissell, Joan, *Schumann*, Dent, London, 1948.
Niecks, Frederick, *Robert Schumann*, Dutton, London, 1925.

Strauss, Richard

Del Mar, Norman, *Richard Strauss, A Critical Commentary on His Life and Works*, Vol. I (up to *Der Rosenkavalier*), Free Press, London, 1963.
Strauss, R., *Recollections and Reflections*, Boosey and Hawkes, London, 1953.
Strauss, R. and Hoffmansthal, H., *A Working Friendship: The Correspondence Between Richard Strauss and Hugo von Hoffmansthal*. Random House, N.Y., 1962.

Tchaikovsky

Abraham, Gerald, ed., *The Music of Tchaikovsky*, Norton, N.Y., 1946.
Weinstock, Herbert, *Tchaikovsky*, Knopf, N.Y., 1946.

Verdi

Toye, Francis, *Giuseppe Verdi, His Life and Works*, Vintage Books, 1946.
Walker, F., *The Man Verdi*, Knopf, N.Y., 1962.

Wagner

Barzun, Jacques, *Darwin, Marx and Wagner: The Critique of a Heritage*, Anchor Books, Garden City, N.Y., 1958.
Burk, J., *Letters of Richard Wagner*, Macmillan, N.Y., 1950.
Newman, Ernest, *The Life of Richard Wagner* (4 vols.), Knopf, N.Y., 1933-46.
Newman, Ernest, *Wagner as Man and Artist*, Vintage Books, N.Y., 1960.
Shaw, G. B., *The Perfect Wagnerite*, Brentano, N.Y., 1916.
Stein, J., *Richard Wagner and the Synthesis of the Arts*, Wayne State Univ. Press, Detroit, 1960.

Weber

Stebbins, Lucy and Richard, *Enchanted Wanderer, the Life of Carl Maria von Weber*, Putnam, N.Y., 1940.

Wolf

Walker, Frank, *Hugo Wolf, A Biography*, Knopf, London, 1951.

Books of General Interest

Artz, Frederick B., *From the Renaissance to Romanticism*, Phoenix Books, University of Chicago, 1962.
Bekker, Paul, *The Orchestra*, Norton, N.Y., 1936.
Boucourechliev, André, *Schumann*, Evergreen Books, N.Y., 1959. (Excellent pictures, not only of Schumann, but also representative of the Romantic Period.)
Bourniquel, Camille, *Chopin*, Evergreen Books, N.Y., 1960. Similar to the Schumann book mentioned above.

Dorian, Frederick, *The History of Music in Performance,* Norton, N.Y.
——, *The Musical Workshop,* Secker & Warburg, London, 1947.
Einstein, Alfred, *Essays on Music,* Norton, N.Y., 1962.
——, *Music in the Romantic Era,* Norton, N.Y., 1947.
Fleming, W., *Arts and Ideas,* Holt, N.Y., 1963.
Kerman, Joseph, *Opera as Drama,* Vintage Books, N.Y., 1959.
Kolodin, Irving, ed. *The Composer as Listener,* Collier Books, N.Y., 1962.
Mellers, Wilfrid, *Romanticism and the Twentieth Century,* Essential Books, Fairlawn, N.J., 1957.
Norman, Gertrude & Shrifte, Miriam Lubell, eds., *Letters of Composers: An Anthology,* Knopf, N.Y., 1946.
Peltz, Mary Ellis, ed., *Introduction to Opera,* Barnes & Noble, Inc., N.Y., 1962.
Prawer, S. S., ed. & translator, *The Penguin Book of Lieder,* Penguin Books, Baltimore, Md., 1964.
Sachs, Curt., *The Commonwealth of Art,* Norton, N.Y., 1946.
Schumann, Robert, *On Music and Musicians,* McGraw-Hill, N.Y., 1964.

ADDITIONAL LISTENING

Mendelssohn
Overtures:
    "The Hebrides" ("Fingal's Cave")
    "Calm Sea and Prosperous Voyage"
    Ruy Blas
Incidental Music to Shakespeare's
    A Midsummer Night's Dream
Symphony No. 3 ("Scotch")
Symphony No. 5 ("Reformation")
Octet for Strings
Elijah (oratorio)

Schumann
Symphonies Nos. 1, 2, 3
"Manfred Overture"
Concerto for Piano and Orchestra
Symphonic Etudes, for piano
Liederkreis: Frauenlieben und Leben
Individual songs:
    "Die beiden Grenadieren"
    "Ich grolle nicht"
    "Der Nussbaum"

Chopin
Piano Concertos Nos. 1 and 2
Various piano compositions:
    valses, mazurkas, polonaises
    impromptus, ballades, scherzi.
    sonatas, etudes, nocturnes, preludes

Berlioz
Romeo and Juliet, dramatic symphony
Requiem
L'Enfance du Christ (oratorio)
Damnation of Faust
Overtures:
    Roman Carnival
    The Trojans
    Benevenuto Cellini
    Harold in Italy, for Viola and Orchestra

Brahms
Academic Festival Overture
Tragic Overture
Variations on a Theme by Haydn
Variations on a Theme by Handel

ADDITIONAL LISTENING (CONTINUED)

Symphonies Nos. 1, 2, 4
Violin Concerto
Piano Concerto No. 1
Double Concerto for Violin and
  Cello
German Requiem
Piano Quintet in A Major
Clarinet Sonatas
Liebeslieder Waltzes
Various piano compositions, es-
  pecially those of Opp. 116,
  117, 118, and 119

Liszt
  Faust Symphony
  Hungarian Rhapsodies, for piano
  Transcendental Etudes, for piano
  Piano Concertos Nos. 1 and 2

Wagner
  Overtures and excerpts:
    Tannhäuser (Venusberg
      scene)
    Lohengrin
    Flying Dutchman
  Prelude and Act II
    Die Meistersinger
    Die Walküre, Act I

Tchaikovsky
  Piano Concerto in Bb Minor
  Violin Concerto
  Symphony No. 4
  Symphony No. 5
  Overtures:
  Francesca da Rimini
  1812 Overture
  Suite for String Orchestra

Jan Sibelius
  Symphonies 1 through 7
  Finlandia
  Violin Concerto

Antonin Dvořák
  Symphonies 2, 4, 5
  Concerto for Cello and Orchestra
  Slavonic Dances
  String Quartet F Major, Op. 96
    ("American")

Bedrich Smetana
  *From Bohemia's Forests and
    Meadows*
  String Quartet ("*Aus Meinen
    Leben*")
  The Bartered Bride (opera)

Alexander Borodin
  Symphony No. 1, B Minor
  Prince Igor (opera)
  "Polovtsian Dances," *from Prince
    Igor*
  On the Steppes of Central Asia
  String Quartet No. 2 in D Major

Nicholas Rimsky-Korsakov
  Russian Easter Overture
  Capriccio Espagnol
  Scheherezade, symphonic suite
  Tsar Saltan, symphonic suite
  Le Coq D'Or

Modeste Moussorgsky
  Night on Bare Mountain
  Boris Godunov (opera)
  Nursery Songs
  Songs and Dances of Death
  Pictures at an Exhibition
    (piano solo, or orchestral ver-
    sion)

Edvard Grieg
  Piano Concerto in A Minor
  Peer Gynt Suite
  Norwegian Dances

ADDITIONAL LISTENING (CONTINUED)

Richard Strauss
  Tone Poems:
    Don Juan
    Death and Transfiguration
    Also sprach Zarathustra
    Ein Heldenleben
  Operas:
    Elektra
    Salome
    Der Rosenkavalier
    Die Frau ohne Schatten
    Capriccio
  Four Last Songs
  Symphony for Wind Instruments
  Burleske, for piano and orchestra
  Suite from *Le Bourgeois
    Gentilhomme*

Gustav Mahler
  Symphonies 1, 2, 3, 8
  Das Lied von der Erde
  Songs from "Youth's Magic Horn"
  Kindertotenlieder

*French Romantic and post-Roman-
    tic Composers:*
  Fauré: *Requiem*
  Chausson: Poem, for Violin and
    Orchestra
  Chabrier: *España Rhapsody*
  Dukas: *Sorcerer's Apprentice*
  D'Indy: *Symphony on a French
    Mountain Air*

Edward Elgar
  "Enigma" Variations
  Falstaff, tone poem

VII THE TWENTIETH CENTURY

HISTORICAL PERSPECTIVE

THE CULTURE OF the twentieth century developed from 1900 onward in three broad phases whose approximate boundaries were the two great wars. Each of these conflicts brought about vast changes in all areas of human action and thought, and each of the cultures they delimited showed rather clearly defined characteristics. Since the development of the twentieth century has followed in the main a technological and scientific path, our historical perspectives will deal principally with that aspect. The course of music and the other arts parallels it well enough.

PHASE I: 1900-1920

The runaway technology begun by the "second industrial revolution" of the 1870's accelerated steadily during the two decades we are considering with the development of new techniques in manufacturing, the increased use of electric power, and important advances

431

in transportation and communication. In 1908 the "Model T" Ford revolutionized both manufacturing and transportation. The mass production methods using assembly-line techniques inaugurated a third industrial revolution, making possible cheap transportation and a uniform, interchangeable set of parts for easy maintainance. Mass production became the standard mode of manufacturing. In transportation, the dirigible, a lighter-than-air craft, was invented by Count Zeppelin in 1900, and the Wright brothers constructed and flew the first practicable heavier-than-air machine in 1903. While both of these inventions took time to develop, they, as well as the automobile, were usable by the time of World War I. In the same year as the first successful flight by the Wright brothers, the first automobile crossed the American continent. In 1914 the Panama Canal was opened, and five years later occurred the first transcontinental and transatlantic flights. The world was on its way to becoming a "global village." The farthest corner was almost at one's elbow, too, for in 1901 Marconi sent the first radio signals across the Atlantic and in 1920 occurred the first commercial radio broadcast in America. And the New York to San Francisco telephone line was put into operation in 1915. The business interests of people and nations were accelerated immeasurably and increased by these inventions, but they seemed to have offered no more persuasive means for agreement and understanding than did the mail coach or the foot courier, for the tensions already strained to the limit exploded in the Russo-Japanese war of 1904 and the first World War of 1914-1918, in which all of the great powers of Europe and the United States were eventually engaged. The Bolshevik revolution of 1917-18 and the Versailles Treaty remade the postwar face of Europe, but the lack of foresight displayed by the "peacemakers" fanned the already heated coals of nationalism and prepared the way for the greater war of 1939-45. World War I was the brutal close of the Romantic period, but its lesson was never fully learned.

Despite wars and disasters, the scientists were busily at work during these years, peering ever more deeply into the nature of matter and the universe. In 1910 and 1911, Rutherford, following up his hypotheses of atomic structure, discovered the electron and proton, basic particles of energy which are parts of the structure of matter. Working with radiant energy, Max Planck had postulated in 1899 that energy was released from radiating sources in bursts, which he called *quanta*. The relation between the energy of a *quantum* and its frequency of vibration was expressed by a constant factor which he called "h." Now known as Planck's constant, this value is the cornerstone of modern physics. Niels Bohr, in 1913, applied this theory to the structure of the atom with spectacular success, laying the foundation of modern atomic physics upon Planck's cornerstone.

The second event of tremendous consequences to occur during these decades was Einstein's development of the general theory of relativity, fully formulated in 1915. This theory, and its experimental verification, thoroughly upset the cosy Newtonian universe which had been so firmly accepted since the seventeenth century. Its significance in the fields of physics and astronomy is incalculable, surpassing almost every other concept in importance in the study of matter and the universe.

The machines, the politicians and the scientists created a new world during these fateful years; the artists and musicians stayed abreast of them and explored new realms of expression as meaningful for the arts of the later twentieth century as the quantum theory or the theory of relativity were for science.

PHASE I: MUSIC FROM 1900 TO 1920

The music composed and performed during the period 1900-1920 reflected uncertainties, conflicts and the passing of Romanticism as an ideal. The most powerful force with which composers had to contend was German Romantic music, personified by Wagner, with the hardly less potent satellites of Brahms and Mahler close behind him. Wagner had collated and appropriated all of the techniques of Romantic music from the leading composers of the period, had produced overpowering works through the mechanistic application of the *leitmotiv* principle, had pushed the tonal system to its furthest limits and, through critical and polemical essays and articles, had forced this image of his imagination upon a public prepared by nationalism, vague religious feelings about the myth and the power of art transmitted through a genius whose prodigious attainments held them in awe. Wagner proclaimed, supported by otherwise quite respectable historians, that his music was the summit toward which all musical evolution had been moving. Many disagreed with him, particularly in France, but others saw no apparent future other than the continuation ——and in some cases, the repetition——of what the master of Bayreuth had done.

These composers adapted the melodic, rhythmic and particularly the potent harmonic techniques displayed by Wagner in *Tristan*, extending them farther into the realm of pure chromaticism than he had

PLATE XXXVI. *"Starry Night" by Van Gogh. The painting is expressionistic in that the artist shows his feelings about the starry night. Note the emotional effect of the upward-leaping cypress tree. (Courtesy of The Museum of Modern Art.)*

done. The psychological interpretation of the orchestra in the music drama they dissociated from the stage and made it express less concretely exemplified ideas. Soon, during these *fin de siècle* years, the name *Expressionism* began to be attached to the music they produced. Expressionism in any art is an intensification of Romanticism in that the extreme subjectivity of the artist is foremost. It presents the inner reality of the composer, a new world with all of the irrationality and fantasy we found in Romanticism, but raised to the nth degree. In Expressionistic art we see and hear experience reconstructed through the emotional responses of another person; it is the presentation of the individual's reaction to life.

Opposed to the self-proclamations of the "gothic North" were composers of the "classic South." Not Italy, caught up in operatic fervor, but the composers of the late French Romantic revival, paradoxically aroused by the French defeat at the hands of the Prussians in 1871. They opposed the emotional fervor of German Romanticism with restrained feeling, ironic wit and clarity of form. They disinvolved both composer and listener from the music, reaching for a coolly classic balance of sentiment and form. While we find this attitude in the music of Fauré (1845-1924), Chausson (1855-1899) and Paul Dukas (1865-1935), the personal and original style of Claude Debussy (1862-1918) epitomized anti-Wagnerianism in a way which became of the utmost importance to succeeding generations of composers. Called "Impressionism" by the newspapers in reference to the vague qualities they felt it shared with the paintings of Monet, Sisely and Pissarro, it could with more reason be called "Symbolism" from examination of Debussy's choices of texts and his manner of setting them to music.

Simultaneously, a new group of composers appeared, more vigorously opposed to Romanticism in general, not merely German Romanticism. These anti-Romantics sought by ridicule, experimentation with dissonance, jazz and primitive styles, and deliberately provocative and scandalous works to make Romanticism an untenable aesthetic. Their leader was that "professional eccentric," Eric Satie, but the movement generally included other notable figures as the young *enfants terrible* of the early twentieth century, Serge Prokofiev and Igor Stravinsky.

A fourth tendency, implicit and sharing in many of the ideals and techniques of the other three, was the ever-present Nationalism. Now, in the persons of the Hungarians Zoltán Kodály and Béla Bartók, the Spaniard Manuel da Falla and the Englishman Ralph Vaughan Williams, the folk element and the national heritage from the past entered the musical arena much more strongly than ever before. These composers were, in a sense, eclectic, for they borrowed from any style the elements which could be of use to them. But the national element was strong, and only toward the ends of their lives did Vaughan Williams and Bartók become truly universal in their utterances.

Chronologically, the order runs: Impressionism, Expressionism, anti-Romanticism and Nationalism. We shall examine them in that order: they constitute the first phase of the musical development of our time.

IMPRESSIONISM: PARIS, 1892-1918

Musical Impressionism is a logical outcome of the development of the Romantic style: it is descriptive, colorful, harmonically exploratory, eager for the exotic and new, and requires unique, nonclassic forms in which to contain its ideas. Instead of exploring an emotional situation thoroughly, as, for example, the *"Liebestod"* in *Tristan und Isolde* does, this technique seeks to capture fleeting images, often necessarily (and preferably) vague, relying upon color and dynamic rather than clear draftsmanship. It avoids Teutonic thematic development, substituting transformation and fragmentation. Impressionistic views of the world essentially are static, the unmoving view of an "action

PLATE XXXVII. *"House of Parliament, Westminster" by Monet. Here we see the deliberate vagueness of Impressionism: only the general outlines of the subject appear. The painting is, of course, much more effective in color, but the essential quality is preserved even in black and white. (Courtesy of The Art Institute of Chicago, Mr. and Mrs. Martin A. Ryerson Collection.)*

shot," a moment of motion frozen. Monet shows the Houses of Parliament partially visible for an instant through the swirl of fog (Plate XXXVII), and Rodin captures in stone the moment when out of a formless mass the hand of God begins to shape humanity (Plate XXXVIII).

The Style of Impressionism

The technical aims of Impressionism might be summed up in the words "exquisite ambiguity." Debussy, the foremost exponent of the style, sought out scales, harmonies, rhythms and sonorities which created out of sound a sensuous haze through which the subjects of his musical discourse appeared and disappeared like the figures of a mirage. They were indeed impressions, and to accommodate them within a musical structure, the composer could only rely upon his intuition, for the music had to give the feeling of being completely free of any restraints, especially those of tradition. It must move in an "arabesque," to use Debussy's term, the curves of a varicolored silken scarf in a gentle breeze.

Melody

This is the most important element in Debussy's music. As in any other style, it is the expression of the scale used. In addition to mildly chromaticized tonal scales. Debussy sought out formations which had no strong tonal tendencies in order to suggest the ambiguity he wanted. For this purpose he adopted the modal scales of the Medieval Period, the exotic pentatonic scales of the Orient and the whole-tone scale of six notes. None of these has a tonic tone in the sense of the major-minor scale system, but only *finals,* tones which, if emphasized by various means, consent to act as final notes of precarious stability. Debussy's melody always *seems* to be singable, whether it actually is so or not. Those which are closest to the tonal scales are often the least characteristic unless combined with the subtle harmony of this style.

Harmony

Again, exquisite ambiguity is attained through the use of nontonal scales and the lattitude of chord movement they permit. But even in tonal works, the deliberate employment of chord successions which do not function to define the key is the general rule. The harmony itself consists of major, minor, augmented and diminished triads, seventh and ninth chords. Seldom do the complex harmonies sound dissonant, for the tones are so arranged that the dissonance is buried within the consonance and gives it richness and depth, like the spices in French cooking. The chromatic style of Wagner and the expressionists is carefully avoided, even though Debussy sometimes uses the same chord progressions.

PLATE XXXVIII. *"The Hand of God" by Rodin. Here is the impressionistic technique adapted, insofar as the medium will allow, to sculpture. It depicts a
moment in creation: we have an impression of fluid, unfixed forms taking shape
out of the amorphous mass of the uncut marble. (Courtesy of The Metropolitan
Museum of Art, gift of Edward D. Adams, 1908.)*

    In Impressionistic music, and soon in Expressionistic music also,
dissonance becomes an independent value, a "higher consonance"
which is not required to resolve. There have been unresolved dissonances before in the history of music, but never used so freely and
frequently. In the piano *Prélude, Feux d'artifice* (Fireworks), the dissonance becomes a color value, a bright spark which stands out from
its sonorous background.

    Both the nonfunctional harmonic successions and the unresolved
dissonance often result from Debussy's practice of doubling the
melodic line at several intervals simultaneously, creating streams of
parallel chords of the same structure. We have encountered doubling
before, usually at the octave or double-octave for thickening the
melodic line, or at the 3rd or 6th in order to add color also. Doubling at
the 5th and 4th was the process of medieval parallel organum. Debussy
often doubled a melodic line at the 3rd and 5th below, creating a major

triad (or minor, as the case might be), which, in its movement introduced chromatic tones in order to preserve the triad quality. For
example, a melodic fragment in the key of C major (scale: C D E F G
A B), might consist of the tones E D C B A. Using major triad doubling,
the chords created would be these:

E	D	C	B	A	G
C♯	B	A	G♯	F♯	E
A	G	F	E	D	C

It will be seen that the three sharped tones are not in the key of C,
and that they contradict unsharped versions of the same tone within
this short succession. No key is defined here; although the V, IV and I
chords are present, their relationship is so weakened by this kind of
doubling that they cannot operate functionally; this is nonfunctional
harmony of a frequently encountered kind in Impressionistic music
(Example VII-1). Streams of more complex chords, sevenths and
ninths, may be obtained by doubling at that interval below the melody
tones; these dissonances do not resolve, but the whole complex chord
moves parallel to a similar chord, followed by another.

With the vagueness accomplished by these means, Debussy is
faced with the problem of fashioning convincing endings to his music.
Some he allows to evaporate in unresolved dissonance and harmonic
ambiguity, but others need bringing down to ground level. For these,
he resorts to traditional tonal formulas depending upon the emphasis
by repetition or organpoint on a tone, usually tonic, to anchor the
airy structure. Sometimes a double organpoint of tonic and dominant
tones provides a more secure and stable sonority. Most compositions
in this style avoid a clear use of IV-V-I harmonic progression at their
conclusions, however.

Rhythm

The rhythmic patterns of Impressionistic music usually are more
original than their romantic predecessors, and often, through syncopations and other dislocations, more ambiguous and elusive. Discontinuous motion is present, but does not have quite the expressive
effect here that it does in the preceding music, no sighing, sentimentality or profundity; all is Gallic, which is to say, feeling and
intellect combined in delicate proportions.

Texture

The texture of this music is unfailingly homophonic, regardless of the sublety of accompaniment or movement to and fro within the chord. At times a countermelody will appear, but it is hardly to be regarded as counterpoint.

Sonority

The lovely sonority of Debussy's orchestra is obtained by the interplay of discreet and soloistic instrumental writing, and the spacing and structure of the harmony he uses. His scoring is usually highly transparent, so that the purpose of doubling is not audibility, but color and a thickening of the line for expressive purposes. Wind instruments are particularly favored in the Impressionistic orchestra, which is large, yet not the huge apparatus employed by Strauss and Mahler. Color is Debussy's main concern in scoring, not quantity of sound. A usually low dynamic level pervades the music, a turning away from the emotional climaxes of German music. The harp comes into its own and the various percussion instruments, almost always played softly for new colors and effects. Every tone is important in Debussy's orchestra and every note is audible.

The piano is also an important instrument for Impressionistic music. Debussy's treatment of the resources of the piano inaugurated another chapter in the history of piano music, for he made demands quite different from those of previous styles, exploiting the coloristic resources of the instrument in all its ranges, pedal modifications of tone, and varieties of touch.

In the search for vibrating color, the Impressionist painters used the technique of *pointillism*, in which dots of pure color were so placed on the canvas as to give the beholder, standing at a little distance away, the feeling of light reflected from the picture (Plate XL). The Impressionist composers adapted this technique to their music, using isolated tones or clusters of tones in various instrumental colors and ranges. The term, pointillism, also applies to this. When a melody was fragmented in a pointillistic manner, we may speak of a *mosaic* type of structure comparable to the bits of glass and colored stone inlaid in a Byzantine mosaic. The effect of color contrast as the fragments pass by is orchestrally effective.

Formal concepts

These may be best defined negatively; there is no thematic presentation and development in the German sense, no counterpoint or fugue, no clear traditional form. The theme transformation devices of the tone poem are employed in some of Debussy's works, but more often the structure is the intuitive succession of sections bound to each other by mood, melody, rhythm, or subtle variation and contrast.

One is always impressed by the relative objectivity of Impressionist music, in contrast with the emotional persuasiveness of the German composers. Toward the end of his life, Debussy's music became even more objective, harder of line, less ambiguous in harmony and form; in a word, more neoclassic. But his most familiar works, Impressionist in style, are the important ones for us to know.

PLATE XXXIX. *Claude Debussy. (The Bettmann Archive.)*

EXAMPLE VII-1: Debussy, *"The Dancers of Delphi."* Parallel chords from doubling.

EXAMPLE VII-2: Debussy, *"Pagodes,"* Pentatonic scale.

SCALE USED

EXAMPLE VII-3: Debussy, *Voiles*. Whole-tone scale.

SCALE USED

EXAMPLE VII-4: Debussy, *Prélude à l'après-midi d'un faune.* Chromaticism, color.

PLATE XL. "La Parade" *by Seurat. Pointillism is best seen in color but the photo-graph does show the mulitude of tiny dots which gives the technique its name. (Courtesy of the Metropolitan Museum of Art, bequest of Stephen C. Clark, 1960.)*

Vocal Music

Debussy wrote some of the most distinguished art songs to be found in the late nineteenth century, as original and characteristic as his instrumental works. The combination of text and music is worth our attention because it links together the explicit information conveyed by the words with the musical images of line and harmony, thus shedding some light on Debussy's methods.

Beau Soir ("Beautiful Evening") is one of the most frequently performed, and merits that popularity. The poem by Paul Bourget is an evening meditation on life's transitory quality and an exhortation to be happy during it. The form is ternary, with a shortened return of the A section. The sonority is full, yet spacious, and consists mostly of 7th and 9th chords. The central portion, in which the poet's feelings are expressed, is more agitated than the outer sections. Note the haunting beauty of the melodic line. The final cadence uses an ambiguous chord in place of the dominant.

The song *Mandoline* (by Verlaine) shows a lighter side——a description of serenaders and their sweethearts in the moonlight, suggesting a painting by Watteau. The mandolin motive, G-D-A, consisting of the tones of the three lowest strings of the instrument, recurs from time to time. The phrases are of odd lengths, giving the feeling of casualness and mobility. The form is A-B-A', in which the A' section contains a passage in rich harmony and a new key.

The richly dissonant harmony of *La Chevalure* ("Her Hair") supports a voice line resembling a recitative throughout most of the song except for the climactic phrase midway in the piece. The feeling of breathlessness and intimacy appropriate to the words is achieved partly by the rhythmic device of beginning the phrases on weak beats of the measure.

Pelléas et Mélisande, Debussy's only opera, was written to the unaltered text of a symbolist play by Maurice Maeterlinck. The theme of the play is the irrationality of fate and the impossibility of avoiding it. All of the characters and incidents are shaped toward this theme and exhibited in a series of scenes which together develop the story by a kind of indirection. Debussy's music provides a sensuous background which reflects the images and symbols of the words sung to a quasi-recitative which resembles the rise and fall of the spoken French language. The music, as might be expected, essentially is reticent, understating rather than emphasizing, and in one scene only, rising to a certain lyric height. It is the antithesis of Wagner's music, yet follows the theories which Wagner stated but did not exemplify in his own music dramas. The Second Act of *Tristan* should be compared aurally with Act IV, Scene 2 of *Pelléas* for the difference to be brought home significantly. However subtle the music may be, it cannot be said to be neutral for an intense passion is felt beneath the surface of the work, an urgency which is all the more effective for being restrained. It especially is noteworthy in the orchestral interludes which provide for the continuity between the scenes. There are recurring *leitmotives* and binding themes for each of the acts, but these never receive the Wagnerian symphonic treatment. Kerman's essay in *Opera as Drama* and Grout's discussion in *A Short History of Opera* are recommended for a fuller understanding of this twentieth century masterwork.

Piano Music

Debussy's piano music not only illustrates the technical devices of his style on an easily comprehensible scale but also the novel style of his writing for the instrument.

Préludes, Book I (for piano)

"*Danseuses de Delphes*" ("The Dancers of Delphi") (Example VII-1): This piece was suggested by a fragment of a frieze from a Greek temple which Debussy saw in the Louvre. It exhibits parallel chords, nonfunctional harmony and exploitation of veiled piano sonorities.

"*Voiles*" ("Sails," or "Veils") (Example VII-3): This piece employs ternary construction, the first and last sections using the whole-tone scale, the middle part written in the pentatonic scale. It is essentially static in feeling. Note the color splashes of rapid notes, and the active rhythmic quality. Both are needed to breathe life into the motionless effect of the harmony derived from these scales. Also note the frequent use of organpoint.

"*Des pas sur la neige*" ("Of Footsteps in the Snow"): This melancholy little vignette uses the repetition of a rhythmic-melodic motive to hold it together. This motive appears almost continuously throughout, providing the harmonic background in many places, and supporting fragments of melody above it. The piece is written in the Aeolian mode, but uses chromaticism to introduce richer chords than occur naturally in that scale.

"*La fille aux cheveux de lin*" ("The Maid with the Flaxen Hair"): This poetic composition uses the pentatonic scale melodically. Harmonies are not pentatonic, and sometimes are functional. Chord parallelism occurs, most notably about two-thirds of the way through, and parallel fourths appear at the cadence.

Préludes, Book II (for piano)

'*Feux d'artifice*' ("Fireworks"): piano sonority, techniques. Dissonant color splashes, nontonal. Possibly a Bastille Day celebration— listen for the fragment of the "*Marseillaise*" at the end.

Orchestral Music

Prélude à l'après-midi d'un faune ("Prelude to the Afternoon of a Faun")

This was one of Debussy's early successes, inspired by a poem of the Symbolist poet, Mallarmé, published in 1876 with illustrations by Manet. In the music, Debussy sought to evoke "the successive scenes in which the longings and desires of the faun pass in the heat of the afternoon." The scene is, presumably, ancient Greece, and the faun, half man, half beast, lies in the shade during a warm afternoon. He drowses, and thinks he sees (or does he dream?) nymphs bathing in the stream. He dreams on. This work is a tone poem, but the painting is anything but literal, either in description or in sequence of events.

To us, it owes more to tradition than do some other compositions of Debussy, but to the people who heard it at the first performance in 1894, it was a revelation, and not always a welcome one. Nothing like it had been heard before. The sonorous yet transparent orchestra was more like Berlioz than Wagner yet the nervous brilliance of the earlier Frenchman was not there. Each instrument provides a specific color which is used with all the care of a painter to capture just the right effect of light and shade. The low, exotic tones of the flute at the beginning of the piece, the answer by the muted horns, the piercingly sweet voice of the oboe—these as well as the colors attributable to various harmonic groupings are handled with the utmost finesse. Theme transformation is used, rather than (horrors!) Germanic development, and section follows and flows into succeeding section with purely sensory logic, disregarding the traditional tenets of musical structure. Many of the characteristics of Debussy's later style are present in this composition.

La Mer ("The Sea")

This, the longest of Debussy's orchestral works, resembles in some respects a three movement symphony, although the middle movement is scherzo-like rather than a slow movement. There is more sharing of themes among the movements than in other works of this composer, but in the atmosphere here created, this thematic transference seems of little significance. Debussy's marine experience consisted of two crossings of the English Channel—hardly sufficient, one would think, to impress him enough to compose a work like La Mer. He wrote to his publisher in 1903 from Burgundy, where he was at work on the composition: "You will say that the ocean does not exactly bathe the Burgundian hillsides—and that my seascapes might be studio landscapes; but I have numberless stores of memories and, to my mind, they are *worth more than a reality which often deadens one's thought.*"[1]

The first movement of the suite is entitled *"De l'aube à midi sur la mer"* ("From Dawn to Noon on the Ocean"), and has a curious static

---

[1] Letter to André Messager, Sept. 1, 1903: *Debussy, Man and Artist*, Oscar Thompson. New York, Tudor, 1940.

quality, perhaps reflecting the essentially unchanging face of the ocean, despite the small squalls which appear from time to time. The primeval undulation of the waves, the gradually clearing atmosphere and a glimpse of the green depths all are here, painted with the utmost subtlety in the orchestra. Notice the mysterious beginning, as the sea begins to become visible, the woodwind figurations, the mosaic of patterns, the parallel chords in the muted lower strings, and the many ways the thematic materials are transformed to provide "mosaic tiles" of various shapes and colors.

The second movement, *"Jeu de vagues"* ("Play of the Waves"), presents us with the same seascape, but with a fresh wind blowing, whipping the surface into small whitecaps. There is a certain element of the fantastic to be noticed here, largely resulting from the rapidity with which the orchestral colors shift, and the qualities of those colors.

The third movement, *"Dialogue du vent et de la mer"* ("Dialogue of the Wind and the Sea"), depicts a stormier ocean scene. Themes from the first movement are recalled, transformed, and the brass "chorale" returns for a climactic section. But, as always, "the whole is more than the sum of its parts," and all the technical tricks are only means to evoke this ideal view of an ocean of the mind.

The three-movement tone painting, *Ibéria*, is a fascinating study in Debussy's use of orchestral color to suggest the atmosphere of Spain. Note the Moorish-sounding melodies, the use of characteristic rhythms and percussion, and the mass *pizzicati* of the strings in the final movement, suggesting a great guitar.

Debussy said that his *Three Nocturnes* were to describe "all the various impressions and the special effects of light that the word (Nocturnes) suggests." The first movement, *Nuages* ("Clouds"), is notable for the use of chord parallelism and harmonic color. The second, *Fêtes* ("Festival"), is more solid, more gay, depicting the "restless dancing rhythms of the atmosphere," and the third, *Sirènes* ("Sirens"), "depicts the sea and its innumerable rhythms; then amid the billows silvered by the moon the mysterious song of the sirens is heard; it laughs and passes." Here, Debussy added to the orchestra a women's chorus which vocalises vowel sounds rather than singing a text. The eerie effect has since been copied by concert and movie composers alike.

Other Impressionist Composers

While Impressionist techniques were borrowed freely by many other composers after Debussy, the Frenchman retained the original patent, for Impressionism depended in the last analysis upon the personality and taste of the composer, and none followed who could reach the standard he had set. Close to it, and individual in his own way was the American, Charles T. Griffes (1884-1920), whose piano piece, *The White Peacock,* and orchestral tone poem, *The Pleasure Dome of Kubla Khan,* are performed frequently. Less known is the music of the Alsatian-American, Charles M. Loeffler (1861-1935). His *Pagan Poem* is worth hearing as is also his *String Quintet,* which adds another violin to the standard string quartet ensemble. The music of the Englishman Cyril Scott (b. 1879) and Frederick Delius (1862-1934) were popular for a time, but have since faded from concert programs. Some of the early works of the Spanish nationalist, Manuel da Falla (1876-1946) are Impressionistic *(Nights in the Gardens of Spain),* while those of his Italian compatriot, Ottorino Respighi (1879-1963) are somewhat too richly Romantic in tone to qualify as genuinely Impressionistic.

PLATE XLI. *"The Cry." Lithograph by Edvard Munch, one of the early German Expressionists. Note the emotional quality which is conveyed by the deliberate distortion and the composition. (Courtesy of the Archive-German Information Center.)*

EXPRESSIONISM: VIENNA, 1900-1923

In addition to the post-Romantic composers working within the Romantic tradition, there were more aggressive spirits who moved along the path Wagner had indicated in *Tristan* toward the outer reaches of tonality. These men were situated in Vienna, the stronghold of Wagner, Bruckner, Brahms and Mahler. Steeped in its musical traditions, yet aware of the implications of the future, these men faced the crisis of vanishing tonality and eventually proposed workable solutions to it. Other composers found their own styles and made peace with the tonality dilemma or resolutely ignored it. One man tenaciously pursued a practical and intellectual solution: Arnold Schönberg (1874-1951). In this difficult task he was aided by two colleagues, formerly his students, Alban Berg (1885-1935) and Anton von Webern (1883-1945).

Schönberg: The Search for Structure

Anyone who doubts Schönberg's sincerity in his quest need only read his letters and articles on the subject: "I am a conservative who was forced to become a radical." And those who doubt his musical skill and imagination must listen to those works written in the now-familiar post-Romantic idiom, *Verklaerte Nacht* ("Transfigured Night") and the *Gurrelieder* ("Songs of the Dove").

Extremely conscious of the soil out of which his music had sprung, Schönberg realized the tonality problem, examined it like the keen theoretician he was, and experimented with it in his teaching and composing. His music had origins in the practices of practically all of the late Romantic composers. From Brahms he received the technique of continuous transformation and thematic variation, and contrapuntal elaboration. From Wagner and Liszt came the concept of unity through the use of germ motives, as well as the important chromatic harmony which was the most obviously important factor in the crisis of tonality. Even the freedom of the dissonance, an impressionist technique, was absorbed, and the mysticism of the chord, sonority for its own sake, springing out of Mahler's "sounding universe" became assimilated. With the expressionistic credo that "the duty of a composer is to express himself," it is easy to see that this man was uniquely fitted to wrestle with the problem.

We have seen how, with the increasing use of chromaticism, tonality abdicates in favor of the twelve-tone scale, a construction without a tonal center. Writing melody and harmony in this scale was not difficult, but the real problem lay in creating clear formal designs. Form is of the essence of music, and a late Romantic composer such as Schönberg wanted to write large and impressive works. But the logical element in his nature required that a form be used. All of the traditional forms except those depending solely upon imitation——especially canon——were impossible because they were predicated upon the establishment and departure from and return to regions of clear tonality. New forms consistent with the nature of the chromatic scale had to be realized if musical composition were to have any logical basis.

Starting from the post-Wagnerian style of the compositions mentioned above, Schönberg pursued an increasingly non-tonal and expressionistic line of development up to 1912. *Pelléas und Melisande,* after Maeterlinck's play, a large symphonic poem in sonata form, and the *Gurrelieder* for an enormous orchestra and multiple choruses, represent the culmination of the post-Romantic period. After these, and actually while working upon the orchestration of them, the composer turned to reduced instrumentation and comparative brevity in length. The *Chamber Symphony in E Major,* Op. 9, written in 1906, is a large sonata-allegro which incorporates into its single form the movements of the traditional symphony. Scored for fifteen instruments, it may be understood on the terms of any late Romantic composition. In it, modulation is so constant as to obscure the tonality over long stretches, and melodies with intervals which will later become most characteristic of this composer's style are to be found. The first important theme of the first "movement" consists of a series of 4ths, an interval which often replaced the third in chord structures of the twentieth century.

Following this work is the *String Quartet No. 2,* in F Sharp Minor (1908), a composition in which tonality becomes attenuated to the vanishing-point during the movement, but returns to the key in the coda. In the last movement, Schönberg added a soprano voice singing two poems, *Litany* and *Release,* by Stefan Georg. The second begins with the words, "I feel an air from other planets . . . I dissolve into tones, circling, wreathing . . ." and in this section tonality is suspended completely.

This style of suspended tonality is characteristic of Schönberg's second period, which includes the violently expressionistic monodrama *Erwartung.* In this "opera for one singer," distortion, chromaticism, dissonance and the most tortured and refined orchestration are used. The work is through-composed, without thematic repetition, and has therefore been called *athematic*. Its intensity and concentration hardly can be surpassed, but certain reflections of it may be found in Berg's opera, *Wozzeck*.

The *Five Pieces for Orchestra*, Op. 16, although Expressionistic, do not have the psychological effect of *Erwartung* perhaps because they are more abstract. In them the motivic interplay of rhythmically complex themes and the abundance of heretofore unheard-of sonorities makes comprehension difficult. Perhaps the most readily accessible is the third movement, *Farben* ("Colors"), in which a single chord is sustained throughout in gradually changing tone colors. This latest example of the "mysticism of the chord" was named *Klangfarbenmelodie* (tone-color melody) by Schönberg.

Perhaps the climactic composition of Schönberg's development beyond tonality is the set of "thrice seven" poems by Albert Giraud entitled *Pierrot Lunaire*, Op. 21 (1912). This is set for speaking voice *(sprechstimme)* and chamber ensemble. The voice part is notated in relative pitches and rhythmic values so as to be synchronized with the instruments. These are piano, violin alternating with viola in some movements, cello, flute interchangeable with piccolo, and clarinet alternating with bass clarinet. By exploiting the different combinations possible in such a group, Schönberg used a different combination for almost every poem, sometimes with one or more of the players silent in many of the movements.

PLATE XLII. *Arnold Schönberg. (Vogue photograph by George Platt Lynes.)*

While intensely Expressionistic, *Pierrot* is more subtle than *Erwartung*, more intimately subjective. This is due in a large part to the gliding voice inflections and the symbolist poetry they project, poetry whose images, eerie or shocking, are placed side by side to convey more than the "scientific meaning" of the words. The musical score enhances this imagery by tone-color, motion, melodic figures and structure. Many of the instrumental phrases seem derived from the *sprechstimme's* gliding, wailing intonations. Despite the thinness of sonority, the settings are extremely intense in effect.

Let us examine the music to see how Schönberg achieves this intensity, as well as to define the style, for this understanding will aid us in comprehending the later twelve-tone serial technique. In view of its complexity, we might define it by noting what it does *not* do.

1. There is an almost total absence of harmonic consonance. While Debussy was first to use free dissonance, Schönberg recognized its emancipation in his *Harmonielehre* ("Harmonic Practice," 1911): "We have progressed so far today as to make no more distinction between consonance and dissonance, or at most the distinction that we prefer to use consonances less . . ."[2]

2. Much of the dissonance occurs as the result of the melodic movements of the polyphonic voices, which Schönberg called "justification only by melody." That is to say, the individual lines are allowed to follow their tendencies, regardless of friction with other parts. Indeed, in the interests of consistency, the counterpoint is so written as to create dissonances in purely accompanying (nonpolyphonic) parts, such as the piano often plays in *Pierrot Lunaire*.

3. Melodies avoid movement from tone to tone of major or minor triads. They are wide in range and employ wide and dissonant skips, with a fondness for sevenths and ninths, never octaves. When a tone is repeated in a melody, it is apt to be an octave higher or lower than the pitch of its previous appearance. There is a strong tendency not to repeat pitches until a large portion of the chromatic tones available have been used. When melodic movement is stepwise, not more than three tones of any scale are used in succession.

---

[2] Austin, W. W., *Music in the 20th Century*, Norton, N.Y. 1966.

When these tendencies are more or less consistently pursued, no feeling of key is present, and the problem of structure confronts the composer. In the short movements of *Pierrot* the structure is not a crucial point, especially since there are words present upon which to attach the music, sometimes through an advanced kind of text-painting. Thus the technique of the through-composed song replaces strictly musical form. Two forms which do not depend upon tonal structure are the ostinato and canon. The first appears in a very developed form in No. 8, *Night*, subtitled *Passacaglia,* where the ostinato figure is subjected to all manner of compression, extension and inversion. The canonic techniques are similarly complex in Nos. 17, *Parody,* and 18, *Moon Spot,* in which the imitations are inverted or backwards. While not audible to the listener, such procedures fulfill a structural need felt by the composer. And if the music is expressively successful without the canons being noticed, all the better!

Schönberg's music from the *Five Pieces for Orchestra* onward is difficult for the listener to comprehend. The complexity of texture, with its crossing parts and overlapping phrases, the extreme variety in dynamics and rhythms, and the high content of unfamiliar and dissonant harmony make understanding possible only upon many repeated hearings. Alban Berg concluded that this difficulty resulted from the compression of the composer's lifelong experience into music of short duration, making it necessary for the listener to spend more time with the music than is customary with "easy" pieces.

During the years between *Pierrot Lunaire* and the twelve-tone compositions of the 1920's, Schönberg did not compose much due to being drafted for military service in 1915 and again in 1917. After this he devoted himself to teaching, conducting and the organization of the *Association for Private Performances,* a group of composers and others interested in the newest in music. This group introduced the works of Ravel, Debussy, Satie, Bartók and Kodály to Vienna, as well as compositions by Schönberg, Berg and Webern. During these years, Schönberg widened his acquaintance with new music of divergent styles, and matured his theoretical thinking about the organization of chromatic elements in nontonal music.

Berg: Synthesis of Old and New

Alban Berg first became associated with Schönberg in 1904, formally studying with him for some six years. Thereafter he shared the intellectual musical circle with Webern and others, having quickly developed a style of a quite personal nature which, after the first two decades, represented a synthesis of the late Romantic idiom with the newer currents which his teacher had set in motion, that is, between Mahler and the Expressionistic works of Schönberg. This synthesis allowed him to use tonality and recognizable triads, chord progressions, diatonic melody, clear rhythms and comparatively clearly audible forms together with the rich chromatic counterpoint and dazzling orchestration characteristic of this Viennese school. Berg was attracted strongly to the theater, and many of his works, both the purely instrumental as well as the vocal ones, reveal a dramatic and theatrical impulse. The *Altenberg Lieder*, Op. 4 (1912), consisting of five songs employing short poems by Peter Altenberg printed on postcards, reveal this dramatic tendency. Despite the brevity of some of them, they employ, in addition to the solo soprano, a large orchestra consisting of woodwinds in threes, four horns, three trumpets, four trombones, tuba, celesta, harp, piano, harmonium, many percussion instruments and strings to balance the above ensemble.

The text of the first Altenberg song may be translated as follows:

> O soul, how much lovelier, how much deeper you are
> after snow-storms.
> You have them too, just like nature.
> And both are still overcast, before the clouds blow away.

The A-B-A' form, corresponding to the three lines of the poem, is preceded by an introduction which presents the basic motive, E-B-F, both melodically and harmonically, decorated in some cases with clusters of other tones. The voice part, after a few tentative, wordless sounds, may be called lyrical despite the large leaps which it contains. Berg's affinity with operatic Expressionism is demonstrated by the violent dramatic gestures of the orchestral part. The A' section is quieter and more transparently scored, with the basic chord sustained in the middle register. Note the harmonic *glissandi* of the strings.

The text of the second song is also in three lines and the music formed accordingly:

> Did you ever see the wood after the rainstorm?
> All is at rest, shining and lovelier than before.
> Lady, you too need such storms!

A smaller ensemble is used in this song, and the voice is given a fairly large share of the eleven measures which constitute it. The intervals and motives are presented melodically at the beginning (*cf.* Schubert:

Symphony No. 8; Liszt: *Les Préludes*), then inverted, played backward and rhythmically transformed during the course of the music in both voice and orchestra. After a complex chord closes the B section, the voice alone delivers the last line in a varied recapitulation of A.

The third song, again A-B-A', with the two central lines as B, runs thus:

> You gaze, thoughtfully, beyond the bounds of the universe.
> You had no care for house or home.
> Life and the dream of life—suddenly all is over.
> Still you gaze, thoughtfully, beyond the bounds of the
> universe.

This song begins with a twelve-tone chord in the brass and woodwind, treated as *Klangfarbenmelodie,* Berg's symbol for the universe. The middle section appropriately is dramatic, ending with the spoken, "it is all over." The last section is notable for the materialization of the twelve-tone chord, now high in the strings, with the celesta sounding at the entrance of each new section of the chord.

The fourth song opens in a mood of Mahlerian nostalgia, with an extremely high, sustained flute tone, while the voice sings in its lower middle register. A poignant, half-sweet chord is treated in *Klangfarbenmelodie* style during the central portion, giving way to a more dissonant chord in the lower register which dissolves with a slow, downward *glissando* in the timpani and a *glissando* in harmonics in the cellos. The song ends in the flute and voice as it began.

> Nothing has come, nothing will come for my soul.
> I have waited, waited, oh waited!
> The days will slip by and my ash-blonde, silken hair
> will be blown about my pale face in vain.

The final song, cast in the form of a passacaglia, is more polyphonic and complex in structure. There are ten rather free variations over the theme which is presented at the beginning. Motives for this song are drawn from the previous ones, thus creating a cyclic series. A twelve-tone countermelody plays an important part in the song, often replacing the passacaglia theme. The following text is marked off according to the variations.

Orchestra:
    Theme and two variations
Voice:
    Hier ist Friede. Hier weine/ich mich aus über alles!

Hier/löst sich mein unfassbares, unermessliches Leid,
    das mir die/ Seele verbrennt.
Siehe/hier sind keine Menschen, keine Ansiedlungen.
 Hier ist Friede!/Hier tropft Schnee leise in Wasser/lachen.
Orchestra:
Two cadential variations.

The translation of the text is as follows:
> Here there is peace, here I weep my fill.
> Here dissolves the unfathomable, immeasurable sorrow
>   that burns up my soul.
> Look: there are no men here, no dwellings.
> Here there is peace. Here the snow drops softly in pools
>   of water.

In these and other compositions of Berg during this period we find the utmost effort to use derived motivic material to provide the substance of each work, a constant attention to the dramatic and expressive values obtainable through tone color and harmony, careful consideration of formal principles and a Romantic Expressionism which is highly effective in the setting of words. These characteristics become even more prominent in the great works of the twenties and thirties.

Webern: Toward the Future

Whereas Berg retained much of the sound of Romantic music through his use of rich harmony and colorful orchestration, Webern typified that growing tendency toward abstraction and intellectualization which has become so characteristic of the arts during and after the second war. He encountered Schönberg and became his student shortly before Berg did. But in 1902 he had already enrolled in the Vienna Conservatory to study musicology under Guido Adler, completing his doctorate in 1906. His study of the abstract polyphony and rhythmic complexity of early music must surely have affected his style: certainly the complete interpenetration of form and content which he gradually achieved paralleled certain of the implications of some of the early styles.

.Even from the earliest published work, the *Passacaglia for Orchestra,* Op. 1, we may note three strong characteristics of all Webern's music: polyphony, the most stringent symphonic economy in the derivation of material from a small number of motives, and continuous variation and elaboration of that material. The second work, an *a cappella* chorus, *Entflieht auf leichten Kähnen,* is canonic throughout, uses suspended tonality and is not Expressionistic in its use of dissonance or dramatic effect. It is a classically poised, serene work, the artifice of which is not at all apparent.

Probably never before did any composer make such marked advances in his art as did Webern during this early period. Opus 1 is tonal, Opus 2 has moved farther away from clear tonality, and the following works are already beyond tonality. Webern recapitulated Schönberg's development of a decade or more in two or three years!

Possibly the most notable of the works written during the next few years is the *Five Movements for String Quartet,* Op. 5 (1909). Requiring about nine minutes to perform, these brief movements employ a dazzling array of coloristic effects ranging from playing the strings with the wood of the bow *(col legno)* to bowing the strings close to the bridge *(sul ponticello)* to obtain a "glassy" tone quality, as well as the more common use of mutes, harmonics and *pizzicato.* Characteristic of his style are the motivic economy, the thin texture and "open" sonority, and the silences which occur from time to time. These silences sometimes indicate formal sections, but at other times are the result of simultaneous rests in the various voices, each pursuing a strictly organized course. They expose, as it were, the framework of silence upon which music is woven. There is a reserved, lyric expression in these pieces, a communication of mood and a sense of integrity which removes from them any taint of experimentalism. They are far different obviously, from the expressionistic fervor of compositions by Schönberg and Berg during these same years.

More than half of Webern's compositions are songs, conceived quite abstractly, yet employing those expressionistic leaps which we find in the music of his two colleagues. Yet Webern's use of the dissonant skips loses the highly charged emotion which characterizes them in the music of Schönberg and Berg, as is well illustrated by his two brief songs, Op. 8 (1910), set to words of Rilke.

Webern wrote his *Five Pieces for Orchestra,* Op. 10 during the same years (1912-13) that Debussy produced his ballet *Jeux* and the cantata *Le Martyre de Saint-Sébastien,* Ravel the ballet *Daphnis et Chloé,* Berg the *Altenberg Lieder,* Schönberg *Pierrot Lunaire,* and Stravinsky *Le Sacre du printemps.* Indeed, the musical world was flooded with significant masterworks. Webern's short orchestral movements were quite incomprehensible to the public, which reacted rather violently for or against the other works.

In the *Five Pieces for Orchestra,* the *Klangfarbenmelodie* technique of shifting instrumentation is now applied to melody rather than harmony. Webern fragments his melodic line into short motives or single tones, each of which is played by different instruments, usually in widely separated pitch ranges. This is *pointillism*, of course, but now carried out with logic and not merely used as colorful decoration. Ultimately, the same tone always will appear in the same color (instrument) and the same register throughout the work. This dissociation of the melodic line increases the abstract quality of the music, for no longer is there a traditionally connected melody supported by harmony: the separate yet motivically related, highly disjunct "lines" of the polyphony cross and recross as the tones appear *pointillistically* in high and low registers. It is entirely new in sound, and it is little wonder that audiences had trouble identifying it as *music* in the traditional sense. No analysis or verbal sketch of this music will be adequate here: the reader must go to the music itself, prepared to meet Webern more than halfway, ready to listen repeatedly with the utmost concentraton, for, as Schönberg romantically stated, these are "whole novels in a single sigh."

ANTIROMANTICISM

The focus of the anti-romantic movement was, as might be expected, in Paris. Here The Diaghilev Ballet Russe commissioned the newest music for its productions, and the theaters and concert halls were the laboratories for trying out all kinds of *avant-garde* experiments, from the Dadaist events of Tristan Tzara to the Futuristic noise music of Russolo and his compatriots. It was the proving ground and scene of the early successes of Ravel, Stravinsky and Prokofiev, as well as the grave of hundreds of failures. Here Erik Satie perpetrated his ironically witty sallies against the self-conscious grandeurs of Romanticism.

Erik Satie (1866-1925)

A friend of Debussy, Satie nevertheless was against the Impressionistic and Romantic modes of expression, and opposed them with a spare neoclassic style of great freedom and originality, despite the ironic and sarcastic titles which he employed. There is much repetition of rhythmic motives in his music, often to the point of hypnotic monotony, free use of chords of all kinds, a gravitation toward the

modal scales, and a mild use of dissonance. His was an art like Debussy's in that it depended solely on the taste of the composer. The
startling titles undoubtedly were used as a shield against critics, but
also often ridiculed the banalities in the music of other composers.
The *Trois Morceaux en forme de poire* ("Three Pieces in the Shape of
a Pear") seems to have been his answer when Debussy remarked that
Satie's music was formless. Similarly his *Avant-dernières pensées*
("Next-to-Last Thoughts") ridicules the salon pieces romantically pur-
porting to be the "last musical thoughts" of Chopin, or Beethoven or
some other composer. The *Sonatine bureaucratique* was a parody of
the mechanical sonatinas turned out for young ladies by Clementi
("brilliant but easy"). Other titles are more obscure, but probably had
their point at the time. The three *Gymnopedies*, dances for the imagined athletic exercises of ancient Greek youths, became his most famous compositions. Originally for piano, they were orchestrated by Debussy. *Parade*, music for a ballet by Jean Cocteau, Picasso and Massine,
was intended to include various noise-makers in the orchestra, but
eventually used only typewriters! Perhaps Satie's most moving and
representative composition is the unfortunately little known symphonic drama, *Socrate*, based upon fragments from Plato's *Symposium*.
Satie influenced a great number of young composers, among them the
famous *Les Six*.

Les Six

This title was bestowed by a journalist upon the half-dozen most
promising young French composers during the years 1910-1918, although they were quite divergent in style and aims. Darius Milhaud
(b. 1892), Francis Poulenc (1899-1963) and Georges Auric (b. 1892)
shared a certain interest in shocking the concert-going public by
employing popular music of the dance halls in their works, later using
jazz in the same way. Milhaud and Poulenc went on to make their
mark in more serious music, the latter becoming the foremost twentieth
century composer of French art-songs. Arthur Honegger (1892-1955)
was more romantically oriented, and developed a highly individual
Neoromantic musical idiom of his own. The other two, Germaine Tail-
lefaire (b. 1892) and Louis Durey (b. 1888) dropped from sight
soon after this publicity.

Milhaud's delightful suite for two pianos entitled *Scaramouche*
employs Latin-American popular idioms which he heard as consul in
Brazil. A somewhat later piece, *La Création du Monde*, may be re-

garded as a primitivistic work, something in the manner of the African masks which were becoming popular among the painters of the period. It uses a fusion of jazz and Bachian counterpoint which is very effective, although the jazz tends to sound quite dated to our ears. A more rowdy work is the ballet entitled *Le boeuf sur le toit* ("The Cow on the Roof"), which has a recurrent jazz section with interludes of other dances. Milhaud's work in the later twenties used polytonality and turned away from jazz and shock tactics.

Maurice Ravel, 1875-1937

Influenced by Impressionism during the first part of his career, Ravel soon turned toward clearer outlines of melody and form, a diamond-hard clarity of line coupled with a mechanistic rhythmic precision which clearly excluded him from the Impressionist style. One of the great orchestral virtuosos of the time, Ravel frequently wrote piano music which he soon transferred to the orchestra. Thus, *Ma Mère L'Oye* ("Mother Goose Suite") and the *Valses Nobles et Sentimentales,* among others, appear in both forms. He accomplished the same feat for Moussorgsky's piano suite, *Pictures at an Exhibition,* with notable results. It is instructive to compare the original piano version with the orchestration to note how little Ravel added. In Ravel's best music, there is a certain intensity, an objective passion. His melody has a characteristic lyricism on the verge of Romanticism, the harmony is often mildly dissonant, and the rhythmic element is strong, particularly in works with a Spanish reference. Such a work is the *Rhapsodie Espagnole,* whose four parts ("*Prélude à la nuit*," "*Malagueña,*" "*Habanera*" and "*Féria*") are interconnected by a scale figure (F E D C-sharp) which is also employed as a melodic germ. Spanish rhythms are most apparent in the last three movements, the *Prélude* acting as an "improvisatory" beginning to introduce the scale figure.

Daphnis et Chloé, a ballet based on the Greek myth, is perhaps one of this composer's most successful compositions. The music has been arranged into two orchestral suites, the second of which is most frequently performed. The three sections, *Lever du jour, Pantomime* and *Danse Générale* ("Daybreak," "Pantomime" and "General Dance") are excellent examples of Ravel's mastery of orchestration, combined with typical melodic warmth and rhythmic excitement. The latter quality is most prominent in the final movement, a crescendo of rhythmic and sonorous excitement in quintuple meter.

Ravel wrote much piano music, (among which is the popular *Pavane pour une infante défunte* ("Pavane for a Dead Princess"), *Jeux d'eau* ("The Fountain"), the *Sonatine,* the suites *Ma Mère L'Oye, Miroirs* and *Gaspard de la Nuit,* as well as two piano concertos, one for the left hand alone. Many of his novel and original effects for the piano and the orchestra have passed into the common practice of film music and arrangements of popular music for "concert orchestra." It is refreshing to hear them in Ravel's music, their natural habitat before they became *clichés.*

Serge Prokofiev, 1891-1953

While Prokofiev arrived in Paris only in 1920, by way of the United States, his anti-romantic tendencies were similar to those flourishing in the French capitol. Among his teachers at the St. Petersburg Conservatory was Rimsky-Korsakov, who lately had tutored Igor Stravinsky. Prokofiev took no part in the revolution of 1918, but secured permission to come to America, where he hoped to make his fortune. When his hopes did not materialize, he moved to Paris, becoming associated for a time with the Diaghelev Ballet Russe. Later, in 1927, he returned to Russia, where he was received with acclaim.

During the period before he came to America, Prokofiev wrote a number of popular works which indicate somewhat the stylistic path he was to take. He himself rather accurately analyzed his directions in a short autobiographical note in 1941. The first was Classical, a heritage from his early training which led him to adopt Neoclassic forms and, in the many gavottes, an eighteenth century manner. The second, which he called "the modern", was characterized by the search for a language of harmony, melody and orchestration with which to express strong emotions. The "motor" tendency, which shows in the *Toccata, Op. 11,* and other works where a percussive rhythmic continuity is present, represents the third direction. The fourth was the concentration upon the lyric element, and this Prokofiev regarded as most important. We shall find that his unexpected harmonies may often be understood in their relation to the melody, much as were the parallelisms of Debussy. The fifth direction he described as "Scherzoish," the mocking, whimsical and witty manner which is often combined with the Classical tendencies, yielding works in which the element of parody is less important than gay spirits and delightful surprises. But other works may be less gay, more ironic or sardonic in their expression.

Prokofiev has an individual melodic style, usually wide in range, with leaps of considerable size, and often changing keys through the adoption of the sharps or flats of another scale through which the melody moves. The harmony varies accordingly, sometimes playing upon the ambiguity of a tone and harmonizing it with a chord other than the one which we expect. The harmony in his music is usually simple, sometimes spiked with dissonance, but more often simply triads or seventh chords of the commonest kinds. But, as we have mentioned, they often are not the precise harmony which we might expect at a certain point, but a rather more interesting one which may turn the melody aside to less predictable paths. The rhythm is most notable in fast movements, where the vigorous movement of melody is required.

The *Classical Symphony* Op. 25 (1918) was an essay in the Haydn style, with twentieth century overtones. Here, Prokofiev sought a measure of security in certain academic disciplines, turning away from the developments of twentieth century music which Debussy and Schönberg had brought to a crisis. The work is in the usual four movements and the expected classical forms except for the third movement, where a *gavotte* in pseudo-eighteenth century style substitutes for the minuet. The second movement abandons a certain parodistic quality present in the first movement, and becomes more expressive and personal. The gavotte exhibits clearly many of the qualities of Prokofiev's style which we have mentioned above. The finale is motoric but not percussively so. The composer set the limitation upon himself in this movement to use no minor chords, a fact which contributes to the bright and cheerful quality which is enhanced, of course, by the orchestration.

The *Scythian Suite* Op. 20, came into being in 1916 through a commission by Diaghilev for a new Russian ballet. Stravinsky recently had leaped into prominence via similar commissions from this Midas of the arts, and Prokofiev hoped to make his reputation in the same way. Impressed with Stravinsky's *Rite of Spring*, Prokofiev and his scenarist chose a story embodying the conflict between light and dark set in prehistoric times among the pagan and barbarian Scythians. It did not please Diaghelev, however, and the composer returned to Russia where, feeling that much of the music was too good to abandon, he converted it into a suite. It is an anti-romantic work of the same stamp as the *Rite of Spring*, but without the striking consistency of material and organization of Stravinsky's masterpiece. The movements are entitled I. "Invocation to Veles and Ala" (the sun, as giver of light, and a sacrifice to Ala an idol which is the daughter of the sun), II. "Chuzhbog and the Dance of the Evil Spirits," III. "Night," IV. "Lolli's pursuit of Chuzhbog and Sunrise." The last movement, in which the Scythian warrior, Lolli, endeavors to save Ala and is rescued from the uneven battle by the rising of the sun god, is the most effective movement of the suite, concluding as it does with a powerful sustained passage describing the rising sun.

One of the most striking compositions for piano of this period is the *Piano Sonata No. 2*, Opus 14. While written during the last of Prokofiev's student days, it reveals an adventurousness of idiom, a demonstration of Prokofiev's understanding of the instrument, and the pursuit of the modern and motoric tendencies which have already been mentioned. The sonata is in the usual four movements. The forms of these, while successful, do not reveal any great understanding of the traditional structures which they presumably follow. But the headlong rhythmic drive and the effective juxtaposition of contrasting sections afford not only interest but also create coherence by means of continuity. The first movement is a highly sectionalized sonata-allegro with a number of themes. It is tonal but highly chromatic. The motoric *Scherzo* which follows is ternary in form, with an intriguing rhythmic figure in the A sections. The structure of the *Andante* is A-B-A'-B', in which the A sections, in clear G sharp minor, contrast with the tonally obscure B sections. The final movement is a scherzo-like sonata-allegro similar to the first movement, but with much ostinato accompaniment. The three-note motive of the first movement (C-B-C) appears throughout the sonata as a cyclic device.

Prokofiev's music is easily understandable against the romantic background, despite its use of dissonance and somewhat anti-romantic tendencies. He never faced the issue of tonality squarely, but found a style which disregarded the dilemma of the times. This style he developed and deepened as time went on, producing some of the most enjoyable music of the first half of the twentieth century.

Igor Stravinsky, 1882-

This pathfinder of modern music was born in the Oranienbaum suburb of St. Petersburg, Russia. The son of a bass singer of the Imperial Opera, he was raised in a musical atmosphere, and became a proficient pianist at an early age. It was not until 1901, when he met Rimsky-Korsakov, that he decided to study composition seriously. After six years of preparatory work, he became a private pupil of the older Russian master. During this time two works of his gained some success: a *Fantastic Scherzo* and a tone painting called *Fireworks*.

These came to the attention of Sergei Diaghilev, the impresario of the Ballet Russe in Paris, who commissioned the young composer to write a score for a ballet, *The Firebird,* based on a Russian legend. With the success of the composition, Stravinsky was commissioned repeatedly by Diaghilev for ballet scores, the results of which were *Petrouchka* (1911), *The Rite of Spring* (1913), *L'Histoire du Soldat* ("The Soldier's Tale") (1918), and *Pulcinella* (1920). During this first period,

PLATE XLIII. *Igor Stravinsky. (Photo by Columbia Records, courtesy of Boosey and Hawkes.)*

extending from *The Firebird* in 1910 to the opera *Mavra* in 1922, Stravinsky produced music which was distinctly national in character, based upon Russian literature and history. At this time he also made the acquaintance of American jazz and composed a few works in which the jazz influence is strong: *Ragtime* (Armistice Day, 1918), and *The Soldier's Tale* of the same year.

Many of the devices of contemporary music first came into prominence in the works of Stravinsky. Not that many of them were new ——far from it——but in his music they were used in entirely novel ways. For each work, Stravinsky created a new musical style, one that was tailored to the style of the subject, whether that subject was as concrete as a ballet scenario, or as esoteric as a musical essay on Bach. But certain constant qualities appear in each work which proclaim its composer. We shall draw attention to Stravinsky's innovations as we examine some of the works which fall into the first phase of our century.

The Firebird Suite, 1910

The story of the ballet is based upon the Russian fairy-tale about the ogre, Kastchei, whom Prince Ivan defeats aided by the magic powers of the Firebird. There are five movements in the suite, some of which employ Russian folk idioms (II: "The Round Dance of the Princesses;" IV: Berceuse; V: Finale). The magic element of the Firebird is represented by the tritone (A♭ to D in the opening ostinato), and serves as a unifying motive. Much use is made of ostinato accompaniments, and the orchestration is brilliant and subtle, combining the flashing colors so typical of Rimsky-Korsakov's technique with the refinements and parallel chord movement of Debussy.

In his next ballet, *Petroushka,* the techniques become more individualized, and the musical profile of Stravinsky emerges more clearly. The orchestration owes less to Rimsky and Debussy, and the characteristic rhythmic virtuosity of Stravinsky becomes more apparent. The use of two keys simultaneously (bitonality, polytonality) appears first in this work and is used more thoroughly in the following one, *Le Sacre du printemps* ("The Rite of Spring"), which signals the end of the Romantic period.

The Rite of Spring, 1913

"I saw in imagination a solemn pagan rite: sage elders, seated in a circle, watched a young girl dance herself to death. They were sacrificing her to propitiate the god of Spring." So Stravinsky described the motivating idea of this ballet. It caused a riot when first performed at the *Théatre des Champs Elysées* on May 29, 1913, but has endured to become numbered in the concert repertory of every major orchestra. What has been most remarked upon is the rhythmic quality of the work, but *Le Sacre* has many other innovations and subtleties, some of which are only becoming appreciated in this second half of the century.

Certainly, the rhythmic element was new; it had to be to satisfy the forward-looking composer, as well as to accomplish the goal of the ballet. This is a primitivistic work, much the same in concept as the painting and sculpture based on African masks which were being brought to Europe (Plate XLIV). Picasso and others found a sophisticated simplicity in them, and adapted elements of this style to their own ideas. Stravinsky paralleled their work, producing a forceful result through rhythm, the most primitive of the elements of music. While the primitive beat may seem monotonous, Stravinsky took care to use certain oriental techniques to create shock and vitality.

The first of these may be called *additive rhythm*, and consists of increasing or decreasing each measure by one beat more or less than the preceding measure. This can be accomplished by changing the meter:

or by the use of strong accents within a neutral, steady metric pulse:

A variation of this procedure, which depends for its effectiveness upon a constant and even basic pulsation, consists of constant metric changes which do not add or subtract smoothly, but vary in a seemingly random way. This creates a total effect of staggering, reeling rhythmic movement:

(Unit of pulsation is the 16th note, ♪).

Regardless of the seeming randomness of these rhythms, they depend upon a mechanical, motoric basic pulse, different from the expressive *rubato* of both Romantic music and jazz. Their brutality in the context of *Le Sacre* is unmistakable and appropriate.

A listener, hearing this work for the first time, is apt to be impressed by the volume, color, and the dissonant quality of the sound, the rhythm, and finally the melodic qualities of some of the sections. It requires repeated hearings to understand. The use of dissonance is essentially Impressionistic, with bold doubling at unusual intervals. Much of the scale material is modal, often with the simultaneous use of two modes with different key signatures (*bimodality*, comparable to polytonality). The melodies are primitive in nature, most of them repetitive within a narrow range of a fourth or fifth, and usually are incomplete, turning upon themselves with rhythmic variations of the same tone-patterns for extension (Example VII-5). The form is, of course, sectional, as would result from the episodic nature of a ballet;

PLATE XLIV. *African Mask from Itumba, The Congo;* "Les Demoiselles d'Avignon" *by Picasso. Examples of primitivism, genuine and imitated. Note the use of the primitive style of the mask by Picasso in the two faces at the right. Note also the distortion in representing the noses as well as other features of the other figures. (Courtesy of The Museum of Modern Art.)*

but it becomes coherent through the family resemblance of the melodic and rhythmic material, as well as by the process which Stravinsky has called "polarity." Essentially, this process, which embraces tonal as well an nontonal procedures, implies the creation of tension by some means, often involving two tones or keys, and the progression toward their resolution throughout the composition. Analysts of this work tell us that the internal tension of tonal sections, dissonant intervals and melodic processes all tend toward resolution upon the tone D, which is the final pitch of the music. However it is accomplished, the formal unity, coherence and progression of *Le Sacre* becomes more and more apparent with each listening, after one recovers from the initial shock of the work.

A detailed analysis of this gigantic and epoch-making composition is beyond the scope of this book, however, so we must be content with indicating a few points of interest as we journey through the first part of the work.

There are two large episodes in the ballet, the first entitled "The Adoration of the Earth," and the second "The Sacrifice." The action depicts the celebration of the coming of spring by a pagan Russian tribe in the dawn of history. To insure the fertility of the earth, a maiden is chosen to be sacrificed; after preparatory rites she dances until she is dead.

Part I, Introduction: The bassoon, in its extreme high register, announces a plaintive theme composed of only a few notes (Example VII-5) which are rhythmically varied upon repetition. An Impressionistic section follows which sets the Neolithic scene, grows to a climax, then subsides with a recollection of the opening melody. This section is not marked by strong rhythms and employs almost entirely the colors of the wind instruments.

EXAMPLE VII-5: Stravinsky, *Le Sacre du printemps.*

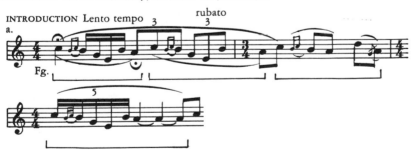

Dance of the Adolescents: This section is introduced by a fragmentary *ostinato* (b), one of Stravinsky's frequent devices, after which a percussive series of polychords assigned to the strings—not the brass or percussion—provides an exciting series of sections in additive rhythms (c) separated by more angular bitonal figures in the bassoons and cellos. A motive outlining the interval of a fourth appears and eventually becomes a primitive scale melody of narrow range (d). This is followed by a more rhythmically active section, still exploiting the *ostinato,* during which the horns announce a variant of the previous melody (e), still narrow in range and primitive sounding. This version is presented with increasing force and instrumentation, always against multiple *ostinato* figures. Such repetition, typical of Russian composers, bears Stravinsky's hallmark in that it is usually rhythmically varied by shifting the theme so that the metric accents fall upon different notes.

The Play of Abduction: This is an active polytonal section which presents a bright theme characterized by leaping fourths in somewhat the fashion of a fanfare (f). Although they are heard with difficulty, changing meters and unequal subdivision of the measure

$$\left(\frac{9}{8}=\frac{4}{8}+\frac{5}{8} \text{ rather than the traditional } \frac{9}{8}=\frac{3}{8}+\frac{3}{8}+\frac{3}{8}\right)$$

add their excitement to that of the highly dissonant sonority. In a sense, there are not themes in this impressionistic section but only scales and *arpeggios* derived from the basic polytonal chords. The interval of the fourth again has an important place in the figures.

Round Dances of Spring: This section presents varied repetitions of two themes, again primitively constructed against a plodding *ostinato* which appears first in the low strings (g). The horns play a colorful version of the theme doubled at the fifth, minor sixth and the octave (h). Later, a rapid section brings back the theme of the previous Play of Abduction, developing it athletically with changing meters and massive chordal interruptions. A quiet solo in the alto flute doubled two octaves higher by the E♭ clarinet leads to the next scene.

Games of the Rival Tribes: Here we find *ostinati,* changing meters, antiphonal exchanges between choirs of the orchestra, and splashes of woodwind color obtained by parallel triads moving in rapid scale figures. The strings again act as percussion instruments. The first melodic ideas (i) are related to those based upon the fourth which were heard previously; they are now followed by a more lyric theme, still narrow and repetitive, which emphasizes the interval of the third both in its shape and in its doubling (j). It is handed around the orchestra, inter-

(g) ostinato

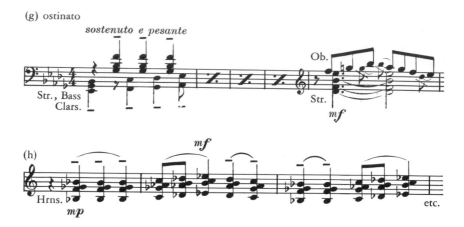

(h)

rupted by Impressionistic fragments and finally returned to prominence in *stretto* imitations.

(i) Molto allegro

Procession of the Sage: A short section of highly dissonant, *ostinato*-saturated Impressionistic writing in which a bugle-call fourth again comes to the fore.

Dance of the Earth: This is the concluding section of Part I, and is essentially choreographic in nature, containing many figures which through energy or direction seem to imply physical motion; these are called "gestic" motives. It is notable for the combination of not only different *ostinati*, but also for the combination of several decorated versions of the same figure. There are added-note chords, fragments of whole-tone scales, doubling at the fifth and octave, and rhythmically compressed versions of the primitive scale theme based upon the fourth.

Part Two consists of an "Introduction," "Mysterious Circle of the Adolescents," "Glorification of the Chosen One," "Evocation of the Ancestors," "Ritual Activity of the Ancestors," and concludes with the "Sacrificial Dance." Much of the same kind of treatment of similar themes takes place here. There is perhaps more obvious use of changing meters, especially in the "Sacrificial Dance," but after being guided through Part I, the listener will find no new problems in Part II.

In summation, then, we find the free use of dissonance, parallel chord movement and doubling at intervals other than the octave, sophisticated rhythmic procedures, polytonality, unusual orchestration and use of instruments, and frequent *ostinato*. Many of these become more refined, some eliminated entirely, in the second creative period.

Most of the works written between *Le Sacre* and 1923 were short, often theater pieces like *L'Histoire du soldat* ("The Tale of a Soldier") and *Renard* which reflected in their small ensembles the more stringent financial situation during and immediately after the war. In both of them, Stravinsky moved farther toward the precision and economical means so characteristic of his work in the second and third phases of the century. His ballet, *Pulcinella*, using material from the works of the 18th century Italian composer, Pergolesi, remains one of the most delightful in the repertory. Rather than just an arrangement, this is a composition which, while retaining the original melodies and chord progressions, becomes more piquant, graceful and interesting through Stravinsky's imaginative orchestration and addition of dissonance. It is as thoroughly of the twentieth century as Prokofiev's *Classical Symphony*, perhaps more so. This type of orchestration, using traditionally unorthodox spacing of chord elements and the omission of certain chord tones also is demonstrated in the *Symphonies for Wind Instruments*, which had its genesis in a chorale written in memory of Debussy and published in the 1920 issue of the *Revue musicale*.

What we have discovered of Stravinsky's musical personality during the first phase of the twentieth century also will apply during the second, becoming a more refined, renewed and continually surprising reflection of the man himself.

NATIONALISM: HUNGARY AND AMERICA

Meanwhile, in other corners of Europe and America, the Nationalistic movement was preparing surprises. Of course, Sibelius was still
writing Finnish musical epics, but now England began to awaken from
the long sleep she had endured since the death of Purcell, and in Spain
arose composers who could realize the national spirit in music. But
these did not affect the mainstream of twentieth century music as yet;
let us look particularly to Hungary for this and to our own country
for surprising developments.

Béla Bartók, 1881-1945

Bartók was born in 1881 in a farming region of Hungary, and from
his earliest years heard the various peasant songs associated with work
and recreation. His father, who was the director of an agricultural
school, died when the boy was seven, and the subsequent lean years
involved many removals from town to town as the job situations of
his mother changed. Arduous as these must have been, they afforded
acquaintance with new folk-songs for the boy. After attending various
grade schools, Bartók graduated and, refusing a scholarship in Vienna,
entered the Royal Academy at Budapest. Shortly after his graduation
from the Academy in 1904, his interest seems to have been focused
more intently upon the folk-songs of his country, and in 1905 he
began, with Zoltán Kodály, a composer-companion who shared his
interest, the first of his life-long researches into the unwritten music of
his country. The effect of the folk-songs upon his personal style was
profound. Previous to this time, his compositions had been strongly
influenced by Liszt, Brahms and impressionism, and programmatically
touched by patriotic nationalism. He writes: "In my studies of folk-
music I discovered that what we had known as Hungarian folk-songs
till then were more or less trivial songs by popular composers and did
not contain much that was valuable. . . . The outcome of these studies
was of decisive influence upon my work, because it freed me of the
tyrannical rule of the major and minor keys. The greater part of the
collected treasure, and the more valuable part, was in old ecclesiastical
or old Greek modes, or based on more primitive (pentatonic) scales,
and the melodies were full of the most free and varied rhythmic
phrases and changes of tempi, played both *rubato* (freely) and *giusto*

PLATE XLV. *Béla Bartók. (Photo by Fritz Reiner, courtesy of Boosey and Hawkes.)*

(strictly). It became clear to me that the old modes, which had been forgotten in our music, had lost nothing of their vigour. Their new employment made new rhythmic combinations possible. This new way of using the diatonic scale brought freedom from the rigid use of the major and minor keys, and eventually led to a new conception of the chromatic scale, every tone of which came to be considered of equal value and could be used freely and independently."[3] From this time on we find innumerable arrangements and transcriptions of folk-songs for piano solo, or piano and voice. In addition, the folk-song idiom so permeates Bartók's thinking that it is reflected in his other compositions, little by little becoming so assimilated that it is impossible to separate this nationalistic flavor from his work.

[3] *Béla Bartók: A Memorial Review of His Life and Works,* Boosey & Hawkes, Inc., New York, 1950. Used by permission.

The *Second Suite,* Op. 4 (1905-1907, revised in 1943), shows a turning point away from the purely romantic sources of Bartók's earlier music and the influence, here rather slight as yet, of his folksong studies. Movements I and III were written in 1905, after which Bartók collected and studied Hungarian peasant music for two years. Upon returning to the Suite, he was faced with the problem of maintaining the stylistic consistency of the composition, for his researches had had the effect of incorporating the folk music into his compositional style. The difference is not marked, however, and the Hungarian flavor of most of the work is rather slight. In its blend of old and new, it might well be compared to the *Chamber Symphony,* Op. 9 of Schönberg, which is, admittedly, a much more advanced work. Bartók's orchestration and use of chromaticism in the *Suite* are strongly reminiscent of Strauss, but certain techniques and sonorities appear from time to time which presage the later Bartók.

These prophetic elements are most strong in certain formal and developmental traits of the *Suite.* Motivic themes, out of which fragments may be drawn for development, are chosen throughout the work, and the contrasting sections of the forms are often devoted to the development of these fragments. This, of course, promotes the unity of the work——another trait of the later style. The fugal development of the second movement is also characteristic, for Bartók assimilated the polyphonic writing of Bach and the later works of Beethoven as an important element of his technique.

Most of the recordings available use the revised version of the score, in which Bartók tightened the structure and recomposed some of the sections, particularly in the third and fourth movements. Nevertheless, the stylistic consistency with the previous movements is maintained, and the whole work undoubtedly is improved.

The form of the first movement (AABA) is highly sectional particularly during the last part which consists of a series of short codas. The important divisions in the structure are made plain by final cadences, and the preluding harp introduces the new sections. The B section consists of the development of a figure drawn from the A theme stated by the cello at the beginning of the movement. The final A begins with the harp and a version of the A theme in which some of the scale steps have been expanded by a half-step, lending the melody an oriental flavor. Throughout the movement the strings predominate recalling the Straussian style of *Der Rosenkavalier* or *Till Eulenspiegel.*

The second movement is more Hungarian, but essentially that of the popular style, well-bred and acceptable to partisans of the nationalistic music of Liszt, Smetana and Dvořák. It is brilliantly scored, rhythmic and forceful. The form resembles a sonata-allegro, with a fugal development of a variant of the accented upbeat figure in the first movement. The recapitulation is varied, and at one place the fugue subject appears in the solo violin as it might be played by an Hungarian gypsy. Possibly Bartók is mocking his listeners who, at that time, regarded the Gypsy music as authentic Hungarian folk song. The scoring of this movement owes much less to Strauss, perhaps due to its later revision. The harmony also is more comparable in places to sonorities heard in later works by Bartók.

The third movement, an *andante*, begins with a long soliloquy by the solo bass clarinet, which introduces the most important motive of the movement, a seventh chord arpeggiated downward (F-D-Bb-G). The movement which follows consists of a statement of thematic material followed by a development devoted principally to the seventh chord figure. A varied restatement begins with the thematic material in the low woodwinds projected against a flickering curtain of celesta *glissandi*, high woodwind trills and rapid scale and arpeggio figures. The coda further develops the arpeggio figure, which supplies the final chord also. The movement, while not strongly Hungarian, reminds the listener of the later *Concerto for Orchestra* (1943).

The final movement was the most drastically revised in 1943, but the orchestration and style seem to have been fairly well retained. The movement is in sonata-allegro form, the first theme of which is divided between the bassoons and clarinets. The second theme consists of a number of motives which are not striking when first presented, but are expanded in the very Straussian recapitulation. The development is concerned wholly with the first thematic material.

What were these folksongs which attracted Bartók and his friend Kodály so greatly? Perhaps the best answer lies in listening to the set called *Eight Hungarian Folksongs* which Bartók arranged for voice and piano in 1907 through 1917, and published in 1922. They bear out his contentions concerning the use of mode and scale, for all except two of them are modal or pentatonic in melody, the implications of which he followed in the accompaniments. The third of them, *Aszszonyok, aszszonyok, haďlegyek társatok* ("Women, women, let me call you comrades"), would seem to provide a basis of the *Allegro barbaro* for piano, and should be listened to in that light.

The *Allegro barbaro (1911)* is Bartók's first large work for the piano which bears the stamp of folk-music upon it. The piece uses the Phrygian and Lydian modes, and is devoted to the working out of two themes, the first of which appears near the beginning and the second, a kind of cadence figure, somewhat further on (Example VII-

EXAMPLE VII-6: Bartók, *Allegro barbaro.*

6). The form is developmental and ternary, A-B-A'. The B section is quieter and somewhat more sustained, while the return of the A section is accomplished by means of a long developmental transition section employing both motives. The A' section proper is very short and consists only of the rhythmic chords in the proper mode without either theme appearing.

From the folk music, certain idioms entered Bartók's music to become so assimilated that they formed a part of his later, less national and more universal style. They may be summarized as follows:

1. The use of modal scales, not only from the old church modes, but derived from folksong and attributable only to them. The pentatonic scale is also important.

2. Certain melodic intervals, particularly the fourth, which probably came from pentatonic scale melodies. The tritone also is important; perhaps its most obvious source is the Lydian mode, which Bartók uses quite frequently. Certainly it occurs in the "folksong modes." The augmented second (E♭ to F♯) occurs in many Gypsy and near Eastern scales; Bartók's researches in Turkish and Arabian music afforded him experience with this

sound. It occurs rather infrequently in his music, probably because of its stereotyped Gypsy sound.

3. The sonority of certain national instruments, such as the *cimbalom* and the *tárogató*. The first is a harp-like instrument with a sound box under the strings. It is played by striking the strings with small hammers held in the hands. Incredible speed can be attained by a practiced player, and, since there are no damping mechanisms to stop the vibration of the strings, a haze of sound surrounds the music, something like piano music when the damper pedal is depressed throughout. Bartók's percussive style of piano music is related to this instrument. The *tárogató* is an ancient woodwind instrument originally with a double reed mouthpiece such as the oboe and bassoon have today. In the nineteenth century it was fitted with a clarinet mouthpiece thus making it a relative of the saxophone. The bassoon and English horn sometimes have passages reminiscent of this instrument in Bartók's music.

4. Certain rhythmic procedures such as alternating triple and duple meters or subdividing a measure in a nontraditional manner. For an example of the last procedure, the reader may look ahead to page 525, where the opening of the *Music for Strings, Percussion and Celesta* occurs. The opening measure of 8/8, usually subdivided into 2+2+2+2, appears here as 3+3+2.

5. There is great use of the chromatic scale, both melodically (see the example just referred to) and harmonically, in which the chord basis is often the second rather than the traditional third, resulting in *tone clusters* or *secundal harmony*. Chords built upon fourths also are used.

6. While the influences of Strauss, Brahms and Wagner gradually disappear, the logical structures of Beethoven and the polyphonic procedures of Bach are notably present in an assimilated form. They do not sound like those composers, but Bartók's methods are demonstrably similar. Impressionism remains in certain movements which are Expressionistic interpretations of "night sounds" by Impressionistic means. One seems to hear in these eerie moments the rustling and chirping of insects, the almost inaudible flight of night birds and the soft sounds of the wind, all disquieting in effect. These movements often are rather terrifying in their intensity, and one imagines that Bartók is not presenting a simple nocturne, but perhaps "the dark night of the soul."

Much piano music embodying many of these characteristics was composed by Bartók during the years between 1907 and 1923 among which are sets of folksong arrangements for piano alone, *Two Elegies, For Children* (a set of eighty-five short pieces based on folksong and arranged simply for young piano students) *Seven Sketches,* the *Sonatina* based on Roumanian folk tunes which was transcribed for orchestra with the title *Transylvanian Dances,* the delightful *Roumanian Folk Dances* (1915) also transcribed for orchestra by Bartók in 1917, and *The First Term at the Piano.* Notable orchestral works of this period after the *Second Suite* are the *Two Portraits,* Op. 5 (1907), *Two Pictures (Images)* Op. 10 (1910), *The Wooden Prince,* a ballet in one act (1914-16), *The Miraculous Mandarin,* a one-act pantomime, Op. 19 (1919), and the *Dance Suite* (1923). During this period Bartók wrote the one-act opera *Duke Bluebeard's Castle,* Op. 11 (1911), employing in it and *The Miraculous Mandarin* a chromatic expressionist technique touched with sonorities from the folksongs. While these works are as Expressionistic as Schönberg's *Erwartung,* their flavor is quite different; the psychological penetration and emphasis upon terror puts them in the same class, however. The subjects themselves here dictated the style, as they always should, however far removed it was from the works embodying what the composer had learned from the peasant songs.

During this period the first two string quartets were written (1909 and 1917), inaugurating the series of six which are often regarded as continuing the line of development and expression which Beethoven began. This medium interested Bartók from his student days to the end of his life, and a study of the six quartets affords a means of following his development, for they are accurately progressive in their growth.

The *Second String Quartet,* Op. 17 (1917), is in three movements and shows most of the salient features of Bartók's style. The movements are: *I, Moderato,* a developmental form derived from the sonata-allegro; *II, Allegro molto capriccioso,* a scherzo which is rondo-like in structure; and *III, Lento,* a chainlike series of sections linked thematically. As Halsey Stevens remarks in *The Life and Music of Béla Bartók* (see biblography), the three movements represent a design of "lyrical——dynamic——reflective," creating an energetic and climactic central movement, and ending with a summary of motives which acts as a cadence to the entire work.

In the *Second Quartet,* Bartók pursued a course of motivic variation and expansion which became a characteristic technique in all of his later works. The basic motive of the entire work consists of the intervals of a 2nd and a 3rd (*e.g.*, G♯-A-C) combined in various ways. From the motive are derived other thematic elements and it is verticalized to form harmonic structures. The interval of the fourth, frequently encountered in Hungarian music, and the tritone also are important in the quartet. Instead of merely repeating the motivic material at different pitch levels and with different harmonizations——a procedure that was the essence of classical developmental procedure ——Bartók expands and varies the material, not only rhythmically, but also by the addition of other tones. This technique is, of course, linked to that of Beethoven's late quartets and to Romantic theme transformation. The three movements thereby are given the closest kind of unity, and a feeling of organic growth and expansion permeates each of them individually as well as the whole sequence.

The two *Violin-Piano Sonatas* (1922, 1923) approach the characteristics of the most advanced Viennese works of the early twenties in their use of chromaticism and avoidance of tonality, their octave displacement of melody tones and the use of motives to integrate the material. They are more international and less specifically Hungarian than some of the previous works.

But in the *Dance Suite* (1923), written to commemorate the combination of the towns of Buda, Pest and Óbuda into the city of Budapest in 1873, the effect of folk elements is especially strong, although the thematic material is original. The compositions consist of five dances separated by a ritornello, and provided with introduction and a coda which summarizes and combines all of the dance themes except that from the fourth dance. The thematic material, as Bartók indicated, resembles Arabian music in the first and fourth dances, while that of the ritornello, second and third are Magyar, and the fifth is Roumanian. The fourth dance is separated from those preceding it by a pause, and consists of a melody given to the woodwinds, each phrase of which is unaccompanied, with small sections of quiet, colorful background in which the harps are especially prominent between each of the phrases. This dance provides a point of relaxation before the fifth dance and large coda, which become increasingly exciting.

Thus we see that a stylistic synthesis was possible using the chromatic scale with tonal implications, together with folkloric materials, which was quite different from either the Viennese or Parisian explorations of the same period. Now let us take a short look at what had happened and was in the process of happening across the Atlantic Ocean in the United States.

MUSIC IN THE UNITED STATES

During the first two-thirds of the nineteenth century, most of the music heard in the United States was imported from Europe. To be sure, there were native composers, but there was no lasting music produced by them. They were products, for the most part, of the European conservatories, principally those of Germany, and the music they wrote was German-Romantic in style with all too little individuality. But these men were important because they showed that there could be American composers and because they established the study of music in the universities and colleges of the country. This group includes the names of William Mason (1829-1908) who studied with Liszt, the conductor Theodore Thomas (1835-1905) and John Knowles Paine (1839-1906) who occupied the first university professorship in music at Harvard in 1873 and whose music to Sophocles' *Oedipus Tyrannus* is sometimes heard. To this list may also be added other composers who were Paine's students: G. W. Chadwick (1854-1931) Arthur Foote (1853-1937) and Horatio W. Parker (1863-1919).

Possibly the first American to make more than a passing imprint upon the musical consciousness of the nation was Edward MacDowell (1861-1908). Born in New York City, MacDowell's talents were recognized early and carefully nurtured, first by private music lessons, later, at the age of 16, at the Paris Conservatoire where he was a classmate of a strange young man named Claude Debussy. Later he studied in Germany and concluded his European sojourn as a member of the informal "class" which met at Liszt's house in Weimar. Here MacDowell met most of the influential men of German and French music. He returned to the United States in 1888 and lived in Boston until 1896, when he moved to New York to become the first chairman of the new music department at Columbia University. He resigned from this position in 1904 due to a conflict in ideals with the university administration, and resumed the role of a private teacher and composer. His mind gradually weakened, however, and he passed his last days in an uncomprehending, trance-like state.

Among the works which are still heard today, in addition to some of his smaller sketches for piano (the omnipresent "To a Wild Rose" was never intended by the composer to reach the public eye; it was thrown in a waste-basket, but rescued by the composer's wife), are four Romantic, heroic piano sonatas in the grand manner and two early piano concertos, the product of his European stay. The Second Suite for Orchestra, based on Indian themes, is probably the work for which he will be longest remembered. Much of his music has a rugged northern quality, somewhat Schumannesque in its dark coloring and rhythmic flow. The music is well made, for MacDowell was a craftsman and aware of the latest stylistic trends of his day. However, the sounds of Impressionism were not for him; rather, he favored the conservative trend as represented by Brahms and Schumann even though he was a member of the Liszt circle. The colony which bears his name at Peterborough, New Hampshire, was established in his memory by his wife and commemorates his love of solitude and nature and offers these necessities to artists and students.

A group of somewhat more familiar composers now fills the scene, beginning with Edgar Stillman Kelley (1857-1944) and including Henry Gilbert (1868-1928), John Alden Carpenter (1876-1951), Daniel Gregory Mason (1873-1953) and Edward Burlingame Hill (1872-1960) among others. There was an increase not only in the number of American composers whose productive years began about 1890, but also a growing interest and pride on the part of the nation in the efforts of these men. To be sure, many of them still found it necessary to study in Europe, but one of the most important, Charles Ives, was taught in the United States.

Charles Ives, 1874-1954

Ives was born in Danbury, Connecticut, taught by his father (the village bandmaster and organist) and at Yale by a number of instructors including Horatio Parker. For a few years, Ives made music his vocation, but in 1898 he entered business and put music aside as an active avocation although he composed continuously until his retirement in 1930. For the remainder of his life he wrote little, and his fame rests upon those works composed between 1890 and 1925.

His music might be called eclectic, if it were not for the fact that he combined musical styles in a most original and daring way. Impressionistic devices, Stravinsky rhythms, polytonality, quotation of popular and folk-tunes, dissonant tone clusters and experiments with sonority are all to be found in this surprising music. And this at a time when the new music was principally confined to Europe, certainly not to be heard in staid and conservative Boston, where Philip Hale, the annotator for the Boston Symphony, wrote "exit in case of Brahms!" Ives' *Concord Sonata,* published in 1919, had to wait until

PLATE XLVI. *Charles Ives. (Courtesy of BMI Archives.)*

1939 for a first American performance. Technically challenging as well as difficult to understand, the work attempts to convey the spirit of transcendentalism associated with the Emerson circle at Concord. Thus, there are impressionistic pictures of Emerson, Thoreau, the Alcotts and a sherzo depicting the fantastic side of Hawthorne's imagination.

Another work which reveals clearly the inquiring mind and experimental method of this surprising man is the first of his suites for orchestra, entitled *New England Scenes,* which consists of three movements: "Boston Common," "Putnam's Camp (Redding, Connecticut)" and "The Housatonic at Stockbridge." The style of all three movements is essentially Impressionistic, recalling the sounds of Bartók's "night music" to a certain extent, but scored more heavily, with divided strings. Thus a harmonic texture is set up composed of a multitude of dissonances, often at a low dynamic level. Such a combination results in opaque harmony of high tension in which no single dissonance is clearly apparent. Often a strong organpoint will seem to act as the root of his harmony, thus making it possible to achieve variety and interest.

The first movement, subtitled "Colonel Shaw and his Colored Regiment," purports to be a ghostly procession, but resembles a march only by a considerable stretch of the imagination. Against the harmonic background mentioned above, fragments of Civil War tunes and drum beats are projected. There is no clear form, and the whole movement resembles a portion of a dream.

The second movement is very much alive with the spirit of rural New England, and is, Ives tells us, a fantasy describing the dreams of a child who falls asleep during a Fourth of July outing within sight of Putnam's old camp. The movement opens with a riotous march, and continues in this vein almost throughout, slowing only once for a section of the "night music" sounds. Many familiar march tunes are quoted, among them the *British Grenadiers, Yankee Doodle, Columbia the Gem of the Ocean,* and, although not a march, *Row, Row, Row Your Boat.* In addition to these, a fragment of a sentimental song appears now and then in the lulls between marches. It is said that Ives heard the effect produced by two bands marching into Danbury from opposite directions and playing different tunes; he has here incorporated this effect into the music, creating not only polytonal combinations, but also polymetric ones of a complexity undreamed of at the time the work was composed.

The third movement again returns to the impressionistic harmony of the first, and generally recalls that movement, although in a calmer fashion. A melodic line which may be derived from a hymn appears against the dissonant harmonic curtain, but other events are not as noticeable. At the conclusion, the music rises to a climax which suddenly vanishes, leaving behind a few instruments to play a quiet and consonant cadence.

Ives also wrote a number of effective songs, among which is the setting of Vachel Lindsay's *General William Booth Enters into Heaven,* with its quotation of the hymn *Are You Washed in the Blood of the Lamb?* Other songs are settings of his own texts or those found in newspapers, and vary in length from the Vachel Lindsay poem to the brief *One, Two, Three* whose text reads:

> Why doesn't one, two, three
> Seem to appeal to a Yankee
> As much as one, two!

Ives also composed four symphonies, of which the third is the most frequently performed, four violin-piano sonatas, two piano sonatas, over two-hundred songs, chamber music, choral works and many miscellaneous piano compositions.

This composer was indeed a prophet without honor in his own land, for had he journeyed to Paris where new artistic ideas of the time were treated seriously he would have become one of the famous pioneers of the style of the twentieth century. But instead, he cultivated his own New England garden, and it remained for an appreciative posterity to recognize his importance.

JAZZ

The central traditions of the improvisatory art called jazz arose in New Orleans near the beginning of the century. Essentially a variation technique, it depended upon a characteristic melodic line, often simple and close to Negro song, supported by traditional harmonies and propelled by a strong duple rhythmic beat. Such a description tells little about the music, however, for certain improvisatory elements must be present. One of these, an important one, is the anticipation or delay in certain tones of the melody by the tiniest fractions of a beat, giving vitality, flexibility and a sense of freedom to the line only approximated by the written notation. The underlying metric pulse must also constantly accelerate by an almost imperceptible amount if the music is to "swing," otherwise rhythmic monotony is the result. The formal unity of the variations depends to a great degree upon the use of the same progression of chords for each repetition. Both melody and harmony soon established a number of *clichés* which made both performance and listening simpler, and later popular music——related in many ways to jazz, but without its vitality——multiplied the clichés to the point where the piece consisted of little else. In its rhythmic and melodic freshness jazz was essentially anti-Romantic and non-European ——a product of the New World unlike anything Europeans had heard before. There was immediately great enthusiasm for jazz in certain quarters, especially Paris, where it was first heard in 1918, and a number of composers, among whom were Milhaud, Satie, Hindemith and Stravinsky, wrote compositions which included elements of jazz. The best known of these are Milhaud's *Création du Monde* and Stravinsky's *Ragtime* for piano.

The instrumentation of the jazz band also was novel, consisting of trumpet or cornet, trombone, clarinet, tuba, and occasionally flute or piccolo. These instruments took turns varying the tune as soloists, sometimes providing background, and frequently playing improvised counterpoint against the firm harmonic and rhythmic support of piano, guitar, banjo, plucked string bass and drums. We call it "Dixieland" now, but it was simply jazz in those legendary days.

Since then, jazz has undergone many transformations, from "hot" to "sweet," together with changes in the ensemble, most notable of which was the inclusion of the saxophone in the twenties, which gave the music the quality memorialized in the novels of F. Scott Fitzgerald. The popular ballad as represented by the songs of George Gershwin from the year of his first success, 1919, to the end of his life in 1937, represented a type of music which could be played as jazz or as a song, never omitting, however, the rhythmic and harmonic stylistic *clichés* of the jazz style. Paul Whiteman created a "symphonic jazz" by adding saxophones to his orchestra and by giving Gershwin the opportunity to compose for such a group. His *Rhapsody in Blue* was the first result of the collaboration.

When one examines the contemporary accounts of jazz in the twenties and thirties, one is struck by the recurrence of the word "blue" in song titles and in descriptions of the music. Certainly much of this came from the Negro lament called "the blues," a chaconne-like set of variations over a standard chord progression of I-IV-I-V-I used in three four-measure phrases. What gave such a piece the authentic "blue" sound was the melodic use of both the major and minor third in the I and IV chords, and the flatted seventh scale degree from time to time, often against the unchanged seventh contained in the V chord. Originally these were vocal inflections which were probably not entirely a half-step flat, but when transferred to the rigid half-step tuning of the piano, were forced into this condition. These were the "blue notes" which gave their name to so many tunes. Later, the spectrum was widened to include every other color and shade, but without any technical musical significance.

Jazz style was and is an individual quality with the performer, since its notation is merely an outline of the musical events for the performer to improvise upon. Thus, while some tunes were important, the history of the style is composed largely of the names of great performers, virtuosi in their own rights, who through their creative imagination as evidenced in performance, or a particular style or quality of playing their instrument, have become memorable. Fortunately, phonograph recordings were made, beginning about 1917, so that a large part of the history in performance has become available. Louis Armstrong (b.1900), Fletcher Henderson (1898-1952), "Ma" Rainey (1886-1939), Bessie Smith (c.1900-1937), Dominic LaRocca (b.1889), "Bix" Beiderbecke (1903-1931), Eddie Condon (b.1904), Tommy Dorsey (1905-1956), "Fats" Waller (1904-1943), "Count" Basie (b.1904), and "Duke" Ellington (b.1899), to name only a few, survive on records and may be compared through their performances rather than from the written notation of the common fund of music which they played.

The influence of jazz upon most American composers has been subtle, intuitively woven into their style as sonorous or rhythmic elements whose origins are buried in the individual's earliest musical experiences. For unlike the European tradition of *Hausmusik* by famous serious composers, the American tradition has emanated from the phonograph, radio and television, largely in the form of popular song and jazz. The budding composer assimilates the stylistic peculiarities of this music, then forgets them, but unconsciously his serious music reflects the influence in many ways. This is the real significance of jazz to serious music, aside from its own importance as a popular branch of the art, for the pieces by Milhaud and Stravinsky tend to sound dated, as of course, does the early jazz from which they sprang. Due to the widespread importation of recordings and orchestras to Europe and Asia, jazz and American popular music now have a pervasive influence all over the world— a fact that would certainly have astonished the early jazzmen such as "Jelly Roll" Morton, "King" Oliver and "Kid" Ory.

PLATE XLVII. *"Mont St. Victoire" by Cézanne. This painting is a forerunner of geometrical abstraction and cubism. Note the reduction of natural objects to quasi-geometrical forms. (Courtesy of The Philadelphia Museum of Art.)*

THE MODERN STYLE IN THE OTHER ARTS: 1900-1920

The first two decades of the twentieth century were years of "isms" not only in politics but also in the arts. In addition to Impressionism and Expressionism, both originating in painting, there were machine-ism, primitivism, cubism, surrealism, futurism, dadaism and realism. Some of these movements correspond in painting and music, while others have no close connection. Sculpture reacted slowly to the isms, and architecture almost not at all for obvious reasons.

The twentieth century was hailed at this time as the "age of the machine." Certain artists, such as Fernand Léger (1881-1955), used mechanistic shapes in his paintings and experimental films, one of which had a score by the American George Antheil (1900-1959) entitled *Ballet méchanique.* Satie had intended to use mechanical noise-makers in his ballet *Parade,* but Antheil surpassed him, employing large sheets of iron, airplane propellers and other hardware. Luigi Russolo (1885-1947), founder of the "Futurist" movement in music, in which all sounds were to be admitted as musical material——prophetic statement——invented various kinds of noise-makers to use in his scores. And, of course, the mechanistic rhythmic elements of Stravinsky and Ravel are easily heard.

Impressionism, as we have seen, treated tone in a manner analogous to the use of color in the paintings of Monet, Degas, Pissarro, Cezanne and others, and drew for pictorial associations upon the literature of the symbolist poets, Baudelaire (1821-1867), Verlaine (1844-1896), Rimbaud (1854-1891) and Mallarmé (1842-1898), among others. Debussy, near the time of his death, was thinking strongly of using a story by the American symbolist, Edgar Allen Poe (1809-1849) as the subject for an opera.

Expressionism, the German counterpart of French Impressionism, is represented in painting by Van Gogh (1853-1890), Oskar Kokoschka (b.1886), Edvard Munch (1863-1944) and in literature by James Joyce (1882-1941), Eugene O'Neill (1888-1953) and T. S. Eliot (1888-1965). The emphasis upon the individual emotional interpretation of the world, together with a certain pessimistic, not to say grim attitude, and the most brilliant use of all available techniques to communicate as intensely as possible is characteristic of all of these artists.

With the importation into Europe of various kinds of native and "primitive" art from Africa, Asia and Australia, many painters and sculptors saw in them a sophistication and freshness of viewpoint——

PLATE XLVIII. *"Girl Before a Mirror" by Picasso. An example of post-cubistic distortion and presentation of several views (clothed, nude, X-rayed) simultaneously. (Courtesy of The Museum of Modern Art.)*

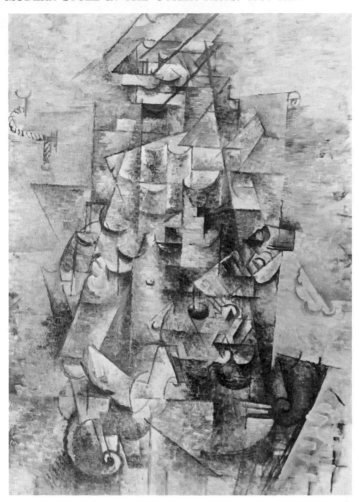

PLATE XLIX. *"Man with a Guitar"* by Braque. A typical cubistic reassemblage of the features of the subject. (Courtesy of The Museum of Modern Art.)

that of a savage or a child——and sought to capture this quality in their art. The vogue thus started reached music eventually, producing at least one important work, Stravinsky's *Le Sacre*. In others, such as Bartók's *Allegro barbaro* and Falla's *El amor brujo* ("Love, the Magician"), there was a strong European folk flavor mixed with the primitivisim which made it more easily digestible for the weak musical stomachs of the public.

Certain painters—Braque, Picasso and Cezanne in his later years ——saw that geometrical shapes abounded in their natural subjects such as bottles, apples, guitars, and so on. In Cubism, they first broke these subjects into assemblies of geometrically shaped figures (Plate XLIX). Later, they broke these apart and reassembled them in ways suggested by their various imaginations. In Picasso's *Girl Before a Mirror*, we see the subject from several angles simultaneously as well as from several imagined points of view. In the same way, Schönberg and his colleagues fragmented the melodic line, assembling these fragments in many ways; they also inverted and turned backward the motives in post-cubistic treatment, and allowed us at least two views of the material——as melody, then assembled into a chord as harmony. Cubistic sculpture offers comparisons even more clearly with music, since it exists in space as music does in time. The use of distortion in rhythm as well may be traced through all of these art works.

Perhaps more than any others, Picasso and Stravinsky personify the seeking spirit of the first two decades of the century. They are much alike in their use of the whole historic range of artistic styles which they use in contemporary fashion. In their work the style itself often becomes the subject, a fact which becomes more plain as we study the compositions of Stravinsky in the following decades. But neither he nor the other men whose work we have studied remained in one place; culture was dynamic, and they moved with it.

TERMS, PHASE I

Impressionism
Expressionism
Antiromanticism
Nationalism
Primitivism
Symbolism
chromatic scale
whole-tone scale
pentatonic scale
modal scales
arabesque
melodic inversion
retrograde
doubling
"blue" third
functional, nonfunctional harmony
Tristan harmony
non-tonal

atonal
suspended tonality
parallel chords
fragmentation of melody
verticalization of melody
pointillism
athematic
polytonality, polymodality
tritone
ostinato
glissando
continuous variation
Klangfarbenmelodie
Sprechstimme
additive rhythm
changing meters
unequal subdivision of the measure
twelve-tone scale

PHASE II: 1923-1946

The first World War was an emphatic cadence to the old culture of the nineteenth century, and the developing twentieth century experienced some of its worst growing pains in that period between the wars. Europe began this phase economically and spiritually depleted, although in Paris the feverish artistic activity continued, and in England a new musical renaissance began to blossom. After about a decade of prosperity, a grinding economic depression descended upon victors and vanquished alike, and in this fertile soil dictatorships took root in Germany, Italy, Russia and Spain. The world moved ever closer to the second great conflict through the Italian campaign in Ethiopia and the Spanish Civil War which was a proving ground for techniques and weapons later unleashed in the Axis assault upon its European neighbors. Science moved ahead rapidly, making discoveries in physics and chemistry which, under the impetus of the second war, created the new world of the second half of the twentieth century.

In music, the twenties saw the emergence of the opposed *neoclassic* and *dodecaphonic*, or *twelve-tone*, systems and the division of composers into factions led by the foremost of each group, Stravinsky and Schönberg. Others, such as Bartók, stood aside from them, but were not unaffected. Prokofiev returned to his homeland, joining an already rising group of composers among whom was numbered Shostakovich. Paul Hindemith, after early successes in the twenties and thirties, came to the United States to write and teach. And, during this period, the United States came of age musically, certainly with the help of foreign aid, but little by little creating an attitude and style quite different from that of any European composer.

EXPRESSIONISM: DODECAPHONY

"Twelve tones related only with one another"

Each composition which Schönberg wrote after his post-Wagnerian period was a highly rational experiment directed toward finding some logical way to use the chromatic scale comparable to the past use of the tonal scale. For him, taste was not enough as it had been for Debussy and scores of lesser composers; there must be a "theory"

which could account for every tone in a composition in the same way
that all the tones in a work by Bach or Mozart could be explained by
tonal theory. Only slowly did the answer reveal itself, but in 1921-1923
he enunciated some guiding principles of a technique for "composing
with twelve tones related only with one another." Notice the phrase
"only with one another." This implied that the tones were not related to
a tonic, and that each was of equal importance to any other. Let us see
how he applied this concept. We shall use the materials of the slow
third movement of Schönberg's *Fourth String Quartet* with which to
demonstrate the technique (Example VII-7).

First, the composer invents a melodic idea which includes each of
the twelve tones of the chromatic scale only once, thus eliminating any
emphasis of a tone which would establish its preeminence over the
others. The tones should not outline any familiar triad or 7th chord, for
this too would have tonal implications. The *tone row*, or *series* chosen
by Schönberg is shown in (a) of the example, and used for the first
movement of the quartet. For the slow movement, he transposed it
down one whole tone. By the time he wrote this work, he had relaxed
his rule concerning triads somewhat, or quite possibly he felt that
musicality was more important than rules, for tones 7, 8 and 9 outline
an augmented triad, and 11, 12 and 1 are the second inversion of an
A-minor triad. Having created a suitable series (b), he proceeded to
write the four simplest variations of it: the *retrograde* version (c), or
the original row backwards; the inversion of the original (d), in
which each interval is matched by the same interval in the opposite
direction; and the retrograde of the inversion (e). These four basic
forms of the row consist of the same intervals, then, but in opposite
directions or orders. They may each be transposed to any other tone
level of the chromatic scale (f, g, h) which the composer desires to
use, analogous to changing key in tonal music. The number indicates
how many half-steps above the original the row has been transposed.

Schönberg now unfolds the original row in the unison tones of the
string quartet. He has assigned a recitative-like rhythm to the notes
which involves some repetitions of tones. Evidently he did not feel that
this emphasis would create a tonal center: such repetitions of tones are
quite frequent in twelve-tone music. Having completed the O(riginal)
version in measure 5, with a suspiciously tonal sounding pattern of
tones 11 and 12, the transposed version IR_5 begins to develop harmonically, with tones 1 and 2 in the Cello, 3 and 4 in the Viola, 5 in
Violin II and the remainder in Violin I. This process is called the
"verticalization of the row," and merely signifies that the "horizontal"
version of the row has been upended so that the tones may sound

PLATE L. *"Painting with White Form, No. 166" by Kandinsky (1913). This is an example of abstract Expressionism. Here Kandinsky, without preparation, paints the feelings that come to him, now abstracted and freed from the necessity of portraying real subject matter. (Courtesy of The Solomon R. Guggenheim Museum.)*

simultaneously as harmony in whatever groupings the composer chooses. Thus, every tone in the composition, whether in the melody, polyphony or harmony, can be explained by reference to the tone row. The reader may follow the use of the various versions of the tone row for himself in Example VII-7. It will be seen that situations of some complexity may occur, as in measures 10 and 11, but that each sonority is in the last analysis the product of the composer's musical sense, for tones may be delayed or gotten through quickly in order to create a sound which the composer has chosen for a particular moment. Thus, the twelve-tone "system" is not as mechanistic as its early detractors would have us believe. It offers a degree of choice comparable to that of the tonal scales, since the materials obtainable from the chromatic scale are so much more numerous. And it offers a logical technique of organization, and, employing the transpositions of the row as changes

EXAMPLE VII-7: Schönberg, *String Quartet No. 4,* Second Movement.

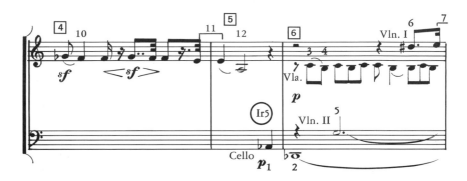

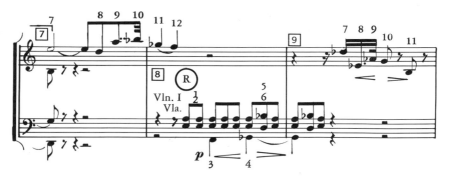

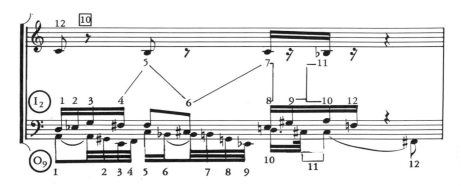

Rows

(a.) Original— O₁ of First Movement.

(b.) Original of Second Movement   (O₁ transposed down one tone)
                                     (Shown in analysis as O)

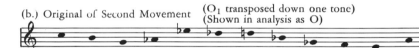

(c.) Retrograde (R)

(d.) Inversion (I)

(e.) Retrograde Inversion (RI)

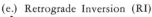

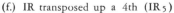

(f.) IR transposed up a 4th (IR₅)

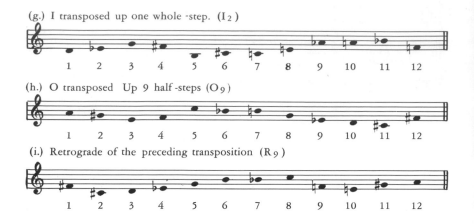

(g.) I transposed up one whole -step. (I₂)

1   2   3   4   5   6   7   8   9   10   11   12

(h.) O transposed Up 9 half -steps (O₉)

1   2   3   4   5   6   7   8   9   10   11   12

(i.) Retrograde of the preceding transposition (R₉)

1   2   3   4   5   6   7   8   9   10   11   12

of level analogous to changes of key, the traditional forms *may* be used. Schönberg, the "conservative who was forced to become a radical," usually worked within the classical structures. Berg was more experimental, and Webern, as we shall see, achieved a synthesis of form and content never before realized in any music.

It is interesting to note that the manipulations of the row fulfill Schönberg's requirement of continuous variation: a twelve-tone composition consists of nothing else! And also his dictum of symphonic economy: the row provides the basis for everything in the work.

During the years from 1917 to 1923, Schönberg was engaged in teaching and wrote no works which have reached the public. Then in 1923 he composed the *Five Piano Pieces*, Op. 23, in which the twelve-tone technique was first used consciously. Something very close to this technique had appeared earlier in his own work and that of his students, Webern and Berg, from time to time but it went by unrecognized. The first four of the *Five Pieces* use tone rows, but they are not completely twelve-tone, as the final one is. The *Serenade*, Op. 24, also approaches the technique in a rudimentary way and seeks to use traditional forms, but the *Suite* for piano, Op. 25, and the *Wind Quintet*, Op. 26, are completely within the new chromatic technique and show the use of extended Classical structures. The first orchestral work to make use of the twelve-tone system is the *Variations for Orchestra*, Op. 31. In listening to these works one is aware of a new spirit, more serene and joyous than the previous Expressionistic compositions, more healthy and objective. One feels that now the composer is sure of himself, having found the heretofore "lost" stream of history and tradition.

PLATE LI. *Alban Berg.* In this heretofore unpublished postcard photograph from the Moldenhauer Archive is included a message to Julius Schloss, Berg's friend and copyist, who made the vocal score of Wozzeck, dated the day of the first performance of that opera, December 14, 1925. The translation of the inscription is: "Julius Schloss The conclusion of Wozzeck: *senza ritard* (without slowing)——up to the end! 14/12. 1925." Note the play on the name *Schloss* and the final word, *Schluss* (end).

Alban Berg: Synthesis of old and new

The music of Berg might be dismissed as eclectic, were it not for its imaginative conceptions, its technical skill and its emotional communication. For Berg, while adopting the techniques of the twelve-tone system, was not a slave to them, and mixed dodecaphonic passages with others derived from Wagner, Mahler, folk-song and jazz in a compelling synthesis. He is a Romantic, whereas Schönberg's orientation, as we have seen, was toward the Classical past. Berg's works are full of opulent orchestration, with fascinating new effects, but these are always in the employ of a scenario, whether stated or not. Such a style could not but succeed upon the operatic stage.

Berg's opera *Wozzeck* was adapted from a play by Büchner (1813-1837) whose theme is the savagery of society toward the underprivileged. As Debussy did with *Pelléas et Mélisande*, Berg set the play with only the exclusion and rearrangement of some of the scenes, thus retaining the shocking rhythm of the original. The story is brutal, psychologically abnormal and filled with tension, well suited for Expressionistic musical treatment.

Wozzeck, a poor soldier, is tormented by three people: by his superior officer, the Captain; by a sadistic physician to whom he surrenders himself for medical experiments in order to obtain money to support his mistress, Marie, and their child; and by the Drum Major, who vaunts his superior physical ability by beating up the helpless and inoffensive soldier. The Drum Major finally seduces Marie, and when Wozzeck, after torturing uncertainty, has convinced himself of her infidelity, he stabs her and subsequently drowns himself, driven mad by events too harsh to withstand.

This drama is set with extreme realism in an opera of three acts, each of which is cast in a purely musical form. Thus, the five scenes of Act I are movements of a suite: rhapsody, military march, lullaby, passacaglia and rondo. Act II is a symphony in five movements: sonata-allegro, fantasy and fugue, largo, scherzo and rondo. Act III consists of a series of "inventions," each of which exploits the development of a single musical concept. In order, they work with a theme, a tone, a rhythm, a chord, a key and *ostinato* movement in eighth notes. Despite this formal approach, the opera moves fluidly, and the forms are not strongly apparent to the listener because they always serve the dramatic purpose. Atonal and tonal writing are mixed according to the effect desired.

Let us examine the final act—the catastrophe. In each of the inventions mentioned above, Berg uses a variety of types of vocal expression: ordinary speaking, *sprechstimme* and singing. The differences between the latter two are often blurred, however, since the *sprechstimme*, when loud, may closely resemble singing.

Scene 1. Invention on a theme: a series of seven short variations ending with a fugue. The scene is Maria's room at night, by candlelight. She reads the biblical passage about the woman taken in adultery, and in an almost hysterical outburst prays that she too might be forgiven. The child enters: she repulses him at first, then sings to him part of a pathetic tale about an orphan, and finally breaks off to read the Bible and to agonize over her betrayal of Wozzeck. The variations are not easily discernible to the ear, which is as Berg intended, for he realized that the real test of music is how it sounds, not how the score appears to the eye.

Scene 2. A woodland path near a pond at dusk. Marie and Wozzeck enter, and he persuades her to sit down. His conversation is sinister, full of dark allusions to innocence and trust. He becomes hysterically excited, and, as the blood-red moon rises, draws a knife and cuts Marie's throat. He stands a moment over her body muttering the word *Tod!* (dead!) before throwing the knife in the pond and running away. This scene is constructed upon the tone B, first heard in the lowest register of the trombones, then gradually shifted to higher registers of the orchestra. It remains at a low level of intensity until after the murder, when a *crescendo* of volume and sonority indicates Wozzeck's madness. This shattering *crescendo* occurs twice in succession, the second time breaking off abruptly to the distorted dance music of the following scene.

Scene 3: A tavern filled with laborers and women who are dancing giddily to the music of an out-of-tune piano. The music and dancing become more hysterical as the scene progresses. Wozzeck enters, seats himself at a table, tries to sing a bawdy song (while the pianist tries to find a key to accompany him, but in this terrifying world there are no keys or accompaniments), spies Margaret, Marie's friend, and dances a few steps with her before pulling her down roughly to sit on his lap. His wild talk alarms her, and when she discovers blood on his hand, shrieks out to the others who crowd around. Wozzeck rushes out in terror. This scene is built upon the tension-accumulating repetition of a rhythm.

Scene 4. The path by the pond again, in the moonlight. Wozzeck has returned to find the knife which he fears he has not thrown far enough out in the water. He is in an hysterical delirium, and speaks to Marie's corpse mockingly, asking her how she earned the red scarf which she wears around her neck. He wades out into the pond, finds that the water has turned to blood, slips and is drowned. As the water closes over him, the doctor and the captain enter, thinking they have heard someone. They are frightened by the moon, the mist and the noises of the pond, and run away. This scene is constructed on a six-tone chord treated in the *Klangfarbenmelodie* technique.

Interlude: "a confession of the author, stepping outside the dramatic events of the theater and appealing to the public as representing mankind." So Berg explained this passage which, in rich orchestration of a Mahlerian cast, recapitulates the main motives of the opera in an elegy on the world of the "little people," Wozzeck and Marie. But one more scene awaits.

Scene 5. Children are playing in the street before Marie's house in the bright morning sunshine, among them Marie's little boy with his hobby-horse. A child runs in with news: "You! Your mother is dead!" The other children run out to see, but the little boy, too young, too innocent to understand, plays a moment, "Hop! Hop!," then follows the others.

PLATE LII. *Anton von Webern. (Courtesy of the Moldenhauer Archive.)*

The expressionistic strength of this opera is powerful: it is a masterwork brought into being by exactly the right techniques at the psychologically right moment of the twentieth century. The leading character is a "non-hero" to whom events happen which he is powerless to resist, and when he is driven to take matters into his own hands, catastrophe results. It is a "progress," a journey without redemption or hope at its end.

Frequently to be met with on chamber music programs is Berg's *Lyric Suite* (1926) for string quartet. In this six-movement work, rapid movements alternate with slow ones, becoming increasingly fast as the composition progresses, just as the slow movements continually decrease in tempo. The first, third, fifth and sixth movements are twelve-tone in construction, while the others are not. The work is cyclic, and employs the entire gamut of effects possible at that time with the string quartet, sounds never used before, but wholly at the service of expression ranging from ghostly to passionate.

Anton Webern

In examining the music written by Webern during the first phase of the century we noted its brevity and its *pointillistic* use of tone colors, its concentration and its originality. All of these characteristics become extreme in the second phase. The scores (Example VII-8) seem to be composed mostly of rests, the notes scattered around the page with seemingly no attempt at continuity, and each movement consisting of but a few pages of this music. Yet when performed it makes perfectly good sense if we can listen to these spatially removed tones as pure sounds linked together in a widespread melody without asking that melody to connote the old romantic feelings. And, doing this, upon repeated hearings one finds a deep sense of integrity in this music.

First of all, we must realize that Webern adopted the twelve-tone technique wholly, not as Berg and even Schönberg later did, with excursions into tonality or free chromaticism. It became second nature to Webern, a way of thinking that fitted his individual approach to music. In each work he explored new possibilities of its employment. Particularly in canonic technique was he able to fuse the form and the material into one indissoluble union, a structure where everything was necessary, where nothing could be added or taken away without violating the entire work. Let us see how Webern did this in his *Symphony,* Op. 21 (1928).

The row which he chose to work with is shown below with the intervals between the tones labeled. It is really the intervallic relationship between the tones which is important, not the tones in themselves.

A   F♯   G   A♭   E   F   B   B♭   D   C♯   C   E♭
  m3 m2 m2 M3 m2 T m2 M3 m2 m2 m3

It will be noticed that if we read the last set of intervals backward to the T (Tritone), we duplicate the first set, read forward. If the row is transposed to begin upon the final E♭, the result is the retrograde of the above:

E♭   C   C♯   D   B♭   B   F   E   A♭   G   F♯   A

This will be true of all transpositions; therefore, instead of the forty-eight possible forms of the row, there are only twenty-four, and in the sense that the second half of the row is the retrograde of the first, intervallically, we have essentially a six-tone row which is transposed and repeated on the other side of the tritone, whatever the transposition of the whole row. This kind of limitation of possibilities was one which Webern pursued in many of his other works.

In the exposition we find four versions of the row used canonically. A glance at the first page of the score shows wide leaps in the instrumental parts, and, if we were to trace the various rows, we should find that the notes are given to different instruments, usually not more than three to any one tone color. Thus, the canons cannot be detected by ear. This "hidden art," reminiscent of the composers of the late Middle Ages, poses an aesthetic problem: of what use is structure in music if you can't hear it? As far as this writer knows, no satisfactory answer has been made. This exposition, comparable to a sonata exposition, is relatively calm and objective, spacious and rhythmically uncrowded. It usually is repeated in accordance with the sign in the score.

The development immediately sounds like a development, with a crowding together of rhythmic patterns and overlapping of parts. It too has a structure: the second eight measures are the retrograde of the first. It can be heard at the point where the cello plays a moderately low C preceded by a grace note below it followed by a low D in the harp; the process is then reversed.

The recapitulation cannot be recognized by ear, so greatly is it changed in sound, but it is a literal repetition of the exposition using the same versions of the row in the same canons. It is generally louder than the exposition, however, and the leaps between tones in one instrument tend to be wider. One has the feeling of a coda near the close, due to the slackening tempo and the thinner instrumentation.

The second movement is a set of variations whose form is derived from that of the row——the second half of the theme being the retrograde of the first; therefore, the variations share this structure. In addition, the seven variations and coda also share this symmetry, as shown in the diagram (Example VII-9). Almost the same transpositions of the rows are used in each of the movements connected by brackets. The diagram also gives the characteristic orchestration, if this is significant for recognition, of each variation.

In this work we see the interpenetration of structure and substance, a completely abstract synthesis of the two with the minimum amount of material used with maximum economy. Nothing can be removed or added. In this respect, the music resembles a mathematical equation in which every term has a meaning, and nothing can be added or subtracted without modifying the total significance. If the music has "meaning," it is not that of the Romantic period, but a new one analogous to the "meaning" of a mathematical expression. It is truth expressed in sounds rather than in x, y and z^2. And this concept proved to be the $E=mc^2$ for music in the post-atomic era.

The later works of Webern all pursue the same ideal of expressing "in tones what can only be said in tones," to quote Schönberg on the subject. After the *Symphony* come the *Quartet,* Op. 22 (1930) for clarinet, tenor saxophone, violin and piano; the two groups of *Three Songs,* Opp. 23 (1934) and 25 (1935), separated by the *Concerto,* Op. 24 (1934) and followed by *Das Augenlicht,* Op. 26 (1935), a cantata for chorus and orchestra; two later cantatas for soloists, chorus and orchestra, Opp. 29 (1939) and 31 (1943), the latter Webern's final composition; and the *Piano Variations,* Op. 27 (1936), the *String Quartet,* Op. 28 (1938), and the *Variations for Orchestra,* Op. 30 (1940). To this list must be added the orchestration of the *Ricercar* from Bach's *Musical Offering* in 1935, done in the Webern *pointillistic* manner in such a way as to bring out the salient motives of the work. It sounds strange, after hearing the original version, but as one listens repeatedly one becomes aware of how Webern has made the structure of the work clear by the use of his orchestra.

In his later works, Webern used what has since been called "total serialization" of his musical materials. In these works, each pitch of the row is assigned to a certain instrument (tone color), appears in a certain register consistently, and has the same intensity, rhythmic position and articulation (*e.g., staccato,* accented, etc.) upon each repetition. This procedure is, of course, merely carrying out the implications of pitch serialism in the other parameters of music. Webern limited the variability of some of these, however, sometimes using only three

EXAMPLE VII-8: Webern, *Symphony,* Op. 21. (Universal Edition.)

Universal Edition Nr. 12198

dynamic levels, or two note values, for example; this was done especially in cases where another element became more complex, as if to compensate. These practices of Webern were taken up enthusiastically by the *avant garde* of the post World War II composers, and extended into electronic music as well. We shall examine some of these works in the section dealing with Phase III of the twentieth century.

NEOCLASSICISM

The dominant style for about twenty-five years after World War I was generally known as Neoclassicism. Rather than being anti-Romantic, it was non-Romantic, often demonstrating the relation of progress to tradition by returning to elements and forms of pre-Romantic periods. Essentially, it might be defined as modern Classicism, much as in Picasso's painting style of *The Lovers* (Plate LIII) with its clean lines, simple color, natural subject, yet contemporary in its sophistication. Both the music and the painting have feeling, but the materials and the expressivity are controlled and intellectually balanced without becoming cold.

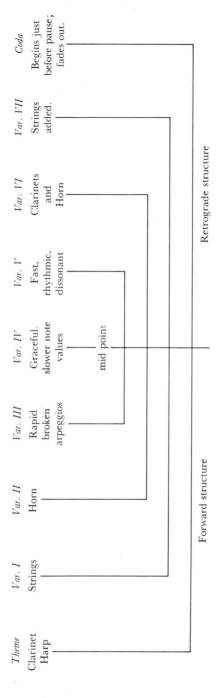

EXAMPLE VII-9: Webern, Structure of Second Movement of *Symphony*, Op. 21.

The total structure is noted by the correspondences shown by the brackets.

Neoclassicism was one of the results of the "back to Bach" movement of the twenties, elevating polyphony, clarity and design to positions of cardinal importance. It was a tonal style, but one clouded with
new concepts of chord relationships, usually avoiding the strongly
functional V and IV chords, or weakening them in various ways if they
did appear. More often, it poised two unrelated chords against each
other, and built the music upon the conflict and resolution of their tensions. The chords are often simple triads or sometimes are built upon
fourths (quartal harmony). Frequently the arrangement of tones is
unusually widespread with spaces between the upper groups of tones
and the lower ones, resulting in new sonorities.

The melodic style usually is angular, often repetitive with rhythmic
variations. The wide leaps are not intended to have the Romantic
fervor of similar intervals in the music of the Viennese Expressionist
composers, but rather constitute a kind of objective musical draftsmanship similar to the lines of a Picasso drawing. They are abstract in
their movement, but not so much so as in the music of Webern.

The polyphony is free to the extent that the harmony which it
produces by the juxtaposition of its lines satisfies the requirements
of the style. Seconds and sevenths are not regarded as dissonant nor
are fourths, therefore they need not resolve, although sometimes the
feeling of resolution is achieved in principle by the movement to less
tense intervals. The only real dissonance available is the half-step
(minor second), and it usually is handled very carefully.

All of the refinements of rhythm are used in this style——changing
meters, unequal subdivision of parts of the measure, syncopations,
additive rhythm, polymeter, and even the motoric pulse of the
Baroque concerto, although it often is varied by changing the meter.
Both harmonic and rhythmic requirements of a neoclassic work often
are served by the *ostinato*. This may take many forms: a constant
repeated pulse, a rhythmic figure, the oscillation back and forth among
a few tones (as in Stravinsky's *Rite of Spring*), or a repeated chord,
perhaps mingled with silences.

The forms of the seventeenth and eighteenth centuries frequently
are encountered in this music, but it is the spirit, not the letter of
tradition that is active in using these structures for the new music.
Thus, we shall discover ritornello forms reminiscent of the concerto,
fugues, ternary arias, sonata-allegros and dance forms among Neoclassic works. What we have learned as formal and generative principles in previous eras will be found at work here——just as valid now
as then.

We must not, however, expect all Neoclassic works to sound alike, for the personal style of each composer will color the result. Prokofiev, Bartók, Hindemith, Schönberg, Piston and Schuman all use versions of the Classic forms, counterpoint, and so on, but all are not Neo-

PLATE LIII. *"The Lovers" by Picasso. The return to Neoclassic simplicity, grace, and naturalness is seen here. (Courtesy of The National Gallery of Art, Chester Dale Collection.)*

classicists, and of those who are usually classed as such——Bartók, Hindemith, Piston and Schuman——the individual style of the composer gives the music a distinctive sound. Perhaps Stravinsky's works of the twenties may best be used as models to illustrate what is meant by Neoclassicism, although many of the outward trappings of these works differ from composition to composition, depending upon what Stravinsky felt to be the requirements of each particular work. There is a certain inner consistency though, which relates all of them, from the *Octet* of 1923 to his opera *The Rake's Progress,* 1950.

Stravinsky created many works that undoubtedly are destined to be remembered as masterpieces during this period. While it requires

some temerity to make such a judgment, the following compositions
would seem to fall into this category:

1923: *Octet for Wind Instruments.*

1927: *Oedipus Rex,* opera-oratorio for chorus, soloists and orchestra,
    words by Jean Cocteau.

1930: *Symphony of Psalms,* for chorus and orchestra

1940: *Symphony in C*

1945: *Symphony in Three Movements*

1947: *Orpheus,* ballet

1950: *The Rake's Progress*

Let us single out three of these works for examination: the *Octet,* the
Symphony of Psalms and a section of *The Rake's Progress.*

Octet for Wind Instruments

This invigorating work is in three movements: *Sinfonia, Tema con
variazioni* and *Finale.* It is "Neobaroque" in its polyphonic texture,
motoric rhythms (to be sure, with typical Stravinskyan dislocations)
and objective and abstract attitude. It is scored for the less expressive
instruments of the orchestra, the winds, and these are used throughout
in this way. They are flute, clarinet, two bassoons, two trumpets and
two trombones. All movements are strongly tonal, although emphasis
techniques rather than functional harmony are used to establish the
tonal center. The thematic materials are angular and disjunct, for the
most part, and many stereotyped Baroque rhythmic figures are used.
Imitation appears from time to time, often distorted rhythmically or
widened intervalically.

The formal plan of the first movement is: *Introduction A B C B A.*
This is an example of the *arch-form,* a rather frequent structure in
twentieth century music. The second movement might almost be
entitled "variations on an interval", so often does the oscillation of
major and minor thirds appear (C♯-A-C♮-A). This Stravinskyan figure
(cf. Rite of Spring) plays an important part in the structure of
the melodic line and the counterpoints. The form is: *Theme—Var.
A—Var. B—Var. A—Vars. C,D,—Var. A—Var. E—cadenza linking to
Finale.* A is of a rather fantastic character, and B tends to be humorous,
at least to this writer. But more interesting than this, Stravinsky has
applied the principle of additive rhythm to the lengths of these
variations. Using A as standard, B=2A, C,D=3A and E=4A. The
Finale might be termed a "sonata-allegro without recapitulation," or
possibly a movement resembling a Baroque orchestral concerto in
which two themes are presented and developed. After a thorough
development section, the coda follows, a section of block chords in

gently syncopated rhythm during which the theme from the first movement appears from time to time. The tonality of the beginning, C major, is reaffirmed strongly enough to give the listener the sense of finality needed to conclude the movement.

Symphony of Psalms

If one were to judge the second period of this composer's works solely by the above, one might think that Stravinsky had lost the elemental power so in evidence in *Le Sacre* and had become a composer of pleasing small works in a strictly Neoclassic style. Such a judgment would be confounded upon hearing the *Symphony of Psalms,* for here one is confronted with a mighty evocation of the religious attitude of an earlier age. This work is such a complete fusion of the medieval and modern that the two become inseparably one. It is austere, yet moving, and has a kind of elemental simplicity for all the modern sophistication of rhythm and harmony it contains.

The work was completed in 1930 and was composed "to the glory of God, and dedicated to the Boston Symphony Orchestra on the occasion of its fiftieth anniversary." The orchestra used is novel: 4 flutes, piccolo, 4 oboes, English horn, 3 bassoons, contrabassoon, 4 horns, high trumpet, 4 ordinary trumpets, three trombones (including bass trombone), tuba, timpani, bass drum, harp, 2 pianos, cellos, double-basses, and mixed choir, preferably of men and boys. The text consists of Latin verses of Psalms 38, 39, and 150, taken from the Vulgate Bible. According to Stravinsky's comments concerning the setting of words, he chose the Latin text precisely because it is a "dead language," and therefore largely meaningless to his auditors. Thus, it will have no emotional connotations, and become only a sounding vehicle for the voices. In the case of the *Symphony of Psalms* one cannot help feeling that the emotion is contained in the music, and that some sort of spiritual communication is intended.

The first movement begins with a percussive E minor chord, scored in such a way that its dissonant quality is emphasized, followed by angular arpeggios in the oboes and bassoons built upon the dominant seventh chords of two tonalities, E♭ and C Major. This process is repeated twice, after which a few measures prepare for the entrance of the voices. The altos enter alone, singing a chant composed of only two tones, E and F, reminiscent of Gregorian chant, but less melodic. Somewhat later, after this narrow range melody has been repeated and the tenors and sopranos have forcefully declaimed a phrase in octaves, another theme, angular in contour, is announced and

developed in the chorus against various *ostinato* figures in the orchestra. The movement cadences on G and is linked to the following one.
The text of this first movement begins: "Hear my prayer, O Lord, and
give ear unto my cry: . . . O spare me, that I may recover strength
before I go hence, and be no more."

The text of the second movement is a testimony to the power of
God: "I waited patiently for the Lord: and He inclined to me, and
heard my cry." In form this movement is a double fugue. The angular
subject of the orchestral fugue is announced first by the oboes, and
answered in turn by the first flute, the second flute, and the second
oboe, after which an episode follows. The orchestral fugue subject
is then announced in the cellos and basses, while the sopranos state
the choral fugue subject, somewhat less angular, as might be expected,
beginning with the downward leap of a 4th. The orchestra and chorus
develop their subjects complementarily. A *stretto* of the choral subject
arrives, unaccompanied by the orchestra, then the development continues, with the first four notes of the orchestral fugue subject
repeated in *ostinato* fashion while the chorus reaches a climax and
a sudden hush at the end of the movement.

The third movement is devoted to singing the praise of God and
begins with an *alleluia,* followed by the words *"laudate Dominum"*
("Praise ye the Lord"). These words are heard frequently during the
movement—each sentence of the Psalm text begins with *"laudate."*
The movement is divided into three clearly defined parts by thematic
and tempo differences. The first and last sections are slow and impressive, the middle is rhythmic and faster. The first section is built on
a modal cadence figure in the choral parts which is developed against
an *ostinato* in the orchestra. The faster second section employs rapidly
repeated chords in the brass instruments against an *ostinato* in the
pianos and low strings. An unexpected touch is the "tearing" chromatic
scale highlighted by the trumpet color which appears from time to
time. The chorus enters after considerable time has been given to the
orchestra, and, while not imitative, the entrances are staggered, beginning with soprano followed by the alto. The melodic line is very like
that of the first movement, and consists of two notes only for most of
the phrase. The altos and tenors now chant rhythmically, using the
repeated chord figures we have heard only in the orchestra up to now.
Then the basses begin a striding theme with wide intervals which
progresses upward, answered by a slower inverted version of the
orchestral fugue subject from the second movement. Then the voices
move more homophonically while the orchestra supports their sound
with various *ostinati* figures. There is an interruption in slower tempo

for an "alleluia," after which a recapitulation of the first part of the middle section ensues, with the chorus used rhythmically rather than polyphonically. Now a return to the tempo of the opening section occurs and an upward-striving disjunct, dotted-note theme is used in the chorus against a sustained background. This is not of long duration, however, for an even slower tempo is soon established with a solemn, bell-like *ostinato* in the orchestra against which the chorus builds a long crescendo of irresistible power. The cumulative effect of this sustained section is tremendous; its sheer weight, together with the dissonant chords in the wind instruments, makes it most impressive. The climax subsides with the repetition of the modal cadence figures on the words *"Alleluia, laudate Dominum."*

The Rake's Progress (1950)

It is necessary at this point to discuss briefly Stravinsky's opera, *The Rake's Progress,* not only because it is one of the outstanding works of the musical stage in the twentieth century, but to act as a counterpoise to Berg's important work, *Wozzeck,* possibly the only other operatic masterwork of the modern period. Opera changed very little after Wagner and Verdi; Strauss still treated it as a symphonic poem, Puccini as sensationalism, and Schönberg's *Erwartung* is hardly material for the operatic stage. In fact, for some time there was real doubt that an opera could be written using contemporary techniques. Berg and Stravinsky proved that it could, and in doing so gave great impetus to an increasing interest in the musical stage.

Stravinsky returned to the conventions of seventeenth and eighteenth century opera, sensing that the old closed forms of *da capo aria* and recitative still contained possibilities for use in the twentieth century. His opera is also an exploration of the sonorities to be obtained from the Mozart orchestra (without trombones) and the harpsichord-accompanied recitative. By accepting these limitations, Stravinsky defined a style for the work, as he has done with every composition since the *Rite of Spring.* Herein lies one of the strengths of the opera.

The other lies in its libretto, by W. H. Auden and Chester Kallman. It has been proclaimed "the most perfect libretto ever written," and——regarded as elegant words, expressive and full of meaning, eminently suitable for musical setting——this undoubtedly is true. Certainly they are couched in an idiom which we would not expect the characters to speak, yet this is an operatic convention accepted since the Camerata. If there is a flaw, it is in the lack of resolution of the progress of Tom Rakewell, the weak, likeable "hero" of the piece, as Kerman points out in his book *Opera as Drama*. For our examination here, as an example of musical style, we shall not go into that aspect of the work; the reader is urged to examine Kerman's book if he is seriously interested in opera.

The story, suggested to Stravinsky by Hogarth's engravings, is concerned with Tom Rakewell, a country lad, who is lured on the downward path by three wishes granted him by Nick Shadow. These wishes, in turn, are for money, pleasure and happiness, and, with Nick as his servant, Tom visits London in search of them leaving behind his faithful sweetheart, Anne Truelove. After sinking deeper and deeper into the clutches of Shadow, Tom finally is redeemed by a fourth wish——for love, which he had disregarded so far——and thus escapes Shadow's clutches; but he is punished by madness, alleviated inexplicably only for a moment near the close by Anne's comforting appearance. After the curtain closes the singers come forward on the stage to point the moral that the Devil will always find mischief for idle hands and minds and hearts.

The first scene of *Act I* illustrates the style. A brass fanfare opens the scene, followed by a lyric introduction to the duet by Anne and Tom. Each sings a stanza, then they join in a couplet: Anne's is in A major and presents the A material, while Tom's is modulatory (B), after which the couplet returns both to the material and key of A. Before the couplet is finished, Anne's father joins the two lovers, and embarks upon a modulatory section of his own, after which Anne and Tom sing together again in A. Thus, a gradually developing trio takes shape, with clearly defined formal distinctions of key and material. The springiness of rhythm, the light woodwind tone color, and the modern lyricism of the vocal lines all provide a sense of freshness to this opening. The orchestra plays a short codetta after which the recitative is accompanied by the classically objective chords of the harpsichord. Tom, alone, sings a recitative with orchestral accompaniment followed by a large binary form aria with four sections and clear cadences. The bassoons give a mocking quality to the beginning of it, but the whole piece has a charming Handelian quality befitting Tom's belief in luck and his high spirits. Immediately after the orchestral conclusion he wishes for money, and, with a dissonant harpsichord arpeggio, Nick Shadow appears. The subsequent conversation is accompanied by the harpsichord, after which comes Shadow's aria, with a suitably Baroque introduction featuring fanfare figures denoting the proclamation of news which Shadow bears. The aria is ternary, with a shortened and altered reprise. It is concluded by an accompanied recitative, the cadence of the whole movement being supplied by the harpsichord.

Tom's following aria is binary, and the material of it is developed in the quartet which is accumulated by the entrances of Shadow, Anne and her father. The next formal section sees Tom's happiness interrupted by Shadow's reminder that his new riches must be attended to, together with Anne's father's agreement that Tom must be off to London, and concluding with Tom's agreement. The music reflects this action, beginning in F major, modulating in Shadow's part, returning to F momentarily at Tom's interjection, then modulatory until Tom's concluding words which close solidly in B♭. The harpsichord accompanies the short recitative which follows, and Anne and Tom sing their farewell in a ternary duet. The pact concerning Shadow's wages is made in recitative accompanied by the harpsichord and cynical laughter by the bassoon. Tom promises to return to claim Anne in a ternary aria in A minor, the reprise of which is given to the orchestra alone. The concluding ensemble is strongly in A major, the key of the opening of the scene, after which Shadow's disquieting announcement to the audience provokes a clouded and dissonant cadence chord in the orchestra.

After listening to this act of Stravinsky's opera, the reader should recall *Wozzeck:* no stronger comparison between Expressionism and Neoclassicism could be made. Berg, in his opera, *is* Wozzeck to all intents and purposes; he illustrates his lacerated feelings with all of the techniques developed from Wagner onward. The emotions are profound and intense. In *The Rake,* we view the proceedings from an aesthetic distance provided by the style; conventions adopted from earlier opera are elegantly presented in twentieth century style. We are moved, but not in the same way as in Wozzeck. There the emotion was visceral——here it is intellectual. In both cases the composers have illuminated the drama with music, made it indispensable to our understanding of the action. Both are modern masterpieces, but how different!

The Rake's Progress undoubtedly marks the high point of Stravinsky's Neoclassical works, but the *Symphony in C,* the *Symphony in Three Movements* and the ballet *Orpheus,* deserve our attention too. The *Symphony in C* is a strongly diatonic work in four movements which are Classic in formal structure. The work is cyclic, employing a motto theme (B-C-G) prominently in the first and last movements.

The *Symphony in Three Movements* is quite different in concept, for it uses additive, or synthetic techniques of development particularly in the first movement, rather than the more usual analytical fragmentation procedures. The first movement, *Overture,* is toccata-like, with a rhythmic drive and complexity that recall *Le Sacre.* The slow central

movement, of chamber music sonority, acts as a foil for the third
movement, which consists of three sections acting as preludes to
a final fugue.

Orpheus, undoubtedly one of Stravinsky's most beautiful scores,
tells the legend in music as grave and tragic as befits a Greek myth.
Over the Neoclassic mannerisms is a veil of deep feeling, in part the
result of the somber and sonorous orchestra. One cannot but sense that
here the adventurous twentieth century composer pays homage to the
shades of Gluck and Monteverdi in the most sincere way he knows——
and homage to the spirit, still alive, of music.

Béla Bartók, 1923-1945   From the national to the universal

Because of the various disappointments connected with the reception of his works and the difficulty of obtaining adequate performances of them, Bartók had retired from public life in 1912, and pursued
his folksong studies for five years. In 1917 the Budapest public favorably received the production of a musical play by Bartók, *The Wooden
Prince,* and in 1918 there took place a performance of a similar stage
work, *Duke Bluebeard's Castle.* But shortly after these promising
beginnings occurred the polical and economic breakdown of Hungary
following the war, and any organized concert activity was impossible.
Since the available areas for folk-song activity were severely limited by
the treaties which cut Hungary into small sections, Bartók sought
concert and recital opportunities, and undertook tours which touched
most of the nations of Europe as well as the United States. In addition,
he gave frequent lectures on folk-music, and published many articles
in this field. He worked as a member of the Hungarian Academy of
Science until 1940, when, because of the increasing tension due to the
Nazis, he was forced to come to the United States, his family following
later. Here financial difficulties beset him which were alleviated somewhat by his recitals and a commission from Columbia University to
edit a collection of Yugoslavian folk-songs. In 1942 he began to suffer
ill health, and was obliged to give up lecturing. The ill-health was due
to the advancement of leukemia, which caused his death on the 26th of
September, 1945, in a New York hospital.

During the period between the wars, Bartók's style embraced two lines of development which heretofore we have regarded as quite separate: Expressionism and Neoclassicism. But he took from each only those techniques which were compatible with his previous stylistic aims, namely expressionistic chromaticism, without adopting the twelve-tone system, and neoclassic formal procedures harking back to Bach and Beethoven. He cannot be classed as a member of either camp, however, for these techniques, combined with the ideas which he had discovered in folk music, resulted in a strongly personal style which became more and more universal as his creative career advanced. During the twenties his emphasis of expressionistic and constructive elements in his composition reached a climax in the *Fourth String Quartet* (1928), which pursues exhaustively the use of motivic transformation and development which we found in the *Second String Quartet*. After this, the sense of mastery increases, and music becomes more universal in appeal. His largest and most representative choral work, the *Cantata Profana* (1930) is an expression of the composer's desire for personal and national freedom which transcends the limits of nationalism.

Between the *Second Piano Concerto* of 1930-31 and the great *Music for Stringed Instruments, Percussion and Celesta* of 1936, Bartók composed the *Forty-four Duos for Two Violins* (1931) and the *Fifth String Quartet* (1934), in addition to many settings of folk songs for various media. These were followed by the *Music for Stringed Instruments* (1936), the *Sonata for Two Pianos and Percussion* (1937), the duo for violin, clarinet and piano dedicated to Benny Goodman and Joseph Szigeti, *Contrasts* (1938), the *Violin Concerto No. 2* (1938) and the set of 153 progressive teaching pieces for piano begun in 1926, the *Mikrokosmos* (1939). Also during that year, Bartók completed the *Divertimento*, for string orchestra, and the *Sixth String Quartet*, the last in the series for this medium that he was to write. The hiatus of three years which occurs between 1939 and 1943, the date of the *Concerto for Orchestra*, represents the departure from his native land and his arrival in America. In 1944 he completed the *Sonata for Solo Violin*, following the example of Bach, and in 1945 wrote the *Third Piano Concerto* up to the last seventeen measures, which were completed according to his sketches by Tibor Serly after the composer's death. The same friend completed the *Viola Concerto* from Bartók's notes.

We have chosen three of these works to examine, but rather than placing them in chronological order, they have been arranged in a sequence which seems to this listener to be one of increasing difficulty.

Piano Concerto No. 3 (1945)

This, the last completed work of the composer, paradoxically is one of the most easily accessible. It is in the normal three movements: *Allegretto, Adagioso religioso* and *Allegro vivace*. The style is one of serene classicism, transparent in orchestration and not obviously a showpiece, but most eloquent and full of an emotion which recalls the last works of Mozart, particularly the *Clarinet Concerto,* K. 622. The first movement is a sonata-allegro whose first theme is in the Bartók folk style, rhythmically lilting, ideally suited to the piano which announces it. There are three short thematic ideas in the second group and a short closing section. The formal divisions are quite easy to find in this movement.

The second movement is a ternary form combining two quite different sections. The first of these consists of descending imitative passages in the strings of an ethereal quality alternating with a fervent chorale in the piano. The central portion, B, is an example of Bartók's "Impressionistic Expressionism" which has been called "night music," although here it is more cheerful than usual. Many of the short motives in the piano and woodwinds are derived from section A. The return of the A part finds the chorale in the woodwinds, while the piano embellishes the chords with Bachian two-part counterpoint. Of particular interest are the rapid scale passages at the cadences, which envelop the chords in a polytonal haze recalling the sound of the *cimbalon.* The music rises to a climax near the close of the movement with a piano development of the chorale theme, then dies away in a last echo of the string figures which began the movement.

The third movement is an interestingly constructed form in which the elements of the sonata-rondo and fugue are intermixed. Were we to assign letters to the main sections, we should arrive at something like the following, in which A is the rhythmic first section and B the fugal part: *A - B - A' - B' - A" - Coda*. The fugal section may be regarded as a "second thematic section." All of the "extra" themes to be found in the usual classical version of the sonata-rondo have been eliminated. The theme representative of A is chordal and syncopated, in contrast to the more evenly running and linear fugue subject of B. At the close of A and A' there is a timpani solo, and the music pauses for a silence of two measures before the *presto* tempo of the coda begins. The syncopations of the A theme, particularly at A" irresistibly remind an American of jazz, particularly that of the Gershwin era.

Concerto for Orchestra (1943)

This work was composed by Bartók shortly after his arrival in America. Because of the difficulties in Hungary and the upsetting conditions attendant upon his leaving that country, it is the first work written after the completion of his *Sixth String Quartet* in 1939. Although the experience of trying to acclimate himself at the age of sixty to a new country and life must have been very difficult, his frustrations may have been somewhat alleviated by the fact that he was composing again, and so the music is not as pessimistic as might be expected. Bartók said that the work represented "a gradual transition from the sternness of the first movement and the lugubrious death song of the third, to the life-assertion of the last."

There are five movements in the work—three important ones and two *intermezzi* separating them. But why call it a "concerto"?

EXAMPLE VII-10: Bartók, *Concerto for Orchestra.*

FIRST MOVEMENT: Andante non troppo

Let us quote further from the composer: "The title of the symphony-like orchestral work is explained by its tendency to treat the single orchestral instruments in a *concertante* or soloistic manner." But far from degenerating into a display piece for orchestra *à la* Rimsky-Korsakov or Ravel, the thematic richness and the logical formal construction preserve its integrity as a serious musical composition. The Hungarian flavor is noticeable throughout, somewhat more so than in music written before or after this piece, and possibly the result of homesickness for his native land.

The first movement is an arch-form with introduction:

Intro.—1st Theme—2nd Theme—Development—2nd Theme—1st Theme

The movement begins with the slow exposition of a theme rich in 4ths, the germ interval of the whole concerto. The theme itself (Example VII-10) is used cyclically. The introduction is of some scope, and includes short passages of "night music," forecasting the third movement, a harmonic theme in the trumpets, and an *ostinato* in the low strings, whose acceleration ushers in the movement proper. The character, tempo and orchestration of the two themes are strongly contrasted, and each is developed somewhat in the exposition. The development begins with the vigor proper to such a section and concludes, after some soloistic passages for woodwinds, with two accompanied brass fugal passages. The recapitulation makes a momentary reference to the first theme, but almost immediately brings in a full reprise of the second theme, this time over chords in the harp. The first theme returns in the strings and winds, concluding with the head of the first theme much in the way that the first thematic area ended in the exposition. Throughout the movement there are fascinating orchestral colors which play a structural part in emphasizing or contrasting themes and sections. The motion is romantic and discontinuous, but the overall effect is one of surging vitality.

Bartók entitled the ternary second movement "*Giuoco delle Coppie*," or a "Game of Pairs." The first section consists of a chain-like structure, each "link" of which is devoted to a like pair of woodwind instruments, and each pair is combined at a characteristic interval: the bassoons in sixths, the oboes in thirds, the clarinets in sevenths, the flutes in fifths and lastly the muted trumpets in seconds. The melodic ideas presented by these pairs are similar, making each section seem as though it is a variation of the preceding one. The middle portion of the movement consists of a brass chorale punctuated by interesting rhythms on a snare drum with loosened snares, a sound which was heard at the beginning of the movement and which follows the last A section. The reprise of this latter part uses the themes of the first A section, but now combines three bassoons in the first "link," oboes and clarinets in the second, clarinets and flutes in the third and flutes with all the woodwinds in the fourth, while the muted trumpets are accompanied with harp *glissandi* and dissonant chordal trills in the strings. The last chord is a seventh chord which, in these surroundings, sounds perfectly consonant and final.

The third movement, *Elegia*, possibly is at once the most Hungarian and the most emotional of the five. It begins with a recollection of the low string theme of the introduction to the first movement, at first interrupted by "night music" passages. These expand and progress with increasing sonority to the main body of the movement. Here are stated, with great passion, declamatory themes of typically Hungarian character derived also from the first movement's introduction. Again Bartók shows his command of the orchestra, indulging in a piccolo solo supported by an an *ostinato* in one place, and a *cim-*

balon-plus-tone-cluster accompaniment for low string themes in another. The declamatory section returns, followed by the coda of "night music" quality, a reference in the violins to the theme in fourths with which the Elegy began and the movement concludes with a piccolo solo against a percussion background.

The "Interrupted Intermezzo" which follows gives us a glimpse of Bartók's humor which is almost Beethovenian in its abruptness, and far more obvious—at least in this instance. The movement begins with a flourish in the strings followed by an intriguing little theme in the oboe, emphasizing the tritone interval by means of repetition. A small three-part section is created by giving a version of this melody to the horns and finally returning it to the oboe. There follows a deeply lyric, folk-like theme which sounds almost too rich to be used by Bartók. It would not be out of place at all in a composition by Tchaikovsky, but here it is treated with reticence, appearing first in the violas then in the upper strings, and never once allowed to create a climax, as the Russian composer surely would have done. The first section of this ternary form is rounded off by a return to the tritone theme, again in the oboe. The low strings now play a series of fourths with accelerating pace and the solo clarinet announces the "interruption," a quotation from the Shostakovich *Seventh Symphony* which contrasts shockingly in its vulgar gayety with the more aristocratic themes of the previous section. The rest of the orchestra seems to think so too, for it bursts out in raucous laughter, interrupting the tune near the cadence. A disrespectful noise is made by the trombones, after which is set up a sort of barrel-organ sound, reminiscent of *Petrouchka*, which acts as accompaniment to the return of the Shostakovich tune. The laughter again follows, concluding the middle section. The emotional lyric theme now appears in the upper strings, accompanied by the harp and string *pizzicato*. It is followed by a woodwind interlude which develops portions of the tritone theme. The movement ends with a cadence phrase constructed from the beginning of the tritone tune followed by the end of the lyric theme.

The last movement is replete with dance rhythms and themes of typically Hungarian character, but these are assimilated in a complex sonata-allegro structure which testifies in its *élan* and flow to Bartók's mastery of his material. The two principal themes are announced within the first few measures of the movement. The horns immediately state the subject of much of the complicated fugal writing in the development section, and the strings begin the rapid, rushing yet melodious passage-work which some commentators have called *"perpetuum mobile,"* or "perpetual motion." There is a rather long section devoted to this material, and as it progresses dance motives in the woodwinds are combined with it. The rhythmic motion is quite exciting, and the music sweeps to full climaxes notable for the use of major chords. There follows a portion which might be called the "closing section," since the bassoon announces the first theme and a short *fugato* develops which disappears in woodwind polyphony. The development begins with the *perpetuum mobile,* followed by a pentatonic section introduced by a timpani *glissando.* A *fugato* now appears, based upon a jazzy version of the fugue subject, works its way through the strings of the orchestra first, and finally develops in the winds in all manner of polyphonic elaboration. The recapitulation brings back the *perpetuum mobile,* dance themes are added, the music grows in sonority, and finally the fugue theme emerges and is used in a brilliant brass passage. The measures following are developmental in character and form an exciting conclusion to the movement.

This work is deservedly one of the most popular in Bartók's entire catalog. Everything about it—the themes, rhythms, orchestration and form— is very clear, and the layman need not have any previous exposure to contemporary music in order to understand it. For this reason it appears on many orchestral programs and forms an excellent introduction to the style of this composer.

Music for Stringed Instruments, Percussion and Celesta (1936)

In contrast with the exuberance of the preceding work, this composition is wholly serious in intent, although the last movement is dance-like. In workmanship and attention to detail, as well as in the thoroughly unified construction, it bears a closer resemblance to the string quartets than to the more varied and more loosely constructed (by comparison) orchestral compositions. It is written for double string orchestra, separated on the stage so that a three-dimensional effect is secured. The additional instruments are harp, celesta. piano, xylophone, timpani, and various percussion instruments including tambourines, cymbals and tam-tam. Bartók gave explicit direction concerning the grouping of the instruments.

The style of the themes is predominantly chromatic, some more so, as in the theme of the first movement, others, like the theme of the last movement, much less semitonal. The work is thematically unified, since all of the important themes of the second, third and fourth movements are derived by transformation from the theme of the first movement. Withal, the rhythms and some of the themes show relationships to Hungarian peasant music, but except for the last movement, the folk music influence is much less obvious than in many other works. Here the process of assimilation of the folk-style into Bartók's personal idiom is complete.

The first movement has been called a fugue, but this is only generally true. No fugue was ever as tightly and continuously thematic as this. There literally is only one subject (Example VII-11), and the entire movement is devoted to imitation of it, sometimes in a simple and direct way, at other times inverted or mirrored. There are no

EXAMPLE VII-11: Bartók, *Music for Stringed Instruments, Percussion and Celesta.*

FIRST MOVEMENT: Andante tranquillo

episodes, and, from the statement of the subject by the violas on the tonal axis of A, alternate imitations at the fifth above and below take place, creating what has been called a "wedge" form (see first part of the following diagram). When the imitations have traversed the various fifths above and below A, they unite on E♭. From here they retrace in inverted form the imitations back to the tonality of A where they cadence. The return is less texturally complex and the celesta, combined with tone-clusters in the strings, is used to throw up a haze of secundal harmony surrounding the subject. It will be noticed that this movement also traces a dynamic curve from the quiet beginning to the intense climax, and drops off rather rapidly after that point. The chromatic tension of the subject assists in the dynamic crescendo in that it creates a concurrent tension crescendo. The diagram (Example VII-12) shows the "wedge" form used.

The second movement, a sonata-allegro with Bartókian modifications, is based on a less chromatic transformation of the fugue subject, plus other versions, and the interval of a fourth, which becomes "stretched" to a tritone or a seventh—an example of Bartók's thoroughgoing developmental procedures. The formal sections, especially those of the theme areas and the recapitulation, are very clear, but the development is much too long and complex to be described here in words. Look for much imitation, sometimes in cross-rhythms between the orchestras, and exciting use of piano sonority in emphasizing rhythms. Two instrumental techniques very characteristic of Bartók appear in this movement: the *glissando* (slide) on the stringed instruments and the percussive *pizzicato*—one with such force that the

EXAMPLE VII-12: Wedge form of First Movement, Bartók: *Music for Stringed Instruments.*

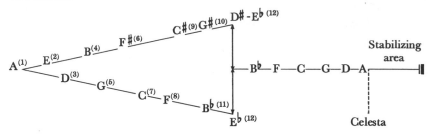

string strikes the fingerboard with a snap. Notice the combined *glissandi* of the harp and piano in the coda, and the use of *glissandi* in the timpani.

The third movement is sectional ("arch" form, *A-B-C-D-C-B-A*) and is the finest piece of "night music" in Bartók's works. From the ghostly tapping of the xylophone at the beginning to its return at the end of the movement, the mood of mystery, almost of supernatural terror, is maintained with the greatest artistry. The themes are derived from the fugue subject of the first movement by drastic rhythmic transformations. The central portion of the movement is less improvisational than the beginning, and the motivic work is less elusive in character. The instrumental combinations exploited are amazing in variety and significance, always treated so as to verify the formal proceedings as well as to be communicative. The vigorous final movement is sectional, corresponding to the plan *A-B-A'-C-A''-D-B- cyclic theme - A,* but all of the themes which characterize the sections are related to each other in that they are all derived in some way from the cyclic theme which opened the first movement. The movement opens with chords strummed back and forth across all four strings of each of the stringed instruments, recalling the sound of the guitar, after which the vigorously syncopated A theme appears, quickly giving way to the percussive B theme in the piano after an introductory passage in 4ths by the timpani. The B thematic section is also quite brief, and A returns in a slightly varied form, but only for a few measures. There is an abrupt pause before the C section, which is devoted to a theme made up of fragments of A and B, but assembled and developed in such a way as to sound entirely new. This section is longer than any of the previous ones, but the A which follows is again short, merely an interlude before D. This section is fairly long, and begins with heavy chords, obstinately accented on the weak beats of the meter, against which a theme straight out of *Mittel-Europa* is played by the violas. This is developed vigorously in two sections, and from it a neighboring-tone figure is derived (C-B-C) which forms the basis for some rather Baroque imitative passages. These become more rhythmic and provide the accompaniment for the return of the B theme, now in dissonant intervals in the piano, and hurried forward by an acceleration of the tempo, to culminate in antiphonal chromatic passages between the string orchestras. This is concentrated and condensed in the lower registers, slows down so that the cyclic theme may be rather grandly brought back and developed. A returns in varying tempos and degrees of rhythmic compression and interval expansion, and closes the work with a descending Lydian scale which cadences firmly on the beginning tone of the first movement, A. Notable throughout this complex work is the sureness of handling the feeling of tonality or modality, particularly at cadence points. Perhaps one of the most striking cadences is that of the first movement, where the medieval *clausula vera* cadence pattern of converging intervals is chromaticized to form a thoroughly modern and satisfactory closing figure.

Paul Hindemith, 1895-1963

It is apparent by now to the reader that all Neoclassic composers do not sound alike. Stravinsky's work in this style, elegant and precise, shows the influences of French music, while the fervor of Bartók's is more Romantic and subjective. In Paul Hindemith we encounter still another shade of Neoclassicism, one which is typically German in its predilection for counterpoint, the processes of Baroque music and in its logic. Hindemith was one of the few composers of the modern era who expounded his concepts about music and its composition. His book, *The Craft of Musical Composition*, reveals in its title one of its author's beliefs: that a composer must be a craftsman, that is, he must have the technical resources at his disposal which will enable him to write well. Hindemith himself was a superb example of this type of composer, and he demanded as much from his students. He was a firm believer in the communicative power of music, and tried to compose in a style which modern audiences could understand. His name was early associated with *Gebrauchsmusik*, compositions which could not only be understood, but also performed by amateurs, thus bringing "modern music" to everyone who could play the recorder, piano, clarinet, etc.

Hindemith produced a great deal of music in all forms and media, including sonatas and concertos for most of the orchestral instruments, particularly those whose solo literature is sparse. The influence of his studies of medieval music appears frequently in his work, most agreeably so in his opera *Mathis der Maler* ("Matthias the Painter"), based upon the life of Matthias Grünewald, and the work for piano and string orchestra entitled *The Four Temperaments*. His first opera, *Cardillac*, deals with a Renaissance subject, his third, *Die Harmonie der Welt*, with the career of Johannes Kepler, and the last one, premiered shortly before the composer's death, is an operatic adaptation of Thornton Wilder's play, *The Long Christmas Dinner*. Notable among his other works are the *Symphony in E Flat*, the *Metamorphoses on a Theme of Carl Maria von Weber*, the *Symphony for Band* and the viola concerto entitled *Der Schwanendreher* ("The 'Swan-herd' "). Most important of his works for piano solo are the three sonatas of 1936 and a set of preludes and fugues entitled *Ludus tonalis* ("Play of Tones"), a modern counterpart to the *Well-tempered Clavier* of J. S. Bach.

Hindemith's style reached a climax of Expressionism in the early twenties, but with the acceptance of *Gebrauchsmusik* during that decade his use of dissonance became increasingly less biting, and the attitude of the music more classical. Shortly before World War II, he was forced to leave Germany, and came to the United States, where he taught at Yale. In 1953 he took up residence in Zurich, and became active in conducting his own works in Europe as well as composing.

Hindemith's style essentially is Neoclassic in the broad sense of the term which includes stylistic elements before the nineteenth century. The neobaroque and medieval elements are particularly strong. The interplay between melody and bass and the dependence upon linear polyphony, with its native procedures of imitation, canon and fugue are Baroque in origin, although in the independent quality of the polyphonic lines, the medieval style is strongly recalled. Also medieval is the modal flavor and the types of cadences he uses, many of which are close derivatives of the *clausula vera* (*cf.*, Bartók, *Music for Stringed Instruments, I*). The forms are most apt to be Baroque or Classic in modern adaptations. His use of these is legitimate, for the music is tonal, as evidenced by the frequent and careful use of cadences, and the close of each composition with a major chord. He uses the chromatic scale freely, however, but in such a way that half-steps seldom follow each other, creating an almost diatonic effect through the frequency of whole-steps. His harmonic language is eclectic, including triads, seventh-chords, and quartal and secundal chord formations. With these, Hindemith creates a feeling of chord movement by carefully graduating the degree of tension in the series, moving through chords of increasing or decreasing dissonance and/or complexity. This technique thus substitutes dissonance for the gravitational pull of non-chromatic tonality. The melody balances skips and steps, frequently using the interval of the 4th. Hindemith had a convincing melodic gift, in part related to plainchant. In his best works, the style is consistent and persuasive.

Piano Sonata No. 3, (1936)

This work is in the usual four movements, marked *Ruhig bewegt* (quietly moving), *sehr lebhaft* (very lively) *mässig schnell* (moderately fast), and *lebhaft* (lively). The first movement opens with a lyric theme (Example VII-13) which the remainder of the movement develops. In order to accomplish this development the theme is broken down into the four motives of the example, each of which receives variation treatment. The movement is divided into three main sections: first, a relatively uncomplicated exposition and development of the theme as a whole, either by making it the leading part, or, later in the section, by combining upper parts with it in a modified cantus firmus technique. The second section is occupied with motive 2 principally, and presents it combined with a brilliant and rapid contrapuntal accompaniment. The third main section returns to the theme as a whole, and is a reworked recapitulation of section one, containing, however, more development of the theme. The movement ends quietly

EXAMPLE VII-13: Hindemith, *Piano Sonata No. 3.*

FIRST MOVEMENT:
    Ruhig bewegt

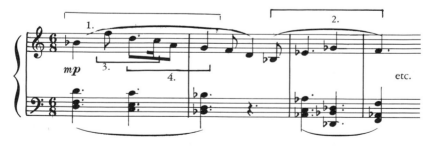

in B♭. Especially noticeable is the lyric quality of the writing, the numerous major triads which appear, and the means of establishing tonality by repetition of the key note and by cadence patterns, often derived from motive 2.

The second movement is a clear ternary form, the first section of which is devoted to the development of the opening rhythmic motive. The music reaches a very definite cadence, after which a humorous little coda brings the section to a quiet close. The second section is devoted to a rapidly running figure over a repeated accompaniment. The theme appears first in the upper register, then in the lower, where it is extended, then again in the treble. A descending quicksilver arpeggio returns the music to the first section which is repeated substantially exactly.

The third movement resembles an asymmetrical ternary form, or perhaps a sonatina form with interior developments differing in the exposition and recapitulation:

A—B: developed—Closing Section—A: developed—
Closing Section—Coda

The A theme is a sturdy and clearly-phrased march which reaches a climax, then comes to a close through several nonfinal cadences, at times interrupted by a curious descending arpeggio figure. The B theme is stated fugally, thoroughly suitable for this treatment, and moves to a climax, at which a decorated version of it appears, leading to the closing section. The restatement of A is considerably more dramatic and developed than before, and, after reaching a series of climactic points, subsides to the decorated version of B, but without the strong projection of this theme needed for a genuine recapitulation of it. The coda makes use of the descending arpeggios and the first theme to close the movement on a luminous E♭ major chord.

The finale is an impressive double fugue. There is an exposition devoted to each subject, after which they are combined briefly. The first subject is angular and rhythmic, and exactly suited to its task, just as are the subjects of the Bach fugues (Example VII-14). It builds up imitatively to four-voice texture, after which an episode appears, to be followed by a forceful counterstatement of the subject. A tranquil episode based on a descending scale passage which is combined with material from the subject provides dynamic relief. Now there comes an exposition of the second subject which is identical to the second theme of the third movement. After completing this exposition, the previous episode with the descending scale figure reappears, now combined with the second subject and followed by a counter-

EXAMPLE VII-14: Hindemith, *Piano Sonata No. 3, IV.*

FOURTH MOVEMENT FUGUE
Lebhaft
SUBJECT I

statement of the same subject. The final section combines the first subject in treble octaves with the second subject in augmentation (note values twice their former length) in the bass. The music then moves to a triumphant repeated cadence on B♭, using thematic motives. The texture of the fugue is rather free and employs chords when needed for harmonic support or dynamic emphasis. Nevertheless, it is an excellent example of the use of the Baroque form in modern dress. We feel that there is nothing academic or forced about this fugue, for it wears its modern garb comfortably.

Mathis der Maler

Probably the most popular of all of the works of this composer, this symphony consists of three orchestral movements drawn from the opera of the same name. The plot of the opera concerns the life of the late medieval German painter, Matthias Grünewald, who painted the triple altar-piece in the church at Isenheim, Germany. Each of the movements of the symphony seeks to describe one of these in music.

EXAMPLE VII-15: Hindemith, *Mathis der Maler.*

FIRST MOVEMENT: Ruhig bewegt

"Es Sungen drei Engel" (INTRODUCTION)

The following outline illustrates the forms to be found in this work.

I. *The Angelic Concert*

    Introduction: establishment of tonality of G major. Trombones present medieval Crusader's hymn *Es sungen drei Engel,* followed by horns, then trumpets (Example VII-15a) with increasing sonority.

Exposition: faster tempo, main theme (b) presented and somewhat developed. Second theme, B major (c) presented with imitative development, cadences. Closing section employs two themes, d and b in the example, closing with some finality in B major.

Development: First theme (b) then second theme (c) followed by combination of the two. Flows without pause into the——

Recapitulation: the Crusader's hymn by the brass as before, in 3/2 time against 2/2 for the rest of the orchestra. The first and second themes are combined polyphonically with the hymn. When the trumpets have their turn, the tempo broadens and the hymn becomes the basis for an impressive chorale. This is followed by a diminishing and slower section using the first theme, which flows into the closing section.

Coda: based upon first and second themes, together with threefold chord which may symbolize the three angels, heard frequently up to this time. These chords, preceded by a short upbeat, finally form the cadential harmonies.

EXAMPLE VII-15, cont'd.

SECOND MOVEMENT:

II. *The Entombment*

This movement is largely based upon the halting scale presented by the strings at the beginning (Example VII-15e). There are a few other themes, notably that announced by the oboe and imitated by the flute about a third of the way through the movement (Example 15f) but these are not used in any important way, and must be regarded as merely contrasting material. In this movement we have an opportunity to sample Hindemith's practice of building chords upon fourths or fifths (quartal harmony), as well as to notice tension modulation principles in action, especially near the climax of the movement about three-fourths of the way through. But on a smaller scale, passages of a similar kind occur all through the other movements.

III. *The Temptation of St. Anthony*

The final movement opens with a fantastic recitative (Example VII-15g) by the string section in unison, punctuated at cadence points by short chords in the winds and percussion. Although it sounds merely introductory, much of the thematic material of the rest of the movement is derived from this recitative, and is in the nature of a tone poem based upon contemporary theme-transformation techniques. The main part of the movement is complex and quite sectional, combining development of brass cadence figures, a lyric theme and massive rhythmic outbursts by the whole orchestra. The picture of the saint being tormented by all manner of fantastic medieval monsters is vivid, but one feels a certain constraint: it is not surrealistic enough, perhaps because of Hindemith's

PLATE LIV. *Paul Hindemith. (Press-foto Köhnert, Berlin.)*

EXAMPLE VII-15, cont'd.

THIRD MOVEMENT:

logical nature and the definite processes of his music. The coda combines an *ostinato* in the horns which is quite clearly related to the opening recitative, with a rapid "perpetual motion" figure in the strings while the woodwinds intone the medieval plainchant *"Lauda Sion salvatorem"* ("Praise to Sion which shall save us"). (Example VII-15h.) When the chant has been presented fully, there is a slackening in tempo and an increase in loudness. The unaccompanied brass choir now plays a chordal *Alleluia "mit aller Kraft"* (with full strength) which concludes the movement in a mood of exalted joy.

NATIONALISM: 1920-1945

Three nations emerged as musically significant during the period between the world wars: England, Spain and the United States. The first two had a rich musical past and a deep well of folk music to draw upon, and this they did, often wedding the two. The United States brought jazz upon the musical scene, one of the most potent forces of the twenties and thirties, and a constant and enduring influence in the life of every American composer.

Because of the inclusion of music under the heading of propaganda, the Russian composers were severely hampered in their efforts to keep up with the musical thinking of the rest of Europe. Instead of developing a fruitful *avant garde*, they were constrained by government criticism, expressed in *Pravda*, to revamp the Romantic styles of their predecessors in order to be sure that their music would be understood by the masses. Within this closed system, it is remarkable that the better composers, such as Prokofiev and Shostakovich, were able to achieve what they did.

A few notable composers from Latin American countries began to appear during these years, of whom Heitor Villa-Lobos (1887-1959) from Brazil, Carlos Chávez (b. 1899) from Mexico, and the Argentinian Alberto Ginastera (b. 1916) were the most eminent. They, too, echoed the folk music of their native lands, blending the twentieth century techniques with Indian melodies, rhythms and percussion sounds.

Three of the composers of *Les Six* continued to be important, but the radicalism of their earlier ventures had now settled down into personal styles. Milhaud continued to exploit polytonality, Honnegger a dramatic Neoromanticism, and Poulenc a style that perhaps can best be termed "Gallicism," so innately French is it in its wit, irony, taste and restrained feeling.

The preeminent style of the period was Neoclassicism, as we have seen, in various personal variants. Dodecaphony slowly made its way in Europe, but was hardly important at all in the United States, where other brands of chromaticism were being developed, despite Schönberg's arrival in the United States in 1933.

Let us begin first with the musical revival in England, a happening of considerable importance for the world of music.

England

The first really important English composer since the death of Henry Purcell in 1695 was Ralph Vaughan Williams (1872-1958). He valued honesty and sincerity above all things in his music, and found expressions of these in English folk song and in the music of the age of Henry VIII and Elizabeth I. Through the assimilation of these, together with certain techniques of parallel chord movement gained from Impressionism, he developed a ruggedly personal style quite aside from the sophistications of dodecaphony and Neoclassicism. He admitted that his technique was often rough and amateurish, but a bluff honesty shines through even these passages.

Perhaps the most well-known of his works are the *Fantasia on a Theme by Thomas Tallis* and the *Folksong Suite* in versions for both band and orchestra. Choral music occupies a large place in his list of works, including a *Mass in G Minor,* a *Magnificat* and a *Te Deum.* Of his five operas, the chamber work *Riders to the Sea,* a setting of the unchanged play by J. M. Synge, is performed frequently. *Sir John in Love,* based upon Shakespeare's character, Falstaff, and *The Pilgrim's Progress,* a setting of the Bunyan work, are presented from time to time in England. He wrote nine symphonies, from the *Sea Symphony* of 1910, which included a choral setting of texts by Whitman, the well-known *London Symphony,* a painting of various aspects of the great city, the *Pastoral Symphony,* the uncompromising *Fourth* and the rugged *Seventh* ("Antarctica"), to the *Ninth* (1957-58). Of these, we should like to discuss the *Tallis Fantasia* and the *Eighth Symphony* as accessible introductory compositions.

Fantasia on a Theme by Thomas Tallis

This work, scored for two string orchestras and solo string quartet, illustrates Vaughan Williams' debt to the great English music of the past. The harmony is almost entirely triadic, modal in flavor, with sequences of unrelated chords and parallel streams of triads which recall the late medieval style of Dunstable. The hymn by Tallis is shown in its original form in Example VII-16; Vaughan Williams uses both the melodic elements and certain of the harmonies, particularly those of the last phrase. The theme is presented first with parallel

EXAMPLE VII-16: Tallis, *Hymn* (1567).

chord interjections at the cadence points, then varied antiphonally between the two orchestras. The third section introduces the string quartet, with viola and violin solos which are imitated and intermixed with the orchestras in a manner somewhat like that of the *concerto grosso*. This expands into a *tutti* of great sonority and a return to the solos of the middle section, followed by an orchestral coda. This mystical serenity is one of the characteristic moods of Vaughan Williams' music, but not too often is it exploited at length as in this work.

Symphony No. 8, in D Minor, (1955)

This symphony is written in the traditional four movements, beginning with a *Fantasia* which the composer labeled "Seven variations in search of a theme." Certain basic material (Example VII-17a,b,c) is expanded in the sections, relating the movement to the old English "fancy": Variation I is scherzo-like, with *staccato* articulation; the second is quiet and lyric, and moves smoothly into the third, which is more impassioned. The fourth variation is similar to the second, but in a new key and with more colorful scoring, while the fifth is faster and more dissonant, after which the full and lyric sixth variation, the climax of the movement leads to the quiet coda with reminiscences of the opening themes and vibraphone and celesta sonorities.

The second movement, a grotesque scherzo, is scored for winds only, and brings to mind certain witty and sardonic movements by Prokofiev. The clean articulations and colorful nature of the instruments are well displayed. The trio is slower and based upon a figure which returns repeatedly to its central tone. The return of the scherzo is short and more fully scored.

The *Cavatina* makes a strong contrast since it is scored for strings only, and is a lyric chain-form (A-B-C-A-B) with three main themes. The A section is rather polyphonic, recalling the *Tallis Fantasia*, while the B section is homophonic, and the C part features a violin solo. The return of the A and B sections is shortened, and the keys are the same as in the first appearance, with the exception that a short coda modulates to E, the key of the opening.

The finale is a *Toccata*, a display piece for the percussion, opening with a broad tune around which the bells, glockenspiel, harps, etc. wreathe a halo of sounds. The motive (a) of the first movement recurs in inverted form here in many guises. A *staccato* counterpoint in the winds offers contrasting sonority and material, still with the bell sounds in the background. The second theme is angular and appears first in the brass. The movement ends rather abruptly with a short statement

EXAMPLE VII-17: Vaughan Williams, *Symphony No. 8.*

of the opening tune, leaving the listener who expected a traditional *finale* somewhat disappointed.

Of the host of composers England now began to produce, once the Muse was reawakened, three have made some claims to international repute. William Walton (b. 1902) is best known for his *Viola Concerto* (1929) and his oratorio, *Belshazzar's Feast.* Michael Tippett (b. 1905) made his greatest impression with the oratorio *A Child of Our Time,* although he has written several symphonies and much chamber music. Perhaps the best known is their younger compatriot, Benjamin Britten (b. 1913), whose operas, particularly *Peter Grimes, Billy Budd* and *The Turn of the Screw* have made his reputation. A number of *Gebrauchsmusik* works such as *The Little Sweep* and *Noye's Fludde* have proved to be popular with amateur groups. The *War Requiem* is a gigantic lament over World War II, and is most compelling in performance.

Spain

Spain began to arouse itself musically during the late nineteenth century through the researches of Felipe Pedrell (1841-1922) in folksong and early music of his country. Through his work, Isaac Albéniz

(1860-1909), Enrique Granados (1867-1916) and Manuel de Falla (1876-1946) were able to create an authentic Spanish music which bears somewhat the same relation to the pseudo Spanish style of Bizet, Rimsky-Korsakov and Chabrier as Bartók's peasant music does to the "Hungarianisms" of Liszt. Albéniz and Granados were primarily composers for the piano, and wrote in a manner recalling the Spanish national instrument, the guitar. Albéniz' chief composition is the suite *Iberia*, a tour of Spain, and that of Granados is his *Goyescas*, based upon paintings by Goya, and subsequently fashioned into a loosely constructed opera of the same name.

Manuel de Falla represents Spanish music in the twentieth century. After early successes with his impressionistic nocturnes, *Nights in the Gardens of Spain* (1909-1916) for piano and orchestra, and his more nationalistic ballets *El amor brujo* ("Love, the Magician," 1915) and *El sombrero de tres picos* ("The Three-cornered Hat," 1917, 1919), his most advanced work, cognizant of trends in modern music, was the *Concerto* for harpsichord, flute, oboe, clarinet, violin and cello (1923-26).

The *Harpsichord Concerto* is cast in three movements, *Allegro, Lento and Vivace*. The first movement begins with a "perpetual motion" figure in the harpsichord, with offbeat accents from the other instruments. This *ostinato* shifts between the keys of D and B, and against it melodic and rhythmic fragments are projected. A more melodic section occurs toward the middle of the movement, with strong chordal punctuations, after which the *ostinato* figure recurs fragmented. The movement closes on B with a series of guitar-like parallel chords. The formal treatment is rather like that of Scarlatti, although with the cadential sections blurred or elided. The second movement has been compared to a cathedral scene, possibly because it was finished on *Corpus Christi* Day in 1926, but it does have a sonorous grandeur and stateliness, and an intensity and passion despite the slow tempo, which recalls the especial character of Spanish Catholicism to mind. Falla achieved gorgeous sonorities in this movement with sweeping arpeggios and colorful spacing of the instruments. From time to time dissonant low tones in the harpsichord make one think of the ringing of great bells which are out of tune with the music within the cathedral. There is a suggestion of modality in the harmony, and the musical past of Spain is evoked in some imitative effects whose technique, however, is modern. The final movement again recalls Scarlatti in its use of short, repetitive motives. It makes much of the division of six pulses into three groups of two and two groups of three, a rhythmic process called *hemiola*. Other more syncopated, almost Stravinskyan passages interrupt the flow from time to time. While this work is not obviously Spanish, in its intensity and spareness, and its hardness and an almost tragic quality, it is very representative of the spirit of the people of the Iberian Peninsula.

American Composers

The composers in the United States, while affected by Stravinsky principally and Schönberg to a lesser degree, essentially were un-aligned with the great European styles. They sought, first, to write American music, then despaired of defining the term. Probably Virgil Thomson summed it up best when he said that to write American music, one first had to be an American and second, had to write music. Styles of all shades were to be found, from Copland's early jazzy Neoclassicism to Sessions' manner of dealing with chromaticism and dissonance in an Expressionistic way. The greater number, however, elected the middle of the road, with overtones of both Neoclassicism and Neoromanticism. The following survey of six composers who came into prominence during the second phase of the century is only a means to suggest the variety of styles which were developed.

Walter Piston, 1894-

Piston began as a Neoclassic composer of the linear counterpoint school, but has since developed a warm and less obviously Neoclassic style in which emotion, though controlled, is very much present. Nevertheless, the dry sonorities and rhythmic energy of his *First String Quartet* still are attractive. He has seven symphonies to his credit, two of which, the third and the fourth, won a Pulitzer Prize and the Naumberg Award respectively.

The *Third Symphony* is a good example of Piston's communicative style. His analysis, printed in the program notes of the premier performance is so clear that quotation of themes is unnecessary. Piston says:

I.   *Andantino*, 5/4: based on three thematic elements: the first heard as a melody for the oboes, the second, more somber in character, played by bassoon, clarinets and English horn; the third, soft chords for brass. These ideas are developed singly and in combination to form a prelude-like movement. Tonality C.

II. *Allegro*, 2/4: a scherzo in three-part form. The theme, stated by violas and bassoons, is treated in contrapuntal, imitative fashion. The middle

PLATE LV. *Walter Piston. (Associated Music Publishers.)*

part is marked by the melody for flute, accompanied by clarinets and harp. Tonality F.

III. *Adagio,* 4/4: the movement has four large and closely connected sections, or rather "phases" of musical development. The first of these is the statement by strings of the theme, which is in three parts (part one by the violins, part two by violas, part three by all except basses). The second section is a variation of the theme with woodwinds and harps predominating. The third section, starting with basses and celli, builds up to the climax of the movement, and the final section returns to the original form of the theme, played by solo viola, the closing cadence recalling the variation by clarinet and bassoon. Tonality G.

IV. *Allegro,* 4/4: a three-part form similar to that of a sonata form movement. There are two themes, the first being developed fugally in the middle section. The second theme is march-like, first heard in oboes and bassoons over a staccato bass, and later played by full brass at the climax of the movement. Tonality C.

In addition to his orchestral music, Piston has written considerable chamber music, of which the charming *Sonata for Violin and Harpsichord* and the solid *Piano Quintet* are good examples.

Roger Sessions, 1896-

One of the most respected of American composers, and a teacher of many young composers whose contributions came during the Third Phase, Roger Sessions developed his present version of atonality and personal idiom without following the path of the Viennese dodeca-

PLATE LVI. *Roger Sessions. (Courtesy of the BMI Archive.)*

phonists. He has had too few performances to make his music really
well known to even those professionally interested in contemporary
music. His production is slow, but this reflects the integrity of his
musical thought. His music is not "easy", for it is an active, highly
colored style, and one must be willing to listen repeatedly to get
beneath the distracting surface of the music. He has written five
symphonies, two concertos——one for violin, the other for piano, an
orchestral suite fashioned out of the music for a production of
Andreyev's *The Black Maskers,* (his first success), a setting for soprano
and orchestra of the *Idyll of Theocritus,* two string quartets, one
quintet, and a violin sonata, two operas——the *Trial of Lucullus,* on a
libretto of Bertolt Brecht (1947) and the large opera, *Montezuma*
(1941-1963), premiered in Berlin in 1964.

  After passing through a Neoclassic phase, Sessions turned toward
a more romantic kind of expression, somewhat Germanic in manner,
rather than the French cast of Neoclassicism. The *Second Symphony*
illustrates this style. The chromaticism is almost constant, although
diatonic melodic lines do occur from time to time (Second Movement).
The orchestration is highly colored, and there is a constant interplay
of motives which agitates the music and makes listening require increased concentration. The first movement, *Molto agitato,* resembles a
sonata-allegro in form, introducing a number of motives in the first section, followed by development. The second thematic section, much
slower in tempo, features a solo violin, accompanied by woodwind and
string figuration. The development deals largely with two themes of the
first group, after which the thematic sections appear in reverse order
and the movement closes quietly.

The second movement, *Allegretto capriccioso,* is a wry little *scherzo* with an intriguing theme. It is in rondo form with short interludes.

The third movement is an elegiac, expressive *Adagio* of extremely involved lyricism which uses the techniques of theme transformation, inversion, retrograde and fragmentation, thus making recognition of formal sections very difficult. Here the expression of feeling is most important, and the music is chromatically eloquent.

The final movement is a rondo-like structure whose recurring element is a gay rhythmic succession of parallel major triads outlining a descending scale of five tones, which sometimes reverses its direction.

Howard Hanson, 1896-

Hanson is a Neoromantic composer who is at his best in those orchestral compositions especially suited by program or text to displays of emotion and orchestral color, such as *The Lament for Beowulf, Three Poems from Walt Whitman* or the *Cherubic Hymn.* He has written five symphonies to date, the most popular of which are the *First* or *"Nordic"* and the *Second,* or *"Romantic."* His opera *Merry Mount,* based upon an event in the early history of Puritan New England, was produced by the Metropolitan Opera in 1934, and from it the composer extracted a suite of movements which is performed rather frequently. In later years, Hanson has been interested in artificial scales, both as a means of understanding certain historical styles of music as well as providing consistent stylistic materials for the modern composer. The *Cherubic Hymn,* which we shall examine, makes use of this technique. In recognition of his extraordinary service to the cause of American music as educator and conductor, he has been the recipient of many awards and honors.

Symphony No. 2, "Romantic"

This work was written for Serge Koussevitzky, conductor of the Boston Symphony Orchestra in 1930, a time when audiences sought reassurance amid the din of experimental music that there were still composers who were writing understandable symphonies. Hence the composer made a definite effort to emphasize Romantic qualities in this work. The symphony is strongly cyclic, and each movement uses thematic material which has been introduced previously. The introduction to the first movement is constructed of the most important

PLATE LVII. *Howard Hanson. (Photo by Ouzer, courtesy of Howard Hanson.)*

of the cyclic themes, a short rising chromatic phrase (Example VII-18a) which develops a dynamic curve before the movement proper begins. The form is that of the sonata-allegro, with distinct sections, and should offer no difficulty to the listener. The second movement begins with a refreshing change of orchestral color, and is based almost entirely upon motive (e) of the example, although the motto theme (a) and the horn theme from the third section of the first movement appear during the central portion. The third movement contains only a small amount of new thematic material, for the themes of the preceding movements are recapitulated in part and are used developmentally. These are more highly colored and dramatically presented now, however, building in waves to the climax near the end. A solo string quartet offers a radical change in tone quality, after which a final climax closes the movement.

Cherubic Hymn

The *Cherubic Hymn,* with text from the Greek Orthodox liturgy of St. John Chrysostom, was composed in 1949, when Hanson was doing research for his book which deals with what we may call artificial scales. As we have seen in the case of the pentatonic and whole-tone scales, the harmonic possiblities of a scale are regulated by the intervals which occur in it. Hanson devised a way to analyze scales for

EXAMPLE VII-18: Hanson, *Symphony No. 2, "Romantic."*

MOTTO AND GERM THEMES

their intervallic content, and then, by the opposite process, to synthesize them according to what intervals were desired to predominate,
thus giving the resulting scale a very characteristic sound. This procedure provided the material for the *Cherubic Hymn;* here, Hanson
wanted to use material which would suggest the quasi-oriental splendor of the Byzantine ritual and accordingly synthesized scale forms
which contained a predominance of colorful intervals of Near Eastern
feeling. These, combined with appropriate orchestration, suit the subject without making it another romantic oriental fantasy. The choral
writing is diatonic despite the chromaticisms which occur in the scale
and is very singable. The thematic materials are very simple, elemental,
in fact, since they consist for the most part of scale fragments—a
characteristic which makes for extreme unity, far beyond that obtained
by theme transference in the symphony. Here Hanson has achieved an
exciting setting of the text without detracting from its solemnity—
indeed, the glory of St. John's vision is more clearly revealed.

Roy Harris, 1898-

The best music of this composer seems highly representative of
pioneer America in its rugged and rough-hewn quality. This is true
of the early *Piano Sonata,* the *Overture "When Johnny Comes Marching Home"* and the fine *Third Symphony.* Other works are not as vital,
although Harris at his dullest still gives the feeling that he is imparting something profound. His reputation rests largely on the music
mentioned above, however, together with a few chamber compositions
such as the *Piano Quintet.*

The *Third Symphony* is a one-movement work cast in five main
sections which differ from each other in themes, sonorities and tempos.
The first section, with which the work begins, has been characterized
by the composer as "tragic—low string sonorities." The long-breathed

melodic lines are combined in counterpoint which relies heavily upon
the intervals of the fifth and fourth, and which, when sufficient lines
have accumulated, creates nonfunctional modal harmony. The motion
quickens, the sonority brightens, and Section II: "Lyric—strings, horns,
woodwinds" arrives. Section III: "Pastoral—woodwinds with a polytonal string background:" here, muted strings play overlapping

PLATE LVIII. *Roy Harris. (Courtesy of the BMI Archive.)*

arpeggio passages, accompanying the solo woodwinds, an entirely new
sound, never before heard in the orchestra. Section IV: "Fugue—dramatic" consists of three subsections: (1) brass and percussion predominating; (2) canonic development of materials from Section II,
providing a background for continuation of the fugue; and (3) brass
climax employing a rhythmic motive derived from the fugue subject.
The fifth section, "dramatic—tragic" first restates some of the thematic
material of Section I, while the brass and percussion continue with
the rhythmic motive of Section IV. This is followed by a coda built
over a constant metric beat in the timpani. The thematic material is
derived from Sections I and II (*i.e.*, the long melodic lines of Section
I appear throughout this entire last section). This work is most convincing in its unity, variety and coherence, and provides one of the
more successful examples of the one-movement symphony written in
the twentieth century.

Aaron Copland, 1900-

This composer was influenced early by jazz, and used it in some of his works—*Dance Symphony* (1925), *Music for the Theater* (1925) and *Piano Concerto* (1926). Since about 1937, however, he has consciously turned toward increased simplicity and a certain use of folk-like materials (the ballets *Billy the Kid, Rodeo, Appalachian Spring, El Salón México,* and concert music *Symphonic Ode, Statements, Lincoln Portrait, Piano Variations, Clarinet Quintet,* and *Third Symphony.* He also has written several fine film scores of which those for

PLATE LIX. *Aaron Copland. (Photo by John Ardoin, courtesy of Boosey and Hawkes.)*

Our Town and *Of Mice and Men* have been outstanding. During the years after the war, Copland worked in his own version of the twelve-tone technique, producing the *Piano Quartet* of 1950 and the *Fantasy* of 1952-57. But whatever the technical mode of composition, Copland's use of form, economy of material and handling of sonority is always individual and skillful. Of all of the American composers, his profile is the most characteristic. A good example of this is the *Third Symphony* (1946):

> *First Movement (molto moderato):* the key is E major; arch form is employed, using three themes, of which the first and third are heard in later movements of the work. Theme A is typically intervallic and wide-spaced, B is more lyric and not

so widely spaced, although it still uses thematic intervals, and C, which first appears in the trombones, consists of triad formations connected by scale passages of a few notes. The three themes are presented in an expository section, developed and recapitulated, although C does not appear in the recapitulation.

Second Movement (allegro molto): the movement consists of a scherzo and trio. The main thematic element of the scherzo is a fanfare figure whose rhythm is as important as the melodic pattern. There are three varied statements of this theme followed by short developments before the trio is reached. In contrast to the climax which precedes it, the trio is quiet and lyric, built on a flowing and only slightly angular theme first stated in the oboe. It is developed in free and imitative counterpoint, after which the scherzo gradually returns by way of a passage of increasing rhythmic motion marked by the use of the celesta (sometimes piano) at first, later by fragmentary development of the scherzo theme and increasing force. The return of the scherzo is abbreviated and recomposed.

Third Movement (andantino, quasi allegretto): this is the slow movement of the work, and employs theme C of the first movement as the subject for the introduction and coda, between which there is a continuous, close-knit series of four variational sections, each of which seems to grow organically out of the preceding one. The theme of these variations is typically angular, tonal and suited to some of the additive rhythmic sections included in the animated variation.

Fourth Movement (molto deliberato (Fanfare)—*Allegro risoluto)*: the fanfare with which this movement opens without pause after the preceding one, is first stated softly in the flutes and clarinets, followed by a forceful repetition in the brass. After this introduction, the main body of the movement, essentially a sonata-allegro, follows. The first theme, a repetitive, rapid note pattern, is stated in the oboe, joined contrapuntally by the other woodwinds and finally by the strings. The theme is thoroughly developed, during the course of which the harmonic-lyric second theme is presented. The development of the fanfare and the first theme continues, coming to a climax on a shrill, dissonant chord which signals the close of the development section. The first theme now is combined with the fanfare theme. Somewhat later, the two harps, piano and celesta are given rapid scale figures against which the solo horn plays the fanfare theme, after which is stated the opening theme of the first movement. The second theme of the finale then appears in even note values in the horns after which the second theme of the first movement (B) is used in the horns and trombones to form the closing section. Interestingly enough, this symphony which began in E major ends in D major.

William Schuman, 1910-

The saga of the films has come true for Schuman, for he began as a Tin-Pan Alley composer of popular songs, and later served a number of years as the president of the Juilliard School of Music. The early days in the "Alley," however, have left their impress on his lively rhythmic sense which is apparent in every page he has written. His style is Neoclassic, economical and spare. One of his most popular works is the *Third Symphony,* and the *American Festival Overture* is frequently played.

The *Third Symphony* of Schuman is divided into two large movements, each of which consists of two sections. The Neoclassic tendency toward Baroque formal patterns is evident here, for the first movement is a passacaglia and fugue, and the second is formed by pairing a chorale and toccata.

PLATE LX. *William Schuman. (Courtesy of the BMI Archive.)*

The passacaglia theme, a rather angular melodic line covering nearly two octaves in span, is first stated in the violas and imitated seven times, each entry a half step higher than the preceding one (*cf.* Bartók: first movement of *Music for Strings, Percussion and Celesta*). At the conclusion of this canonic section, the thematic idea is developed simultaneously in the strings, trumpets and trombones, concluding with a passage for the brass alone. The following sections are devoted to development and transformation of the theme, not as a ground bass, as in Baroque style, but as a melodic element.

The fugue subject is announced by the unison horns and *pizzicato* strings, and followed by the violins, violas and cellos, basses and tuba, woodwinds, trombones and trumpets. After the first imitation, there is a short episode between the succeeding entries, each of which is a half step higher than the preceding one. A climax is accumulated, not only dynamically, but also through the increasing number of instruments participating, followed by a brilliant canonic passage based on the subject and played by the four trumpets. A quiet section employing the woodwinds ensues to which the strings add their sound, again reaching a high point at which the timpani has a variant of the fugue subject. During the rest of the movement, strings and woodwinds supply developmental backgrounds to thematic motives in the brass; the passage culminates in a statement of the subject in augmentation (long note values) by the horns which leads to the coda where similar procedures bring the movement to an impressive close.

Part II, Chorale and Toccata, begins with a set of chorale variations on a theme first presented by the trumpet after a rather polyphonic introduction by the low strings. The variations work up to a considerable climax, subside to a low, sustained B♭ and lead to the statement of the rhythmic toccata theme by the snare drum. The bass clarinet in its low register invests these rhythmic fragments with pitch contours which chase each other in various transformed patterns throughout the movement. As befits the title, the movement is a rhythmic display piece for orchestra. There is an interesting passage for the cellos which introduces a new theme that is worked out briefly before the movement gathers momentum and rushes toward its conclusion.

Ernest Bloch, 1880-1959

One other composer we must mention who, although a naturalized American, received his musical formation in Europe. A Swiss Jew, he came to the United States in 1917, where he taught and composed. One of his successful students is Roger Sessions. Perhaps his most interesting works are Nationalistic, those in which he expressed the "Jewish soul, the complex, glowing, agitated soul" in works such as *Schelomo, A Hebrew Rhapsody for Cello and Orchestra; Baal Shem: Three Pictures of Chassidic Life,* for violin and piano; and the *Avodath Hakodesh,* or Sacred Service, for solo baritone, chorus and orchestra.

His style was a fusion of Romanticism, Impressionistic techniques, full-blooded orchestration and a leaning toward open, rhapsodical structures. The Hebraic style is perhaps most convincing in *Schelomo,* where Solomon is portrayed as a brooding and exhorting being, passionate and vital. The melodic line contains many oriental sounding skips of the augmented 2nd, and has a near-Eastern sinuosity. The movement grows organically through the repetition and extension of important motives. The orchestration recalls in its colors *The Old King* of Rouault in its glowing yet somber coloration. One hears the *shofar* and the temple instruments in it, even though he knows that these are ordinary French horns and bassoons.

In addition to these, Bloch composed a large number of works in an idiom difficult to classify neatly: perhaps the nearest would be a warm Neoclassicism, although issue could be taken with this in individual cases. But the two *Concerti grossi of* 1925 and 1952, the *Piano Quintet,* the *Violin Concerto* and the *Concerto Symphonique* for piano and orchestra, the five string quartets and the opera *Macbeth* are all individual, expressive and well-wrought, as characteristic of one side of Bloch's character as the Jewish pieces are of another.

Prokofiev, from 1935 to 1953

In 1935, after a sojourn in Paris, with frequent visits to Russia, Prokofiev returned to his homeland for the remainder of his life. He was welcomed enthusiastically by musicians and brother composers as an accomplished master and one whose music was Nationalistic to the core. In 1936 and in 1948, however, Prokofiev, Shostakovitch and some other composers were publicly reprimanded in *Pravda* for "formalistic tendencies" and "pursuit of novelty" rather than writing music which followed the traditions of the music of the people. In this way, the Soviet was able to preserve in the strongest manner the romantic tradition, relieving its composers of the necessity of solving the dilemma of tonality. All of the accused composers apologized in public letters, promising to follow the ideas of Socialist realism more closely

PLATE LXI: *Serge Prokofiev. (Photo courtesy of MCA Music.)*

in the future. These letters are most interesting to read in the light of the subsequent works by these men, and may be found in Nicolas Slonimsky's book, *Music Since 1900*[4].

During the decade after 1935, Prokofiev produced some of his best works: the familiar *Peter and the Wolf* (1936), the ballet *Romeo and Juliet* (1934-36), the cantata drawn from the film score to Eisenstein's *Alexander Nevsky* (1938-39), the opera *War and Peace* (1941-43) and another ballet, *Cinderella* (1940-44). During World War II there appeared the *Fifth Symphony*, the *First Violin Sonata*, the *Sixth, Seventh* and *Eighth Piano Sonatas*. Before his death in 1953, he completed *The Stone Flower*, a ballet, and the *Sixth* and *Seventh Symphonies*, among other compositions.

One of Prokofiev's most popular works is the suite drawn from the film music of *Lt. Kijé*, a fictitious officer brought into being by the Czar's mistaken signing of a commission. Kijé's various adventures, including his wedding, are depicted delightfully in the movements of the suite. His existence becomes embarrassing to his superior officers, and they decide to dispose of him with a mock funeral. Prokofiev concludes the suite by bringing back all of the themes of the previous movement combined contrapuntally in a finale.

[4] Coleman-Ross Co., Inc., New York, 1949.

Symphony No. 5

The style of this work is Romantic, but with the particular flavor of the composer's personal style——the humorous indirection in regard to key, the witty themes and the deeply-felt lyricism. It is easily accessible to anyone familiar with the nineteenth century idiom, so that we shall merely offer a "road-map" of the forms to assist the musical traveler.

The first movement is a sonata-allegro which employs four themes made up of similar motives, thus insuring unity. Each time the themes are repeated, they are varied subtly.

The second movement is a sectional form containing six distinct themes arranged in the following scheme:

Section 1		Section 2		Section 2'		Section 1
A-B-A	C	D-E	C	D-E	C	A-B-A

It will be noted that C acts as a sort of refrain during the central portion of the movement. It is only about eight measures long. The A theme is accompanied by a rapid-note *ostinato*, and illustrates Prokofiev's amusing way of deflecting the course of a melody so that it traverses several keys before ending.

The third movement is a species of sonata-allegro with a quite regular exposition and abbreviated recapitulation, but with new thematic material in place of the development section, a form that both Haydn and Mozart experimented with briefly. A quotation of a theme from the first movement makes the work cyclic, but more notable is the mocking laughter of the coda, a whirlwind finish which is not a little enigmatic in significance.

Dmitri Shostakovitch, 1906-

After the death of Prokofiev, Shostakovitch became the most important contemporary Russian composer, although the number of his works performed outside Russia is not nearly as great as that of the older man. He has a consistent but less readily identifiable style than Prokofiev, but one which can be easily understood in terms of the Romantic Era. Out of thirteen symphonies, the *Fifth* is the strongest and is quite representative of Shostakovitch's style of melody, harmony, orchestration and form at its best. He is extremely prolific, having written eight string quartets, many choruses and songs, a rather frequently performed *Piano Quintet* (1940) and an opera, *Katerina*

Izmailova, formerly entitled *Lady Macbeth of Mtsensk,* which, in this first version, aroused the critics of *Pravda.* Unfortunately, much of Shostakovitch's music, especially the choral works, glorifies some aspect of Soviet life which stereotypes it for consumption elsewhere. One cannot help wondering what kind of music would have come from Russia if the arts had not been subverted to the purposes of the state.

THE AVANT-GARDE

The radically progressive composers of the inter-war period advanced ideas and wrote experimental music which became the basis of much of the electronic music after 1945. But these pioneers were hampered by the relative crudity of their equipment, for the tape recorder and the electronic sound synthesizer had not yet been invented. The Theremin and Ondes Martenot, two electronic machines capable of producing new sonorities, were available during the late twenties, but did not seem to answer the needs of the experimentalists. Instead, they found ways of producing new sounds from standard instruments, or extended their investigations to include those produced by "non-instruments," such as flower-pots, brake-drums, sirens, sheets of metal and oriental percussion instruments, to name but a few. Colin McPhee (b. 1901), Lou Harrison (b. 1917) and John Cage (b. 1912) produced compositions which employed these means. Their interest in Asiatic and African music, especially the philosophical bases as well as the musical techniques, introduced a new dimension into western musical culture. The Javanese *Gamelan* orchestra especially fascinated McPhee, and his compositions reproduce many of the sounds of this percussion ensemble. Harrison was early associated with modern dance. and produced some interesting music for this activity. John Cage, one of the serious *avant-garde* philosophers, began his career in new sounds with the "prepared piano," a piano which has had pieces of felt, wood or metal placed on or between the strings so as to produce different percussive sounds of tuned pitch when the keys were depressed, thus affording the player a miniature percussion ensemble. Another experimenter, Henry Cowell (1897-1965), had made efforts to bring the music of Ives and Ruggles to a wider public hearing, as well as using new sonorous techniques in his music. His name probably always will be associated with the *tone cluster,* produced by playing several keys of the piano at one time by pressing them down with the palm of the hand, the forearm, or with measured blocks of wood. He was not the first to do this——Ives had written such clusters——but the music appeared at the right time for the technique to be effective and adopted by others.

In Europe, the guitar and mandolin were included in ensembles by Schönberg, Berg and Webern, who already had introduced new sonorities by the extension of playing techniques of standard instruments. The waves set up by Russolo and the Futurists had not yet subsided, for, in France particularly there was much experimental music written which, in addition to projecting novel musical philosophies which affected the structural and temporal bases of the music, employed noise-makers of various kinds. George Antheil's (1900-1959) *Ballet Mèchanique*, written to accompany a ballet by the painter Léger, included sixteen pianos, a player piano, airplane propellor (and motor), anvils, bells, automobile horns and a large sheet of galvanized iron. Other Europeans were less vociferous: Alois Hába (b. 1893), a Czech composer, wrote much music based upon quarter-tone and sixth-tone divisions of the octave. This technique perhaps has been superseded since the advent of continuously variable pitch available in electronic instruments, but it was one of the important speculations concerning scale divisions smaller than the half-step.

The most consistently important *avant-garde* composer of this and the post-war period was Edgard Varèse (1885-1965), who came to the United States in 1915. A musical prodigy, he was first intended for an engineering career, and the studies pursued during this time probably strongly influenced the experimental music which he composed later. It certainly is reflected in the titles of his compositions—— *Hyperprism, Intégrales, Ionisation* and *Density 21.5*, for example. He early had prophesied that contemporary music would have to await the collaboration of the composer and the engineer in order to produce new sound sources with infinitely variable pitch, quality and intensity: this was fulfilled during the years of the war and those immediately after, for the tape-recorder and the electronic sound synthesizer were developed——the instruments for which he had been waiting all his life. In 1951-54 Varèse composed *Déserts* for winds, percussion and tape-recorded noises of industrial origin. He received a commission from the Phillips Corporation in 1957 to compose a work for their Brussels Exposition pavilion, designed by Le Corbusier. The *Poème électronique* was the result, recorded on multiple channel tapes which were projected to the listener by four hundred speakers located on all sides of the pavilion.

Almost all of the Varèse compositions are available on recordings, and demonstrate his radical and progressive innovations in the handling of sound. They combine percussion of wide varieties with wind instruments, and use sirens as well as the Theremin and Ondes Musicales.

Density 21.5 (1936), the density of platinum, was commissioned by George Barrère, a noted flutist whose instrument was made of that metal. The intervallic material is presented in the opening phrases and is later extended and varied in pitch level and intensity. Notable are the changes of tone quality due to the use of harmonics and extreme registers, as well as new sounds such as that produced by tapping the keys without blowing.

Intégrales (1926) employs a wind group of eleven players and a percussion ensemble of seventeen. It is essentially monothematic, based upon variations of the opening motive stated by the clarinet, a procedure reminiscent of the *maquamat* of the Arabs or the *ragas* of Hindu music. The rhythmic pulse often is discontinuous, and the motives frequently are projected in dissonant counterpoint preceded and followed by silences——a technique similar to that of Webern in that the silence becomes a musical value as important as the sound. The entire composition shows little of the passing fads of the twenties, but is original and unique.

Poème électronique uses only electronic sound generators and modified tape recordings of bells and the human voice. It has few associations with our ordinary experience, and should not be listened to in a traditional way, but open-mindedly for new experiences. Nevertheless, it has a sense of rhythmic movement, almost one of harmonic and melodic flow despite the fact that it is abstract and non-human. Many such works are static, lacking any sense of movement or flow, thus depriving or inhibiting one of the natural human responses to music.

These, then, were the important *avant-garde* composers: they and their students and followers were to extend their work into the complex techniques characteristic of the post-war Phase III.

PHASE III: AFTER 1945

Music: "the corporealization of the intelligence that is in sound." (Hoëne Wronsky, 1778-1853, quoted by Varèse)

Music after the war saw the emergence of the twelve-tone technique into its rightful place in musical development, and the cessation of hostilities between the neoclassicists and the dodecaphonists. It was recognized to be a "method of composing," just as Schönberg had insisted all along, and composers realized that it could be combined with other, non-serial methods, or that a specific style could be set up merely by the choice of intervals within the row.

The discovery that Webern had been writing pure music which used serialization of other factors in addition to pitch, created a school of total serialization which moved rapidly toward the total control of material offered by electronic music. At last the dream of the nineteenth century composer had become a reality: the creation of a piece of music in which everything was necessary and nothing could be changed!

Stravinsky

While this serialization was going on, Stravinsky finished *The Rake's Progress*, and in the wake of it a number of vocal pieces, some in English, others in Latin. Among the English works were the *Cantata* (1951-52), three songs from Shakespeare (1952), *In Memoriam Dylan Thomas* (1954), *A Sermon, a Narrative and a Prayer* (1960-61), *The Flood* (1961-62), a dance-drama, and a setting of T. S. Eliot's *The Dove Descending* from the *Four Quartets* (1962). The two Latin works are the *Canticum sacrum* (1955-56), dedicated "to the City of Venice in praise of its Patron Saint, the Blessed Mark, Apostle," and *Threni (Dirges, that is, The Lamentations of the Prophet Jeremiah,* 1957-58). It will be noted that out of these eight works, five of them are religious in nature. Instrumental compositions of the same period were *Agon* (1954-57), an abstract ballet, a *Septet* (1952-53) for three strings, three winds and piano, *Movements* (1960-61) for piano and orchestra, and some essays based on the music of Bach and of Gesualdo.

In these compositions Stravinsky began working with serial procedures, not twelve-tone, and not necessarily chromatic in nature. Possibly his interest in contrapuntal manipulation of melodic lines had led him to this, for, considering it abstractly, a melody is a series, and the theme transformation technique was essentially a manipulation of the series. To go farther back in history, the polyphonic tricks of Ockeghem, Obrecht and Des Prez in the late fifteenth century——the use of inversion, retrograde and retrograde inversion of melodic lines as well as all kinds of complicated canons——were also serial procedures. The ballade *Ma fin est mon commencement,* of Machaut, provides an earlier precedent. Stravinsky worked with five, seven and ten tone series in various compositions during this decade finally using the twelve-tone series, but in a very individual, almost Neoclassic way——which could have been expected, for a composer does not shed completely the preferences for sound and rhythm which he has been using for the past twenty-five years. He discovered the music of Webern also, and had only the highest words of praise for it. Long the outstanding opponent of the twelve-tone technique, Stravinsky did much to reconcile others by his recognition of Webern and the technique and many other composers began to work with it also. While our analysis of the *Cantata* will reveal only its structure, without necessarily relating this to the moving concept of the whole composition, it still will provide an entry into the microcosm of the particular work which otherwise might remain sealed to the casual listener.

Cantata (1952)

This touching work uses fifteenth and sixteenth century anonymous English texts, and is set for soprano and tenor solos, women's chorus and a small ensemble of two flutes, two oboes (one interchangeable with English horn) and cello. The seven movements consist of three long movements named *Ricercari,* prefaced, separated and concluded by the choral refrain of the *Lyke-Wake Dirge* (Example VII-19). The four verses of the dirge describe the progress of the soul after death, the reliance on charity for the attainment of purgatory, and ends each verse with *"And Christe receive thye saule."* The words of the first verse appear also at the end, following the fourth verse, to close the sequence. This dirge is set to the same music each time, a poignant and simple harmonization with a modal feeling about it.

The significance of the words of the first *ricercar* (b) for soprano and ensemble is difficult to understand. Given the religious attitude of the whole cantata, these words tend to be obscure in the symbolist manner, calling forth images whose relation to the whole seems important but unfathomable. The form, as defined by cadences and the beginning of new canons (b), may be indicated thus:

A: inverted canon between Flute I and English horn.

B: a pause separates these sections; then an inverted canon between the voice and Flute I, with a later canon in the oboe beginning with the upward scale line in faster notes.

A: a recapitulation of the opening melody, now in the oboe; momentary imitation between voice and clarinet.

EXAMPLE VII-19: Stravinsky, *Cantata.*

"LYKE-WAKE DIRGE"
(MOVEMENTS 1,3,5,7)

a. Tempo (♩ = 52)

mf
This   ae   nighte,   this   ae

nighte,   E - ve-ry   nighte   and   alle,

etc.

RICERCAR I: Tempo (♩ = 69)

A.
b.   Fl.

p

VOICE: The   mai-dens came when   I   was   in

Cor. Angl.

CANON INVERTED, RHYTHMICALLY CHANGED

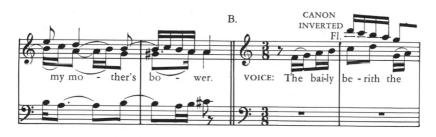

B.   CANON
INVERTED
Fl.

my mo - ther's bo - wer.   VOICE: The bai-ly be-rith the

bell   a - way,   The   li - ly,   the rose, the   rose I   lay

etc.

Ob.
CANON, ORIGINAL FORM

B: a similar short recapitulation of the B section with canons between the voice and Flute I (inverted) and the oboe.

A: a rhythmically altered canon between the voice and flute; the low oboe plays a mirror reflection of the flute line simultaneously with it.

Recitative: *"Right mighty and famus Elizabeth, our quen,"* etc.

Prayer.

After the repetition of the *Lyke-Wake Dirge*, the central and most elaborate *ricercar* of the work occurs. The text is Christ's account of His life, death, resurrection and ascension, with the symbolic refrain as the recurring ritornello between canons, *"To call, to call my true love to my dance,"* the significance of which is plain. The opening section states the canonic subject in the instruments, after which it is exposed by the tenor voice in its original, retrograde, inversion and retrograde inversion (Example VII-19c). These are not apparent to the listener since they overlap and there are no pauses between the forms of the series. The row comprises six tones with one chromaticism, and some of the tones are repeated in the row. There are three rhythmic variations of the row as first presented, differing in length and scoring, and separated by two *ritornelli* ("To call, to call. . ."); then follow nine canons, each scored for voice, two oboes and cello, each separated by three-measure *ritornelli* scored for the full ensemble. The movement concludes with such a *ritornello*. The canons are complex and varied rhythmically so that they cannot be clearly heard or identified; Stravinsky here evidently wants to conceal the structure and make it subservient to the expressive aims of the work. If so, he succeeds admirably.

The duet on the famous *Westron Wind* (d) is gay and dancelike (the dance referred to in the previous *ricercar*?) and exhibits a formal pattern somewhat resembling the arias and duets in *The Rake's Progress*. The A section opens in C minor and concludes in C major just before an abrupt pause. A B section which is modulatory follows, suiting the impassioned words, after which a section in C minor but with wider harmonic rovings occurs, concluding with long-sustained notes in the voice parts and rhythmic chords in the instruments. The last section is a literal repeat of the opening A. The verses IV and I conclude the work in a most poetic and expressive way.

Listening to the delightful ballet music of *Agon*, one becomes progressively aware of the use of the twelve-tone system as the work moves on. But Stravinsky's "negative criteria" in the choice of harmonic quality obviously are not those of the Viennese school, and above all, the rhythmic and orchestral clarity are his own. It consists of three large

EXAMPLE VII-19, cont'd.

c.

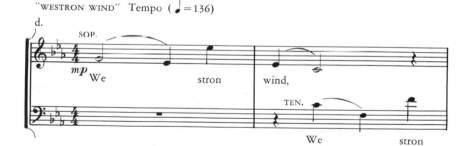

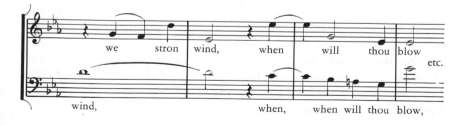

sections, each of which contains a number of dances for male and female dancers, solo or in various combinations. There is no plot or program.

The later, and especially the Latin works become more difficult of penetration, and one often must take them on faith until repeated listening has revealed their expressiveness and logic. The *Sepet* and the *Movements,* however, once one understands the previous instrumental compositions, offer little resistance.

We may expect many more works from Stravinsky, for he continues composing with practically unabated vigor, and the spirit of the works reflects this vigor.

Other Post-War Composers

Not all composers after the war became dodecaphonists, nor did they all embrace the new electronic and experimental musics which were appearing with prophets and apostles as passionate as the earlier twelve-tone advocates. Many rightfully "cultivated their own gardens," advancing steadily according to the nature of their own talent, and producing music that has been obscured too often by the newest fads. To even list the names of all of the composers who were working through the war and beyond would require more space than we have available; but, let us mention the most prominent.

In Germany, Carl Orff (b. 1895) produced a sensation with his *Carmina Burana* (1939) and subsequent operas which continued the percussive and simple melodic appeal of that work. Ernst Krenek (b. 1900) traversed the path from the early jazz opera *Jonny spielt auf* (1927) through total serialization to electronic music after the war. Wolfgang Fortner (b. 1907) has produced music of solid worth, as has Gottfried van Einem (b. 1918). Works by Giselher Klebe (b. 1925) and Hans Werner Henze (b. 1926) are having increasing performances outside of Germany, particularly the operas of the latter.

In France, Olivier Messiaen (b. 1908) produced orchestral religious music of a particularly arresting quality. To the post-war generation, however, his fame rests mainly on the fact that he was the teacher of Pierre Boulez, whom we shall encounter shortly. In Switzerland, Frank Martin (b. 1890) was one of the first French-aligned composers to use the twelve-tone technique, bringing it finally to a synthesis with tonality that suited his expressive needs. His *Petite Symphonie Concertante* (1945), the setting of Hoffmannsthal's *Jedermann* texts (1943), the opera *The Tempest* (1955) and several concertos attest to his importance as a composer.

In Italy, the veteran twelve-tone composer Luigi Dallapiccola (b. 1904) has found a lyric style which lends itself to vocal and choral compositions of great warmth and lyricism, traditional Italian musical ingredients which might not be expected to thrive on dodecaphonism. The first work of his to reach the United States was the *Quaderna Musicale di Annalibera* ("Musical Notebook of Annalibera"), short piano pieces dedicated to his daughter, so named because she was born in the "year of liberation" (1944). Perhaps his most powerful composition is the opera *Il prigionere* ("The Prisoner," 1944-48).

The resurgence of English music continued, and a lively national appreciation and pride has grown up over it. Britten has not ceased composing, but Walton's production has fallen off. New composers, who have not yet made their way to the United States, but whose music is less insular and eclectic than that of their elders, are Peter Racine Fricker (b. 1920), Iain Hamilton (b. 1922), Alexander Goehr (b. 1932), Peter Maxwell Davies (b. 1934), Richard Rodney Bennett (b. 1936) and Cornelius Cardew (b. 1936).

Because we are submerged in our own musical life in the United States, it is rather difficult to assess the lasting value of our own composers other than those who have been around for some time. Names which have risen to prominence during the last fifteen to twenty years, however, are Norman Dello Joio (b. 1913), Lukas Foss (b. 1922), Elliott Carter (b. 1908), Mel Powell (b. 1922), Gunther Schuller (b. 1925), Easley Blackwood (b. 1933), Peter Mennin (b. 1923), Milton Babbitt (b. 1916), Ben Weber (b. 1916), Arthur Berger (b. 1912) and Robert Palmer (b. 1915), among many, many others. Their styles vary from Neoromantic to total serialism, with a typical American tendency toward individualism in the use of twelve-tone techniques.

Perhaps one of the most notable figures is Elliott Carter, whose music reflects the complexity of our period in its rhythmic and harmonic detail, yet carries a total impression of integrity and significance. The early music is Neoclassic-American in melody and rhythm, and might fairly be represented by the *Symphony* (1942). In the three movements of this work, the composer says that the thematic material "suggests the folk-lore of the American rural past," a quality most noticeable in the final movement. The forms are developmental, but easily followed and functional, and the whole work is a pleasant example of what the better American composers were writing in the forties.

The *Piano Sonata* (1945-46) shows a distinct departure from the Neoclassic idiom into something more serious, a different kind of expression which, chromatic and rhythmic, is distinctly new. The *So-*

nata is in two large movements, an opening *Maestoso* of great breadth which progresses through proclamatory octaves and chords contrasted with rapid figuration and lyric sections which possess this quality more through sonority than melodic line. Two chordal polarities are placed in conflict throughout: B major and B-flat minor, one half-step lower. The piano writing is idiomatic and of the virtuoso variety, but it definitely is subservient to the expressive aims of the movement. Notable are the sonorities obtained by sympathetic vibrations of higher strings excited by harmonics of low tones. The second movement is a large ternary structure of which the central section is a fugue. The tempos are *Andante-Allegro-Andante,* and the material of the first section reappears in the final one, but in a different order. One of the rather surprising things in this work is that Carter is not afraid of using consonance when it will best suit his purpose. Many of these are derived from the basic chords of the work, but others do occur, possibly by analogy with them. The fugue theme is fragmentary in short rushes of patterns, giving it the expectant quality of good subjects from Bach to the present. The working out is bold and decisively rhythmic with rather jazz-like touches from time to time, not only in the softer episode, but in some of the surrounding sections. Altogether, it is an invigorating and vital section. The *Andante* releases the tension which has been built up, and closes thoughtfully with the implication of B major.

The *String Quartet* (1951), which comes after the *Sonata for Cello and Piano* (1948) and the interesting *Eight Etudes and a Fantasy* for woodwind quartet (1950), is undoubtedly one of the major pieces of chamber music of the present period. Anyone familiar with the Bartók, Berg and Schönberg essays for the string quartet cannot but realize its importance. The next best thing to listening to it perhaps is to read the composer's own analysis, provided in the program of a concert at the University of Illinois in 1953.

"The first movement, a contrapuntal fantasy, is built on four main and several subsidiary themes each in a different speed and character. Various polyrhythmic combinations of these are made and this resolves into a rapidly flowing scherzo, 'allegro scorrevole,' with a dramatic trio section. The scherzo is interrupted, before it is concluded, with a pause of the kind that usually comes between movements. It is resumed briefly after the pause and leads into an Adagio that features a vigorous recitative between viola and cello answered by a quiet duet between the muted violins. Later the duet and the recitative are heard together leading to a shadowy, fast coda that prefigures the variations of the last movement. These variations are made up of a number of ideas which become slightly faster at each repetition. The one heard in the cello at first appears frequently from beginning to end of the movement where it finally becomes so fast that it turns into a tremolo; other themes reach the vanishing point sooner and give place to new ones. The work ends with a variation in the form of a cadenza for the first violin that is also a continuation of the one heard in the cello at the very opening of the work."

The *Sonata for Flute, Oboe, Cello and Harpsichord* (1952) is a lighter and easier work, followed in 1961, by the *Double Concerto* for harpsichord and piano with two string orchestras, a much more difficult work it seems to this observer, and one that might best be heard in live performance rather than on records.

Elliott Carter is only one of the American composers writing in new and individual idioms. Many of these styles are traceable back to the end of the nineteenth century, although their attitude is modern and what they have to say has no contact with those times. But, advanced as they are, these men do not constitute the *avant-garde* of today; the newest music is the province of the electronic sound generator, the tape recorder and the men who carry on the imaginative processes of Varèse.

PLATE LXII. *Elliott Carter. (Photo courtesy of the BMI Archive)*

THE POST-WAR AVANT-GARDE

Progressive composers since the war have produced music in three rather large categories: post-Webern, including totally serialized works; electronic music, including that performed wholly electronically as well as that which is produced by manipulations of magnetic recording tape, and the combination of traditional instruments with either of the foregoing; and chance music, which may use either traditional or electronic sounds, but whose mode of creation uses to some degree the principle of chance.

Karlheinz Stockhausen (b. 1928) and Pierre Boulez (b. 1925) first came to general attention as post-Webern composers of totally serialized music. Both studied with Olivier Messiaen (b. 1908), and both have worked with electronic music as well as that written for traditional instruments.

Le Marteau sans maître, by Boulez, is a nine-movement setting of René Char's three short poems for alto voice, flute in G, viola, vibraphone, xylorimba, guitar, and a number of percussion instruments including bongos, maracas, claves, tambourines, bells, tam-tam, triangle, gong and cymbals of various pitches. Its ancestor is obviously *Pierrot Lunaire,* but the abundance of percussion, almost like a Javanese *gamelan* orchestra, gives it a quite different sonority from Schönberg's work. In this composition, the combinations used for each of the movements are varied——as in *Pierrot*——but the voice is present only in the third, fifth, sixth and ninth movements, and it sings rather than uses *sprechstimme,* except in the ninth movement, marked *recitative* in part. The fragmentary nature of the patterns in the instruments, together with the lack of a perceptible continuous pulse, makes the music stationary, without rhythmic movement or sense of progression. It goes without saying that the serialization cannot be apprehended by the listener, any more than the sense of the words, which, in their dispersal throughout the music, become merely vehicles for vocalization rather than intelligible combinations. Indeed, the surrealistic imagery of the poetry is rather difficult to understand even when it stands before one on the printed page!

The organization of the movements is more apparent from their titles than from the music itself; the following diagram shows the plan.

I. *Avant "L'Artisanat furieux"* (Before "The Furious Artisan," a prelude, wholly instrumental).

PLATE LXIII: *Pierre Boulez. (Courtesy of the composer.)*

    II. *Commentaire I de "Bourreaux de solitude"* (Commentary on "The Hangmen of Solitude," ABA form, instrumental).

    III. *"L'Artisanat furieux"* ("The Furious Artisan," with voice and instruments).

    IV. *Commentaire II de "Bourreaux de solitude"* (AB form, instrumental.)

    V. *"Bel édifice et les pressentiments," version premiere* ("Beautiful Building and Premonitions," first version. Voice and instruments.)

    VI. *"Bourreaux de solitude"* (voice and instruments).

    VII. *Après "L'Artisanat furieux"* (After "The Furious Artisan," instrumental postlude).

    VIII. *Commentaire III de "Bourreaux de solitude"* (sectional form, instrumental.)

    XI. *"Bel édifice et les pressentiments," Double* (Variation on "Beautiful Building and Premonitions," for voice and instruments.)

Thus, a prelude, song and postlude *("L'Artisanat furieux")* is interlocked with a theme and variation *("Bel édifice et les pressentiments)* and a series of sectional movements *(Commentaires de "Bourreaux de solitude")* which Robert Craft likens to sonata movements.

The disappearance of audibly discernable form behind the complexity of extreme formal organization is one of the aesthetic paradoxes of twentieth century music. The knotty question it raises concerning the value of structure if it cannot be heard is one which has not yet successfully been answered. Indeed, many chance and improvisatory "compositions" sound exactly like those whose composers have painstakingly organized the material in all possible ways. What value, then, is such precise structure, other than to the composer's ego, and the fact that he can account for everything in the music if asked? Perhaps the remaining years of our century will provide a satisfactory answer.

Electronic music admits of two subdivisions, differentiating that which employs purely electronic sound sources, and that which uses tape recordings of various "natural" sounds which have been speeded up, slowed down, or otherwise electronically manipulated to give results different from the "raw" original. The latter was developed in France about 1948 by Pierre Schaeffer, a sound technician and amateur musician. He called the result *musique concrète*. His work, and that of a colleague, Pierre Henry, aroused enough interest for the French National Radio to create a research studio especially for him. Similar studios were soon instituted in Cologne, Hamburg, Milan and Brussels, and composers such as Boulez, Stockhausen, Maderna (b. 1920), Berio (b. 1925) and Nono (b. 1924) began producing works which rather quickly abandoned *musique concrète* techniques in favor of purely electronic sound sources. Pioneers in tape-recorder music in the United States were John Cage (b. 1912) and Otto Leuning (b. 1900), soon joined by Vladimir Ussachevsky (b. 1911) and Edgar Varèse. In 1955, the RCA Sound Synthesizer was constructed, and in 1959 an improved model of it formed the original equipment of the Columbia-Princeton Electronic Music Center.

Both purely electronic and *musique concrète* compositions are recorded on magnetic tape, and, while the processes of the former are quite complicated, those of the latter are easy enough to understand. In both cases the composer first must establish a vocabulary of sounds analogous to the traditional composer's memory of intervals, chords and tone colors derived from his experience with instruments. In the case of *musique concrète*, he records various sounds that seem to have possibilities for use. Ussachevsky decribes such a process, using sounds from a gong, a piano, a cymbal, a kettledrum, a jet plane, a chord from an organ and the click of a tape-recorder switch. These sounds may be manipulated by speeding the rotation of the reels of the tape recorder, or slowing them to any degree, thus raising or lowering the pitch. The sounds may be prolonged, also, so as to be able to use only a certain part of them.

PLATE LXIV. *Karlheinz Stockhausen. (Photo courtesy of the BMI Archive.)*

The results of these manipulations, recorded on a series of other tapes, forms the vocabulary. The composer then decides upon a formal plan for the work, perhaps something as simple as a gradual *crescendo* of loudness, which can be controlled completely, of course, together with increasing density of sound produced by adding elements of the vocabulary; then a *diminuendo* following a reverse of this pattern. This done, he may record and re-record the vocabulary to produce the finished work. A more common practice, since not all composers have facilities for the multiple recording technique, is the splicing together of short pieces of the vocabulary tapes, each piece cut to last a definite amount of time and to enter and leave the composition in a specified way (i.e., abruptly or gradually). This is a laborious process, frustrating in the extreme, and can only be regarded as primitive. Still, composers use it and manage to create some interesting works.

In the case of the pure electronic music, a score may be written which notes the vibrations per second of the sound on a graph, the horizontal axis of which represents the duration of the sound in fractions of a second. A supplementary graph may show relative dynamic levels of various sound planes and is coordinated with the larger graph. The sounds are recorded directly on a master tape from the vocabulary tapes, re-recording as many times as necessary. They also may be stereophonic, or, as in the case of one of Stockhausen's works, be multichanneled so as to play through thirty speakers arranged around the audience. Another technique involves the programming of a computer with punched cards which direct it to produce the sound frequency complexes directly on tape. And, of course, there is the improvisatory technique of manipulating the controls of the sound vocabulary manually, composing the work "live" on the master tape. Many compositions use both natural and purely electronic sounds mixed. Stockhausen's *Gesang der Jünglinge* ("Song of the Youths in the Fiery Furnace") employs an electronically manipulated voice together with electronically generated sounds. And Henk Badings (b. 1907) has produced a *Capriccio* in which a solo violin is accompanied by a prerecorded tape. Stockhausen and others have combined performance by chorus or conventional ensembles with tape-recorded sound.

The complete control over the materials is a factor of electronic music which attracts post-Webern composers of the school of total serialization, for it expands the tonal palette to an infinite degree, and it assures perfect results, untouched by the all-too-fallible human hands. It also attracts experimentalists like Varèse, interested in new sound qualities and new ways of arranging them. The electronic composer is usually a blend of the two, plus a knack for electrical engineering. More and more recordings of this kind of music are becoming available to open our minds and ears to the possibilities of today, for they probably will be of great importance tomorrow. They should be listened to with stereophonic earphones for the best effect, for this music, like that of Gabrieli, often uses physical space as one of its dimensions, and can manipulate that space much more effectively than Gabrieli or any other previous composer could possibly do.

Chance music means just that: music put together by chance procedures such as flipping a coin or throwing dice to choose rhythms, tones, patterns or chords. Mozart made just such a device whereby amateurs could write minuets! Of course, he wrote the patterns from which the choices were made. John Cage probably has worked with this aspect of music more than any one person alive today, and has gathered a group of followers dedicated to his ideas. His ideal is to "free musical continuity from individual taste and memory, and from the literature and traditions of the art." His is interested in the "natural music" of everyday sounds which penetrate what we ordinarily think of as silence, and his music shows a concern for the dynamics of silence, the relativity of silence to sound. This is exhibited in much of his music by silences of varying durations during the course of a composition, so located as to seem part of the work——a composition of silence and sound, not just sound. The sounds themselves may have no traditional sense of continuity or coherence; it is enough for Cage that they follow each other in time, establishing only this neighboring relationship.

The ways in which Cage employs chance are fascinating in their diversity. In some cases he used the ancient Chinese *Book of Changes* (the *I-Ching*) to guide the results of tossing coins. In others, such as the *Imaginary Landscape,* twelve radios, controlled by two performers each for volume and station tuning, are directed in these capacities by a conductor with a score prepared according to the *Book of Changes* technique. Obviously, due to differences in programming, the result is random, and can never be repeated. Other composers have experimented with what might be called "controlled chance." Stockhausen's *Klavierstücke XI* presents a series of fragments of piano music printed on a roll of paper. The pianist plays them in any order at any tempo he wishes, not repeating any fragment. Here, each performance will consist of the same "events" but the order will, within the range of probability, be different. Other compositions may unite fixed and improvisatory elements. Cage performs a work which uses two prepared tapes of sound obtained by rubbing and scraping a phonograph pickup over various surfaces. These are not coordinated with each other every time they are played, so the net result is different to some degree. While they are playing stereophonically, he improvises in the same way that the tapes were prepared, but varies the sound by whatever means may be at hand, such as scraping a chair across the floor with or without the phonograph pickup attached.

It will be seen from the descriptions of some of the *avant-garde* experiments described above that many composers feel that we must widen our definition of what music is, just as Picasso and Braque expanded the meaning of the word *painting* by inventing collages, or other artists by making constructions out of everyday materials comparable to *musique concrète* as well as the "noise music" produced by some of Cage's experiments. It would seem, given our advancing state of technology, that the genuine music of the end of the twentieth century and the beginning of the twenty-first would be electronic. But, we shall probably have the old instruments and the old music at the same time, for do we not go to museums to see the paintings of Giotto, Da Vinci and Carvaggio? In many respects, our concert halls and opera houses are museums right now, with seldom a display of contemporary work. Hopefully, we shall achieve a balance in some future day when we feel the response to electronic song, when we come to regard it as art.

THE OTHER ARTS IN THE POST-WAR ERA

Both painting and sculpture became increasingly abstract during the 1920-1945 period, first using distortion of the geometrical, cubistic kind, or that of Expressionism. The result was a nonobjective, sometimes dehumanized kind of art in which natural objects did not appear, or only faintly made their presence felt, although they may have formed the original basis of the work. Music followed suit, first in the abstract compositions of Webern, then in the totally serialized music of his successors, together with the electronic and chance music which developed as extensions of or reactions against these various manifestations. The private realities of Miró, Klee and Kandinsky, expressed in varying degrees of abstraction and distortion, might be seen to be comparable to similar tendencies in the music of Berg, Bartók and Varèse. Art of a more geometrical kind, such as that of Mondriaan, where the relationship of each element is shown clearly, is comparable in a way to the music of Webern and his followers——although certainly the structure can be plain only to the musician who has painstakingly analysed the composition. And even random techniques, often involving improvisation, occur in both music and painting.

The mobiles of Alexander Calder, as well as sculptures by Epstein and Giacometti, involve spatial elements as well as abstract or distorted shapes, analogous to the stereophonic recreation of space in the music of Stockhausen and others who dream of auditoriums with ceilings studded with loudspeakers activated by multi-channeled tape recordings, so that the music may move around the listener, wholly enveloping him in sound. Of course, the correlation between the various collages and montages of two and three dimensional material with the natural and manipulated sounds of *musique concrète* is fairly obvious to anyone who will take the time to look and hear.

Perhaps the music and art of our time are in closer relation to each other than in any previous era. It remains to be seen if the "Pop Art" movement will have a parallel in music, although certainly the "Op(tical) Art" of visual illusions may be compared with certain stereophonic electronic compositions. We are living in a most interesting period of change in which the artistic responses of creative spirits reflect the amazingly rapid developments in technology. Experimentation is the order of the day; whether it will evolve a "common practice" or something resembling that unanimity of technique and attitude remains to be seen. The other alternative, of increasingly diverging lines of development and experimentation, lies in the impenetrable future, about which we can only guess. It becomes a game of artistic chance, guided undoubtedly by forces which we either cannot perceive, or at best, sense only dimly. But what a fascinating game, all the more so because each of us has a part in it as watcher, listener and critic.

TERMS USED IN PARTS II AND III

Neoclassicism	abstract Expressionism
dodecaphonism, twelve-tone technique	tone row
	tone cluster
unrelated triads	arch form
quartal harmony	wedge form
serial technique	clausula vera
total serialism	*Gebrauchsmusik*
musique concrète	free chromaticism
electronic manipulation of sound	"artificial" scale
electronic music	gamelan orchestra
chance music, aleatory music	*ricercar*

BIBLIOGRAPHY

Music since the turn of the century has excited so much critical writing and biography that it would be a hopeless task for a book such as this to try to cover the subject thoroughly. Possibly one of the best bibliographies is contained in William W. Austin's fine book, *Music in the 20th Century* (Norton, 1966). We shall present here only a few of the best titles dealing with the foremost composers.

Bartók

Fassett, Agatha, *The Naked Face of Genius,* N.Y., 1958.
Stevens, Halsey, *The Life and Music of Béla Bartók,* Oxford University Press, 2nd. ed., N.Y., 1963.

Berg

Redlich, Hans F., *Alban Berg: The Man and His Music,* N.Y., 1957.
Reich, Willi, *The Life and Works of Alban Berg,* London, 1965.

Cage

Cage, John, *Silence,* Middletown, Conn., 1961.

Carter

Goldman, Richard Franko, "The Music of Elliott Carter," *Musical Quarterly,* XLIII (1957), 151.

Copland

Berger, Arthur, *Aaron Copland,* N.Y., 1953.
Copland, Aaron, *Music and Imagination,* Cambridge, Mass., 1952.

Debussy

Debussy, Claude, *M. Croche, the Dilettante Hater,* in *Three Classics in the Aesthetic of Music,* N.Y., 1962.
Lockspeiser, Edward, *Debussy,* London, 3rd ed. 1951.
Seroff, Victor, *Debussy, Musician of France,* N.Y., 1956.
Vallas, Léon, *The Theories of Claude Debussy,* trans. O'Brien, Oxford, 1929.

Hindemith

Hindemith, Paul, *A Composer's World,* Cambridge, Mass., 1952.
Strobel, Heinrich, *Paul Hindemith,* Mainz, 3rd ed., (in German), 1948.

Ives

Cowell, Henry and Sidney, *Charles Ives and his Music,* N.Y., 1955.
Ives, Charles E., "Essays Before a Sonata," in *Three Classics in the Aesthetic of Music,* N.Y., 1962.

Křenek

Křenek, Ernst, *Music Here and Now,* trans. B. Fles, N.Y., 1939.

Prokofiev

Hanson, Lawrence and Elisabeth, *Prokofiev, the Prodigal Son,* London, 1964.
Nestyev, Israel V., *Prokofiev,* trans. by Jonas, Stanford, 1960.

Ravel

Seroff, Victor, *Maurice Ravel,* N.Y., 1953.

Satie

Myers, Rollo H., *Erik Satie,* London, 1948.

Schönberg

Leibowitz, René, *Schoenberg and his School,* N.Y., 1949.
Newlin, Dika, *Bruckner, Mahler, Schoenberg,* N.Y., 1947.
Schönberg, Arnold, *Style and Idea,* N.Y., 1950.
——, *Letters,* N.Y., 1965.

Schuman

Schreiber, Rheta and Persichetti, *William Schuman,* N.Y., 1954.

Shostakovitch

Seroff, Victor I., *Dmitri Shostakovitch,* N.Y., 1943.

Stravinsky

Lang, Paul H., ed., *Stravinsky: A New Appraisal of his Work*, N.Y., 1963.
Stravinsky, Igor, *Poetics of Music*, Cambridge, Mass., 1947.
Stravinsky, Igor, and Robert Craft, *Conversations*, Garden City, N.Y., 1959.
——, *Memories and Commentaries*, Garden City, N.Y., 1960.
——, *Expositions and Developments*, Garden City, N.Y., 1962.
——, *Dialogues and a Diary*, Garden City, N.Y., 1963.
Strobel, Heinrich, *Stravinsky: Classic Humanist*, N.Y., 1955.

Vaughan Williams

Dickinson, A. E. F., *Vaughan Williams*, London, 1963.
Vaughan Williams, Ralph, *National Music and Other Essays*, London, 1963.
Vaughan Williams, Ursula, *R. V. W., a Biography*, London, 1964.

Webern

"Anton Webern," in *Die Reihe*, special edition, 1958.
Moldenhauer, Hans, *The Death of Anton Webern: A Drama in Documents*,
    N.Y., 1961.
Moldenhauer, Hans, and Irvine, Demar, *Anton von Webern: Perspectives*,
    Seattle and London, 1968.
Webern, Anton, *The Path to the New Music*, Bryn Mawr, Pa., 1963.

The careful peruser of the above list will note the startling omission of
many important names. In some cases this is due to the fact that no
biographical works or informative articles exist in English at the layman's level. Not listed here, for similar reasons, are articles in professional journals. More of the gaps are filled, however, and we may hope
that eventually every important twentieth century composer will be
discussed in print. We look forward to Newlin's projected biography of
Berg and Moldenhauer's definitive work on Webern.

General Readings in Art, Aesthetics, History and Theory

Abraham, G., *This Modern Music*, Norton, N.Y., 1952.
Austin, W. W., *Music in the Twentieth Century*, Norton, N.Y., 1966.
Barnes, H. E., *An Intellectual and Cultural History of the Western World*,
    Volume III, Dover, N.Y., 1965.

Bauer, M., *Twentieth Century Music*, Putnam, N.Y., 1947.

Chase, G., *America's Music from the Pilgrims to the Present*, McGraw-Hill, N.Y., 1955.

Chavez, C., *Toward a New Music*, Norton, N.Y., 1957.

Copland, A., *Copland on Music*, Doubleday & Co., Garden City, N.Y., 1960.

Dallin, L., *Techniques of Twentieth Century Composition*, Wm. C. Brown, Dubuque, 1957.

Dewey, J., *Art as Experience*, G. P. Putnam's Sons, N.Y., 1934.

Dorian, F., *The History of Music in Performance*, Norton, N.Y.

——, *The Musical Workshop*, Secker & Warburg, London, 1947.

Edman, I., *Arts and the Man*, Mentor, N.Y., 1949.

Eisler, H., *Composing for the Films*, Oxford, N.Y., 1947.

Fleming W., *Arts and Ideas*, Holt, N.Y., 1955.

Graf, M., *Modern Music*, Philosophical Library, N.Y., 1946.

Grosser, M., *The Painter's Eye*, Mentor, N.Y., 1955.

Hansen, P. S., *An Introduction to Twentieth Century Music*, Second Edition, Allyn & Bacon, Boston, 1967.

Hindemith, P., *A Composer's World*, Harvard University, Cambridge, 1952.

Hunter, S., *Modern American Painting and Sculpture*, Dell, N.Y., 1959.

——, *Modern French Painting*, Dell, N.Y., 1956.

Kerman, J., *Opera as Drama*, Vintage, N.Y., 1959.

Kolodin, I., ed., *The Composer as Listener*, Collier Books, N.Y., 1962.

Lang, P. H., ed., *The Problems of Modern Music*, Norton, N.Y., 1960.

Langer, S., *Philosophy in a New Key*, Harvard University, Cambridge, 1951.

McLuhan, M., *The Gutenberg Galaxy*, University of Toronto, Toronto, 1965.

——, *Understanding Media*, University of Toronto, Toronto, 1965.

Mellers, W., *Romanticism and the Twentieth Century*, Essential Books, Fairlawn, N.J., 1957.

Newmeyer, S., *Enjoying Modern Art*, Mentor, N.Y., 1955.

Norman, G. and Shrifte, M., *Letters of Composers*, Knopf, N.Y., 1946.

Peltz, M., *Introduction to Opera*, Barnes & Noble, N.Y., 1961.

Reihe, Die, No. 1: Electronic Music, Presser, Bryn Mawr, 1957.

Sachs, C., *The Commonwealth of Art*, Norton, N.Y., 1946.

Santayana, G., *The Sense of Beauty*, Collier, N.Y., 1961.

Sargeant, W., *Jazz, Hot and Hybrid*, Dutton, N.Y., 1948.

Schwartz, E. and Childs, B., eds., *Contemporary Composers on Contemporary Music*, Holt, Rinehart & Winston, N.Y., 1967.

Sessions, R., *The Musical Experience of Composer, Performer, Listener*, Princeton University, Princeton, 1950.

Slonimsky, N., *Music of Latin America*, Crowell, N.Y., 1945.

Thomson, V., *The Art of Judging Music*, Knopf, N.Y., 1948.

Walter, Bruno, *Of Music and Music Making*, Norton, N.Y., 1960.

INDEX